The Hardisons

A SOUTHERN ODYSSEY

The Hardisons

A SOUTHERN ODYSSEY

Elizabeth Shreve Ryan

The Reprint Company, Publishers
Spartanburg, South Carolina
2004

Copyright © 1997 by Elizabeth Shreve Ryan
All rights reserved.

An original publication, 1997
Second printing, 2004
The Reprint Company, Publishers
Spartanburg, South Carolina 29304

ISBN-087152-501-1
Library of Congress Catalog Card Number 96-44359
Manufactured in the United States of America

Book design by Harriet Miller Correll

Illustrations by Thomas Sully

Photograph of cotton field courtesy of Vanishing Georgia Collection, Georgia Department of Archives and History

∞ The paper used in this publication meets the requirements of American National Standard for Information Science—Permanence of Paper for Printed Library Materials, ANSI Z-39.48-1984.

Library of Congress Cataloging-in-Publication Data

Ryan, Elizabeth Shreve.
    The Hardisons : a southern odyssey / Elizabeth Shreve Ryan.
        p.   cm.
    Includes bibliographical references and index.
    ISBN 0-87152-501-1 (alk. paper)
    1. Hardison family. 2. Southern States—Biography. 3. Southern States—Genealogy. 4. Migration, Internal—Southern States—History. I. Title.
CT274.H357R93   1996
975'.04—DC21   96-44359
                                                                            CIP
                                                                            r97

Dedication

To the daughters and granddaughters of John Randolph Hardison, Winnifred Cornelia Davis Hardison, and Mary Fletcher Northington Hardison, whose values and ambitions gave shape to my life,

To my husband, John Morris Ryan, whose assistance and forbearance were invaluable,

And to the friends and kin who have made this book possible.

↜ *Preface* ↜

> Life must be lived forwards,
> but it can only be understood backwards.
> Sören Kierkegaard

Since ancient times people have asked questions about their origins—who am I, where did I come from, who is my family? These are heavily freighted questions and they may be answered in a variety of ways. From the ancient Egyptian pharaohs, depicted in tomb and temple carvings with scrolls in their hands representing records of their ancestry, to the many thousands of contemporary Americans combing public and private archives for their roots, the recording of family patriarchs and matriarchs represents a deeply significant effort to answer these questions. As students of history we learn that the quest acquires much greater significance when placed in the context of the local, national, and world events which shaped the lives of the people from whom we are descended. *The Hardisons, a Southern Odyssey* is an attempt to address both of these facets of the family's history. The founding and growth of the family of Jasper Hardison in colonial North Carolina, the movement of several of its members to Georgia shortly after the American Revolution, and the subsequent relocations of Jasper's most adventurous descendants throughout the South have been narrated both as the history of a particular family and as a case history of migration in the American South in the eighteenth and nineteenth centuries.

An odyssey is defined as a long wandering, usually marked by many changes of fortune. The Hardisons' movements and their alternating successes and reverses qualify as an odyssey and their story is representative of the migrations from Virginia through the Carolinas, Georgia, and Florida and westward into Tennessee, Kentucky, Arkansas, the Gulf coast states, and finally Texas, which peopled the American South. The area's agricultural economy, labor system, culture, and class structure made it unique in the developing nation and fostered the sectional rivalry which erupted tragically in the Civil War. With the South's defeat in that conflict, the way of life which had evolved from its plentiful and fertile lands was permanently altered. Hardison family members increasingly looked to the professions, particularly law, medicine, and teaching, rather than the land, for a livelihood. The narrative of their odyssey ends with the generation which came of age in the quarter century following the Civil War.

My own odyssey in pursuit of the information on which the Hardisons' story is based began in childhood as I studied the faded photograph of the great-grandfather whose middle name I shared. Confederate veteran John Randolph Hardison and his second wife, Mary Fletcher Northington, stared with solemn gaze from their heavy multi-layered Victorian frame. They were the parents of my grandmother, Amelia Randolph Hardison Granade, and the grandparents of my mother and her three sisters, the graces, and occasionally the furies, of my youth. For five years during the 1930s I lived in Sandersville, the county seat of Washington County, Georgia, where the Hardisons and Northingtons had settled after migrating from North Carolina in the early years of the nineteenth century. The Old South was a palpable presence amidst the faded ante-bellum homes and continuing reverence for the sacrifices made for the Lost Cause of the Confederacy. My family lived in a rambling old house which had survived Sherman's assault during his March to the Sea. An elderly neighbor, Mrs. Sophronia Bayne, who had lived in the house as a child, told me stories of the stationing of a Union soldier to guard the milliner who was living there when the invaders wrought destruction in the town. My interest in history grew after I moved a short distance away to Milledgeville, the ante-bellum capital of Georgia, and it led to my major in college. After graduate school, I pursued a career in history for ten years and it has continued to be an abiding interest.

Fifteen years ago, when my children were well out of the nest and settled into college, I felt the urge to dust off my long-shelved skills and to research and write a bit of history. I knew that John Randolph Hardison had migrated to Texas before the Civil War with his first wife, Winnifred Cornelia Davis, and that my grandmother was born there, to his second wife, Mary Fletcher Northington, in 1869. Since I was living in Texas, it seemed to be the ideal place to begin my research. Inquiries among family members in Georgia led to knowledge of two collections of letters written from Texas by John, Winnifred, and Mary. Their owners graciously shared their letters and knowledge of the family and I was off and running. The research which has produced this study has at times proceeded at a desultory pace as other interests and concerns have made claims on my time, but I never lost sight of the ultimate goal which this book represents.

My original intention was to edit the letters in the framework of the family's move from Georgia to Texas and back to Georgia. However, as my knowledge of their lives grew I became curious about the generations of Hardisons, Davises, and Northingtons which had produced John, Winnifred, and Mary, all of whose families had migrated from North Carolina to Georgia. My knowledge of Southern history gave added interest to my pursuit of their past and led me on an odyssey which has taken me with varying degrees of success from Maine to Texas and, in pursuit of the letters, to Nebraska and Georgia. From Kittery and Berwick, Maine, to Devil's Gut and Roses Plantation, North Carolina, to Davisboro and Bay Spring, Georgia, and on to China Hill, Florida, and Tarkington's Prairie and Cotton Gin, Texas, it has been a joyful journey.

Ideally the journey would have begun or ended with research in Great Britain and the uncovering of the Hardisons' pre-American roots. But as the poet Robert Burns warned, "the best laid schemes o' mice an' men gang aft agley," and that phase of the study will have to wait for a later day and probably another researcher. The failure of such a search by another family member has been shared with me, but I am sure that there will be success in the future among the several interested descendants. The motivations for emigration from Britain are writ large in the seventeenth and eighteenth history of that nation and the ambitious Hardisons took advantage of the opportunities offered to them by a new land. It is very likely that Jasper Hardison was an Englishman whose American migrations began in New England, but positive proof of that connection is still lacking to me and all of the other Hardison researchers whom I have encountered. The circumstantial evidence of that connection will be presented in the Prologue.

This study is not a comprehensive history or listing of all the Hardisons in the United States, in the South, or in North Carolina, where they are still most numerous. Rather it is the story of the earliest documented Southern Hardison, Jasper, whose purchase of land in 1723 in North Carolina is recorded in colonial archives, his seven sons and two daughters and their children in eighteenth century North Carolina, and the family descended from Jasper's great-grandson John Hardison who migrated to Georgia about 1800. A narrative of John's three sons and four daughters and their children makes up the nineteenth century portion of the study. Since my own descent came through John's second son, Seth, and Seth's son, John Randolph Hardison, and I had access to a body of data and correspondence from that branch, it has been the focus of my research. However, an effort has been made to provide information on the families of all of John's children. Descent charts of these lines of descent from Jasper have been provided in the appendices and a number of blank pages included on which family members are encouraged to record the names of their own particular branch of the family tree.

Just as this is not a comprehensive study of all the American or Southern Hardisons, the sources on which it is based are by no means inclusive of all that are available. In spite of courthouse fires, the loss of Federal Census records (most notably those for Georgia for 1790, 1800, and 1810), and the ravages of time and conscientious housekeepers on a multitude of public and private records, our ancestors have left an amazingly large paper trail. Limitations on time and opportunity, as well as knowledge, did not allow me to make use of all the available resources, but for each stage of the Hardisons' odyssey I attempted to search the major sources in order to document their personal and public lives. Rather than list these in a comprehensive bibliography, I have included them in the notes at the end of each chapter and readers who are interested in a particular time or place of the family's story are directed to this documentation.

The letters of 1857-1882 are the most appealing and personal sources and genealogical information gathered from family members has provided data on the identities and relationships of the writers and the people they wrote to and about. The framework within which the letters are set and which explains the movements bringing members of the family to Texas on the eve of the Civil War is derived from a variety of county, colonial, state, and national records, particularly those which document the acquisition of land. These have been augmented by the resources in a number of libraries, particularly the James C. Bonner Collection of the Georgia College Library, Milledgeville; the Clayton Library, Center for Genealogical Research, Houston Public Library; and the North Carolina Collection of the University of North Carolina Library, Chapel Hill. Newspapers, church records, and cemetery surveys have added additional dimensions to lives of family members and the eras in which they lived. For beginners in family research, I recommend *The Source* by Arlene Eakle and Johni Cerny as a guide to the many resources available in this country and abroad. In addition to primary sources, I have used a number of histories to provide the background for the various periods covered by the study.

In attempting to document the Hardisons' lives I fear I have been guilty of a sin I once pointed out in reviewing another family history—the inclusion of a quantity of seemingly extraneous minutiae. Based on frustrations experienced in using family and local histories, I decided to err on the side of excessive documentation, both as a means of verification and a guide to further inquiry. Another source of annoyance may be the excessive use of such qualifying words as possibly, probably, and most likely. I exhausted my vocabulary of equivocation in order to avoid the many erroneous conclusions and statements of "fact" which I have encountered in my research. A feature which I believe will be applauded is the index, which I hope will facilitate the location of data about specific family members, particularly those allied to the Hardisons through marriage.

Whether readers join me in experiencing the Hardisons' entire Southern odyssey or search the study for knowledge of a particular person or period, I hope that they will share a measure of the excitement and satisfaction of the search and will be inspired to learn more about their own families and the history which shaped them.

Elizabeth Randolph Shreve Ryan
Chapel Hill, North Carolina
1996

↭ *Acknowledgments* ↭

If it had not taken so long to bring my narrative of the Hardisons to completion, I would be tempted to write another about the experience of researching and writing such a book. The process has acquainted me with formerly unknown family members, fellow sleuths, librarians, local historians, and archives personnel. It has taken me to obscure rural settlements which were once thriving communities when the vast majority of Americans lived on farms. I wish to express my appreciation to the numerous individuals who have made my search a rich and rewarding experience. Because of the number of years through which the process has gone on I may fail to acknowledge helpers whom I should remember and I beg forgiveness for such omissions.

Since readers will receive my work in its finished form, I wish to open my remarks with an expression of thanks and admiration to Harriet Miller Correll, who is responsible for its handsome format. Our friendship developed during years of shared enthusiasm for literature and, as I struggled with my meager computer skills, Harriet offered to use her expertise to help produce a well designed book which would represent our joint contribution to the printed word. Her patience, skills, and encouragement have been memorable and my gratitude is great.

Writing often takes a heavy toll on domestic life and I wish to recognize the support and forbearance of my husband, John Morris Ryan. In spite of my declining attention to the culinary arts, he has remained enthusiastic about the research, has read and edited the text at every stage of its evolution, and has cheerfully chauffeured me from Texas east to Georgia and Florida and north to

Maine (he has threatened to write a memoir entitled "Driving Miss Lizzie"). He has generously supported my desire to present *The Hardisons, a Southern Odyssey* in a format commensurate with the work it represents and its significance to our family. Thanks are due also to our daughters, Nancy Elizabeth Ryan and Susan Randolph Ryan Sully, who have never lost faith in the value or eventual completion of my undertaking.

I am indebted to my son-in-law, Thomas Alfred Sully III, for the drawings which embellish and inform the section title pages. As a fellow lover of the South and of family lore, he has shared his talent with the Hardison descendants and enriched this study of their lives.

Beyond my immediate family, I wish to express my gratitude to the cousins who shared their collections of family letters, pictures, memorabilia, and genealogical data—Nancy Louise Brown Slaughter, a daughter of Annie Mary Hardison Brown, the youngest child of John Randolph Hardison and his second wife, Mary Fletcher Northington Hardison, and the Cain family, descendants of John and his first wife, Winnifred Cornelia Davis Hardison, through their second daughter, Winnifred Cornelia Hardison Wood. I am particularly indebted to George Wood Cain and his niece, Cornelia Winnifred Cain Bien, who have made their collection available and to Lilly Mary Cain for the confidence and support represented by her generous monetary gift.

The letters went from often barely legible originals to photocopies and then to beautiful typescripts through the kindness and skill of my friend, Sara Stone Smith. John, Winnifred, and Mary Hardison became such intimates during the many hours we worked on their letters that Sara and I produced a dramatization, "A Dream of Texas," which was well received by several audiences in Houston. The letters finally made their way into my computer through the skills of Lois Boynton, a graduate student in Journalism at the University of North Carolina, Chapel Hill.

Alma Walker Jackson is a special friend who came to me through a chance discovery of our shared interest in the Hardisons, from whom her husband, Andrew Talley Jackson, is descended. I have benefited greatly from her genealogical skills and we have shared many happy hours at the Clayton Library in Houston and memorable trips to Florida, Maine, and New Hampshire.

I launched my original research in the early 1980s on two fronts, from my home in Texas and my former home in Georgia. To my aunt, Helen Granade Long, I am grateful for providing my Georgia base of operation and for making the overtures which brought me in touch with the Cain family. She has been opening doors for me all of my life and she remained loving and patient whether hurtling down a rutted red clay trail in search of a country graveyard or listening to recitals of my latest findings. I am sure she will be thankful when I move on to another enthusiasm.

Among the facilitators of the Georgia research I wish to acknowledge Donald Hodges for information on the town of Oconee, the childhood home of my mother and her sisters in Washington County; Elizabeth P. Newsom, whose years of research enriched and promoted the study of that county's history; Mary Alice Jordan, editor of the county's fine history, *Cotton to Kaolin*, produced by the Washington County Historical Society; Nonie C. Veal, who has willingly and efficiently searched newspapers and courthouse archives for me; and Catherine Everett Thurston, collector and preserver of the history of Bay Springs Methodist Church, where five generations of my family worshiped. Thanks are due also to Nancy Davis Bray, Head of Special Collections, Georgia College Library, Milledgeville, who recommended many useful sources unknown to me and guided and encouraged my research in numerous ways.

My contacts in Texas were many and varied. Residents of Houston who are interested in family research are particularly fortunate to have ready access to one of the finest collections of genealogical data in the South, the Clayton Library, Center for Genealogical Research, Houston Public Library. The information it yielded provided the framework within which I constructed my narrative of the Hardisons and related families. Its staff was always helpful and efficient. Among the numerous courthouse archives I visited, the clerk and staff of Polk County, Livingston, were most memorable for their helpfulness and efficiency. The county's land records were the first I researched and the organization and availability of the records set high standards for my expectations elsewhere. Robert L. Schaadt, Director of the Sam

Houston Regional Library and Research Center, Liberty, encouraged my research and aided it with a variety of resources on the history of Liberty and Polk counties. Efforts to reconstruct the lives of the Hardisons in Limestone County introduced me to a branch of the family previously unknown to me—the descendants of John Randolph Hardison's half brother, James Harvey Hardison, who was a child at the time of John's death. Garvis Hardison of Limestone County and Linda Hardison Smith of Dayton, Liberty County, have been particularly helpful and supportive.

Although I started my research with the Hardisons' nineteenth century history in Georgia, Florida, and Texas, I eventually went back to their North Carolina roots and again encountered numerous descendants previously unknown to me. Ysobel DuPree Litchfield of Washington, a descendant of Jasper through his son Joseph, provided useful information and guidelines for my North Carolina research and produced the clue which enabled me to connect the Georgia and North Carolina Hardisons. Doris L. Wilson of the Martin County Historical Society has been most generous with her store of information and in making photocopies of documents in the Society's collection. My research in the Martin County and Tyrrell County courthouses has been facilitated by patient and efficient staff members. Hardison descendants are numerous in North Carolina and elsewhere and have done extensive research on the family's beginnings in that state. The excellent study by Fred L. Hawkins and Dorothy Westmoreland Gilliam, *Hardison and Allied Families*, was invaluable in informing and guiding my search of North Carolina records. I am indebted also to Verena Hatch, a descendant of Jasper's son Charles, for sharing her extensive research.

Although my research in the state archives and libraries of the states of Hardison residence has not been nearly as extensive as I would have liked, I am grateful for their fine work of preserving and making available the records of our past. It has been my pleasure to visit these facilities in Florida, Texas, Maine, New Hampshire, and North Carolina and to receive prompt and useful responses from the Georgia Department of Archives and History.

And finally for my knowledge and enthusiasm for history, I wish to pay tribute to my teachers, most notably Dr. Helen I. Greene, Dr.

Amanda Johnson, and Dr. James C. Bonner at Georgia State College for Women, now Georgia College, Milledgeville; Dr. Thomas C. Clark and Dr. Clement Eaton of the University of Kentucky, Lexington; and Dr. Albert Ray Newsome, University of North Carolina, Chapel Hill. The two years I worked as a staff member of the Southern Historical Collection of the University of North Carolina Library, Chapel Hill, whetted my taste for the materials of which history is made, particularly the personal papers of men and women of the nineteenth century. It was my privilege to become acquainted with the founder of this outstanding manuscript collection, Dr. J. G. deRoulhac Hamilton, and to work with his successor as director, Dr. James Patton, and his assistant Anna Brooke Allan. To Dr. Venila L. Shores, Florida State University, Tallahassee, I am grateful for the confidence which enabled me to learn through teaching. These associations took place in the 1940s and 1950s but they are ever-green in my memory and in their influence on my life. A recent academic acquaintance, Dr. Norman D. Brown, University of Texas, Austin, has encouraged my research in the Civil War career of John Randolph Hardison and informed it with *One of Cleburne's Command*, his editing of the reminiscences and diary of one of John's fellow soldiers in Granbury's Texas Brigade.

The interest and useful suggestions of Thomas E. Smith of the Reprint Company and his expertise in publishing have brought *The Hardisons, a Southern Odyssey* to its final form. To him and his assistant, Dr. Margaret H. Cannon, who has produced the index, I wish to express my appreciation for making real my dream of a finished book.

The poet John Donne has rightly said "No man is an Iland, intire of it selfe; every man is a peece of the Continent." We live in community with each other whether we like it or not and we are influenced daily by all the people, living or dead, who have touched our lives. Writers should be particularly aware of their indebtedness to others for they must work within the framework of human accomplishments, failures, and aspirations. In calling the names of those whose generous sharing of knowledge and skills has enabled me to produce this study, I have become increasingly aware both of the number of people to whom I owe a debt of gratitude and the richness of their gifts. They have helped me to breathe new life into long deceased men and women and to tell their story as a part of the fabric which has shaped all our lives. I regret only that I may have failed to recall or to cite others to whom thanks and credit are due.

CONTENTS

	Prologue	3

THE ODYSSEY—Part 1
North Carolina, 1723-1800

I	The Southern Odyssey of the Hardisons Begins in North Carolina, 1723-1733	13
II	The Second Generation Comes of Age in the Albemarle, 1733-1775	31
III	The Hardisons in the Era of Revolution and Early Statehood, 1775-1785	65
IV	North Carolina at the Close of the Eighteenth Century, 1785-1800	83

THE ODYSSEY—Part 2
Georgia and Florida, 1800-1857

V	From the Albemarle to the Land of Cotton Washington County, 1800-1828	113
VI	A Sojourn in Florida Jefferson County, 1828-1835	145
VII	A Return to Georgia Early County, 1835-1845	163
VIII	Back to Florida Gadsden County, 1845-1857	179

THE ODYSSEY—Part 3
Texas and the Confederacy, 1857-1875

IX	On to Texas Polk County and Liberty County, 1857-1862	201
X	The South at War John Hardison's Service in the Confederate Army 1862-1863	231
XI	The South in Defeat John Hardison and the Texas Brigade from Georgia to North Carolina, 1864-1865	255
XII	New Beginnings in Texas during Reconstruction Limestone County, 1865-1875	287
XIII	Family Life in Texas during Reconstruction Letters of John and Mary Hardison Part 1, 1866-1870	309
XIV	Family Life in Texas during Reconstruction Letters of John and Mary Hardison Part 2, 1871-1875	343

THE ODYSSEY—Part 4
Georgia, 1875-1889

XV	Home to Georgia Washington County, 1875-1889	379

Epilogue	409
Photographs	413
Appendices	429
Index	451

The Hardisons

A SOUTHERN ODYSSEY

ಌ *Prologue* ಌ

The westward transatlantic movements of people is one of the greatest events in recorded history. Its magnitude and consequences are beyond measure. From 1500 to the present, it has involved the displacement and resettlement of over fifty million people, and it has affected indirectly the lives of uncountable millions more. It forms the foundation of American history and is basic, too, in ways we are only now beginning to understand, to the history of Europe, Africa, and even, to a lesser extent, of Asia.

Bernard Bailyn, *The Peopling of British North America*[1]

The Hardisons, a Southern Odyssey is the story of a particular family who participated in a particular phase of the peopling of British North America and the American South in the eighteenth and nineteenth centuries. Their British origins have yet to be documented but in all probability they were English men and women who with thousands of their countrymen looked upon America as the land of new beginnings. The dominance of England's rural economy by large estates and the depression which was a consequence of the conversion of much of the land from agriculture to wool production created a large body of dispossessed and displaced men and women who were eager to take advantage of the opportunity to acquire land of their own. In the late sixteenth and early seventeenth centuries, commercial and industrial advances and England's growing sea power provided the means for colonizing the recently discovered and explored continent of North America. These circumstances combined to produce a remarkable new empire along the Atlantic coastline. Following several failed attempts in the late 1500s, the settlement of colonies from

Maine to Georgia got underway with Britain's first permanent settlement at Jamestown, Virginia in 1607. The second successful settlement began in Massachusetts in 1620 and then slowly, painfully, but steadily the immigrants from Great Britain moved north, south, and west, pushing the native population out of its hunting, fishing, and farming lands and occupying the new Eden claimed in the name of their king. With varying degrees of success they sought to acquire a share of the vast lands in their new home.

The focus of this study is the family founded by Jasper Hardison in North Carolina in the early 1700s and a branch of his family which began its migration through the lower South about 1800. Jasper's purchase of several tracts of land, including a 1,000 acre plantation, within a decade of his first appearance in the land records of North Carolina in 1723 seems to indicate that he had either acquired wealth elsewhere in the colonies or had migrated directly from England with the means for acquiring land. Obviously he was a mature man at the time he came to North Carolina, for when he died in 1733 he left a family of nine children, some of whom were already adults. The presence of a Hardison family in Maine in the seventeenth century and the fact that one of Jasper's daughters was married to a member of the Carkeet family, also early settlers in Maine, makes it highly likely that Jasper had lived in New England before removing to North Carolina. Unfortunately none of the family researchers, including this author, who have attempted to find proof of the link between the Maine and North Carolina families have been able to document Jasper's presence in New England. There was a great loss of early records in Maine in the late 1600s and early 1700s as the native inhabitants destroyed nearly all of its towns in their effort to drive out the settlers. Records of the Carkeets in Massachusetts in the early 1700s suggest the possibility that Jasper might have lived there before going south and a search of that state's voluminous colonial records should be made.

Maine had a very troubled history in the seventeenth and early eighteenth centuries. Both the French and British claimed the lands which the native population called "Mayne" and each used Indian allies to discourage settlements by the other. Grants of land by the British crown led to conflicting claims over various portions of the relatively unknown and unsurveyed lands. The most important grants were made to John Mason and Ferdinando Gorges and to James, Duke of York, but by 1700 their lands had come under the jurisdiction of Massachusetts. There remained, however, a number of overlapping land grants along the coast whose ownership continued to be contested. Maine did not achieve statehood until 1820 and during most of the colonial era York County, in its southernmost area, was its only functioning county. At the end of the seventeenth century there was a large out-migration as attacks by the French and their Indian allies left only four towns inhabited by 1691, Wells, York, Kittery, and Appledore. Berwick, the town in which the Hardisons lived, had been completely destroyed in the previous decade. A measure of stability developed at the close of the seventeenth century as Massachusetts came under the authority of its first royal governor, but Indian attacks again took a heavy toll in the early 1700s and many settlers abandoned both New Hampshire and Maine, migrating to other British colonies along the Atlantic coast and in the West Indies. In addition to the turmoil of warfare and political upheaval, the harsh climate and rocky soil and growing resentment toward the Puritan dominated colony of Massachusetts were factors in the continuing out-migration. The early settlers in Maine had been drawn to America more by their desire to exploit the forests and the wealth of fish in the coastal waters than the Puritans' desire to establish a community based on their religious convictions.

The early presence in Maine of both the Carkeets and Hardisons is documented in records of the seventeenth century.[2] Members of the Carkeet family appear in the late 1500s and early 1600s in Plymouth, St. Andrews Parish, Devonshire, England, and in Maine records from the 1630s.[3] The spelling of Carkeet varies greatly, including Carkete, Curkeete, Curkeitt, Kirkeet, and Kerkeitt. Ellis Curkeitt, whose English baptismal record is dated 1596, appears in a list of settlers who arrived in Maine in the 1630s. In 1654 William Curkeete purchased in Saco, Maine, the plantation (the name used for a large land holding) of Thomas Redding on which he was already living. William's purchase places him in the northern portion of what is today York County. A later William, probably son of the first William, was married in Salem, Massachusetts in 1686 to Lydia Glanfield, the daughter of Lydia Ward and Robert Glanfield. The second William was identified as a mariner and in 1689 he was mate of the ketch Friendship, of which Robert was the master. In 1712 William was master of the sloop Endeavor, which sailed from Boston to Virginia. Children of William and Lydia were Lydia, born in 1686, William, 1689, Robert, 1697, and Benjamin, 1706. In all probability the last of these was the Benjamin Carkeet who was married to Jasper Hardison's daughter Mary. Their children's names repeated those used by William and Lydia. North Carolina records refer to Benjamin as a mariner and indicate that he continued to pursue the family's calling of sailing in the coastal trade of the Atlantic colonies.[4] William was deceased by 1720 when his widow, Lydia Kerkite, sold his property in Saco, long occupied by another tenant. Evidently the Carkeets were among the families of Maine who had looked elsewhere for safer, more promising lives.[5]

The Hardisons appear in the records of southernmost York County, primarily in Kittery and Berwick, in the latter half of the seventeenth century and in Berwick and Portsmouth, New Hampshire in the eighteenth century. As with Carkeet, the name takes various forms and it is difficult to know if they refer to the same family. The most common variations are Hardeson, Hardiston, Hardisson, and possibly Hareson, Harison and Harrison. The name Hardison is obviously a patronymic, meaning son of Hardi or Hardy. Families with varied spellings have been found in several counties in England, but none definitively associated with the American families. The New England Hardisons settled on the lands lying between the Merrimac River, in what is now New Hampshire, and the Kennebec, in southeastern Maine, which were granted in 1622 by King James I to Ferdinando Gorges and John Mason. Gorges was responsible for the settlements east of the Piscataqua River, which separates the present states of New Hampshire and Maine. Kittery, on the coast, was the first incorporated town of Maine and it originally had jurisdiction over the areas occupied by the towns of Eliot, South Berwick, Berwick, and North Berwick. The original town of Berwick was located at the head of navigation of the Piscataqua River and was known by the Indian name Newichawannock. The site's attraction was its great stands of pine trees and an early industry, which Berwick claims as the first saw mill in America, was begun after Mason and Gorges shipped cutting and processing machinery from England in the 1630s. The town of Berwick grew up around this industry, augmented by river traffic, boat building, fishing, and hunting.[6]

Records of the Hardison family's presence in York County date from the 1680s and continue into the nineteenth century. Stephen Hardison headed the earliest documented Hardison family of Maine. The first record for Stephen pertains to a lawsuit of 1685 in which he was plaintiff in a case involving a lot of pine timber. He married Mary Taylor of Berwick and their sons John and Stephen were born in 1691 and 1693. A record of 1696 suggests that Mary and Stephen may have been typical of the independent minded colonists of York County who resented the Puritan regulations of Massachusetts. They were called on to appear in court in Kittery "to answer for not frequenting public worship of God upon the Lord's Day" and were admonished and fined four shillings. The elder Stephen died in 1697 and his wife was twice remarried. Their son John established himself in the maritime trades in Portsmouth, New Hampshire and he and his son Stephen were identified in the eighteenth century deed records of Portsmouth, Rockland County, as mariner and boat builder.[7] John's brother Stephen remained a resident of Berwick, as did his descendants, well into the nineteenth century. Family historians have listed five Maine Hardisons who participated in the American Revolution—John, Peter, Stephen, Thomas, and Benjamin.[8] In the nineteenth century descendants of the second Stephen began to move from Berwick to other areas of Maine and were pioneers in Kennebec and Aroostook counties. From their home in Caribou, Aroostook County, some of the more adventurous Hardisons migrated from Maine in the late nineteenth century. Notable among them were Allen Crosby Hardison (1869-1965) who was active in the citrus industry and in promoting agricultural education in California and Wallace Libby Hardison (1850-1909), who was a pioneer in the oil industry in Pennsylvania and California.[9]

A third New England family with whom the Hardisons of the South may have a tie is the Hardy (varied spellings including Hardie and Hardee) family of Maine and New Hampshire. Their presence in Maine is documented from the mid-1600s and by the end of the century in New Hampshire.[10] The marriage record of Theophilus Hardy of Durham, New Hampshire to Mary Sullivan of Berwick in 1768 is recorded in the Berwick Record of Marriages.[11] As will be noted in the chapters which follow, Hardy families were living in northeastern North Carolina at the same time as the eighteenth century Hardisons and in Washington County, Georgia and Jefferson County, Florida at the time family members settled in those areas. Several Hardison children in North Carolina were named Hardy and in 1829 and 1830 the wedding ceremonies of two descendants of Jasper Hardison in Florida were performed by a Baptist minister named Theophilus Hardy. Another descendant, Elizabeth Hardison, and her husband Abner Jackson named their son Theophilus Hardee Jackson (1836-1917).

The lack of proof for a time of residence of Jasper Hardison and his family in New England before their settlement in North Carolina needs to be repeated—and remedied by future research, particularly in the early eighteenth century records of Massachusetts. However, circumstantial evidence is strong because of the presence of a well established Hardison family in Maine before the time of Jasper's arrival in North Carolina and the relationships between the Southern Hardisons and the Carkeet and Hardy families. Of course these relationships may have developed after the families migrated to the South and it is possible that the two Hardison families shared no kinship. It is significant, however, that Stephen and Jasper and both branches of the Carkeets shared interests in the timber industry and maritime trades. If Jasper first settled in New England, he had the opportunity for travel to the Southern colonies in ships in which the Hardisons and Carkeets had an interest. Throughout the colonial era, there was a lively trade between North Carolina and New England, particularly involving the sale of tobacco. English trade laws forbid or restricted such trade, but the colonists generally ignored these regulations and the coastal trade was of great value to both areas. A number of New Englanders settled in the Albemarle Sound area of North Carolina, particularly during the Indian wars at the close of the 1600s and in the early 1700s. It is highly probable that Jasper and his family were among their number.

NOTES

1. Bernard Bailyn, *The Peopling of British North America* (New York: Vintage Books, a Division of Random House, 1988; originally published by Knopf, 1986), p.5.
2. Sybil Noyes, Charles Thornton Libby, and Walter Goodwin Davis, editors, *Genealogical Dictionary of Maine and New Hampshire* (Portland: Southworth-Anthoensen Press, 1928-1939), p.128 (Carkeets) and p.309 (Hardisons). This valuable source, which was originally published in 5 volumes between 1928 and 1939, is based on the body of data known as the Lists, a compilation of the records of the communities of Maine and New Hampshire in the seventeenth century; church records; and the deed records of Maine and New Hampshire. The multi-volume York Deeds, published by the Maine Genealogical Society, was searched, but no proof of Jasper's presence in New England or a relationship to the Hardisons of Maine or New Hampshire was found. An unsuccessful search for Jasper was also made in the Provincial Deed Records, New Hampshire Records and Archives, Concord.
3. Data furnished by Verena Hatch, a descendant of Jasper Hardison's son Charles.
4. Tyrrell County, North Carolina, Deed Book 1, pp.88-89, 121-22, and 153; Robert J. Cain, editor, *The Colonial Records of North Carolina*, Second Series, Records of the Executive Council, 1735-1754 (Raleigh: Department of Cultural Resources, Division of Archives and History, 1988), vol.8, pp.376-78.
5. Richard D. Pierce, editor, *The Records of the First Church in Salem, Massachusetts, 1629-1736* (Salem: Essex Institute, 1974), p.244, record of the baptism in 1716 of "Lydia Karkett Junior." The Essex Institute has produced extensive collections of the records of Salem and Essex County.
6. J. Wilfred Albert, *et. al.*, compilers, *The Story of Berwick* (Berwick: 250th Anniversary Committee, 1963), pp.3-7.
7. Noyes, Libby, and Davis, *op. cit.*, p.309.
8. Florence Collins Porter and Clara Wilson Gries, *Our Folks and Your Folks* (Los Angeles: Fred S. Lang Company, 1919), chap.3.
9. Rena V. Grant, *Three Men from Aroostook* (Berkeley: Brazelton-Hanscom, 1963). The book, based on the research of Allen Crosby Hardison, is a study of the Stephen Hardison family of Maine from its beginnings to the descendants living in California in the twentieth century.
10. Noyes, Libby, and Davis, *op. cit., p.309.*
11. Town of Berwick, Record of Marriages, Book 1 (transcription from originals made in 1933), p.118, Theophilus Hardy to Mary Sullivan, May 4, 1768.

THE ODYSSEY
෫ Part 1 ෫

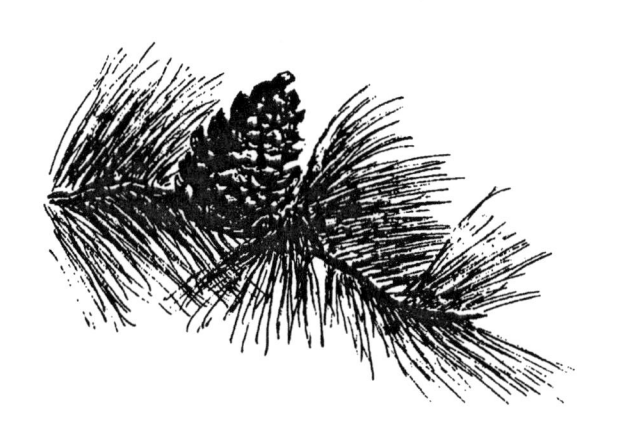

North Carolina
1723-1800

I

The Southern Odyssey of the Hardisons Begins in North Carolina, 1723-1733

*I*n the first quarter of the eighteenth century, the vast forests and fertile land of North Carolina's Coastal Plain drew Jasper Hardison to the newly developing portion of that region lying between Albemarle Sound and Pamlico Sound. Within the ten years between his first documented acquisition of land in 1723 and his death in 1733, Jasper, his wife Mary, their seven sons and two daughters established themselves as a family of large land holdings. Jasper's major purchase and the place where he established his home was Roses Plantation, a 1,000 acre tract in the northeast corner of Martin County, just to the west of the present boundary between Martin and Washington County. His land lay south of the Roanoke River, near its entry into Albemarle Sound, in the vicinity of two of the numerous waterways which threaded this plain on the western fringe of the Tidewater—Devil's Gut, the large creek paralleling one of the great bends of the Roanoke, and Welches Creek, to the south of the river near its opening into the sound.[1] The area was characterized by alternating swamps and ridges of dry land and by thick forests. It was a mysterious terrain which provided a dramatic setting for local folklore, inspiring tales of devils and witches, particularly among the black population, which

Lea's New Map of Carolina, 1695

History of North Carolina by Samuel A'Court Ashe,
1908 Greensboro, North Carolina.

grew as plantations were carved out of this wilderness.[2] Fearful and mysterious as the swampy land might be, its numerous creeks provided access to the river and the sound, which were lifelines to trade with the other colonies and with England.

The native population of North Carolina had prized the Coastal Plain for its abundance of fish and game and for the fertile soil and mild climate. The French, Spanish, and English explorers of the 1500s searched it for gold and precious gems. Each nation had attempted a settlement along the Carolina coast, the most notable being the "Lost Colony" founded by Sir Walter Raleigh in the 1580s on North Carolina's Roanoke Island. By the time of the Hardisons' arrival, about sixty years after the founding of the colony of Carolina in 1663, the steady stream of settlers from Virginia and other colonies valued it more realistically for its cheap and fertile land, its stands of giant pine trees, its long growing season, and its suitability for tobacco and a variety of food crops. Jasper and his sons, particularly the eldest, John, were aggressive in the acquisition of land and they were successful in establishing lumber and grist mills. Their names appear in the public records of the eighteenth century as juror, justice of the peace, sheriff, militia officer, and representative in the colonial and provincial legislatures, again with John as the most noteworthy.[3] A contemporary map of Martin County includes reminders of their lengthy presence—Hardison Creek, Hardison Mill, the village of Hardison—and a look in the current telephone book for Williamston, the county seat, reveals over one hundred Hardison entries for that town and its vicinity. The majority of these listings are for the town of Jamesville, which is located in the eastern area of the county, where the Hardisons originally settled in the early 1700s. The nineteenth century portion of this study will tell primarily of the branch of John's family which left North Carolina for Georgia in the early years of the century, a time when thousands of North Carolinians emigrated to states to the south and the west. Obviously, however, many of the Hardisons found the Albemarle area to their liking and planted roots which were deep and lasting.

Early Carolina History

A brief review of North Carolina's development in the colonial era provides a background for the lives of the Hardisons in the eighteenth century. At the time of their arrival, the major area of settlement was the Coastal Plain, that broad swath of land which occupies two-fifths of the present state, stretching from Virginia's southern border to South Carolina. The great German and Scotch-Irish migration which filled in the central two-fifths, the Piedmont, was yet to come, in the middle decades of the eighteenth century. In the preceding century, from the mid-1600s, settlement had begun in the northeastern corner of the Coastal Plain, with a small trickle of the curious, the land-hungry, and the discontented from Virginia spilling into the Chowan River-Albemarle Sound area. The native population, with whom they at first co-existed and sometimes paid for their land, was made up of a number of tribes, the most outstanding being the Tuscaroras, a branch of the Iroquois. As the flow of these settlers increased, confusion arose over the jurisdiction into which their lands fell. The original charter of the Virginia Company, which had planted England's first successful settlement in North America at Jamestown, had included the area which was later known as North Carolina. After this charter was revoked, confusion grew out of the granting of land by both King Charles I and Charles II, the Virginia legislature, and native American chieftans. In addition to these "legitimate" claims, many of the settlers were squatters, holding no title.[4]

The confusion resulting from conflicting claims was one of several reasons for founding the colony of Carolina. In 1663, King Charles II, who had recently been restored to the throne of England at the conclusion of the bloody civil war which had resulted in his father's death, was pressed by a group of his supporters to repay them with a large grant of land in America. These eight wealthy and powerful men, designated the Lords Proprietors of Carolina, were granted the whole of what is today North and South Carolina. In addition to paying a debt and consolidating Charles' political support, the colonizing scheme was a significant part of England's effort to make good her claim to the Atlantic seaboard stretching from French Canada to Spanish Florida. The Lords Proprietors were given enormous powers, including the right to establish and administer government, to lay and collect taxes, to grant lands, and to confer titles of nobility. Residing in England, they formulated various elaborate and impractical plans for organizing and governing their colony, including "The Fundamental Constitutions of Carolina" which have been attributed to the philosopher John Locke, secretary to the proprietors. They envisioned the establishment of enormous feudal estates which would yield products needed by the mother country and create great personal wealth. Two factors doomed this dream from its inception—the abundance of land for the taking in an area remote from the proprietors and the limitations which had been placed on the proprietors' powers. The settlers were guaranteed the rights of Englishmen and were promised taxation based on their consent through some form of representative body. The seeds for resistance to authority, for which North Carolina was particularly notable throughout the colonial era, were planted early in its history. Their sprouting and flourishing led eventually to the end of the proprietary project in 1729 and to independence from the mother country in 1776. John Hardison was among the members of the Provincial Congress held in Halifax in November, 1776 which prepared North Carolina for statehood and participation in the Revolution.

Soon after receiving their charters, the first in 1663 and a second in 1665, the proprietors divided their vast lands into three "Counties," each named for one of the proprietors: Albemarle, consisting of the land in present northeastern North Carolina east of the Chowan River and north of Albemarle Sound; Clarendon, including the lands south of the Sound through the valley of the Cape Fear River; and Craven, continuing south through what is today South Carolina. Although their charter granted lands southward from Virginia to Spanish Florida and westward to the South Seas (the Pacific Ocean), the seventeenth century settlements were small colonies in the tidewater area of the Coastal Plain. In spite of the proprietors' generous land policy, the "Counties" grew slowly. In the case of Albemarle County, the shallowness of the Sound and the treacherous waters surrounding the islands along the coast made it impossible for large ships to bring in the settlers who were needed to realize the proprietors' scheme of feudal estates. Albemarle County was primarily attractive to an overflow of settlers from Virginia, who came down the rivers from the southern counties of that colony. An attempt at colonization in Clarendon County failed, but prospects were more promising in Craven County with the beginnings of a coastal settlement eventually known as Charleston, which attracted a number of wealthy immigrants from the Caribbean islands.

Albemarle's history as a separate colony lasted less than twenty years and was marked by strife and instability, created by the proprietors' failure to establish a strong government or a satisfactory plan of land distribution. Although the name continued in use well into the next century, Albemarle officially ceased to exist as a separate entity in 1689, when a governor was appointed for the whole Carolina colony. He was to reside in Charles Town, later Charleston, which received more attention from the proprietors than the other settlements because of its relative prosperity. The plan called for the residents of the Albemarle area to send delegates to Charles Town to participate in a representative body, but this arrangement proved unworkable and for all practical purposes North Carolina became a separate colony, with its own legislative body and a deputy governor. In 1710 the proprietors recognized its separate status and appointed a governor.

A period of relative calm and stability was enjoyed in the last decade of the 1600s and first of the 1700s and North Carolina's population began to grow from the meager 5,000 estimated by 1700. Settlers began to migrate beyond the original bounds of Albemarle County into the lands south of the Sound. Old Albemarle County was divided into the precincts which later became counties. They maintained the names which the natives had given them—Chowan, Pasquotank, Perquimans, and Currituck. New counties were created as settlers occupied the Coastal Plain to the west across the Chowan River and the south below the Roanoke River and Albemarle Sound, toward Pamlico Sound and eventually the Cape Fear River Valley. Towns were founded, including Edenton, Bath, and New Bern, but they were mere villages and none was designated as a permanent seat of government. The majority of the population lived in crude houses in isolated clearings of the forest. Locations on creeks and rivers were prized because of the absence of roads.

The relative growth and prosperity of the first decade of the 1700s were broken in the second as Thomas Cary led a rebellion against the newly appointed governor, Edward Hyde. Numerous issues were at stake, among them were political rivalries and resistance of the widely diverse population, which included numerous Quakers and Presbyterians and what an Anglican missionary called "anythingarians," to the establishment of the Church of England as the official and tax supported religious institution of the colony. The native population, most notably the Tuscarora tribe, took advantage of the disturbance to address a long history of usurpation of their lands by a steady stream of settlers. Added to this grievance were the numerous instances of kidnapping and enslaving of members of this and other tribes, particularly women and children. North Carolinians had an unsavory reputation for cheating and dealing harshly with the native population. In September of 1711 there was a well coordinated attack on white settlements and a massacre of over one hundred men, women, and children. The ensuing hostilities lasted two years, resulting in hundreds of deaths and widespread destruction of property. Help came to the colonists from South Carolina and the inevitable defeat of the natives followed. A reservation was created west of the Chowan River, but many of the Tuscaroras who had managed to survive left to join their Iroquois kinsmen in the North.

The early decades of the 1700s were troubled also by the widespread piracy which plagued shipping on the South Atlantic coast. North Carolina became notorious for the great frequency of acts of piracy along its coast, a natural site for such activities with the numerous inlets and treacherous sand bars. The colonists' desire to evade English taxes on trade had promoted smuggling and the ongoing warfare of England with France and Spain made the seizure of ships of those nations respectable. Both proprietary officials and colonists were at times involved in these activities. Such attitudes and actions encouraged thievery and flagrant lawlessness. In the late 1710s a concerted effort was made by the Virginia and Carolina authorities to curb the menace to shipping. With the capture and execution of such famous pirates as Edmund Teach (Blackbeard) and Stede Bonnet in 1718, the "Golden Age" of piracy ended. Treasure seekers still search for hidden casks of gold on North Carolina's islands, known as the Outer Banks.

The defeat of both the natives and the pirates, accompanied by a lull in the ongoing hostility between the proprietary authorities and the colonists, created conditions which encouraged prosperity within the colony and made it attractive to new settlers. Several thousand arrived in the 1720s, the Hardisons most likely among them since the founder of that family in North Carolina, Jasper, made his first recorded purchase of land in 1723. At the end of the 1720s the often arbitrary and ineffective rule of the eight Lords Proprietors was brought to an end as King George II bought out all but one, the Carteret family. Their land became known as the Granville District and the Hardisons received several large grants from it.

From 1729 until the beginning of the Revolution in 1775, North Carolina functioned as a royal colony and, despite the ongoing contentions between the governors and the colonial legislative delegates, enjoyed a more stable government and economy than it had previously known. When the proprietary era ended in 1729, North Carolina was one of the most sparsely settled of England's North American colonies and most of its population, about 30,000 whites and 6,000 blacks, lived in the tidewater area. By 1775 the white population was estimated at 265,000 and the black at 80,000, making North Carolina the fourth most populous of the colonies, exceeded only by Virginia, Pennsylvania, and Massachusetts. At the time of the Hardisons' arrival, North Carolina's white population was primarily of English stock, but in the next forty years it was to be augmented by the arrival of thousands of Scotch-Irish (Scottish Protestants from northern Ireland) and Germans, who came both from their native lands and from Pennsylvania and other colonies, and Scotch Highlanders, who migrated directly from their homeland. English immigrants from both England and other colonies continued to arrive throughout the remainder of the colonial period. These numerous and varied settlers filled in the Coastal Plain to the south of Albemarle Sound and then settled in the upper Cape Fear Valley and the Piedmont, moving on toward the mountains. This westward shift of population concentration from the coastal area eventually led to challenges of the dominance of the older settlements. The grievances culminated in a rebellion in the early 1770s known as the Regulator movement. The rebellion was brutally supressed by royal and colonial militia units from the eastern counties shortly before the American Revolution began. Soon the same militia companies were mobilized to fight for independence from the mother country.

The Hardisons began their participation in the colonial history of North Carolina in the 1720s when Jasper and his family settled in the area just to the south of the Roanoke River and Albemarle Sound. The occupation of this area by white settlers represented the first expansion of the original Albemarle County beyond its designated boundaries. Throughout the 1700s the Hardisons were a prolific and prosperous family, with most of them remaining in the area between Albemarle Sound and the Pamlico River and Sound—today's Martin, Washington, Tyrrell, Beaufort, and Hyde counties. A few family members ventured away from the original Hardison lands to Craven and Onslow counties to the south in mid-century.

Jasper Hardison Founds the Family in the Albemarle

The land records of the thirteen original colonies are one of the most valuable sources of information about the individuals and families who peopled British North America. North Carolina is rich in these records and they, in turn, are rich in data about the Hardisons in the eighteenth century, since they were very successful in the immigrants' obsessive pursuit of land. The Lords Proprietors to whom King Charles II had granted the vast lands of Carolina were eager to have them settled and they devised various schemes for attracting immigrants from the other colonies as well as Great Britain. The instrument by which the proprietors gave title to land was known as a patent.[5] There were two types of patents, purchase patents for persons who paid a fee for their land and headrights patents. As in most of the southern colonies, many of the original titles to land were acquired through the headrights system, with from 50 to 100 acres being given to the head of a family who paid his own way and 50 acres for each person he was responsible for bringing into the colony.

Throughout the colonial period the proprietary and the royal authorities in England tried to prevent the establishment of large estates in North Carolina, however some of the governors and other influential and powerful men were able to acquire vast acreages, among them Thomas Pollock, whose will of 1722 recorded his possession of parcels totaling 22,000 acres plus ten additional plantations and seventy-five slaves.[6] By the time the Hardisons settled in the Albemarle in the 1720s, the crown authorities were trying to stop the rapid disposition of land by the Proprietors and many acquisitions by new settlers were made by purchase from those who had received the original grants. Jasper's major purchase of that decade, Roses Plantation, was from the huge estate which Thomas Pollock left to his sons Cullen, Thomas, and George. The elder Thomas, a native of Scotland and an early settler in North Carolina, had served as Acting Governor of the colony, in his capacity as President of the Council, during some of its most troubled times in the second decade of the eighteenth century.[7] The sons inherited numerous tracts of land to the south of the Roanoke River and both Jasper and his son John acquired large acreages from them. The wording of the documents for these transactions seems to indicate an ongoing personal relationship between the Pollocks, particularly Cullen, and the Hardisons. One of John's grandsons was named Cullen.

A search of the colonial land records of North Carolina indicates that Jasper Hardison was the first member of his family to acquire land in that colony, with his earliest recorded purchase being 100 acres from William Morris for 14 pounds "Current Money" on January 7, 1722/23.[8] The deed was recorded in Chowan Precinct, later Chowan County, a subdivision of the original Albemarle County, which at this time included the lands of Bertie, Martin, Washington, and Tyrrell counties. This land and Jasper's subsequent acquisitions were in the northeastern portion of today's Martin County on its border with Washington County, in the vicinity of Welches Creek, adjoining property of Cullen Pollock. His first purchase also adjoined the land of John Browning, from whom Morris had recently purchased the land, and Thomas Lee. It is possible that this was not Jasper's original acquisition of land in North Carolina for the deed refers to him as Jasper Hardison of Chowan Precinct, "planter." This designation was usually reserved for men with holdings of at least several hundred acres.

Jasper's purchase in 1729 of a 1,000 acre tract on the south side of the Roanoke River certainly put him in the planter category. He purchased the land, at that time in Bertie County, which was created in 1722 from Chowan Precinct, for 120 pounds "sterling money of Great Britain" from Cullen Pollock.[9] The deed describes it as "a certain plantation & Tract of Land containing by Estimation one thousand Acres be it more or less Scituate lying and being on the South Side of Morattuck [Roanoke] River commonly known by the name of Roses plantation adjoining to the Land of Mr. John Blount." Jasper's will and subsequent Hardison deeds indicate that this plantation became the family homestead. The past history of this parcel of land and the origin of its name are found in patents of 1716 and 1717 from the proprietary government to Richard Rose and Thomas Pollock, Cullen's father.[10] Rose, also spelled Ross, was granted three parcels south of the Roanoke River in the vicinity of Welches Creek totaling 1,570 acres. The descriptions of the land includes names of locations often mentioned in later Hardison deeds—Gum Swamp, Deep Run, and "Rosses Creek." Possibly these patents augmented land already in the possession of Rose. A few months after Rose was granted his patents of 1717, Thomas Pollock received a patent for 3,250 acres which included land on both sides of "Roses Creek" adjoining former land of Richard Rose. Apparently the ever acquisitive Pollock had come into possession of some or all of Rose's land and son Cullen sold a portion of it to Jasper after his father's death.

Information on the subsequent history of Jasper's purchase from Cullen is found in the Tyrrell County deed records, the land having come under the jurisdiction of this county after its creation in 1729. In 1740, seven years after Jasper's death, Cullen registered an "Assignment of Contract," with John Hardison as one of the witnesses. He affirmed a transaction of 1726 with Jasper in which for "considerable consideration" he had made a deed of sale of about 1,000 acres on the northeast side of Roses Creek and the southeast side of the Morratock (Roanoke) River. He noted that before his death Jasper had made a deed for 100 acres to Benjamin Carkeet (husband of Jasper's daughter Mary) and had willed the rest of the land to his sons. He noted also that Jasper's sons Jasper and Charles had subsequently sold their inheritances from this land, totaling 300 acres, to Benjamin. In his 1740 affidavit, Pollock assigned 400 acres to Benjamin, since he had deeds from Jasper and sons Jasper and Charles covering their transactions, and he disclaimed any right to the remaining 600 acres. Pollock gave as his reason for recording the transaction that, not having been heretofore acknowledged, it "became void and of none effect and thereby the honest purchasers not entitled to what they have paid their money for." He wished that "justice may be done to everyone concerned."[11] It is probable that this document of 1740 referred to the same 1,000 acres of the deed which had been recorded in 1729 in Bertie County, the jurisdiction in which the land lay at that time. Possibly the original transaction had taken place in 1726, with registration at a later date, as was often the case because of the difficult travel between plantations and county courthouses. Cullen's verification in the Tyrrell County deed records of the original Bertie County transaction and the subsequent disposal of portions of the 1,000 tract by Jasper and his sons served as a guarantee of the titles of both the Carkeets and the Hardisons.

Jasper's last recorded land acquisition was a patent of April 22, 1730 for a section (640 acres) in the vicinity of his earlier purchases —"southerly of Morattock River joining William Rhodes and west side of Deep Run."[12] The patent was granted during the administration of the last of the proprietary governors, Sir Richard Everard, who ignored the prohibition on land grants which the crown had ordered during the term of the previous governor, George Burrington.[13] As the reality of a transtion from ownership and government by the Lords Proprietors to the status of crown colony became obvious, Everard issued a great number of "blank patents." These titles were signed by the proper officials but they were inadequately recorded and deliberately left blank the size and location of the parcel of land being granted, thus thwarting future collections of the land tax, the quit rent, owed to the crown. Jasper's patent may not have have been of the "blank" variety, since as recorded in Patent Book Three it mentions both the size and boundaries of the grant, but it was made at a time during the transition from proprietary to royal status when the British authorities had expressly forbidden new distributions of unoccupied land. Among the records in Patent Book Three are a number of patents for sections of land to Cullen Pollock, who was taking advantage of Everard's largesse to add to his already vast acreages. The name Richard Everard appears often as a witness in the transactions recorded in Patent Book Three, including a patent for land which adjoined Jasper's boundary.[14] It may be assumed that this Richard was the son of Governor Everard, who is known to have remained in

North Carolina after his father left for England when George Burrington, serving now in the capacity of royal governor, arrived in the colony in 1731. A personal relationship between the younger Richard and the Hardisons is revealed in a document of 1730 recorded in Craven County, in which Richard made a gift of land in what was at that time Bath County to "my God son Richard Hardison, son of Jasper Hardison." The land, located between the present towns of New Bern and Kinston, later fell in the jurisdiction of Craven County. Richard was probably a child at the time of the gift and there is no evidence that he ever laid claim to the land.[15]

Within three years after receiving his patent of 1730, Jasper Hardison died, but in the preceding decade he had succeeded in the eighteenth century version of the American dream—the acquisition of an estate which would provide a livelihood for his family and would be an impetus to them to enlarge and develop their holdings. In a period when the vast majority of the residents of the southern colonies derived their livelihood from the land, the possession of it determined political, social, and economic status. Jasper and his sons were accorded the titles planter, esquire, and gentleman and they joined the landed citizens who ran the affairs of the colony. They had established ties with two powerful families, the Pollocks and the Everards, who could help them realize their ambitions, and they intermarried with the planter families of their neighborhood.

On May 8, 1733, Jasper made his last will and testament and died shortly thereafter, the will being probated on November 5, 1733. All matters pertaining to wills, probate, and administration of estates were a function of the proprietary and later the royal officials in the early colonial period, rather than the precinct or county courts. The official copy of Jasper's will was signed by Governor George Burrington and filed in the office of the Secretary of State, the official keeper of the colony's records. He is referred to as a resident of Albemarle County, rather than Tyrrell County, in whose jurisdiction his lands actually lay after the formation of that county in 1729.[16]

The opening paragraph of his will is an elaborate version of the usual introduction to such documents in this era:

> In The Name of God Amen The 8th day of May 1733 I Jasper Hardison of the County of Albemarle planter being very sick and weak in body but

of perfect mind and memory thanks be given to God for it therefore calling to mind the mortality of my body and knowing that it is appointed for all men once to die do make and ordain this my last will and testament that is to say principally & first of all I give and recommend my soul into the hands of a loving God that gave it and my body I recommend to the earth to be buried in a decent Christian burial at the descresion of my Ex [executors] nothing doubting but at the general resurrection I shall receive the same again by the mighty power of God and as to such worldly estate wherewith it hath pleased God to bless me in this life I give, devise & dispose of the same in the following manner and forme . . .

The will names Jasper's wife Mary, seven sons, and two females, Mary Carkeet and Judah Sutton, presumed to be his married daughters. Wife Mary and John, most likely the eldest son, were named as executors. To Mary he left "one negro and all my goods and chattles all and singular debts and moveable effects" except those specifically willed to others. Also, as noted below, he provided Mary the use of his plantation during her life. To John he left a tract of land containing 640 acres on the south side of Deep Run and one horse, one dish, one bason [basin], a case of bottles, and one pot. The remainder of his land was divided among his other six sons—to Jasper 200 acres in Cheat Neck, to Charles a parcel known as Cheat Neck Island, to Joshua and Thomas a tract running from the upper part of "Mr. Carkeat's line" to Cheat Neck Branch, and to Richard and Joseph "the plantation and remainder part of the land after the decease of my well beloved wife known by the name of Roses plantation."[17] To Mary Carkeet he bequeathed one cow and calf, having already given 100 acres to her husband Benjamin, as noted in the previously cited Cullen Pollock document of 1740. He gave to Judah Sutton "fifty pounds current money of North Carolina" and a mare branded B. Judah's given name was probably Judith.

A rather curious will which relates to the Hardison family was written by William Garrett (also spelled Garrott and Garrat), shortly after Jasper's death. Like Jasper, William was identified as a planter of Albemarle County.[18] The will is dated March 23, 1734, which in terms of our current calendar falls in the year 1735, March 25 being considered the first day of the new year until the English adopted the Gregorian calendar in 1751. Apparently William died shortly after writing the will, for it was signed by the royal governor, Gabriel Johnston, on March 27, 1735 and recorded the following day. William's wife, like Jasper's, was named Mary and the will mentions five of Jasper's sons. John and Jasper were witnesses, John was co-executor with Mary, and Thomas, Richard, and Joseph were given small bequests of livestock. Family researchers have raised the possibility that Mary was Jasper's widow, perhaps a second and younger wife than the mother of the older children.[19] The major portion of the estate was left to Mary, with provision being made for a possible unborn child, though the wording indicates uncertainty as to whether Mary was pregnant. If she were not pregnant or if the child died, the parcel of land set aside for it was to go to James Chason, who like the Hardison brothers had been given a small bequest earlier in the will.[20] The nature of the relationship between the Hardisons and the Garretts is not known, but the deeds of Tyrrell County indicate that they lived in close proximity and bought from and sold land to each other throughout the 1700s. Members of the Garrett family were prominent landowners in the portion of Tyrrell which became Washington County, after its formation in 1799. They built a house at some time between 1750 and 1760 on land known as Garrett's Island, acquired by Daniel Garrett, about three miles southeast of the town of Plymouth. The residence, named Island Home, is considered the oldest house in Washington County.[21]

During the forty years between the time of Jasper's death and the beginning of the Revolution in the 1770s, his children developed and enlarged the Hardison holdings, became noted for their grist and saw mills, held public offices, and participated in the life of the planter class in the tidewater area of North Carolina. With varying degrees of success the Hardison sons and the Suttons and Carkeets pursued the acquisition and exploitation of land, North Carolina's most abundant and valuable resource, establishing families primarily in Tyrrell and Martin counties. The following chapter will tell of the fortunes of Jasper's sons and daughters as revealed by the land records of the last four decades of the colonial era.

NOTES

1. Place names as well as family names in eighteenth century records have many variations in spelling and there are often two or more names for natural features, such as rivers and creeks. Welch's Creek and Rose's Creek appear often in the Hardisons' records. They were generally spelled "Welches" and "Roses" in their deeds and this spelling will be used in the following chapters. I am indebted to Mr. F. W. Smith of Martin County for information on the location of Roses Creek, which is one of the boundaries of his land. It is a small black-water creek which crosses State Road 1563 north of Highway 64. It flows into the Roanoke River in the northeast corner of Martin County, just below the river's last great loop before entering Albemarle Sound. The Roanoke was frequently referred to in Hardisons' land records since it formed the northern boundary of the area in which they lived. Its original name, the Morratock (many spelling variations), which was drawn from the name of the native inhabitants, was often used in the eighteenth century, but Roanoke will be the designation in the chapters which follow.
2. Louise Robertson Booker, *Ghosts and Witches of Martin County* (Williamston: Enterprise Publishing Company, 1971).
3. Material on the early history of the Hardisons in North Carolina is drawn from P. W. Fisher, *One Dozen Pre-Revolutionary Families of Eastern North Carolina and Some of Their Descendants* (New Bern: New Bern Historical Society Foundation, Inc., 1958), pp.129-30; Francis M. Manning and W. H. Booker, *Martin County History*, (Williamston: Enterprise Publishing Company, 1977) vol.1, pp.1-22; *Colonial Records of North Carolina*, 10 volumes (Raleigh, 1886-90), edited by William L. Saunders; *State Records of North Carolina*, 16 volumes (Winston, Goldsboro, Charlotte, 1895-1905), edited by Walter Clark (these volumes will hereafter be referred to as *Colonial Records of North Carolina* and *State Records of North Carolina*; Fred L. Hawkins and Dorothy Westmoreland Gilliam, *Hardison and Allied Families* (Columbia, Tennessee: privately published, 1992); and the deed records of Chowan County (Edenton), Bertie County (Windsor), and Tyrrell County (Columbia).
4. Hugh Talmage Lefler and Albert Ray Newsome, *North Carolina, The History of a Southern State*, 3rd edition (Chapel Hill: University of North Carolina Press, 1973), chaps.1-4. These chapters cover the early years of North Carolina as a colony.
5. Margaret M. Hofmann, *Province of North Carolina, 1663-1729, Abstracts of Land Patents* (Weldon: Roanoke News Company, 1979), in the foreword Hofmann explains the process by which a potential owner received a title, known as a patent. This volume is the first of a series in which Hofmann abstracted the proprietary, royal, and Granville records of colonial land grants.
6. *State Records of North Carolina*, vol.22, pp.290-96, Thomas Pollock's will; Lefler and Newsome, *op. cit.*, pp.89-91.
7. Samuel A. Ashe, editor, *Biographical History of North Carolina* (Greensboro: Charles L. Van Noppen Publisher, 1925), vol.1, pp.411-12.
8. Chowan County Deed Book C, number 1, p.361. In the introduction to her volume of abstracts of Chowan deeds, Margaret Hofmann notes that the English did not adopt the Gregorian calendar until 1751, continuing to count March 25 as the first day of the year. This fact accounts for the use of both the years 1722 and 1723 on the deed, the latter being the correct year in terms of our present calendar. Margaret M. Hofmann, *Chowan Precinct, North Carolina, 1696-1723* (Weldon: Roanoke News Company, 1972).
9. Bertie County Deed Book C, p.159.

I. THE SOUTHERN ODYSSEY BEGINS, 1723-1733

10. Hofmann, *Province of North Carolina, 1663-1729, Abstracts of Land Patents*, Abstracts 2841, 2842, 3338, and 3340, the originals from Patent Book 8, pp.152, 153, and 292, for Richard and Thomas Rose/Ross; Abstract 1321, the original from Patent Book 2, p. 331, for Pollock.
11. Tyrrell County Deed Book 1, pp.121-22 (Cullen Pollock); pp.88-89, (Charles and Jasper Hardison).
12. Hofmann, *Province of North Carolina*, 1663-1729, Abstract 2620, original in Patent Book 3, p.265.
13. William S. Powell, editor, *Dictionary of North Carolina Biography* (Chapel Hill: University of North Carolina Press, 1986), vol.2, pp.171-72.
14. Hofmann, *Province of North Carolina, 1663-1729*, Abstract 2601, original in Patent Book 3, p.261.
15. Hawkins and Gilliam, *op. cit.*, p.60.
16. North Carolina State Archives, Raleigh, Secretary of State Will Book 876, p.279. In the quotation, the original spelling is reproduced but punctuation has been added to improve readability.
17. Tyrrell County Deed Book 4, vol.2, pp.372 and 375, deeds of Thomas Stewart in 1770 locate Cheat Neck Island as lying on the south side of the Roanoke River.
18. North Carolina State Archives, Secretary of State loose wills, #1388.
19. Hawkins and Gilliam, *op. cit.*, p.22.
20. J. Bryan Grimes, editor, *Abstract of North Carolina Wills* (Baltimore: Genealogical Publishing Company, 1980), p.71, the will of Anne Chesson, Perquimans County, 1727, lists sons James, John, and Joshua and brothers Daniel and William Garrett.
21. Washington County Historical Society, *Historic Washington County* (Plymouth: Washington County Historical Society, n.d.).

II

The Second Generation Comes of Age in the Albermarle, 1733-1775

The nine children of Jasper Hardison lived the major portion of their adult lives in North Carolina during the years, 1729-1776, when it was a royal colony.[1] Jasper died in the early 1730s just as the transition was being made from the colony's proprietary status, as a personal possession of the eight Lords Proprietors, to a crown colony with a governor appointed by the king. As a family the Hardisons prospered and, as members of the planter class, the sons played active roles in the colony's economic and political life. They left numerous records of their acquisitions of land in the deed books of Tyrrell and Martin counties and the public career of John Hardison is well documented in the official records of North Carolina.

Relatively little is known of the women in the family—Jasper's wife and two daughters and his sons' wives and daughters. Few of the eighteenth century marriage records which would have given their maiden names have survived and in the instances in which their names appear in deeds only their husbands' surnames are used. Scant attention was given to education in North Carolina in this century, particularly for women, and many had to sign their legal documents with an "X." The children of the planters were generally educated at

JASPER HARDISON I
(?? - 1733)

JASPER	CHARLES	JOSHUA	THOMAS	RICHARD	JOSEPH	MARY	JUDAH
JOSEPH	CHARLES JR.	JOSHUA JR.	??	JAMES	MILLICENT		
FREDERICK	Catherine	Mark		Thomas	JUDITH		
JOSHUA	Gabriel	Mary		Margaret	NANCY		
JASPER JR.	William	William J.		William	CHARLES		
Isaac	Elijah	Sarah		Charles	WIGGINS		
Samuel	JOHN	Cloah		Frances	Wiggins Jr.		
Hannah	Jesse Sr.	Robert		Joel	Mary		
John	Elzey	Jemima		Delilah	Joseph		
Jessie	Samuel	Daniel		Humphrey	Martha		
Noah	Lamb	Joshua III		Ezra	James W.		
David	Jesse Jr.	Hannah		Penelope	Nancy		
James	Alcy	Nancy		Asa	WILLIAM		
Jessie Jr.	Hardy	Joshua IV		Richard B.	Lavinia		
Charles	Elizabeth	Mary		James Y.	William Jr.		
James	Nancy	Sarah		Emily J.	Robert		
Hannah	ROBERT	Martha		FREDERICK	Hansel		
Harmon	JOSEPH	Edward		RICHARD JR.	Mittie		
Martha	ISAAC	Ira			Churchill		
William		Eliza			Luther		
Frederick		Joseph H.			Wm. Jonathan		
Judah		Lewis W.					
LEMUEL		George W.					
JUDY		Ezra					
DAVID		Simon					
		Luke					
		Joseph					
		Nancy					
		Charlotte					
		Louisa					

JOHN
WILLIAM
Benjamin
Cullen
Elizabeth
Hannah
Sarah
Mary
BENJAMIN
John
William L.
Seth
Winnifred
Temperance
Elizabeth
Nancy
John M.
William
Ezekiel
Hardy
Seth
Samuel
Martha
Thomas
Elizabeth
JOHN
MARY
ELIZABETH
SARAH
ANN
HANNAH
FRANCES
ROBERT(?)

Descendants of Jasper Hardison

Fred L. Hawkins and Dorothy Westmoreland Gilliam, *Hardison and Allied Families*. Used by permission of Fred L. Hawkins.

home by their parents, with the major share of attention given to the male children. Early death due to childbirth and the hardships of colonial life was common among women of the colonial era. The eighteenth century was truly a man's world; however, the few existing Hardison wills and the deed records of this family and a number of their contemporaries offer many examples of provisions for the support of widows and the care and education of children.

The Hardisons' way of life was probably like that of the majority of the planter families of moderate wealth in the Albemarle area of North Carolina. They generally secured for their residences sites along the numerous rivers and creeks of eastern North Carolina. These waterways were their means of transportation to markets for their goods and to the social, political, and economic activities of the colony, in an era when roads were few and generally in poor condition. The term plantation was used for the tract of land on which they built their homes, with the "manor" being the residence. Plantation does not necessarily imply extensive agricultural development, particularly in the case of the Hardisons, whose major interest was in milling. Many planters owned fewer than ten slaves, the Hardisons among them, with nine being their greatest number. Plantation gardens and orchards; their numerous livestock, which were generally left to roam in the woods; and the plentiful wild game yielded bountiful food for the planter families. They were noted for their hospitality to each other and to travelers, but relatively few lived in luxury. Manufactured goods were scarce and expensive and most furniture, clothing, and household goods were produced on the plantation.

A small number of the wealthiest planters built homes which might be called mansions, but the majority lived in simple wood houses of the plentiful native pine, often left unpainted and added to as families grew. The earliest settlers had lived in log houses of one or two rooms and these houses remained the most common type of habitation for the small landowners.[2] Judging from their frequent mention as bequests in wills, bedsteads and their feather mattresses were the most prized of household furnishings. Most of the homes were modestly furnished and possessions such as desks, pewter, and dishes were given special mention in wills. Jasper left his "moveable effects" to his wife but specified "one dish, one bason [basin], a case of bottles, and one pot" for son John.

Dances were the most popular form of social gatherings and provided opportunities for young people who lived on widely separated plantations to meet. In the next century religious gatherings were one of the major forms of social life in the South, but churches grew slowly in North Carolina in the colonial era, partly because of the difficulties of travel and because of the ongoing controversy over Great Britain's attempts to make the Anglican Church the official religious body of the colony. The dissenting Protestant groups, most notably the Presbyterians, Quakers, and Baptists, dominated the religious life of colonial North Carolina. but their churches were few in number and small in membership. The Hardisons may have been Anglicans at the time they came to North Carolina, possibly indicated by one of Jasper's sons having been referred to as the godson of Richard Everard; however most of their descendants probably became members of the Methodist, Baptist, and Disciples of Christ churches which dominated the religious life of the nineteenth century. Their names appear often in the histories of churches of these denominations in Martin County.[3]

The deed records of Jasper's children reveal that, with the exception of Charles, they lived out their lives in close proximity to each other on lands in the vicinity of Jasper's acquisitions. These lands lay in what had been Albemarle County and briefly Chowan and Bertie counties in the proprietary era, then in Tyrrell County after it was created in 1729, and finally in Martin, Washington, and Tyrrell counties after portions of Tyrrell were taken to form Martin in 1774 and Washington in 1799. All of these lands lay in the swampy, heavily wooded area south of the Roanoke River and in the eastern area of North Carolina, which dominated all phases of life throughout the colonial era. The Hardisons were in the right place at the right time with adequate wealth to take advantage of the colony's expanding economy and the relative stability of the royal government. Of the brothers, only Charles moved away from the Albemarle area, settling to the south in Craven and later Onslow County. Apparently he did not prosper, judging from a pathetic appeal for tax relief in Onslow County in 1780.

The Hardison brothers, along with Mary and her husband Benjamin Carkeet, appear to be a close-knit clan. They bought from and sold land to each other and served as witnesses to each other's transactions within the family and with neighbors. Their lands came from a variety of sources, the first being inheritance, each having been left a portion of land in Jasper's will of 1733. He did not follow the English practice of primogeniture, but divided his estate among his seven sons, as well as making provisions for his widow and daughters. The Hardisons' major acquisitions came through purchases from owners in the area where they lived, who had gotten the land through grants from the proprietary or the royal authorities or through purchase or inheritance from the original owners. A third source was a direct grant from the colonial government. These grants, known as patents, had been numerous during the proprietary era when unclaimed land was most plentiful; however the tracts of land had been so inadequately surveyed and so poorly recorded that the first of the royal governors, who arrived in the colony in 1731, inherited a serious and ongoing problem as he attempted to register all lands for purposes of taxation. As noted in the preceding chapter, Sir Richard Everard, the last of the proprietary governors, had exacerbated the problem by issuing numerous "blank patents," with inadequate descriptions of the location and size of grants. The elder Jasper received a patent for a section of land during Everard's administration and this was probably the 640 acres he left to his son John in 1733. Both John and Charles received additional patents at a later time.

The fourth major source of land was the extensive holdings of the only one of the eight Lords Proprietors who refused to sell to the crown when the proprietary charter was revoked in 1729. In compensation for his share Lord Carteret, Earl Granville, was given an enormous land grant known as the Granville District. The district covered the area just south of the Virginia boundary which represents the upper half of today's North Carolina. At the time it was created, it included well over half of the colony's population. John Hardison applied for grants in the District both for himself and for the children of his sister Mary Carkeet and in the 1760s served as a surveyor and collector of rents for Earl Granville in Tyrrell County.

To the confusion resulting from North Carolina's multiple sources of land ownership and its chaotic record keeping were added the constant controversy over taxation and the old, inexact method of surveying, known as "metes and bounds." Surveyors used neighbors' lines and physical features, such as trees and streams, to describe the boundaries of a tract. A land tax, known as a quit rent, was due to the crown on all lands which fell in the royal domain and to Granville for all lands granted from his District. Both the proprietary and the royal periods of the colony's history were marked by bitter disputes between the governors and the elected representatives over the amount of the tax and the type of payment. Gold and silver coins were scarce since North Carolina carried on little direct trade with the outside world. The colonists insisted on paying with commodities they produced, while the governor insisted on payment based on the colony's official currency, known as proclamation money. Proclamation money, as defined by William S. Powell in *North Carolina Through Four Centuries*, was "not so much a definite kind of money as it was a practical though fluctuating value placed on various types of foreign coins circulating in the colonies." It functioned as a rate of exchange against the pound sterling and also was related to marketable commodities, such as tobacco, which might be used as barter money. When paper money was issued by the colony, its value was set by proclamation.[4]

The wrangles over land and taxes escalated during the royal period and, coupled with the British Parliament's tightening of the trade laws after the end of the French and Indian War in 1763, led to increasing erosion of loyalty to the mother country. Due in part to their interests as land speculators and developers, the Hardisons became supporters of the revolutionary cause. John Hardison was active at both the state and county levels in establishing new forms of government after independence was declared in 1776. Several Hardisons served in North Carolina's Revolutionary forces, including one who died in service.

The Hardisons in the Records of the Colony of North Carolina and of Tyrrell and Martin Counties 1730-1780

The acquisition of land and its productive use were the major economic concerns of the colonists of North Carolina. At least ninety-

II. THE SECOND GENERATION COMES OF AGE, 1733-1775

five percent of the colonists were engaged in agriculture and other uses of the land. The abundant deed records in the county archives include numerous entries for the children of Jasper Hardison. The majority of their deeds are recorded in Tyrrell County, created in 1729, in whose jurisdiction most of the Hardison lands lay until Martin County's creation in 1774, on the eve of the Revolution. An analysis of the records of these two counties makes it possible to learn much about the nature of the family's involvement in the colony's economy and the relationships among the members of the family. All of Jasper's children owned tracts of land which were referred to as plantations, but the deed, census, tax, and will records indicate that they had few slaves and thus were not extensively involved in agriculture. Their major and most successful undertakings seem to have been in milling, both grist mills and lumber mills. John, with his purchase of thousands of acres of land and numerous sales was obviously involved in land speculation. He also had an outstanding career in public service. The forest products industry was the most significant of North Carolina's colonial industries in terms of trade with the other colonies and the mother country and in generating income for the colony. It continues to be a major industry in contemporary North Carolina, particularly in the Albemarle area where the Weyerhaeuser Paper Company owns an 11,000 acre tract of timber land near the town of Plymouth. Their holdings lie in the swampy area south of the Roanoke River in the portions of Martin and Washington counties, originally Tyrrell County, which were home to the Hardisons in the eighteenth century. Of the nearly 5,000 acres of land which John Hardison acquired through inheritance, purchase from individuals, royal patents, and Granville grants, a considerable portion was probably devoted to his milling operations. Grist mills were a significant part of the Hardisons' undertakings, since bread was a major staple of the colonial diet, but forest products were far more important as producers of wealth for the individual and the colony. As noted earlier, the Hardisons of Maine of the late seventeenth century and early eighteenth, who are thought to be Jasper Hardison's kinsmen, were involved in both the lumber business and in the shipping of colonial products along the Atlantic seaboard. It was probably the potential in these industries which drew Jasper to North Carolina.

The significance of the lumber industry and the production of naval stores, the latter leading to North Carolina's designation as the "Tar Heel State," is noted in the following quotation from Hugh Talmage Lefler and Albert Ray Newsome's *North Carolina, the History of a Southern State*:

> The lumber industry was more widespread than that of naval stores and in some respects more important and of greater monetary value. Since the only statistics available for colonial manufactures are export figures it is impossible to grasp the magnitude of of lumber products in colonial North Carolina. In every community there was a great demand for wood in the construction of houses, barns, and other buildings, as well as for making furniture, farm implements, and a variety of wooden utensils for home use. In some years, as many as 100,000 barrels were used for the exportation of naval stores, and more than half this number for the shipment of "provisions" and other articles. The cooperage industry was one of the colony's largest industries.
>
> Lumbering, which began as a household industry, had assumed commercial proportions by the beginning of the eighteenth century. At an early date saw-mills were established. These were usually water-powered, and were encouraged by colonial and local authorities, in the form of land grants, tax exemption, and other favors. By the middle of the century they were in operation throughout the province, and in 1766 there were over fifty in the Cape Fear Valley alone. Lumbering, like naval stores, was usually carried on in connection with ordinary farm operations, and these two industries supplemented the income of some individual operators as much as one thousand pounds a year.[5]

The children of Jasper Hardison succeeded in varying degrees in taking advantage of the economic opportunities which the colony of North Carolina offered in the last four decades preceding the American Revolution. In the remainder of this chapter the information gained from a survey of the official records of the colony, the county deed records of the 1730s-1770s, and county tax lists will be summarized for each of the sons and daughters. The order in which they are discussed is based on the previously cited version of the will of Jasper which is found in the records of the Secretary of State in the North Carolina State Archives. It is presumed that this order indicates their relative ages, with John eldest and Joseph youngest.

John Hardison

Of the nine children of Jasper Hardison, John has the largest number of entries in the land records of colonial North Carolina. His acquisitions came from all the sources previously cited. Milling, land speculation, and politics were the major concerns in his career. He was an adult at the time of his father's death in 1733 and was probably born about 1710. He died in Martin County some time between 1778, when he made his will, and 1780, when it was probated.[6] The importance of milling in his family is indicated by provisions for his saw mill and his third interest in a grist mill and by his first bequest, to his wife Olive, "one pare of mill stones that she brought here with her." The owners of the other two-thirds of the grist mill are not specified, but they may well have been his brothers Joshua and Joseph, whose lands adjoined John's and who along with John's son Benjamin had the highest property valuations of all the Hardisons in the Martin County tax list of 1779.[7]

John acquired his estate through inheritance, grants from both the royal government and the Granville District, and purchase. As Jasper's eldest son, he received the largest bequest of land, 640 acres, which was probably the land his father had received in his patent of 1730. This land was in the vicinity of Jasper's original acquisitions in the western portion of Tyrrell County which later became a part of Martin County. According to its description in the patent, it lay south of the Roanoke River and on the west side of Deep Run, a swamp in eastern Martin County. Also John received a patent from the colonial authorities in 1743 for 300 acres in Tyrrell County in the vicinity of Swift Creek and Bentley Swamp, and four grants, between 1753 and 1762, from the Granville District, totaling 1,000 acres.[8] To this land John made numerous additions through purchase. The majority of his land records are found in the deed books of Tyrrell County. Unfortunately the earliest records of that county seem to have been lost for, although the county was founded in 1729, the first entries date from 1735 and the first for John is dated 1744. However, he does appear in a list of Tyrrell taxpayers who were in arrears in their property taxes in 1735. He was being taxed on 640 acres.[9]

Between 1744 and 1770 John was the grantee (purchaser) in eighteen deeds totaling 3,885 acres and the grantor (seller) in thirteen deeds with an acreage of 2,670 acres.[10] The total sum of land purchased should probably be at least an additional 1,000 acres, since several of the deeds did not give the size of the tract and the purchase price of one of these was the substantial sum of 750 pounds. The price per acre varied greatly, sometimes averaging a pound per acre and sometimes far more and far less. It is difficult to know if the land in each case had been improved or was undeveloped and to know the value of the currency cited in the deed, since it fluctuated throughout the colonial era. Usually the sums quoted were in proclamation money, the official currency of the colony, but in several cases the land was paid for in the currency of the colony of Virginia, which appears to have had a higher value.

The over 5,000 acres of land which John acquired, in addition to his inheritance of 640 acres, were apparently intended for both re-sale and for his and his family's use in their milling and other undertakings. His largest single purchase was 1,280 acres, for 600 pounds proclamation money, from the Pollock family. Cullen and Thomas Pollock's deed of 1768 implemented a bond made in 1762 between John and George Pollock, who had died before the transaction was complete. The land, located on Swift Creek in Tyrrell County, had originally been granted to the Pollocks in two patents and, when purchased by John, included a saw mill and its appurtenances.[11]

A series of five Tyrrell County deeds and a bond negotiated in 1766 between James Johnson on the one part and John Hardison and Benjamin Gainer on the other appear to illustrate the interplay between political and economic ambitions and, as will be noted in the discussion of the Carkeets, family connections.[12] The total acreage of the lands which Johnson sold to Hardison and Gainer cannot be determined since the acreage is missing from two of the deeds, but the purchase price of the five amounted to 1,075 pounds, a very large sum. The bond was a guarantee to the amount of 1,000 pounds "sterling money of Great Britain" for Johnson, who was to be the sheriff of Tyrrell County in 1767. Among the sheriff's most important duties was the collection of taxes for the royal authorities, a percentage of which he received as compensation. Johnson put up as security for

Hardison's and Gainer's guarantee of his bond five slaves, four horses, a riding chaise and harness, and various household furnishings. Apparently Johnson's expectations of monetary gain from his undertakings were disappointed or he may have misappropriated the funds he collected, for during the ten years after his term as sheriff parcels of his land were sold in sheriff's sales as the result of a judgment against him by William Tryon, the royal governor.[13] Within a few years, time brought a change in fortunes for all three men involved in the transactions. Benjamin Gainer was spoken of as deceased in a Martin County deed of 1772 and John Hardison was playing a leading role in that newly formed county, including holding the office of sheriff.[14]

The Tyrrell and Martin County deed books record several sales of land by John to his brothers and to his sons and, toward the end of his life, a gift of land to a granddaughter. To brother Joshua he sold 100 acres in 1749 and 50 in 1754 and to brother Joseph, 200 acres in 1756.[15] John's will indicates that he had three sons, Benjamin, William, and John. The first two seem to be the eldest since John transferred land to them in the 1760s and 1770s, before writing his will. To William he sold 100 acres for the nominal sum of 5 pounds in 1764 and to Benjamin 600 acres for 100 pounds in 1774. The land transferred to Benjamin may have been a portion of the 640 acres which John had inherited from his father. Its boundaries included Gardner Creek and Deep Run Swamp. In the year he wrote his will, 1778, John made a gift of 200 acres to his granddaughter Rosanna "for love and affection."[16]

The most frequently mentioned place names which appear in John's Tyrrell and Martin County deeds provide vivid descriptions of the wooded, watery kingdom of the Hardison family—Deep Run Swamp, Beaver Dam Swamp, Sawmill Swamp, Swift Creek, Gum Swamp, Great Pine Bottom, Hardison Mill Swamp, Henderson Island, Mirey Branch, and Devil's Gut. The names of the families who were the neighbors of the Hardisons appear throughout the deed records, since the owners of adjoining properties, along with natural demarcations, were used in descriptions for the surveys. Smithwick Creek and Gardner Creek, named for families of the area, were often mentioned along with lands owned by the Pollocks, Carkeets, Garretts, Griffins, Cherrys, Hollidays, Hudsons, Ryans, Lees, Blounts, and Brownings. As would be expected in an era when social life was limited to a relatively small surrounding area, the Hardisons became related by marriage to several of these families.

In addition to his activities and success in the acquisition of land and in milling, John carried on a career in public life which culminated in outstanding service to Martin County and to North Carolina in the decade of the American Revolution. His public career and the family which he left as he died at the end of the 1770s will be discussed in the two chapters which follow. John, through his son Benjamin, was the grandfather of John Hardison who migrated to Georgia about 1800. The younger John and his descendants will be the subject of the nineteenth century portion of this study.

Mary Hardison Carkeet

Mary Carkeet, assumed to be Jasper's elder daughter, follows John in the listing of bequests in her father's will. Mary was the wife of Benjamin Carkeet, probably a son of William and Lydia Carkeet of Massachusetts and Maine, whose children were Lydia, Benjamin, Robert, and William, names which are repeated in the Carkeet family in North Carolina. The elder William was identified as a mariner in the early eighteenth century records of Massachusetts and in a 1741 deed of Tyrrell County, North Carolina, Benjamin was also given that identity. An incident in Benjamin's maritime career in North Carolina, recorded in the minutes of the Executive Council of the colony in 1741, indicates his involvement in the coastal trade along the Atlantic seaboard. He reported to Governor Gabriel Johnston on the fate of the sloop Guarnsey of which he was the commander. On June 7, 1741 the ship had sailed from the port at Edenton, bound for Boston with a cargo of 600 barrels of pitch and tar, 50 bushels of corn, and 400 pounds of dressed deer skins. As it was being piloted through the channels leading to Ocracoke Inlet and thence to the Atlantic, it ran aground on Horse Shoe Shoal and sank after running over the anchor, which had been used in an attempt to secure it. While Benjamin and his crew were salvaging the cargo and the ship's sails and rigging, they were set upon by about sixty men from two vessels which sailed through the inlet from the Atlantic. Benjamin reported that one of the ships was flying a Spanish flag. He and his crew

II. THE SECOND GENERATION COMES OF AGE, 1733-1775   43

fled the scene in a boat but their attackers then proceeded to set fire to their cargo and the equipment from the stricken ship. Benjamin's report ended with a protest on behalf of the crew and the investors in the Guarnsey.[17]

Such mishaps may have made a career as a planter more appealing and the land records of eastern North Carolina indicate the acquisition of a considerable amount of land by the Carkeet family. As with the family name in New England, there are a number of variations in its spelling, among them Cerkeet, Karkeet, and Kerkeet. An affidavit given by Cullen Pollock in 1740 in the Tyrrell County deed records indicates that Jasper gave 100 acres of land to Benjamin at some time before his death in 1733. Pollock filed the affidavit in order to verify Benjamin's title to the land, which was part of the larger tract Pollock had sold to Jasper in the 1720s. The affidavit referred also to other portions of the tract which Jasper had left to his sons Charles and Jasper and which they had sold to Benjamin in 1739.[18] Having already given land to the Carkeets, Jasper's only bequest to Mary was a cow and a calf, a typical gift to a daughter in that era.

Members of the Carkeet family appear in the records of Tyrrell and Martin counties during the remainder of the eighteenth century. Benjamin and later his son William are referred to as "planter" and they married into the planter families of the area. In 1746 Benjamin, along with his brother-in-law John Hardison, was commissioned as Justice of the Peace in Tyrrell County, a colonial position which carried a number of administrative duties.[19] The deed records of Tyrrell County indicate that from the 1720s through the 1740s Benjamin acquired 700 acres of land, primarily from the Hardisons. Initially he had come into possession of 400 acres, the 100 acre gift from Jasper and the purchase in 1739 of the lands Jasper had left to sons Jasper, 200 acres, and Charles, 100 acres, in an area south of the Roanoke River known as Cheat Neck. To these tracts Benjamin added 100 acres in the vicinity of Roses Creek, by purchase from Cullen Pollock in 1741, and 200 acres, bordering his own land and that of brothers-in-law Joshua and Joseph Hardison, by purchase from Joshua in 1746.[20]

The estate records of Tyrrell County reveal that by 1751 Benjamin Carkeet was deceased. There is no will for Benjamin, but the estate records include a bond for John Daley (also spelled Daly), who was appointed as guardian of Sarah Carkeet, identified as the orphan of Benjamin. In a document of 1751 Daley was named as guardian for Lydia, Mary, and William Carkeet. Nine slaves were divided among Daley and the children, Daley and William receiving three each and the daughters one each. The document for this division is signed by the Carkeets' kinsman, John Hardison. Further evidence of John's involvement in the affairs of the Carkeets is provided by records of three Granville grants for land in Tyrrell County, totaling 750 acres, which he applied for in 1751 in the names of Mary, Lydia, and Sarah Carkeet. The grant procedure was completed by November, 1753. The use of the term "orphan" for Sarah implied that both her parents were deceased, but the records of Tyrrell County include a marriage bond for Mary Carkeet, Widow, and John Daly for 1752.[21]

While the Tyrrell deed records of the 1730s and 1740s record Benjamin's acquisition of 700 acres of land, those for his and Mary's son William in the next two decades indicate the sale or mortgaging of 1,000 acres. Since the Tyrrell records do not include deeds for purchases by William, the additional land may have come to him through the Granville grants and by marriage. In 1756 William sold 100 acres adjoining Roses Creek to Charles Hardison. In 1764 and 1768, he sold to other purchasers 300 additional acres south of the Roanoke River, in the vicinity of Joseph and Richard Hardison's lands.[22] In the 1764 transactions, it was noted that Mary Carkeet surrendered her right of dower. This Mary is probably the Mary Carkeet who is identified in a 1775 deed in Martin County as the daughter of Edmund Smithwick and sister of Edward and John Smithwick. A Tyrrell County marriage bond indicates that Mary Smithwick was married to William Carkeet in 1753. The Smithwicks were outstanding landowners and political leaders in Martin County.[23] A relationship existed also between the Carkeets and the Stewart family, another planter family prominent in the affairs of Tyrrell and Martin counties, as indicated in the will of Thomas Stewart and several deeds of the late eighteenth century. Thomas' will includes a bequest to Lydia Carkeet and mentions his ownership of a part interest in a saw mill and grist mill in the vicinity of Beaver Dam Swamp, one of the areas of the Hardisons' operations in Martin County.[24]

II. THE SECOND GENERATION COMES OF AGE, 1733-1775   45

William Carkeet's sales of land in the 1760s and his mortgaging of 600 acres in the Cheat Neck area, along with "a negro fellow Arch," in 1768, were probably related to his involvement in the legal and financial woes of James Johnson.[25] Johnson (also spelled Johnston) was the previously discussed Tyrrell County sheriff who had sold several large tracts of land and mortgaged his personal possessions to John Hardison and Benjamin Gainer in 1766, at the time he was appointed to the position of sheriff. A Tyrrell County deed of 1769 for land owned by Johnson, which had been sold in a sheriff's sale, states that the 290 acre tract had formerly belonged to Carkeet, now deceased.[26] It adds that Carkeet had left the land, called Davises Neck. to his daughter Lydia Carkeet, identified as the wife of Johnson. Several other Tyrrell deeds of 1769 and 1770 pertain to sales of Johnson's lands by the current Tyrrell County sheriff Edmondson Samuel Smithwick,[27] Ironically, one of the confiscated tracts, a 400 acre Granville grant, was referred to as "Johnston's Folly."

The deeds which are cited above indicate that the Johnsons' and Carkeets' problems resulted at least in part from a judgment in 1768 by Governor William Tryon against Johnson, William Carkeet, and John Lewelling. A factor in the judgment may have been Johnson's failure to make a return of the taxes he had collected as sheriff. Both he and John Hardison are included in the official list of sheriffs and other revenue collectors who were in arrears in their accounts during the 1760s. Tryon was a particularly able and active governor, who attempted to force the colony into compliance with British taxation and regulation. His complaints against "the irregular conduct of the officers of the Revenue" were strongly expressed in a speech before the assembly in December, 1770.[28]

The former sheriff Johnson/Johnston may be the James Johnston whose wrangle with Edmund Smithwick is recorded in the Legislative Journal of the colony's Assembly of January, 1768. According to the record, Johnston "grossly abused and aspersed the character of Mr. Edmund Smithwick, one of the members of this House." It adds that he was arrested, investigated, and forced to apologize both to the Assembly, on bended knee, and, standing, to Smithwick, since his charges were considered unfounded. Unfortunately the nature of his charges against Smithwick are not recorded.[29]

A second William Carkeet, probably the son of the previously discussed William and thus a grandson of Mary Hardison Carkeet, appears in the records of Martin County of the 1770s as witness to several deeds. Apparently some of the Carkeet lands had been salvaged after the Johnson debacle, for William is listed in the Martin County tax list of 1779 with property worth the considerable sum of 3,192 pounds. William is listed as a resident of Martin County in the North Carolina State Census of 1784-87 and the Federal Census enumerations of 1790 (spelled Karkeet) and 1800. A Benjamin Carkeet is also listed for Martin County in 1800. A search of the variant spellings of the name did not reveal any listings for the family in the 1810 census.[30]

Judah Hardison Sutton

Judah (probably originally Judith) Sutton follows Mary in Jasper's will, receiving "fifty pounds current money of North Carolina and a mare branded B." It is likely that she was the Judith whose name appears in Bertie County records of the 1730s as the wife of Thomas Sutton. The Suttons had been among the early settlers of Perquimans County, an area just to the south of Virginia which was settled primarily by families from Virginia. Patents issued to Deborah Sutton, widow, in 1684 refer to land she already owned on the east side of the Perquimans River.[31]

By the early eighteenth century members of the family had settled in Bertie County, to the north of the Roanoke River and the lands which later became Martin County. They appear as grantor and grantee in nearly fifty deeds in Bertie County's records of the 1700s. Thomas Sutton received a patent for land in the county from the Lords Proprietors in 1722.[32] Subsequent Bertie records indicate that in the decades preceding the writing of his will in 1751 Thomas was married three times, with Judith as his second wife. It is possible that these records pertain to more than one Thomas Sutton, given the repeated use of names within a family. A deed of 1729 in which Thomas was a grantor includes the name of a wife named Elizabeth.[33] Two subsequent deeds of 1734 name Judith as wife and record her giving up her right of dower in a 640 acre tract of land.[34] In the second of the 1734 documents, Thomas deeded 200 acres to "my Loving Friend Isaac Gregory Mariner," yet another reference to the family's ties with the maritime profession.

By the time Thomas wrote his will in 1751, Judith had apparently died and another wife named Elizabeth, along with six sons and four daughters, were listed as beneficiaries.[35] The children were named Thomas, William, George, Joshua, Jasper (spelled Jesper), John, Parthenia, Mary Elizabeth, Sarah, and Judith. It is difficult to know which of the children were Judith's, but judging from the repetition of favorite Hardison names probably most of them were hers. Judith's brother John was named as one of the executors of the will and was referred to as "my trusty & well beloved friend John Hardison of Tyrrell County."

The bequests in Thomas' will total 958 acres in Bertie County, nine slaves, and household furnishings and livestock, which were apportioned among his wife and children. A 640 acre tract was to be divided among sons Thomas, William, and George, and Joshua was given 150 acres adjoining the "mannour plantation." The plantation, including 168 acres, was given to Jasper, with wife Elizabeth retaining right of dower during her lifetime. She was also given all the estate which she had brought to the marriage, but the nature of this property is not specified. Son John was given a Negro man named Andrew. Eight other slaves were left to eight of the children, excluding John and Thomas, but ownership was to be deferred until the end of six years, during which time their services were to be used to help provide for the rearing and schooling of the five youngest children (not specified). The household furnishings and livestock were to be divided among Elizabeth and the children, with the provision that sons Thomas and John were each to receive a "good new feather bed," bed clothes, and some pewter and cattle.

In addition to providing for his family, Thomas made a gift of 100 acres in Tyrrell County to a man who had been responsible for the care of his livestock in that county. Thomas' legal records reveal him as a moderately prosperous member of the planter class, with a fair and generous nature toward both family and friends. Since he named his former brother-in-law John Hardison as co-executor of his will, he apparently maintained close ties with Judith's family after her death.[36]

Jasper Hardison

Jasper, the namesake son, was bequeathed a 200 acre tract in the Cheat Neck area of the 1,000 acre tract his father had purchased from Cullen Pollock. As noted previously, Jasper (Jasper, Sr. after his father's death) sold this land to his brother-in-law Benjamin Carkeet in 1739, a few years after his father's death.[37] Jasper's other appearance in the records of the 1730s is as a witness to the William Garrett will of 1735, which is evidence that he was an adult early in this decade.[38] Apparently searching for land more to his liking than his inheritance, Jasper purchased two tracts in Tyrrell County from a neighboring family, the Lees, early in the next decade. He bought 90 acres on the east side of Beaver Dam from Stevens Lee in 1741 and the following year a 460 acre tract in the vicinity of Reedy Branch from Thomas Lee. The deed for the latter indicates that the land had originally been a proprietary grant of 1715, a fact which is noted concerning several other tracts which the Hardisons purchased.[39] Within a few years, Jasper sold 460 acres in Tyrrell County, probably the land he had purchased from Thomas Lee, in two tracts of 230 acres each, the first to Philip Ward in 1746 and the second to James Garrett in 1753.[40] He realized a considerable profit, with the sale to Ward bringing 150 pounds "current money" and the tract to Garrett, 15 pounds "Virginia currency." The Ward deed indicates this land had been part of a 1715 patent and was the portion known as "Browney's [probably Browning] Old Field," a name which appears in several of the Hardison deeds. The land adjoined Daniel Garrett's property. Although the Tyrrell County deed records do not include additional acquisitions for Jasper prior to 1770, he apparently had other lands in the portion of the county which became Martin County, for in 1772 he sold 160 acres in the Beaver Dam area to his nephew Joshua Hardison, Jr., a blacksmith of Bertie County.[41]

The year of Jasper's death is not known but he is believed to have lived well into the 1790s. Either he or his son, Jasper, Jr. was both grantor and grantee in Tyrrell County deeds of the last two decades of the eighteenth century. Jasper Hardison "Gentleman" purchased 320 acres for 50 pounds from Thomas Everett in 1786 and sold the tract in 1789 to Leven Bozman in 1789 for 30 pounds.[42] The only identification of its location is "beginning at a pocoson at a pine . . . ." Another transaction with Bozman was the transfer to him of one acre of land on the east side of Beaver Dam "for sett a mill on."[43] The final eighteenth century entry for Jasper in the Tyrrell records was a deed of 1794 from John and Anne Stubbs for three slaves, a woman named Bell and her children Annee and Winny, for 25 pounds.[44] Later records indicate that the Bozmans and Stubbs were related to the Hardisons, probably through marriages of Jasper, Jr.'s daughters.

Jasper, Sr. did not leave a will and the name of his wife is not known. His deed records and his inclusion in the Tyrrell County tax list of 1784 indicate that he lived in the portion of Tyrrell County which remained a part of the county after Martin County was created from Tyrrell in 1774.[45] The names of at least some of his children have been derived by family historians from records of the dispersal of his property. They are Joseph, Frederick, Joshua, Jasper, Lemuel, Judy, and David. Jasper, Jr. is one of the few eighteenth century Hardisons for whom a marriage record has been found. He married Alse Evins in Tyrrell County in 1763.[46] Records pertaining to the division of his property in 1807 and to members of his family, particularly Frederick, who was probably his son, are found in the Washington County deed books.[47] This county was formed in 1799 from the westernmost portion of Tyrrell County and included the area where Jasper, Sr. and Jasper, Jr. lived. Subsequently descendants settled in Hyde, Bertie, Duplin, Lenoir, and other North Carolina counties. The Frederick who migrated to Washington County, Georgia is believed to be a son of Jasper, Jr.[48]

Charles Hardison

Of the seven Hardison brothers, Charles was the only one to move away from the original family lands in the Tyrrell and Martin County area. Like his brothers, he received a portion of land from his father Jasper, a parcel which was known as Cheat Neck Island. In the same year, 1739, when the younger Jasper sold his tract in this vicinity to Benjamin Carkeet, Charles sold his to Benjamin. He was paid 100 pounds for 100 acres.[49] From 1739 through 1756, Charles purchased four tracts totaling 601 acres in Tyrrell County. The grantors were Daniel Garrett, John Browney, Henry Robinson, and William Carkeet. Charles' new acquisitions were located in the vicinity of his brothers' lands, with Welches, Roses, and Smithwick creeks being mentioned in the deed descriptions.[50] By 1759 he had sold three of these tracts, totaling 501 acres, the last being the 100 acres he had purchased from William Carkeet in 1756, which he deeded to his brother Richard.[51]

Charles' disposal of most of his land in Tyrrell County indicates his intention to settle elsewhere and the purchase by a Charles Hardison of 720 acres in Craven County in 1759 seems proof of this intention.[52] As will be noted below, evidence drawn from the records of Craven, Onslow, and New Hanover counties raises the possibility of more than one Charles Hardison and the presence of other Hardisons whose relationship to Jasper's family has not been established. These counties were created from Bath County, the very large county established by the Lords Proprietors in 1694 as settlers began to move into the area south of Albemarle Sound. It originally included all the land south of the sound to the Cape Fear River and was gradually divided into the counties which now fill the Coastal Plain from Beaufort County to New Hanover County. None of the counties was given the name Bath. The land which Charles purchased in 1759 from Harding Jones for 120 pounds lay on the south side of Brices Creek on the Trent River. It was located in the vicinity of land which had been patented to Robert Shreves (various spellings), an early settler in Craven, as was William Brice.[53] Almost a decade after his first purchase, Charles and Isaac Fonville were granted a royal patent to 207 acres in the same area of Craven County.[54]

The tax records of Onslow County, located just to the south of Craven at this time before the creation of Jones County, indicate that a Charles Hardison was living in Onslow by the early 1770s. Charles was included in the tax lists for 1770 and 1771 and "Hardeson, Charles & Son Charles & Son Jn.[John?] —- 3 White Polls" were listed for the year 1774.[55] Two Craven County deeds of 1772 and 1774 record the purchase and sale by a John Hardison of Craven County of a 200 acre tract of land, which, like the earlier purchase of Charles, mention its relationship to land which had formerly been patented to Robert Shreves (spelled Sreaves).[56] The possibility of two or more John Hardisons in this area of North Carolina arises from the fact that a John Hardison is listed in the tax rolls of New Hanover County

II. THE SECOND GENERATION COMES OF AGE, 1733-1775

at an earlier date.[57] A John Hardison of Onslow County made his will in 1785, mentioning his wife Ann and children Jesse, Hardy, Nancy, and Elizabeth. A Charles Hardison, possibly Charles, Jr. wrote his will in Craven County in 1807, dividing his property among his wife and children, Gabriel, Elijah, William, and Catherine. Several Gabriel Hardisons appear in the records of Craven and Onslow counties in the eighteenth and nineteenth centuries. A deed of 1835 in the Onslow records refers to the sale of lands which had previously been patented to a Charles Hardison in 1726, too early to have been an acquisition of Jasper's son Charles, unless this land was given to him as a child, as was the gift of land in Craven to his brother Richard by Richard Everard in 1730.[58]

An Onslow County document of 1780, believed by family researcher Verena Hatch to pertain to Jasper's son Charles, indicates that prosperity did not ensue from his move away from the family in the Albemarle area. It also raises the possibility that, given his age as stated in the document, the young children he referred to came from a second marriage and he had older children who might have been the Charles, Jr. and John referred to in the 1774 Onslow County tax list. In the following petition he asked for tax relief from Onslow County.[59]

> June the 26th 1780. This to the Worshipful Court of Onslow to let you know my circumstances that I am a old Man sixty od years of age and is in a por state of Health and a crasy Woman at times and five small children the oldest not nine years old and it is very hard scufling for Me to keep them from sufrance and if the Honorable Court is pleased to clear me from paying taxes for I have nothing to Give but only one small old horse and about a hundred acres of land that {is} very por. Was I well and Hearty I would not desire the Releaf But I am not so.
>
> I Subscribe myself   Your Humble Servant. Charles Hardison, Senr.

The Hardisons of Craven and Onslow counties left numerous descendants, a number of whom are currently living in this area of North Carolina. Charles' movement into the southern portion of North Carolina's Coastal Plain was part of a major extension of the original colony. The creation of new centers of population, power, and wealth challenged the dominance of the Albemarle planters and helped to make the colony more complex and diverse—and more contentious.

Joshua Hardison

On the basis of property valuation listings in the Martin County tax list for 1779, Joshua was one of the most prosperous of the Hardison brothers. His and Joseph's property had the highest valuations, 3,820 pounds and 4,151 pounds respectively, of any of the Hardisons except John's son Benjamin. Joshua had started his career with land left jointly to him and brother Thomas by their father's will of 1733. The bequest was described as "a parcel of land from the upper part of Mr. Carkeet's line to Cheat Neck Branch." The number of acres in the parcel was not indicated. The boundary line mentioned probably referred to Benjamin Carkeet's land, since Jasper had already given land to him before his death. In 1746 Joshua sold land to Benjamin, probably from his inheritance, as had his brothers Jasper and Charles several years before. For 200 pounds he deeded 200 acres to Benjamin, adjoining his own and Benjamin's lands and those of brother Joseph.[60] Between the year of his sale to Carkeet and 1760, Joshua acquired three tracts of land in what is today eastern Martin County. Two of the parcels, first 100 acres and later 50, were purchased from his brother John.[61] They were portions of Henderson Island in the vicinity of "the Great Gum Swamp" and "the Great Pine Bottom." Henderson's Island was one of the so-called islands south of the Roanoke River, which are areas of high ground rising above the surrounding swamps. Apparently there was some confusion about the boundaries of the first of these purchases, for many years later, in 1792, two of John's sons, John and William, made an entry in the Martin County deed records to clarify the original deed of 1749.[62] Following Joshua's purchases from John, he added 320 acres in the Beaver Dam Swamp area from James Bently in 1760.[63] A number of years later, in 1779, he bought 320 acres from Francis Ward, bordering Buck Branch and Beaver Dam Swamp.[64] Still later he was a party in a transaction involving the widow and sons of his brother Richard, which will be described in the section of this chapter on Richard.[65] Apparently Joshua was satisfied with his lands, for other than his 1746 sale to Benjamin Carkeet, he sold only two small parcels—25 acres along their joint border to brother John in 1754 and a 30 acre tract, called "Back Island," near the mouth of Devil's Gut, to Edward Mizelle in 1780.[66] The boundaries of his land were frequently mentioned in deed descriptions of other parcels in the area and he was often a witness in his neighbors' transactions. Place names mentioned in Joshua's deeds, Beaver Dam Swamp, Hardison's Mill Swamp, Cedar Branch, and the Pine Bottom, indicate the nature of the land and the probability that Joshua, like his older brother John, was engaged in the timber business.

Joshua prospered and lived out his life in the vicinity of the homestead founded by his father and the lands of his brothers and sister Mary. He did not leave a will and thus it has been difficult to know the names of his children, other than a son, Joshua, Jr., who appears as a grantor and a grantee in two Tyrrell County deeds of the 1770s, a purchase from Jasper Hardison and a sale to Francis Ward.[67] Hardison family researcher Fred L. Hawkins, whose primary interest is the North Carolina Hardisons who migrated to Tennessee, believes, but has not been able to document, that Joshua, Jr. was the father of three Hardison brothers, Mark, Joshua, and Edward, who went to Tennessee in the early 1800s.[68]

Thomas Hardison

Thomas is the brother about whom the least is known, there being few deed records for him and no will. As noted in the history of brother Joshua, they jointly inherited a tract of land from their father, in the vicinity of other family lands. Thomas, along with Richard and Joseph, assumed to be Jasper's youngest children, received a small bequest of livestock in the 1735 will of William Garrett. Thomas was a witness in many of the Tyrrell County deeds of his brothers, but the only one in which he appeared as a principal was a deed of 1769 which recorded his purchase from Benjamin Corey of 165 acres in the vicinity of Welches Creek adjoining the land belonging to his brother Joseph. This was land which had previously been owned by Charles Hardison.[69] The Hardisons apparently liked to keep land in the family, for in a Martin County deed of 1789 Thomas sold the land to David Hardison, probably the son of Jasper, Sr.[70] With no will and few land records, the names of Thomas' wife and children are not known. A Thomas Hardison appears as a buyer and seller of slaves in several Martin and Pitt County deed records.[71] His property was valued at 2,076 pounds in the Martin County tax list of 1779, about half the valuation of Joseph and Joshua. A Thomas Hardison, assumed to be Jasper's son, is listed as a head of household in Martin County in the North Carolina state census of 1784-1787 and the federal census enumerations of 1790 and 1800.[72]

Richard Hardison

Richard and his brother Joseph were probably minors at the time of their father's death in 1733, for they were to have Jasper's plantation after the death of his wife Mary. The will specified "the plantation and remainder part of the land after the decease of my well beloved wife known by the name of Roses plantation." Both were also named legatees in the William Garrett will, receiving small bequests of livestock. Richard was the recipient of another more substantial gift, which probably carries with it the origin of his given name. A Craven County deed of 1730 records the gift of a tract of land in Bath County from Richard Everard to "my Godson Richard Hardison son of Jasper Hardison."[73] As noted earlier this Richard Everard was probably the son of Sir Richard, the last of the proprietary governors, who served in that capacity from 1725 to 1729 and then as acting governor until the royal governor arrived in the colony in 1731. Sir Richard used his position to make numerous grants of land, in defiance of crown regulations, and most likely his son benefited and shared his good fortune. The younger Richard remained in North Carolina after his father departed for England and was active in the colony's political life until he died in 1742.[74] There is no indication that Richard Hardison ever settled on or laid claim to the land given him by Everard. As previously noted, the name Bath was given in 1694 to a county covering a wide expanse of the Coastal Plain to the south of Albemarle Sound, which was formed as settlers began to move into the area. Craven County was created from a portion of the area in 1712 and the town of New Bern became its county seat and one of the official locations of the colonial government.

Richard's mother Mary, like most married women of the period, did not leave a will, having only a life interest in the husband's property. Thus the year of her death and of Richard and Joseph's possession of Roses Plantation is not known. In the 1750s each sold his share to John Daly, who is identified in one of the deeds as a merchant. Joseph sold first, in 1756, and Richard in 1759. The deed for Richard's sale speaks of the land as "the plantation whereon I now live" and describes the 100 acre parcel as being north of Joseph's share and bounded on the southwest by the Roanoke River, on the north by Cheat Neck Branch, and the east by the lands of William Carkeet. John Hardison and William Carkeet were witnesses to this sale of the last of Roses Plantation in Hardison possession.[75] Richard did not move far away, for in the year of his sale he purchased 100 acres in the upper fork of Roses Creek from his brother Charles.[76] His land lay in Martin County after its formation from Tyrrell and in the 1780s he acquired additional land in Martin County in three parcels. The deed for the first, in 1780, was for 400 acres in the vicinity of Roses Creek. reading simply "Richard Hardison enters 400 acres." Since it was signed by Governor Richard Caswell, the deed represented a grant from the state.[77] In 1783 he purchased two tracts, the first, 150 acres, for 8 pounds and the second, giving no acreage, for 20 pounds, both adjoining the property of Silvanus Buttrey. As usual with the Hardison purchases, waterways are mentioned, Wolfpit Branch and Cedar Branch.[78]

Apparently Richard was fairly prosperous, for in the 1779 Martin County tax list his property was valued at 2,445 pounds. He did not leave a will, but a Martin County deed of July 3, 1787 indicates that he had died by that date and gives the names of his wife and two of his sons.[79] In this deed Joshua Hardison sold to James and Frederick Hardison, sons of Richard, deceased, 101 acres in the vicinity of Hardison Mill Swamp and Joshua's boundary line. Joshua stated that he had signed the document in the presence of Rebecca, the widow of Richard, whose interests were protected in "as full and ample a manner" as if her husband had signed the deed. The meaning of this remark is not explained in the document, but it probably refers to previous dealings between Richard and Joshua and a settlement which had been made to provide for Rebecca. There were several James Hardisons in the generation of Richard's son, but his James is believed to be the one who migrated to Tennessee in the early 1800s.[80]

Joseph Hardison

Joseph was the youngest son of Jasper, based on the order of children in his will, and became one of the most prosperous. As noted in the discussion of Richard, both were legatees in the will of William Garrett and the two were to have title to Jasper's home place, Roses Plantation, after the death of their mother. Like their older brothers, Charles and Jasper, they sold portions of the land inherited from their father, Joseph first, in 1756, to John Daley, and Richard to Daley in 1759.[81] In the year of his sale, Joseph purchased from his brother John 200 acres on the west side of Welches Creek for 20 pounds proclamation money. As with several of the Hardison to Hardison transactions, the purchase price was small and probably the sum mentioned was more token than a measure of actual value. Welches Creek forms the border between today's Martin and Washington counties and Joseph's new land thus lay in what is now the far eastern portion of Martin.[82] He sold another tract of land, possibly a remainder from his inheritance, to John Daley in 1764.[83] Judging from the fact that the Tyrrell and Martin deed records do not indicate further acquisitions of land by Joseph and that he had the highest property value of any of the Hardisons, 4,151 pounds, in the Martin County tax list of 1779, Joseph apparently prospered with the land he had purchased from John, the remainder of land from his inheritance, and possibly land acquired through marriage. He was probably involved in the Hardisons' milling operations.

Joseph and John, the youngest and the eldest of Jasper's sons, were the only ones to leave wills. Joseph's was written and probated in 1788, ten years after the writing of John's. He left his estate to his wife Mary, known to be Mary Ann Collins from their Tyrrell County marriage bond of 1765, and to his children, Millicent, Judith, Nancy, Charles, Wiggins, and William. He left most of his land and personal property to Mary for a ten year period for the "Raising and Schooling [of] my Children Only," a slave to each child, and a parcel of land in the Welches Creek property and two town lots in the newly founded town of Plymouth to his sons. The founder of Plymouth, which became the county seat of Washington County after its creation from Tyrrell County in 1799, was Arthur Rhodes, one of the executors of Joseph's will and probably the husband of his daughter Millicent, who is listed in the will as Millicent Rhodes.[84]

Numerous descendants of Joseph and Mary Ann live in Martin

County, particularly in Jamesville and the Farm Life Community in the eastern area of the county, and in adjoining Beaufort County. Ysobel DuPree Litchfield of Washington, Beaufort County, has done extensive research on the Hardisons and on Beaufort County, where Joseph's son William settled.[85]

The Hardisons at the End of the Colonial Era

The above summaries of the information from public sources available for the Hardison brothers and sisters fall far short of what descendants would like to know about their personal and family lives. The writer and the reader of this history would welcome the insights which letters and diaries would offer, but relatively few such records of ordinary folk have survived from the eighteenth century and none for the Hardisons are known to this writer. Their most numerous records are those of land transactions, found primarily in the county deed books, and of the value of their holdings as reflected in the tax records of the counties. Land, livestock, and slaves were the main sources of the wealth recorded in the tax rolls of the eighteenth century in North Carolina. Since the various records of this century—deeds, tax rolls, census, and wills—indicate that the Hardisons owned few slaves, it may be assumed that their wealth derived chiefly from their land and the uses to which they put it for speculation and for exploitation of its timber.

The surveys of the land records of Jasper and his children show that they were successful in the acquisition of land. North Carolina was a colony whose liberal policies had made it possible for a majority of the settlers to become landowners and Jasper's sons and sons-in-law achieved the status of planter. They put their lands to various uses, including speculation. In historian Bernard Bailyn's study of the forces which shaped what he has called "the peopling of British North America," he cites the role of land speculation in the settling of America's vast lands and in the accumulation of wealth by settlers who had the means and the ambition to exploit the country's most abundant and valuable resource. Bailyn generalized that every farmer with an extra acre of land became a speculator and stated further, "There was never a time in American history when land speculation had not been a major preoccupation of ambitious people."[86]

Undoubtedly Jasper Hardison was an ambitious man and he was drawn to North Carolina by its vast unsettled lands. Within less than ten years, from 1723 to 1730, he acquired nearly 2,000 acres by purchase and patent. His sons made various uses of their inheritance, with John using his, the largest share, as a spring-board to a long career in land speculation. On a smaller scale, his younger brothers were engaged in the buying and selling of land. Jasper, Charles, Richard, Joseph, and Joshua sold all or portions of the land they inherited and bought and sold other tracts of land in transactions chiefly involving their neighbors and members of their family, including brother-in-law Benjamin Carkeet. Charles purchased and sold parcels totaling 600 acres and then set out on his own to acquire several tracts in Craven County.

The earliest extant tax roll of Martin County, prepared in 1779, a few years after the county's formation, provides an insight into the relative wealth of Jasper's descendants, both within the family and among the residents of the county.[87] The valuations are expressed in pounds rather than dollars, as continued to be the case well into the period following the Revolution. The basis of value is not indicated, but most likely it was land, livestock, and slaves. In the miscellany of information at the end of the list which bears the heading, "An Account of Insolvents in Martin County," several notations concerning slaves gives the value of each at 700 pounds. This miscellany is particularly valuable in listing the names of fourteen Martin County men who were away from home at the time the tax returns were made, serving in the Revolutionary armed forces.

Among the 538 names in the main body of the 1779 list are twelve Hardisons and William Carkeet, a grandson of Jasper's daughter, Mary Hardison Carkeet. Although the repetition of names in the family makes it difficult to identify its members, four of the twelve were probably sons of Jasper—Joseph, Joshua, Richard, Sr., and Thomas. (Two other of the seven sons were living elsewhere—Jasper in Tyrrell County and Charles in Onslow County.) There are three John Hardisons in the list, designated as John Esquire, John, Jr., and John. Since the will which Jasper's son John wrote in 1778 was not probated until 1780, it is possible that he was one of the Johns; however the relatively small valuation of the property of John Esquire

II. THE SECOND GENERATION COMES OF AGE, 1733-1775   59

makes it more likely that the elder John had died and that his son John was now given that designation since he had been willed the family plantation. With this identification, John, Jr. would then be his son. The third John, who had the smallest Hardison valuation, was probably the son of the elder John's son Benjamin and possibly the grandson John named in John's will of 1778. The judiciary system of the state was in such disorder during the Revolution that a delay in the probating of John's will would not be surprising. His older sons, Benjamin, who is given the title Esquire, and William, are included in the tax list, with the former's relatively high property valuation probably reflecting the 600 acre tract which his father had transferred to him in 1774. The remaining names on the list are grandsons of Jasper—a second Benjamin (possibly the son of William), David (a son of the younger Jasper), and Richard (son of Richard, Sr.).

Below are the Hardison names in the list and the value of their property in pounds. All lived in District One except John Hardison Esquire and John Hardison, Jr., who were listed in District Two. Because of the known location of their lands, it may be assumed that these are the two easternmost districts in Martin County. The names are listed in descending order of valuation.

Joseph Hardison	4,151
Benjamin Hardison, Esquire	3,895
Joshua Hardison	3,820
William Carkeet	3,192
John Hardison, Esquire	2,678
Richard Hardison, Sr	2,445
Thomas Hardison	2,076
William Hardison	1,515
John Hardison, Jr.	621
David Hardison	602
Benjamin Hardison	400
Richard Hardison	305
John Hardison	301

In the list of "Insolvents" at the end of the lists for the seven districts are fourteen men who are described as "in the Service," obviously those serving in the Revolutionary armed forces. Among them are

James and John Hardison, each assigned a property value of 400 pounds. Also among this list are seven described as "Gone, Nothing Found," including a Benjamin Hardison, also assigned a value of 400 pounds. As will be noted in the following chapter, which contains a discussion of the Hardisons who served in the Revolutionary forces, it is difficult to know whose sons or grandsons these men are. John had a son and a grandson named Benjamin and the names James and John were used repeatedly by the brothers in naming their sons.

The standing of the Hardisons in relation to the property values assigned to their fellow citizens in Martin County may be seen in the following analysis:

Valuation over 10,000 pounds . . . . 22 . . . . no Hardisons
Valuations between 5,000 and 10,000 . . . 24 . . . . no Hardisons
Valuations between 3,000 and 5,000 . . . . . 47 . . . . . 4 Hardisons
Valuations between 1,000 and 3,000 . . . . 121 . . . . . 4 Hardisons
Valuations under 1,000 . . . . 324 . . . . . 5 Hardisons
plus the 3 in the insolvent list

The combined valuation of the property of the three men believed to be the sons of John—Benjamin Esquire, John Esquire, and William is 8,088 pounds.

The Martin County resident with the highest valuation was Whitmel Hill, with 115,124 pounds, far exceeding the next highest, Thomas Hunter and Samuel Williams, with 29,151 and 21,113 respectively. As will be discussed in the following chapter, these wealthy men played leading roles in organizing Martin County and guiding it through the difficult times of the Revolution and early statehood. Also among the most affluent and most prominent in public life were Kenneth McKenzie, William Slade, and Edward and Samuel Smithwick. They and other large landholders of the eastern counties dominated the political and economic life of North Carolina throughout its early years of statehood. Although not one of the wealthiest of these men, John Hardison was among their ranks as a leading citizen in the Revolutionary era.

II. THE SECOND GENERATION COMES OF AGE, 1733-1775

NOTES

1. The major sources of material for this chapter are Hugh Talmage Lefler and Albert Ray Newsome, *North Carolina, The History of a Southern State*, chaps.6-10; Hugh T. Lefler and William S. Powell, *Colonial North Carolina* (New York: Charles Scribner's Sons, 1973); Fred L. Hawkins and Dorothy Westmoreland Gilliam, *Hardison and Related Families*, chaps.1-3, which contain a section on each of Jasper's children and, on p.23, a chart of his descendants; William S. Powell, *The North Carolina Gazetteer* (Chapel Hill: University of North Carolina Press, 1968) which includes a number of the creeks and swamps mentioned in the Hardisons' deeds; and the deed records of Tyrrell (Columbia), Martin (Williamston), Bertie (Windsor), Chowan (Edenton), Craven (New Bern), and Washington (Plymouth) counties. See maps in Chapter 3 for the location of these counties.
2. Catherine W. Bishir, *North Carolina Architecture* (Chapel Hill: University of North Carolina Press, 1990), chap.1.
3. Francis M. Manning and W. H. Booker, *Religion and Education in Martin County, 1774-1974* (Williamston: Enterprise Publishing Company, 1974).
4. William S. Powell, *North Carolina Through Four Centuries* (Chapel Hill: University of North Carolina Press, 1989), p.89
5. Lefler and Newsome, *op. cit.*, p.100.
6. Martin County Will Book 1, pp.61-63.
7. "Martin County: Tax List of 1779," *Journal of North Carolina Genealogy* (Raleigh: William Perry Johnson) vol.11, no.2, Summer 1965, pp.1461-68.
8. Margaret M. Hofmann, *Colony of North Carolina, 1735-1764, Abstracts of Land Patents* (Weldon: Roanoke News Company, 1982), vol.1, p.163, abstract 2302, original in Patent Book 5, p.98; Granville grants in Secretary of State Land Grants, North Carolina State Archives, Raleigh, microfilm 1334 A and B.
9. *State Records of North Carolina*, vol.22, pp.240-41.
10. Tyrrell County Deed Books 1-5.
11. Tyrrell County Deed Book 4, vol.2, pp.355-57. I have been unable to find the location of Swift Creek from current maps, but have been told by Mrs. Doris Wilson of the Martin County Historical Society that it is another name for Gardners Creek, a major creek in eastern Martin County.
12. *Ibid.*, pp.185-91, 325.
13. *Ibid.*, pp.361-71 (1769); Martin County Deed Book A, pp.85 and 159 (1774 and 1779).
14. Martin County Deed Book A, p.19 (reference to Gainer); Manning and Booker, *Martin County History*, vol.1, pp.9-14, for data on John's career.
15. Tyrrell County Deed Book 2, pp.105-06 and Book 4, vol.1, pp.57-59 (Joshua); Book 2, pp.236-38 (Joseph).
16. Tyrrell County Deed Book 4, vol.1, pp.360-61 (William); Martin County Deed Book A, p.17 (Benjamin); and pp.187 and 349 (two entries for the gift to Rosanna).
17. Sybil Noyes, Charles Thornton Libby, and Walter Goodwin Davis, editors, *Genealogical Dictionary of Maine and New Hampshire*, p.128; Tyrrell County Deed Book 1, p.153: *Colonial Records of North Carolina*, Second Series, vol. 8, pp. 376-78.
18. Tyrrell County Deed Book 1, pp.88-89 (Charles and Jasper) and pp.121-22 (Cullen Pollock).
19. Tyrrell County Deed Book 2, p.134.
20. Tyrrell County Deed Book 1, p.153 (Cullen); Book 2, p.355 (Joshua).

21. Stephen E. Bradley, Jr., editor, *Tyrrell County, North Carolina Estate Records, 1734-1800* (Keysville, Virginia: privately published, 1991), abstracts 72 and 73; Margaret M. Hofmann, *The Granville District of North Carolina, 1748-1763, Abstracts of Land Grants* (Weldon: Roanoke News Company, 1987), vol.2, pp.111-12; Tyrrell County Marriage Bonds Index, p.35.
22. Tyrrell County Deed Book 2, p.255 (1756); Book 4, vol.1, p.457 (1764); and Book 4, vol.2, p.227 (1768).
23. Martin County Deed Book A, p.156; Tyrrell County Marriage Bonds Index, p.26.
24. Tyrrell County Deed Book 4, vol.2, pp.372 and 375; Martin County Deed Book A, pp.85 and 159; Stephen E. Bradley, Jr., editor, *Tyrrell County, North Carolina Wills, 1729-1811* (privately published, 1990), p.77.
25. Tyrrell County Deed Book 4, vol.2, p.156.
26. *Ibid.*, p.365.
27. *Ibid.*, pp.304, 361, 363, 365, 367, and 370; see also Martin County Deed Book A, pp.85 and 159 for sales in 1774 and 1777.
28. *Colonial Records of North Carolina*, vol.8, pp.278-81, revenue officers in arrears in 1760s; vol.8, pp.282-86, Governor Tryon's speech; vol.9, pp.572-73, revenue officers in arrears in 1771.
29. *Ibid.*, vol.7, pp.626-29.
30. See census data analysis in Chapter 4; also will of Benjamin Carkeet (1808), Bertie County Will Book F, p.77.
31. Margaret M. Hofmann, *Province of North Carolina, 1663-1729, Abstracts of Land Patents* (Weldon: Roanoke News Company, 1979), abstracts 233 and 239, originals in Patent Book 1, pp.86 and 88.
32. Bertie County Deed Book B, p.161.
33. Bertie County Deed Book C, p.277.
34. Bertie County Deed Book D, pp.70-71 and 73-74.
35. North Carolina State Archives, Secretary of State, North Carolina Wills, 1663-1789, Thomas Sutton will (1750/51).
36. Hawkins and Gilliam, *op. cit.*, pp.73-74, includes information on Judith and her descendants based on research of Verena Hatch of Provo, Utah and Ima Eula Mewborn of Farmville, North Carolina.
37. Tyrrell County Deed Book 1, pp.88 and 121-22.
38. North Carolina State Archives, Secretary of State loose wills #1388. William Garrett will (1734/35).
39. Tyrrell County Deed Book 1, pp.133 and 173.
40. *Ibid.*, p.348 (Ward); Book 2, p.206 (Garrett).
41. Tyrrell County Deed Book 5, vol.1, p.79.
42. Tyrrell County Deed Book 10, pp.88-89; Book 12, vol.2, p.293.
43. Tyrrell County Deed Book 12, vol.1, p.211.
44. *Ibid.*, p.29.
45. Tyrrell County 1784 Tax List, microfilm, reel S-50-10, North Carolina State Archives, Raleigh.
46. Tyrrell County Marriage Bonds Index, p.55; other Hardisons included on p.55 are Asa (to Nancy Garrett in 1792), Jesse (to ? Leggett, 1793); Joseph (to Mary A. Collins, 1765), William (to Mary Mizell, 1760) and William (to Hetty Hatfield, 1836). Colonial law required the groom to post a bond before marriage, but numerous marriages took place without it. Many of the original bonds have been lost in various ways. Martin County's marriage records were destroyed in the courthouse fire of 1884. The bonds of Tyrrell County are indexed by the name of

II. THE SECOND GENERATION COMES OF AGE, 1733-1775

the groom. The present (1995) county archives include only the index, not the original bonds. For a discussion of marriage customs, laws, and records, see Helen F. M. Leary and Maurice R. Stirewalt, *North Carolina Research, Genealogy, and Local History* (Raleigh: North Carolina Genealogical Society, 1980), pp.131-43.

47. Washington County Deed Books A and B; see Book B, p.435 for division of Jasper's land among Frederick, Lydia Bozman, and Levi and Mary Stubbs.
48. Hawkins and Gilliam, *op. cit.*, pp.35-51;. Martha Mewborn Marble of Washington, D.C. (see unpublished manuscript in North Carolina State Library, Raleigh) and James Hardison of Lenoir, North Carolina have done extensive research on Jasper and his descendants. Fred Watkins of Fayetteville, Georgia is researching the Frederick who migrated to Georgia in the early nineteenth century.
49. Tyrrell County Deed Book 1, pp.88 and 121-22.
50. *Ibid.*, p.59 (Garrett), p.175 (Browney), and p.349 (Robinson); Book 2, p.255 (Carkeet).
51. Tyrrell County Deed Book 1, pp.151 (Dwight) and 353 (Cory); Book 2, p.381 (Richard Hardison).
52. Craven County Deed Book 2, p.207.
53. Alan D. Watson, *A History of New Bern and Craven County* (New Bern: Tryon Palace Commission, 1987), p.4.
54. Margaret M. Hofmann, *Colony of North Carolina, 1765-1775, Abstracts of Land Patents* (Welson: Roanoke News Company, 1984), vol.2 of two volumes which cover 1735-1775, abstract #7146, original in Patent Book 23, p.353.
55. Clarence E. Ratcliff, compiler, *North Carolina Taxpayers, 1701-1786* (Baltimore: Genealogical Publishing Company, 1987), vol.1, p.88, Charles on 1770 Onslow County roll; Ratcliff, *North Carolina Taxpayers, 1679-1790* (Baltimore: Genealogical Publishing Company, 1987), a supplement to the above and considered vol.2, p.85, Charles on 1771 list; Hawkins and Gilliam, *op. cit.*, pp.54-55, data on Charles including 1774 Onslow tax roll, citing C.R.072.703.1 in North Carolina State Archives, Raleigh.
56. Craven County Deed Book 20, pp.280-82 and 331-33.
57. Ratcliff, *op. cit.*, vol.1, p.88 lists John Hardison for 1742 in New Hanover County, but does not include a roll for that year in its list of data for New Hanover, the years covered being 1755, 1762, 1763, 1765, and 1767. If 1742 is a misprint for 1762, the listing may refer to John, a son of Charles.
58. Hawkins and Gilliam, *op. cit.*, pp.54-57, data on wills of John and Charles and the 1726 deed.
59. *Ibid.*, p.54, cites "Petitions for Exemption from Tax, 1780-1785," C.R.072.703.1, North Carolina State Archives. Verena Hatch, a descendant of Charles, has done extensive research in the North Carolina State Archives and the genealogical collections of the Church of Latter Day Saints, Salt Lake City, Utah.
60. Tyrrell County Deed Book 1, p.355.
61. Tyrrell County Deed Book 2, p.105; Book 4, vol.1, p.57.
62. Martin County Deed Book C, p.144.
63. Tyrrell County Deed Book 4, vol.1, p.44.
64. Martin County Deed Book A, p.238.
65. Martin County Deed Book B, p.13.
66. Tyrrell County Deed Book 2, p.426; Martin County Deed Book A, p.244.
67. Tyrrell County Deed Book 5, vol.1, p.79.
68. Hawkins and Gilliam, *op. cit.*, p.58 and chaps.20-22, Joshua's connection to Mark, Joshua, and Edward in Tennessee..

69. Tyrrell County Deed Book 4, vol.2, p.328.
70. Martin County Deed Book B, p.227.
71. Hawkins and Gilliam, *op. cit.*, p.58.
72. See Chapter 4 for data on Thomas in the state census records of 1784-87 and federal census records of 1790 and 1800.
73. Craven County Deed Book 1, p.234.
74. Samuel A. Ashe, *Biographical History of North Carolina from Colonial Times to the Present*, vol.1, pp.270-71; William S. Powell, *Dictionary of North Carolina Biography*, vol.2, pp.171-72.
75. Tyrrell County Deed Book 2, p.230 (Joseph) and p.392 (Richard).
76. *Ibid.*, p.381.
77. Martin County Deed Book A, p.276.
78. *Ibid.*, pp.386 and 467.
79. Martin County Deed Book B, p.13.
80. Hawkins and Gilliam, *op. cit.*, see chaps.4 and 5 on James and his settlement in Tennessee.
81. Tyrrell County Deed Book 2, pp.230 and 392.
82. *Ibid.*, p.236.
83. Tyrrell County Deed Book 5, vol.1, p.72.
84. Tyrrell County Marriage Bonds Index, p.55; Martin County Will Book 1, pp.143-44.
85. Shelby Jean Nelson Hughes, editor, *Martin County Heritage* (Williamston: Martin County Historical Society, 1980), see for numerous articles on the descendants of Joseph and the other sons of Jasper Hardison.
86. Bernard Bailyn, *The Peopling of British North America*, p.67.
87. "Martin County: 1779 Tax List," *Journal of North Carolina Genealogy*, vol.11, no.2, pp.1461-68.

III

The Hardisons in the Era of Revolution and Early Statehood, 1775-1785

The world in which the Hardison brothers and sisters had matured and prospered went through a dramatic transition in the 1770s as the American colonies declared their independence and rebelled against the mother country.[1] Divided loyalties toward the revolutionary cause tore at the fabric of the planter class society in the eastern counties, while the resentments of the more recently settled counties of the Piedmont against the political dominance of this class and of the eastern counties continued to fester. In the east, the original leadership in colonial affairs wielded by the settlers in the Albemarle area was now shared with planters and merchants from the counties to the south of Albemarle Sound, through the lower Cape Fear River Valley. While most of the colonists had resisted or at least resented English taxation and trade regulations, differences of opinion over the degree of opposition and over the way in which the new state government should be organized and financed led to civil strife and near anarchy. The future for the numerous grandchildren of Jasper Hardison, who were coming to maturity in the 1760s and 1770s, held both challenge and opportunity as the colony moved into statehood and took its place in the newly established United States of America. As the re-

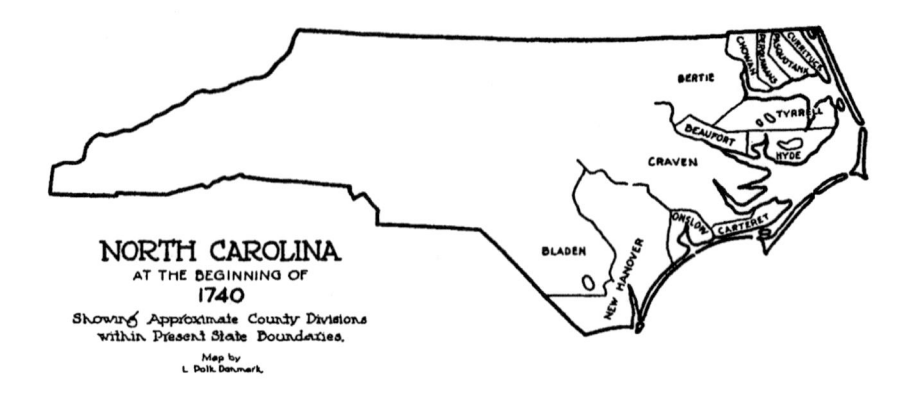

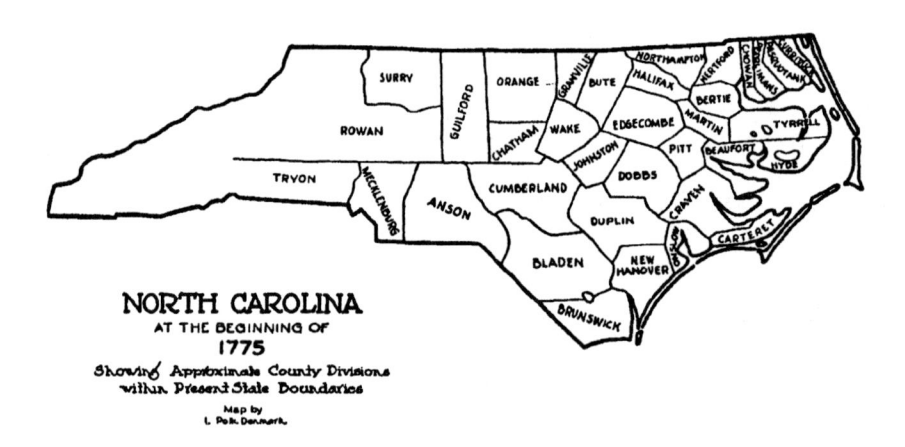

NORTH CAROLINA
AT THE BEGINNING OF
1740
Showing Approximate County Divisions within Present State Boundaries.
Map by
L. Polk Denmark

NORTH CAROLINA
AT THE BEGINNING OF
1775
Showing Approximate County Divisions within Present State Boundaries
Map by
L. Polk Denmark

Reprinted with permission of North Carolina Division of Archives and History maining chapters of this study will show, for a number of these descendants the problems at home and the opening of vast new lands to the south and the west after the Revolution led to a leave-taking from their family and lands in North Carolina.

John Hardison's Career in Public Service

For Jasper's eldest son, John, the 1770s provided the opportunity to bring decades of experience as a successful entrepreneur and public office holder to the service of North Carolina and to newly created Martin County.[2] During the years when the eastern portion of Martin County, where John and most of the Hardisons lived, was a part of Tyrrell County, John had pursued a career as land speculator and developer and had held a variety of public offices. In 1761 he was appointed as a collector of revenues for the lands in Tyrrell County which had been granted by Earl Granville, the remaining proprietor of the original eight Lords Proprietors, and during the decade of the 1760s he served as a surveyor of Granville lands.[3] For his service as collector, he was to receive five per cent of the funds collected. These revenues corresponded to the taxes, known as quit rents, levied by the royal government on all other lands. The taxes were hated and resisted and it is not surprising to find John's name in a list of public officials in arrears for monies collected during the 1760s. In a speech of 1770 to the Assembly, Governor William Tryon spoke out against the common practices among collectors of "taking monies at pleasure from one fund to make up the deficiencies of others" and "employing the public money as a stock in private trade."[4] John's name appears in a subsequent list of "Sheriffs of the North District," among six men from Tyrrell County who owed balances to the royal authorities up to the year 1771.[5] The particulars of his appearance on the lists of delinquent collectors are not known, but his role in the movement toward independence is indicative of his sentiments toward royal authority. Certainly resistance took many forms and often served personal as well as patriotic interests.

John's career in public life in the 1760s also included service in 1764 as a representative from Tyrrell County in the Assembly, the legislative body of the colony.[6] He was assigned to several committees, including those concerned with the colony's defenses at Fort Johnston and Fort Granville. North Carolina had suffered heavy damages during the various wars for empire among England and her enemies during the first half of the century and defense of her lengthy coastline was a constant source of concern. In the decade before his service in the Assembly, John had served as captain of a militia company in Tyrrell County.[7]

In 1774, on the eve of the Revolution, John was offered a new opportunity for leadership as Martin County was created from the western portion of Tyrrell County and the southern portion of Halifax County.[8] For several years the residents of these areas had petitioned the colonial authorities for a new county whose seat of government would be more accessible to them. It was named for the current governor, Josiah Martin, the last of the royal governors, who was soon to be the subject of calumny as the movement toward revolution escalated. After statehood and independence, the residents of the county designated Alexander Martin, an early governor of the state, as the honoree.

John Hardison was one of the leaders of the new county from its beginning, serving in a number of positions to help organize and run the county during the chaotic years of the Revolution. He was chosen also as a representative to the Provincial Congress of November, 1776 which created the new state government and prepared North Carolina for war.[9] When the county was formed, he was a member of the commission to erect the first courthouse, jail, and stocks. There being no towns in the county, these facilities were erected on lands belonging to Thomas Stewart near the Roanoke River landing known by its Indian name, Skewarkey. In 1779 the town of Williamston, named for the prominent and wealthy Williams family, was founded in the vicinity of the landing and it became the seat of government, with a courthouse whose main access was a rope ladder let down to the banks of the river, the area's chief highway. John was one of the three men, along with Kenneth McKenzie and Thomas Hunter, nominated to be the county's first sheriff, with McKenzie, then Hunter, and finally John holding the position in succession. He was also appointed by the Assembly as one of the county's two grand jurors to serve on the Superior Court of the Edenton District, one of the colony's six judicial districts.

III. REVOLUTION AND EARLY STATEHOOD, 1775-1785

Martin County soon became active in the movement toward open rebellion against England and sent representatives to the series of Provincial Congresses which began in 1774 to take over the government of the colony. The battles at Lexington and Concord in April of 1775 and North Carolina's first battle of the Revolution, Moore's Creek Bridge, in February of 1776, brought the colonies to an official break with the mother country. Already in the spring of 1775, citizens of Mecklenburg County had adopted a "Declaration of Independence," proclaiming the rights of its citizens to be free and independent, and the Provincial Congress meeting in Hillsborough put North Carolina on a war footing. The dramatic victory at Moore's Creek Bridge of North Carolina's militia over the Tory forces assembled by Governor Josiah Martin helped to overcome the reluctance of the colonists to make an official break with Great Britain. When the fourth Provincial Congress met in the town of Halifax in April of 1776 there was strong support for independence. The Congress is famous for its passage of the Halifax Resolves, the first recommendation of a vote for independence sent by a colony to its representatives in the Continental Congress. Soon Virginia called for independence, other colonies concurred, and the Declaration of Independence became official on July 4, 1776.

The exhilaration which the prospect of freedom from British control brought to those who had called for independence soon gave way to consciousness of the multiple problems which lay ahead for North Carolina and the other former colonies. Primary were the need to organize state and local governments, to prepare for war, and to deal with the very large minority of the North Carolina populace who had opposed independence. A fifth Provincial Congress met in Halifax in November and December of 1776. John Hardison was one of the representatives from Martin County, serving with Whitmel Hill, Thomas Hunter, Samuel Smithwick, and William Williams. He was appointed to the committee which was directed to inquire into the number of troops which could be raised in the various counties. In addition to concerns over preparation for war, the Congress addressed the need to establish governments for the state and the counties. A committee was appointed to write a state constitution and a bill of rights. Richard Caswell, who had been one of the writers of the constitution, was chosen as the first governor.

Early in 1777 North Carolina changed its status from colony to state and the new governments went into effect. Sheriffs and justices of the peace were appointed by the state Assembly to conduct the affairs and administer justice in each county. Again John Hardison was among those chosen for leading positions, being one of the twenty-two justices of the peace appointed to govern Martin County, and among the seven of them who met in January to reorganize the county. The latter group appointed John as sheriff, Thomas Hunter as clerk, and Edward Smithwick as coroner. John had earlier served as sheriff during a portion of 1776, after Hunter had resigned the position. These men, like the others appointed to office in the county, were members of the eastern planter class who had long dominated the political affairs of their localities and of the colony and would continue to do so well into the nineteenth century. Not all of the planters or the wealthy merchants shared their enthusiasm for the Revolution and many of this group remained loyal to the mother county, suffering fines, imprisonment, and loss of property during and after the war.

North Carolina and the Hardisons in the American Revolution

After the battles of Lexington and Concord in 1775, the county militia companies were ordered to a state of preparedness. North Carolina was divided into six military districts, each of which was to have a battalion of ten companies. The militia, known as Minute Men, were to defend their local area and help recruit two regiments for the Continental Army, called the Continental Line, which North Carolina was asked to raise. As the war progressed, additional regiments were called for. William Williams of Martin County was briefly the adjutant of the First Regiment when it was organized in 1775, then the commanding officer of the Martin County militia until his resignation in 1778. At this time he recommended a slate of officers to the governor which included his nephew Whitmel Hill as First Colonel, Kenneth McKenzie as First Major, and John Hardison as Second Major. It is not likely that John served long in this position for in November of 1778 he wrote his will and he died some time before

September, 1780, when it was probated. It is possible that the John who was nominated for the office of Second Major was the son of the elder John. In the official records of the recommendation he is referred to only as John Hardison, Esquire.[10]

There was little military activity in North Carolina after the Battle of Moore's Creek Bridge in 1776 until the southern campaign of General Charles Cornwallis led to an invasion of the state in 1781. In the intervening years men from North Carolina served in Virginia and South Carolina and under General George Washington's leadership in New York, New Jersey, and Pennsylvania, with more than a thousand of them suffering through the winter of 1777-1778 at Valley Forge. After failing to defeat Washington in the northeast, the British turned their efforts toward occupying the southern states, where there were strong Tory sympathies, and cutting them off from the remainder of the states. In December of 1778 they launched their campaign with the capture of Savannah and then went on to take Charleston and attempt to occupy South Carolina. Numerous North Carolinians fought in the battles at Camden, Cowpens, and Kings Mountain and the many smaller confrontations. Such a large portion of the state's soldiers had been committed to the South Carolina campaign that North Carolina was ill prepared when it became evident that Cornwallis would invade. Fortunately the British general was so dilatory in launching his offensive to the north, that North Carolina had the opportunity to recruit men for the state's defense. General Nathanael Greene, whom Washington assigned to the campaign in the Carolinas, with able assistance from North Carolinians such as William R. Davie and William Davidson, skillfully outwitted and outfought the British in the Carolinas. After the Battle of Guilford Courthouse in central North Carolina in March of 1781, Cornwallis, although technically the winner of the battle, was too weak and disorganized to pursue Greene's army and he withdrew his forces to Wilmington and then on to Yorktown, where he surrendered to Washington in October, 1781.

Estimates of the number of North Carolinians who served in the Continental Line range between 5,454 and 7,663, a relatively small percentage of the estimated 235,000 enlistments in the national army. However, the state had a great number of men in its militia units, possibly as many as 10,000. Both national and state records were so poorly kept during this chaotic period that it is impossible to find the names of all who served and the nature of their service.[11] A search of the official army records in the *State Records of North Carolina*, the archives of the Daughters of the American Revolution, and the list of men in service attached to the Martin County Tax List of 1779 yielded the names of at least five and possibly seven Hardisons from North Carolina—Benjamin (possibly two men with this name), Hardy, James, Jesse (possibly two). and Joseph. All were probably Jasper's grandsons or great-grandsons, but their identity is difficult to determine, since there are two or more persons among Jasper's descendants with each of these names.[12]

There were at least two and perhaps three Benjamin Hardisons living in the last quarter of the eighteenth century—the son of John Hardison, the son of John's son William, and possibly another based on the fact that the name appears three times in the 1779 Martin County Tax List.[13] Two Benjamins are included in the main body of that list as heads of household, one of whom was undoubtedly John's son, cited as Benjamin Hardison, Esquire. The third is found in the addendum at the end of the list which includes men in service and insolvents. The notation by this third Benjamin's name is simply "gone, Nothing found." Additional evidence for the existence of three Benjamins lies in the fact that two, one living in Martin County and one in Washington County, are listed among the heads of household in the 1800 Federal Census enumeration, fifteen years after the death of John's son Benjamin.[14] Two documents provide proof of the participation of one or more Benjamins in the Revolution. The first is the inclusion of the name in a list of men from Martin County who volunteered in June, 1780 for "the present Expedition" (the nature of the expedition is not indicated, but was probably part of North Carolina's attempt to prepare for an expected British invasion).[15] The second is the pension application of James Hardison in which he stated that he had served under Captain Benjamin Hardison in Colonel Hill's Regiment in the Battle of Guilford Courthouse in 1781.[16] The Benjamin who volunteered in 1780 is identified in the Daughters of the American Revolution records as the son of John Hardison, but no mention is made of his service in 1781.[17] In Manning and Booker's

History of Martin County, reference is made to Captains Benjamin and Joshua Hardison as members of one of the prominent families of the county, but no information is given concerning the nature of their service.[18] Probably both men were captains in the Martin County militia. The reader may choose among the possible identities of the various Benjamins—that each is the same man or that one is the son of John and the other a younger man, possibly the son of William Hardison. It is interesting that there was another Benjamin Hardison, a private from Berwick, Maine, most likely a distant cousin of the North Carolina Hardisons, serving the Revolution in a Massachusetts unit. This Benjamin was captured in Canada and remained a prisoner until the end of the war.[19]

Hardy Hardison is listed in the Roster of the Continental Line from North Carolina, 1783, as a quartermaster sergeant in the Seventh Regiment who enlisted in April, 1777 and died on December 18 of that year.[20] No information is given as to the place or cause of his death, but it is possible that he was among the North Carolinians at Valley Forge. There were at least two Hardisons named Hardy, a grandson of John through his son Benjamin and a grandson of Charles, with the latter being the more likely identity since the former is referred to in deeds of Washington County in the post-Revolutionary period.

James and John Hardison are among the fourteen persons appearing in the list of men in service which is attached to the 1779 Martin County Tax List. No further references to service by a John Hardison, other than the inclusion of the elder John in the Daughters of the American Revolution Patriot Index for his participation in the Provincial Congress of November, 1776, have been found.[21] James has been identified by family researcher Fred Hawkins as the son of Richard Hardison and the founder of one of the Hardison families which migrated to Tennessee early in the nineteenth century.[22] James was drafted for several tours of duty and served as a private at various times between 1778 and 1781. He participated in the 1779 campaign in South Carolina and during his last tour he served in 1781 under Captain Benjamin Hardison in Colonel Whitmel Hill's regiment. In the latter capacity, he was on guard duty during the Battle of Guilford Courthouse. He applied for a pension from the federal government after his move to Tennessee.[23]

There are two men named Jesse Hardison who appear in the Revolutionary records of the *State Records of North Carolina*. One of them, spelled "Jese," and Joseph are included in the same roster of the Continental Line as Hardy and both enlisted on July 20, 1778 and served in the Tenth North Carolina Regiment. Jese was a sergeant in Baker's Company and served nine months and Joseph was a private in Bradley's Company, enlisting for nine months and being discharged May 7, 1779.[24] The record of service by another Jesse is found in the roll of the officers in the Third North Carolina Battalion from the U.S. Pension Office, in which he is listed as an orderly sergeant. This document is undated but a note in the *State Records* states that knowledge of the careers of commissioned officers whose names appear in the roll indicates a date after June 1778.[25] The names Jesse and Joseph appear often enough among Jasper's descendants to make it difficult to know from which sons they were descended, though Jasper and Charles are educated guesses.

In summary, the Hardisons with proven service to the Revolution are:

Benjamin—volunteered for service in 1780

Hardy—enlisted and died in 1777, quartermaster sergeant in the Seventh N.C. Regiment

James—private in various units

Jesse—enlisted for nine months in 1778, sergeant in the Tenth N.C. Regiment

Jesse—orderly sergeant in the Third N.C. Battalion

John—member of the Provincial Congress of November, 1776

Joseph—enlisted for nine months in 1778, private in the Tenth N.C. Regiment

The Death of John Hardison

As has been previously noted, John, the eldest of Jasper Hardison's seven sons, died at some time between the writing of his will on November 27, 1778 and its probate in the September, 1780 court of Martin County.[26] To use a hackneyed but appropriate expression, his passing marked the end of an era in the Hardison family. The relatively easy acquisition of good land in the Albemarle area and the as-

III. REVOLUTION AND EARLY STATEHOOD, 1775-1785

surance of a ready market for its produce no longer prevailed in the post-colonial years. At the time John wrote his will, the revolutionary cause was far from victory, as Washington struggled to drive the British from the northeastern states and the enemy launched an offensive in the south. John might well have wondered about the wisdom of the break with the mother country, for at the time he wrote his will the state's and nation's economies were a shambles. Their protected British markets were closed, public confidence was eroded by the virtually worthless paper money issued by both North Carolina and the Continental Congress, and both governments were weak and inefficient.

John and his brothers who shared in the lumber industry must have suffered during the war, since the major markets for forest products, Britain and her West Indies colonies, were cut off. The economy of Martin County, particularly the eastern area in which the Hardisons lived, was centered around what was known as "swamping," the felling and processing of the bountiful forests south of the Roanoke River to produce lumber, shingles, and barrel staves. As noted earlier, the Hardison lands lay primarily in the swampy areas south and east of the present town of Jamesville and among John's major interests were his saw mills and grist mills. Outlets for some of his products may have been provided by the demand for timbers to build the many North Carolina privateer ships which preyed on British vessels and by the need for processed grain to feed the army, but his various economic interests must have suffered in the dislocations of war.

As John attempted to set his affairs in order, he had a large family to provide for. It is interesting that while most wills of the period begin with statements that the writer, though in sound mental state, was in failing physical health, John began by saying that he was "in bodily Health and perfect mind and Memory." If he were the John who was nominated to be Second Major of the Martin County militia in 1778, he may have expected to perform military service and wanted to be sure his property would be divided as he wished in case of death.

John's family consisted of a wife, Olive; three sons, William, Benjamin, and John; six daughters, of whom four were married—Mary Beasley, Elizabeth Moore, Sarah Meazle, and Ann Mizell, one an unmarried adult—Hannah, and one a minor—Frances; an unborn child, who was to be named Robert if a son; and a grandson who lived with the family, John Hardison. The great range in ages of the children probably indicates that Olive was a second wife. John had transferred land to son William as early as 1764, indicating that he, apparently the eldest son, was well into adulthood at the time John wrote his will.[27] Benjamin had also had land transferred to him, in 1774.[28]

The term plantation, which appears often in the will, should not be construed in this case to mean a large, cultivated acreage producing a staple, such as tobacco or rice, as a money crop. For many land owners in the Albemarle area, it referred to their home place, the acreage varying greatly, on which their residence, augmented by various outbuildings, stood. With their orchards, vegetable gardens, and livestock—including sheep for wool, these plantations produced most of the food and clothing needed by the family. There were, of course, a number of plantations in eastern North Carolina which were engaged in large scale agriculture, particularly the production of tobacco, but John's major interest was lumber milling and tracts of forested land provided his staple crop. As the will indicates, he owned tracts of land other than his plantation, some of the many acquisitions which are reflected in his Tyrrell County deed records and probably held for their timber. The fact that only four slaves are mentioned in his will is further indication that he was not engaged in large scale agriculture. In land and in wealth, he stood somewhere in the middle among the planters of his area. His plantation home was probably typical of that group—a rambling two story wooden house, often left unpainted and added to as the family grew.

John's will provides a record of the large family for whom his plantation was home and begins with bequests to his wife. Ample provision was made for Olive and for the care of the two youngest children, the daughter Frances and the unborn child; however, in each case that Olive was given an interest in the property, the qualification was made that she was to enjoy the benefits only as long as she "sees fitt to live" on the plantation. One bequest which had no strings attached was the return to her of "one pare of mill Stones that she brought here with her." Perhaps these stones had been a sort of dowry, a highly valued possession for a family engaged in milling, and

III. REVOLUTION AND EARLY STATEHOOD, 1775-1785

perhaps Olive had not been satisfied in Martin County and wished to return to her former home. Later census and land records place her in Virginia and it is probable that this had been her place of origin.[29]

The bequests in John's will are as follows:

To Olive
1. the pair of mill stones which formerly belonged to her
2. one-half of the household goods and furniture
3. one gray mare
4. one-third of "all my horse kind Cattle and Sheep and all my hogs"
5. the use of one-half of the plantation, all the buildings on the plantation, and one-half of the produce of the orchards, "for and During her Nattrall life or as long as she sees fitt to live on the said plantation and no longer"
6. the work and labor of "negro Hannah" for six years to help raise the two young children
7. the work and labor of Manger (not identified as a Negro), toward raising and schooling the two young children, during her life or as long as she lived on the plantation
8. one-half of the benefit of John's third of the grist mill during her life or as long as she lived on the plantation.

To son William—a Negro boy named Bob and one-half of a tract of land lying in the Narmouth Neck and Brovens [?]Neck (this tract may have been John's 300 acre grant of 1761 from the Granville District which mentions Narrow Mouth Neck, Deep Run, and the line of William Gardiner in its description).[30]

To son Benjamin—a Negro man named Caksky and the other half of the above mentioned tract of land.

To son John—the Negro woman named Hannah after the expiration of her six years of labor for Olive; the plantation and the land belonging to it, with the provision that Olive was to have the use of half of it during her life or time of residence; and a tract of land known as Mannings Old Field.

Jointly to sons William, Benjamin, and John—the saw mill and grist mill interests, with the limitation that wife Olive was to have one-half of the income from the elder John's one-third interest in the grist mill during her life or the time of her residence on the plantation. (The will does not indicate to whom the other two-thirds belonged.)

To daughters Mary Beasley, Elizabeth Moore, Sarah Meazle, Ann Mizell, and Hannah Hardison—twenty pounds each. (The name Meazle was probably a variation of Mizell, a prominent family of the area on whose lands the town of Jamesville was founded in 1785.)[31]

To daughter Frances and the unborn child—a parcel of land lying between Deep Run, Benjamin Hardison's line, and the mill pond, to be equally divided.

To grandson John Hardison "that lives with me"—one cow and calf and one ewe and lamb. (Both sons John and Benjamin had sons named John, but this grandson is more probably Benjamin's son, for as Benjamin's will indicates his John was the son of his first wife and he might have been displaced by the second wife and her large family. As will be discussed in later chapters, Benjamin's John and his half brother Thomas migrated to Georgia in the early nineteenth century.)[32]

Joint distributions of property—a rather confusing provision concerning household goods, livestock, and other possessions reads as follows, "I give all my House hold good[s] furniture to my son John Hardison and my daughter Hannah Hardison to [be] Equely divided between them all that is not before [mentioned?] and I also give all the Remainder of Horses Cattle Sheep and every other thing that is not mentioned to be equally divided amonst my Ten Children that is above named"; the value of any children of the slave Hannah was to be equally divided among the ten Hardison children.

The will ended with the appointment of John's three sons, William, Benjamin, and John as executors. It was witnessed by William Carkeet, a descendant of John's sister Mary, and William Ushere, whose relationship is unknown. The will was probated at the September, 1780 session of the Martin County Court and recorded by John's colleague in county affairs, Thomas Hunter.

The reader of this document has the impression of a husband and father attempting to make a fair distribution of his worldly goods among members of a large and rather complex family.[33] The high mortality rate among women of child-bearing age in the eighteenth century made for frequent re-marriages and consequent rivalry for the family possessions among two or more sets of children. John made numerous provisions for his two minor children, Frances and the unborn child, but the major portion of his estate, including the valuable mill properties and the plantation were left to his three existing sons. William and Benjamin were evidently well advanced into adulthood, but John may have been a very young man, still living at home. The monetary gifts to the four married daughters and to Hannah were nominal, but husbands were expected to provide for their wives and Hannah was given a share of the household goods. The disposition of these goods is rather confusing, with the provision early in the will that Olive was given, not lent the use of, one-half of all the household goods and furniture. One can imagine that the day on which they were divided was not a peaceful one! It is interesting to make such speculations, but it must be pointed out that there is no proof that Olive was a second wife. As noted earlier, she is believed to be the Olive Hardison who appears in the records of Princess Anne County, Virginia, from the 1780s.

John can be pictured as a vigorous but aging man, proud of his material possessions and of his large family, possibly dubious about the outcome of the Revolution which he had supported and helped further in North Carolina, and anxious about the future well-being of his many dependents. He had taken advantage of the opportunities for economic advancement in the portion of the British Empire in which his father Jasper had planted the family and he had served in the effort to make the transition of North Carolina from colony to state. His descendants faced a time of crisis and challenge in the decades following his death as North Carolina and the United States attempted to set their courses in the era of independence.

NOTES

1. Background information on North Carolina in the period of its early statehood and during the American Revolutionhas been drawn from Hugh Talmage Lefler and Albert Ray Newsome, *North Carolina, the History of a Southern State*, chaps.13-15.
2. Confusion has arisen among genealogists and local historians who have written about the Hardisons as to the identity of the John who played a prominent role in the public life of Tyrrell and Martin counties in the eighteenth century. Was it John the son of Jasper, born about 1710, or his son John, Jr.? In their history of Martin

County, Francis M. Manning and W. H. Booker, *Martin County History*, vol.1, seem to be of two minds concerning the identity of the John who was a public figure. In their initial chapter, which deals with the founding of the county in the 1770s, there are numerous references to the positions held by John. In Chapter 9, entitled "Prominent Men," pp.232-33, the John who filled these roles is referred to as John, Jr., son of Jasper's son John. I believe the latter identity to be an error, for none of the references to John's public service in the official records of North Carolina include the designation "Jr." and the elder John did not die until sometime between the writing of his will in 1778 and its probate in 1780. Deeds and other public records of the time indicate strict attention to identifying father and son as "Sr." and "Jr." when both were living. Manning and Booker remark on p.233 that few records have been found about John Hardison, Jr., after 1778. References to the younger John in the 1778 will of his father seem to indicate that he was the youngest of three sons and was possibly still living at home. His name does not appear in Manning and Booker's discussion of the leading men in Martin County in the years following the Revolution and no will has been found for him. Even though the elder John was of considerable age in the 1770s, having been born about 1710 since he was old enough to be his father's executor in 1733, he is the more likely choice as the office holder both in Tyrrell County in the 1750s and 1760s and in Martin County's formative years in the 1770s.

3. Tyrrell County Deed Book 4, vol.1, pp.107-10 (John's appointment); Margaret M. Hofmann, *The Granville District of North Carolina, 1748-63, Abstracts of Land Grants*, vol.2, includes frequent mention of John as surveyor.
4. *Colonial Records of North Carolina*, vol.8, pp.278-86 (lists and Tryon's speech).
5. *Colonial Records*, vol.9, pp.572-73.
6. *Colonial Records*, vol.6, pp.1105, 1148, 1153, 1176, and 1217.
7. *State Records of North Carolina*, vol.22, p.390.
8. Manning and Booker, *op. cit.*, chaps. 1-3 provide information on the early history of Martin County and on the roles played by John Hardison in the 1770s.
9. *Colonial Records*, vol,10, pp.913-17 (John in the Provincial Congress of Nov., 1776); *State Records*, vol.15, p.693 and vol.23, pp.992-94 (John's Martin County appointments).
10. *State Records*, vol.12, pp.600 and 707-08, and vol.13, p.393 (John's nomination to be Second Major of the Martin County militia).
11. Lefler and Newsome, *op. cit.*, pp.239-40.
12. Hawkins and Gilliam, op. cit., see their chart of descendants reproduced in Chapter 2.
13. "Martin County: 1779 Tax List," *Journal of North Carolina Genealogy*, vol.11, no.2, pp.1461-68. (Benjamin Hardison, Esquire, and Benjamin Hardison in District 1 on pp.1461 and 1462; Benjamin, "gone, Nothing found" on p.1468.)
14. Ronald Vern Jackson and G. R. Teeples, editors, *North Carolina 1800* Census (Provo: Accelerated Indexing Systems, 1974), p.388.
15. *State Records*, vol.14, pp.838-39.
16. National Society of the Daughters of the American Revolution (afterwards cited as DAR), Register General, Washington, D.C., record copy of National Number 742397 (James).
17. DAR, National Number 243-704-A428 (Benjamin of N.C.).
18. Manning and Booker, *op. cit.*, pp.232-33.
19. DAR, National Number 200140 (Benjamin of Maine).
20. *State Records*, vol.16, p.1077 (Hardy).
21. DAR, National Number 243-704-A421 (John).

III. REVOLUTION AND EARLY STATEHOOD, 1775-1785

22. Hawkins and Gilliam, *op. cit.*, chap.5 (James); see also pp.35 and 42-43 for data on another James Hardison, identified as a son of Jasper, Jr., whose widow Lucretia applied in 1853 for a widow's pension for his service.
23. DAR, National Number 742397 (James).
24. *State Records*, vol.16, p.1079 (Jese) and p.1080 (Joseph).
25. *State Records*, vol.13, p.343-44 (Jesse).
26. Martin County Will Book 1, pp.61-63.
27. Tyrrell County Deed Book 4, vol.1, pp.105-06 (1764, William); Martin County Deed Book A, p.234 (1779, William).
28. Martin County Deed Book A, p.17 (1774, Benjamin).
29. Hawkins and Gilliam, *op. cit.*, p.29; S. N. D. North, director, *Records of the State Enumeration: 1782 to 1785, Virginia* (Washington: Government Printing Office, 1908), p.102, Oliff Hardison is listed in the Lower Precinct of the Western Shore of Princess Anne County, a county which covered the southeastern coastal area of Virginia, just to the north of North Carolina, but no longer exists. Oliff is the only Hardison listed in the census and may be a misreading of Olive from the handwritten original, such errors being numerous in the transcriptions of the manuscript records for early census records. The Virginia records for the First Federal Census, 1790 have been lost and the state enumeration serves as a substitute.
30. Tyrrell County Deed Book 4, vol.1, p.115.
31. Manning and Booker, *op. cit.*, p.104 (Jamesville); John's son William also married a member of the family, Mary Mizell, in 1760, Tyrrell County Marriage Bonds Index, p.55.
32. Martin County Will Book l, pp.118-19 (will of Benjamin).
33. Martin County Deed Book A, pp.187 and 349, see for two entries for a gift of 200 acres from John to granddaughter Rosanna in 1778, the year he wrote his will. Her name does not appear in the wills of John's sons William and Benjamin, so she may have been the daughter of son John.

IV

North Carolina at the Close of the Eighteenth Century, 1785-1800

In the last two decades of the eighteenth century, the Hardisons and their fellow North Carolinians experienced the cost as well as the blessings of liberty and independence. The domestic problems which had plagued the new nation during the Revolution became more acute after the armed conflict ended.[1] With the defeat of the British at Yorktown in 1781, the men in service were free to return to their homes; however, after years of little or no pay, they returned to a daunting accumulation of problems which affected all areas and all classes. Most pressing were the need to create a stable economy, with a dependable currency and new markets to replace the favored status the colonies had enjoyed in Great Britain and her possessions, and to establish fair and stable governments on every level, from county to nation.

The decade of the 1780s was a time of crisis for North Carolina as attempts were made to address both her economic and political ills. The state suffered from rampant inflation, which accompanied the totally discredited state and Continental currency; the loss of traditional and subsidized markets; the problem of dealing with the confiscated property of the many people who had remained loyal to Britain; and a

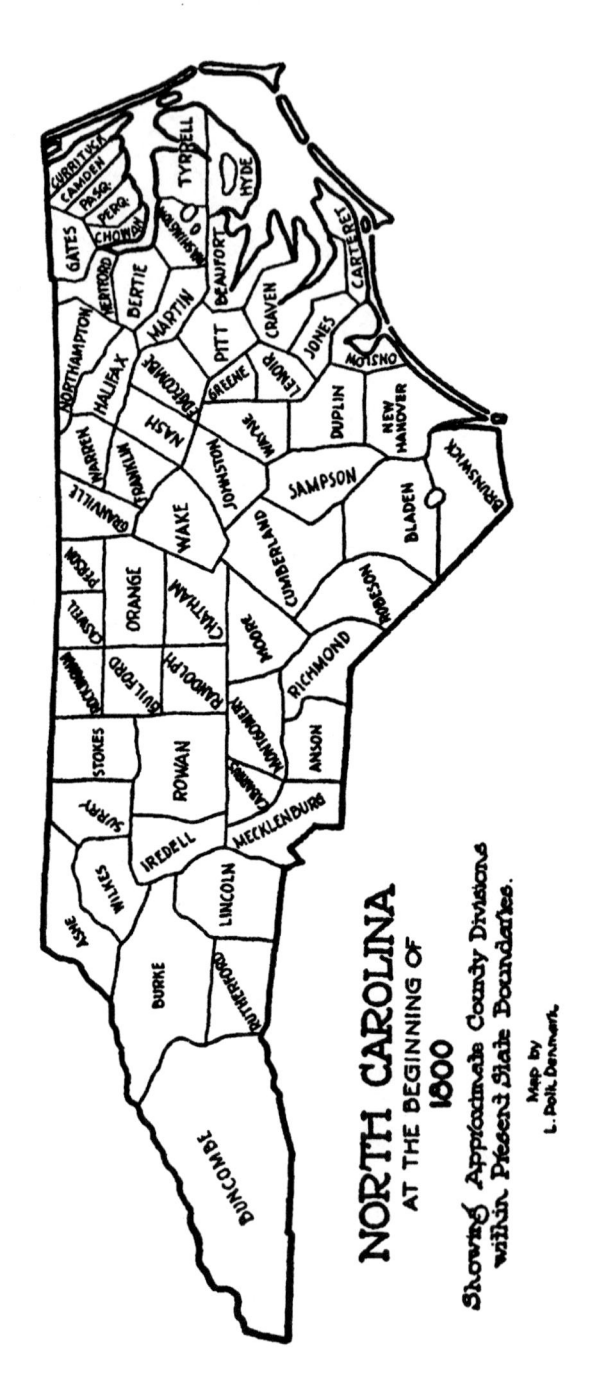

Reprinted with permission of North Carolina Division of Archives and History

weak and inefficient government. Every area of life in North Carolina, from education and religion to government and economy, was in a state of disarray.

As producers of forest products which had found their markets primarily in the British Empire and as business men who needed a stable economy with a dependable currency, the Hardisons were undoubtedly hit hard by the depression which became severe in 1785 and 1786. As will be noted, the will which John Hardison's son Benjamin wrote in 1785 has a tone of discouragement, which may well reflect the gloom of that time. Toward the end of the 1780s conditions improved as new trade patterns developed and the major portions of North Carolina's exports found markets in other American states, particularly New England, and in the West Indies. Naval stores, lumber, and tobacco remained the chief exports and their quantities increased; however, the colonial problem of the inadequacy of North Carolina's ports, due to the nature of her coastline, became more acute due to the increasing size of ocean-going vessels. The interior of the state lacked adequate roads to bring goods to the coast and its crops found their chief markets in South Carolina, using transportation by the inland rivers as much as possible. Marketing problems, along with a number of other ills, caused North Carolina's economy to lag behind the rest of the nation in the post-Revolutionary era.

The systems of government on all levels from county to nation, which had been quickly fashioned during the Revolution, reflected the fear and hatred of a strong executive, resulting from experience with the royal governors. Added to North Carolina's problems with a weak executive was the sectional rivalry growing out of the dominance of the legislative branch by the planter elite of the older eastern counties. As the 1780s progressed, the relatively high level of cooperation among the political factions in North Carolina, which the Revolutionary crisis had forced, broke down. Sectional and class rivalries led to a polarization of political factions into the Conservatives and the Radicals. When the first state constitution was written in 1776, the eastern leadership, which had long dominated political affairs, was able to create a legislature whose membership was based on equal representation for each county and not on population. As the population of the Piedmont area, fed by massive migrations of the Scotch-Irish and Germans in the middle decades of the eighteenth century, grew at a more rapid rate than that of the eastern counties, this system generated increasing dissatisfaction. Leadership in the Piedmont was drawn from the ranks of the dominant yeoman farmers and this group fashioned an alliance with the small farmers and artisans of the eastern counties, whose interests the planter elite generally ignored. The leadership of the Radicals included Timothy Bloodworth, Willie Jones, and Thomas Person and of the Conservatives, William R. Davie, James Iredell, and Samuel Johnston.

The sectional enmity, which had erupted in armed conflict in the Regulator movement shortly before the Revolution, was to continue for years. It helps to explain why there was no fixed capital city for the state for ten years after the Revolution. With all the trundling of official records among the seven different place of meeting, it is a wonder that any state records of the period survived. Finally a site in centrally located Wake County, which became Raleigh, was agreed on in 1792. North Carolina's reputation for contentiousness in the colonial era continued to be well deserved.

The Conservative faction included not only the big planters but also the other monied interests, the merchants, money lenders, lawyers, and land speculators. On both the state and national levels, they called for stronger and more efficient governments, a dependable currency, high prices for land, and conservative credit policies. The Radicals addressed the needs and concerns of a majority of the population, who wanted "cheap" money, easy credit, and liberal distribution of public lands. They feared strong, centralized government on both the state and national level.

The issues which divided the population in the state did so on the national level as well. With the growing controversy of the 1780s over replacing the ineffectual Articles of Confederation with a new, more centralized form of national government, the Conservatives became part of the Federalist faction and the Radicals, the Anti-Federalist. The latter group was by far the more numerous in North Carolina and was able to defeat the state's ratification of the new national Constitution in a vote taken in Hillsborough in 1788. In this vote only the representatives from the Albemarle and Pamlico Sound counties and four scattered counties voted for ratification. Great pressure was brought to bear on opponents of the Constitution by both state and national Federalist leaders and heed was taken of the demands of North Carolinians and others for a body of amendments which would protect personal rights and liberties. In a second convention, held in Fayetteville in 1789, ratification of the Constitution was secured with a major shift in the votes of nearly half of the state's counties.

As the Constitution went into effect in the 1790s, the national Federalist faction, led by Alexander Hamilton, was so successful in fashioning policies which favored the nation's monied interests that animosity against the Federalists caused the party to be discredited in North Carolina. It lost favor among many of the planters as well as the small farmers, for it leaned toward the interests of the urban wealthy of the North. Increasingly the majority of North Carolinians looked to the party, known as the Democratic Republicans (eventually the Democrats), which Thomas Jefferson created. Its economic policies were more compatible with agricultural interests and its political philosophy with the states rights sentiments of the South. Toward the end of the eighteenth century, North Carolina became a one-party state in national politics, though bitter factionalism between sections and classes on the state level continued into the next century.

It is interesting to speculate on the stands which the Hardisons might have taken on all of these issues. The family, though never among the wealthiest planters, had been a successful part of the planter society in the colonial era. However, after the Revolution, as the best lands in the eastern portion of the state had been settled and the estates of Jasper's sons and daughters were divided among their numerous descendants, the future did not hold the promise which had drawn Jasper to North Carolina. John Hardison, as land owner and speculator, entrepreneur producing goods for export, and county official, would undoubtedly have been a part of the Conservative faction in the early national years and probably a supporter of the Federalists in the debate over the national Constitution. However, it is likely that he, like most of the planters of moderate means, would have looked with increasing favor on Jefferson's Democratic Republican Party.

The Hardison Family in Transition

As the American Revolution was bringing to a close the colonial era, in which Jasper and his nine children had established the Hardison family in North Carolina, the eldest son, John, died. Jasper's daughter Judah/Judith was deceased by 1750 and it is likely that daughter Mary and John's six brothers, Joseph, Richard, Jasper, Joshua, Thomas, and Charles were deceased by the end of the century.[2] All of the sons were included in Jasper's will of 1733 and thus were aging men in the last decades of the eighteenth century. As the century had progressed, their sons and grandsons had become heads of families and their daughters married members of the planter families of Martin and Tyrrell counties.

The year of death for most of Jasper's children is not known. Only two wills for his sons have been found, those written by the eldest and the youngest, John and Joseph. John's, written in 1778 and probated in 1780, has been discussed in the preceding chapter. Joseph, believed to be the youngest son based on the order of his appearance in Jasper's will, was one of the most prosperous, judging from the value of his property in the Martin County tax list of 1779. In his will of 1788 he left his estate, primarily "Lands in the Piney Woods on Welches Creek" and lots in the newly founded town of Plymouth, to his wife Mary, sons William, Wiggins, and Charles, and daughters Millicent, Nancy, and Judith.[3] An approximate year for the death of a third son, Richard, at some time in the 1780s, may be drawn from provisions made for his widow Rebekah (Rebecca) and sons by Joshua Hardison in a deed of 1787.[4]

The names of the other four sons, Jasper (who will be referred to as Jasper, Sr. to identify him in relation to his son Jasper, Jr.), Joshua, Thomas, and Charles appear in the North Carolina State Census which was taken in 1784-1787 and the Federal Census enumerations of 1790 and 1800. Since all except Thomas are known to have namesake sons and all the age categories of these censuses are so broad, it is difficult to know if the listing is for father or son.

Wills have been found for only two of Jasper's grandsons in the Martin and Tyrrell County archives for the closing decades of the eighteenth century. These were written by two of John Hardison's three sons—William, Benjamin, and John. Benjamin's was written in

1785 and William's in 1797. The information in these wills is particularly useful for this study since Benjamin's sons John and Thomas established the Georgia family which is the focus of the nineteenth century chapters. One of William's sons, Cullen, and Frederick, probably a son of Jasper, Jr., also migrated to Georgia early in the 1800s. Benjamin's and William's wills will be discussed at the end of this chapter as an introduction to the Georgia portion of the study.

The size and location of the various Hardison families in North Carolina at the end of the eighteenth century are revealed in the state and federal census records of the closing decades. The following abstracts from the North Carolina State Census of 1784-1787, the First Federal Census, 1790, and Second Federal Census, 1800, list the names of each of the Hardison heads of household in North Carolina and their county of residence. Also included is information about each family within the categories called for in these enumerations. Not until 1850 did the Federal Census list by name all members of each household.[5]

The names of heads of household of the Carkeet and Sutton families who are likely to be descendants of Jasper Hardison's daughters have been listed at the end of the discussion of the Hardison households for each of the three censuses. No attempt has been made to include the households of Jasper's granddaughters and great-granddaughters since the married names of most are not known.

1784-1787 Census of North Carolina

In 1784 the North Carolina Assembly passed a law, on recommendation from the national Congress, calling for an enumeration of all black and white inhabitants of the state.[6] Any head of household who refused to participate was liable to a fine of 50 pounds. Over the next three years the census was taken in a majority of the counties. Unfortunately one of the exceptions was Craven, where members of Charles Hardison's family lived. The inhabitants were listed by households, with only the name of the head of the family recorded. Five categories of information were called for—the number of white males from age 21 to 60, white males under 21 and over 60, all white females, blacks from 12 to 50, and blacks under 12 and over 50. After the responsibility for census taking became a function of the federal government in 1790, increasing amounts of information on the population and on the economy and other aspects of national life were collected, but, as noted, the names of all members of each family were not listed until 1850.

The North Carolina Census of 1784-1787 includes fourteen Hardison households, ten in Martin County, two in Onslow County, and one each in Tyrrell and Hyde counties. The census was taken in Martin County in 1787. Below is the information for each of the Hardison families.

1784-1787 State Census
North Carolina

COUNTY	Head of Household	White Males 21 to 60	White Males under 21 & over 60	White Females	Blacks 12-50	Blacks under 12 & over 50
MARTIN	David	1	2	2		
	James	2				
	John	1	3	2		
	John	1	1	3	2	4
	Joseph	1	3	4	4	3
	Joshua		4	3	4	4
	Rebekah		2	1		
	Richard	1	1	5	1	
	Thomas	1		5	3	2
	William	2	4	4	1	1
HYDE	Jasper	2	2	5		
ONSLOW	Charles	1	4	1		
	Gabriel	1		3		
TYRRELL	Jasper	1	2	5		

Of the Martin County heads of household, only three were possibly sons of Jasper—Joseph, Joshua, and Thomas. Former Martin residents John and Richard had died before the census was taken. The two Jaspers were father and son, with Jasper, Sr. most likely the resident of Tyrrell and Jasper, Jr. of Hyde County. Charles of Onslow County was either Charles the son of Jasper or one of his sons, with Gabriel another member of the Craven-Onslow County Hardison branch. Rebekah was the widow of Richard, as indicated in the pre-

IV. THE CLOSE OF THE EIGHTEENTH CENTURY, 1785-1800   91

viously cited Martin County deed of 1787, between two of their sons and Joshua Hardison. Richard was Rebekah's and Richard's son and the two Johns, David, James, and William were sons or grandsons of the seven brothers. William and the John with the slaves were most likely two of John's three sons, the third, Benjamin, having written his will and probably died in 1785. The other John was either the son of the younger John or of Benjamin, possibly the grandson John who is mentioned in the eldest John's will of 1778. James was a son of Richard and David, a son of Jasper, Sr.[7]

Descendants of the first Jasper through his daughters Mary and Judah/Judith are represented by male members of the Carkeet and Sutton families. William Carkeet of Martin County, a grandson of Mary and Benjamin Carkeet, was the only Carkeet listed. Two Suttons, John and Thomas of Bertie County, were probably sons or grandsons of Judah and Thomas Sutton. There were five additional Sutton families living in Perquimans County, the area where the Suttons first settled in the seventeenth century, and one in Granville County.

1790—The First Federal Census

Within three years after the State Census was completed, the first Federal Census was taken. A national population enumeration was necessary since the newly operative Constitution of the United States called for a House of Representatives whose membership was apportioned by the population of each state. Unfortunately the records of the 1790 enumeration for several states, including Georgia and Virginia, have been lost, but North Carolina's have survived and they yield the names of nineteen Hardison heads of households, including eight in Martin County.[8] The population of North Carolina has been estimated at 350,000 in 1786, while the Federal Census total for 1790 was 393,751.[9] Martin County's population in 1790 was 6,080, about two-thirds white and one-third black.[10]

Nineteen Hardison households are included in the 1790 enumeration as compared with fourteen in the State Census. Eight of the households resided in Martin County and were headed by the same persons listed in the State Census excepting Joseph, who had died in 1788, and Rebekah, widow of Richard, who was possibly living with one of her sons, had remarried, or had died. As in the state enumeration, there were Hardisons in Hyde, Onslow, and Tyrrell counties, and in addition there were now families listed for Craven, Dobbs, and Pitt counties. The data for each of these households under the categories called for in the 1790 census are as follows:

1790 Federal Census
North Carolina

COUNTY	Head of Household	White Males 16 & older	White Males under 16	White Females	Other Free Persons	Slaves
MARTIN	David	1	1	3		
	James	1	1	1		2
	John	1	3	2		
	John	1	1	1		4
	Joshua	2	1	3		6
	Richard	2		4		3
	Thomas	1	1	4	7	
	William	2	2	3		1
CRAVEN	James	2	1	4		
DOBBS	James	2	1	4		
HYDE	Charles	2		2		1
	Isaac	1		3		
	Samuel	1		1		
ONSLOW	Charles	1	4	3		
PITT	Joseph	1	1	4		
	Joshua	1	3	2		
TYRRELL	Benjamin	2		2		2
	Jasper	1	3	3		2
	Mary	1	2	3		8

The identities of the Martin County Hardisons have been included in the discussion of the State Census. James of Craven County was probably a member of the Charles Hardison family and James of Dobbs, a son of Jasper Jr. (see below for data on Lucretia Hardison in the Federal Census of 1800). The Hyde County households were part of the Jasper, Jr. family and Charles of Onslow was either the eldest Jasper's son Charles or one of his descendants. Both Joshua and Jasper, Sr. had sons named Joshua and Jasper, Sr. had a son named

Joseph, the names of the Pitt County heads of households. The three Tyrrell County members were Benjamin, probably the son of William, one of John Hardison's sons; Jasper, either Jasper, Sr., if still living, or his son; and Mary, most likely the widow of Joseph, who had died in 1788. It should be noted that all three of the Tyrrell County heads of household are found in the Washington County list for the 1800 census. Obviously they lived in the western portion of Tyrrell which was formed into Washington County in 1799.

An interesting entry in the Martin County data is the listing for Thomas of seven persons under the "other free persons" heading. This category included free black persons. The information may indicate that Thomas, who had five slaves listed in the State Census, had freed his slaves. In the 1800 enumeration his household had three persons in this category.

William Carkeet (spelled Karkeet) of Martin County was the only member of that family listed. Forty-five Sutton households, spread over a number of counties, particularly Perquimans, Tyrrell, Bladen, Dobbs, and Pitt, were included. The two in Bertie County, Thomas and William, were probably of Judah and Thomas Sutton's family.

The 1800 Federal Census

The population enumeration for the Federal Census of 1800 called for a much more specific break-down of age groups for both white males and females than the 1790 census and thus provides better insight into the make-up of the families.[11] Slaves, as in 1790, were counted under one heading and the "all other free persons" category was changed to "all other free persons except Indians not taxed." The total North Carolina population had increased from 393,751 in 1790 to 478,103, but Martin County's had declined from 6,080 in 1790 to 5,629.[12]

The number of Hardison households had grown to twenty-eight, from fourteen in the State Census of 1784-1787 and nineteen in the Federal Census of 1790. Of the twenty-eight households in 1800, seventeen lived in the old family strongholds of Martin County and what had formerly been western Tyrrell County, now Washington County. Seven additional families lived in nearby Hyde and Beaufort counties, all being in the tidewater areas of Albemarle and Pamlico sounds. Three families resided in the more southerly tidewater counties of Craven and Onslow, where Charles Hardison had migrated in the mid-eighteenth century. One newly established family had moved a little to the west of the tidewater, to recently created Greene County, named for General Nathanael Greene in honor of his service in North Carolina during the Revolution. The names and data for these families are shown in the table on the following page.

The names of the four sons of Jasper who might still have been alive in 1800, Joshua, Jasper, Thomas, and Charles, appear in the above listing, but it is more likely that these names belong to their namesake sons and grandsons. Thomas is a good candidate for an exception to this generalization, for his household included only a male and a female in the highest age category. As in the 1790 census, he was the only Hardison with an entry in the "other free persons" category, having three in 1800 and seven in 1790. In 1802 Thomas Hardison of Martin County sold a parcel of land on the east side of Roses Creek "whereon I now Dwell," along with his plantation house. In 1805 he acted as agent for two of John Hardison's grandsons (John and Thomas—sons of Benjamin) in a Washington County deed of 1805. His relationship to John and Thomas was not specified in this record.[13] Thomas' name does not appear in the Federal Census listings for Martin County in 1810, and presumably he had died by that year.

As indicated by the use of Jr. and Sr., the two Johns in Martin County are the son and grandson of the eldest John. The two Benjamins, one each in Martin and Washington counties, present a problem of identification. As was noted in the discussion of the 1779 tax list of Martin County, the name Benjamin appeared three times in that list. Deed records and wills identify two of the three, the eldest (wrote will in 1785) being the son of John (son of Jasper) and a younger Benjamin, the son of William (wrote will in 1797), who was another of John's sons. An educated guess is that the Benjamin of Washington County in the 1800 enumaration was William's son. David of Martin County was a son of Jasper, Sr. and James and Richard were sons of Richard. Luke, Mark, and possibly Joshua were sons or grandsons of Joshua, and Wiggins was a son of Joseph.

The Beaufort County families were headed by Cullen, who with

1800—Federal Census
North Carolina

COUNTY	Name of Head of Family	Free White Males Under 10	10-16	16-25	26-45	45 and over	Free White Females Under 10	10-16	16-25	26-45	45 and over	All other free persons except Indians	Slaves
MARTIN	Benjamin	2			1		3	1					
	David		1		1			1		1			
	Jas., Sr.	3	1		1		2			1			4
	John, Jr.	2	2		1		1	1	1	1			9
	John, Sr.	1	1	1		1							
	Joshua			2	1			1			1		8
	Luke			1				1		1			
	Mark	2			1		2			1			2
	Richard		1			1					1		1
	Thomas					1					1	3	
	Wiggins		1		1		1	2					3
BEAUFORT	Cullen			1			1	1					1
	Frederick				1			1					
	William				1					1			
CRAVEN	Jasper			1					2		1		
GREENE	Lucretia	1	1				1	1		1			
HYDE	Anna	1							1	1			
	Joseph	1				1	2		2	1			
	Lemuel			1									2
	Isaac	1			1		2	1		1			
ONSLOW	Charles			1									
	Charles	2	1	5		1		1	1	1			
WASHINGTON	Asa		1		1		1	2					5
	Benjamin	2		2	1		1			1			9
	Ezekiel			1					1				3
	Jasper		1	1		1	1	1	1				2
	Jessey	3			1			1		1			
	Mary			2					2		1		3

Benjamin was a son of William (son of John); Frederick, either a son or grandson of Jasper, Sr. or son of the elder Richard; and William, either the son of Joseph or of the elder Benjamin (son of John).

The identity of Jasper of Craven County is not known but it is likely that he and the two men named Charles in Onslow County are descendants of Charles, the son of Jasper, who had migrated in mid-century to Craven County. Lucretia of Greene County has been identified through a pension application of 1853 as the widow of James Hardison, a Revolutionary War veteran who, in one of his tours of duty, served as a substitute for his brother Isaac. Jasper, Jr. had sons named James and Isaac, making Lucretia his daughter-in-law.[14] The Hyde County Hardisons were also members of the family of Jasper, Jr.

As noted, Washington County was created in 1799 from the western portion of Tyrrell County, which had been the home of Jasper, Sr. Jessey and Jasper were members of his family and the name Asa appears among the sons of James, son of Richard. Ezekiel was one of the sons of Benjamin (son of John) and Mary was probably the widow of either Joseph or William (son of John), each deceased by 1800 and each having had a wife named Mary.[15]

Two Carkeet (spelled Carkeete) households, headed by William and Benjamin, were listed for Martin County. The Sutton households had increased to fifty, living in a number of counties. Again the only two in Bertie County, where Judah and Thomas Sutton had lived, were Thomas and William. Two others likely to be members of this family were Lemuel and William, living in Washington County.

A comparison of the data in the three censuses which have been abstracted shows the growth of the Hardison family in the last decade and a half of the eighteenth century and the beginning of the movement, begun by Charles a number of years before, of some of its members away from their Albemarle roots.

CENSUS	HOUSEHOLDS	COUNTIES	WHITES	FREE BLACKS	SLAVES
1784-7	14	4	86		29
1790	19	7	103	7	30
1800	28	7	133	3	52

If slave-holding may be taken as a measure of wealth, the Hardisons in the original family homelands of Martin and western Tyrrell (later Washington County) were the most prosperous. John's grandson John; Benjamin of Washington County, presumed to be another grandson through John's son William; and Joshua had the largest number of slaves in 1800. Mary, probably the widow of Joseph, had the highest number in 1790. However, none of these holdings exceeded ten slaves and the numbers indicate the continuing status of the most prosperous Hardisons among the planters of moderate means. Of the approximately 660 heads of household in Martin County in the 1784-1787 State Census, only thirty-three owned more than ten slaves. Only two of the thirty-three owned over fifty—Samuel Williams, with ninety, and Whitmel Hill, with one hundred sixty-two. The black population in Martin County was about one-third of the total at the end of the eighteenth century. In the years immediately following the Revolution, there had been public expressions of opposition to the institution of slavery and particularly to the continuation of the importation of slaves. However, as the nineteenth century progressed, slave labor became an increasingly integral part of North Carolina's economy and by the time of the Civil War blacks made up almost half of Martin County's population.[16]

The Inheritance Passes From the Third to the Fourth Generation

The majority of Jasper Hardison's descendants remained in North Carolina after the Revolution, but in the early years of the 1800s a few were drawn to the newly opened lands of Georgia and Tennessee. Three of these adventurers were grandsons of Jasper's son John—two sons of Benjamin, named John and Thomas, and one son of William, named Cullen (also spelled Cullin). These three, along with Frederick, probably a greatgrandson of Jasper through his son Jasper, and a female head of household, Elizabeth, who has not been identified, appear in the records of Washington County, Georgia (excepting Cullen who settled in Jones County) in the first two decades of the nineteenth century. Their story will be told in the chapter which follows, with the remainder of the study following John and his family in their migrations to Florida, western Georgia, and Texas. While the above named Hardisons were making their journey southward to Georgia, others were seeking their fortune in Tennessee. Their lives are chronicled in the previously cited *Hardison and Allied Families* by Fred L. Hawkins and Dorothy Westmoreland Gilliam.

Land was the lure which had drawn Jasper Hardison to North Carolina in the early eighteenth century when it was plentiful and cheap. He had acquired three tracts totaling 1,740 acres in the decade before his death in 1733 and had passed 640 acres to his eldest son, John, dividing the remainder among six other sons.[17] As noted, the Tyrrell County records for the next forty years provide ample proof of John's acquisitive abilities as he purchased thousands of acres of land, both for speculation and for his saw mills and grist mills.[18] John lived a long life and when he died his estate was divided among his wife, nine children, and an unborn child. His will of 1778 does not include the acreages of the lands which he left primarily to his sons William, Benjamin, and John and it is impossible to know how much of the land he purchased had been retained. Certainly these sons had far above the average inheritance of their contemporaries, but the division of their father's property came at a time of economic chaos during the Revolution, which was followed by a depression in the early post-war years. The possibility for them and for their sons to expand their holdings was not promising. The best lands in the Albemarle area had passed out of the public domain into private ownership and the generation of young men who were entering their maturity after the Revolution faced a future of diminished opportunity. The eastern areas of North Carolina, which were increasingly dominated by the wealthiest of the planters, had the highest rate of out-migration for the state as families began to leave for Georgia and Tennessee at the end of the century.

Since two of Benjamin Hardison's sons migrated to Georgia soon after 1800, it is interesting to look at the make-up of his family, as revealed by his will of 1785, and at his life in North Carolina. As elder sons of John, he and his brother William were probably born in the 1730s, giving Benjamin an age between fifty and sixty when he wrote his will. As a young man he was a militia volunteer in 1748 "for the present expedition," at the time when the Spanish were attacking and plundering settlements along the North Carolina coast.[19] The name Benjamin appears again as a militia volunteer "for the present expedition" during the Revolution, when the state was preparing for a Brit-

IV. THE CLOSE OF THE EIGHTEENTH CENTURY, 1785-1800 99

ish invasion in 1780.[20] Since there were possibly three Benjamin Hardisons in Martin County at that time, there is some question as to this volunteer's identity; however it is most likely that the Captain Benjamin Hardison of the Martin County militia, under whom James Hardison stated that he served in the Battle of Guilford Courthouse in 1781, was Benjamin, son of John.[21]

Benjamin's will indicates that he had been married two times, since he first made bequests to sons John and William and then to a wife named Elizabeth and their five sons and two daughters. The name of his first wife is not known, but an estimate of the time of their marriage may be made from the age of son John in the Federal Census of 1830. This data places his birth between 1760 and 1770.[22] It is possible that this son was the grandson named John who was mentioned as living with Benjamin's father John at the time he wrote his will in 1778, perhaps during a time of transition in Benjamin's household. Benjamin's second wife was Elizabeth Duggan, the daughter of William Duggan and Mary Smithwick. Elizabeth married John Collins after Benjamin's death. According to descendants who have written their history for *Martin County Heritage*, William Duggan was a native of Ireland.[23] The Smithwicks were early settlers in the Albemarle area and were prominent as land owners and political leaders. Benjamin was a witness to several of their land transactions in the 1770s and 1780s and was a member of a committee chosen in 1782 to settle a land dispute between John Smithwick and John Roberson.[24]

Few land records have been found for Benjamin and his brother William and none for their brother John in the years before the writing of their father's will in 1778. It is probable that they were engaged with John in his milling and other interests. William married Mary Mizell in 1760 and in 1764 John transferred to him 100 acres in the fork of Swift Creek, on the south side of the Roanoke River, for the minimal sum of 5 pounds.[25] Together William and Benjamin purchased three slaves, a woman aged twenty-seven, an infant girl aged four months, and a twelve year old boy, for 82 pounds and 10 shillings. The date of the deed for this purchase, as recorded in the copy of the original in the Tyrrell County archives, is 1756, but it may have originally been dated 1765 since the deed was not registered until 1769.[26] In 1774, a few years before his death, Benjamin's father

John sold a large tract of 600 acres to him for 100 pounds. The land lay in the heart of John's homeland—in the fork of Gardner's Creek, below the Mill Branch and Deep Run Swamp.[27]

At some time between the elder John's writing of his will in 1778 and its probate in 1780, Benjamin, William, and John came into their inheritance of land, slaves, and interest in the mills. In the intervening year, 1779, a tax list was prepared for Martin County and it includes Benjamin, with a property valuation of the very substantial sum of 3,895 pounds; William, with 1,515 pounds; and three John Hardisons—John Esquire, with 2,678 pounds, John, Jr. with 621 pounds, and John with 301 pounds. Probably the eldest John had died by the time the tax list was made and the Johns were his son, now in possession of the family plantation; his son, John, Jr.; and possibly Benjamin's eldest son, John. The fact that Benjamin's property valuation far exceeds that of the other brothers may reflect his father's transfer of 600 acres to him in 1774. Other than provisions for his wife Olive, the major bequests in John's will were to his three sons. Benjamin and William were each given a male slave and equal shares in a tract of land in the vicinity of Narmouth Neck, acreage not mentioned, and John was given the plantation and another tract of land. The sons were to share in the saw mill and grist mill interests. It is obvious from the wording of the will that John was in partnership with others in the mills, probably brothers Joshua and Joseph, but their names are not mentioned.[28]

In 1779 both Benjamin and William added to their inheritance with purchases of 100 acre tracts of land. Benjamin's purchase was made from Francis and Sarah Henry for 200 pounds and included Cedar Branch and the Mill Pond in its description.[29] William's new acquisition was made for 100 pounds and its boundaries included the Great Swamp, Swift Creek, Devil's Gut, and John Smithwick's Island. The purchase was made from John Hardison, probably his brother.[30] After James Town (now Jamesville) was founded in 1785, William purchased a one-half acre lot.[31] The town was established on the lands of William Mackay and Luke Mizell, a member of the family into which William had married. It was one of the so-called "river towns," Williamston, Jamesville, and Blountsville, which were the oldest towns in Martin County. The last was chartered in the same

IV. THE CLOSE OF THE EIGHTEENTH CENTURY, 1785-1800   101

year as Jamesville, but has since disappeared.[32] Jamesville, located on Highway 64 in eastern Martin County, continues to be the home of numerous Hardisons

On March 25, 1785, seven years after his father had written his will, Benjamin, "Being Very sick and Weak in body," wrote his last will and testament.[33] The date of probate is not recorded on the document as it now appears in Martin County's archives. Benjamin may have lived for some time after writing the will, for he was witness to a deed of Edmund Smithwick in September, 1785; however he is not listed in the 1784-1787 State Census, which was taken in Martin County in 1787.[34] The will is relatively short and will be quoted in its entirety so that readers may draw their own conclusions as to family relationships and the state of Benjamin's mind at the time of writing. Original spelling and punctuation have been reproduced as nearly as possible.

> In the name of God Amen the twenty-fifth Day of March 1785 I Benjamin Hardison Being Very sick and Weak in body and Wherein it is appointed for all men once to die thanks be to God for it Calling to mind the Mortality of my body & knowing that it is appointed for all men once to die Do make & Ordain this my Last will & Testament that is to say Principly & first of all I Give & Recommend my Soul into the hands of God that Gave it and my body I recomend to the Earth to be buried in A Christian like manner at the Discretion of my Executors and as for my worldly Goods wherewith it hath Pleased God to bless me I Give & Dispose of them in the following Manner I give and bequeath to my Sons John Hardison & William Hardison the Negro Woman Called Phibb and her Children Charity Simon and Easter I Also Give to my son John Hardison one feather bead & Furniture & one Cow and Calf, I also Give to my son William Hardison one feather bead and furniture and one Cow and Calf. Item I lend to my beloved Wife Elizabeth Hardison all the Rest of my Estate both within Doors & without for the Support of the Family and Raising of the Children for the term of Eight Years to be Equally Divided According to Law I Give to my beloved wife Elizabeth Hardison one third Part of the Mills and also one third Part of the Plantation thereunto belonging to her & to her heirs forever and all the Rest of my Estate to be Equally Divided between the children I had by

my Wife Elizabeth Hardison Ezekiel Hardison Hardy Hardison Seth Hardison Samuel Hardison Martha Hardison Thomas Hardison and Elizabeth Hardison and the executors to do as they think best with the Negrows that is Contending for Freedom & Do Constitute and Appoint my beloved Brother Wm Hardison and I Do hereby Appoint my friend John Stewart and my beloved Wife Elizabeth Hardison my hole and Sole Executors of this my last Will & Testament. In Witness Whereof I have hereunto Set my hand & Seal—
Signed Sealed Pronounced & Declared by me the sd.
Benjamin Hardison as my last will & Testament
In the Presence of
Test Isaac Gardner Jurat   Ben'n Hardison
Edmund Smithwick
John Hardison

The will is evidence of the meagerness of the inheritance of the elder sons, John and William, and of the consequent appeal which the lands of Georgia might offer. John and one of the younger sons, Thomas, followed that lure at the end of the century. Benjamin's wife Elizabeth was given, rather than loaned, one-third part of the mills and of the plantation and, as noted earlier, she later remarried, her second husband being John Collins.

Relatively little is known of the life of Benjamin's "beloved Brother" William other than his few previously cited deed records in Tyrrell and Martin counties, his marriage to Mary Mizell in 1760, and his appearance in the Martin County tax list of 1779 and the census records of 1784-1787 and 1790. However, his will of 1797 tells much about his property, his family members, and the relationships among them.[35] Like Benjamin's will, it bears no date of probate as it exists in the Martin County archives, but William probably died within a relatively short time after writing the will, for his name does not appear in the list of Martin County heads of household in the Federal Census of 1800. Unlike Benjamin's and more like his father John's will, William's contains detailed bequests to his wife Mary; two sons, Benjamin and Cullen (spelled Cullin in the will); and four daughters, Mary, Elizabeth Everitt, Hannah Gardner, and Sarah Blount.

On February 6, 1797, William wrote that he was "in a very Pore State [of] health but thank be to god Att present In my Right mind." His bequests were as follows:

To wife Mary:
1. gave the use of the plantation and houses during her lifetime
2. lent a horse named Jupiter and mare called Fanny for her use
3. lent a Negro woman named Phibea, with the provision that any additional children of Phibea would be divided among William's children
4. lent the use of his stock of hogs and cattle to support her during her lifetime
5. lent the use of "one Small Negro girl named Rose," who was to belong to daughter Mary Hardison after her mother's death
6. lent one feather bed and furniture together with all household furniture as long as she lived.

To son Benjamin, who may be presumed to be the elder son since he is mentioned first, William bequeathed:
1. 120 acres of land out of the survey "whereon I now live lying up the Swamp joining Old man Edward Cooper's line"
2. "one Ridge of my Island land with all the low Swampy land lying on this Ridge"
3. 50 acres lying on the north side of Devil's Gut
4. one-half of "my Negro boy named Bob" (John had given a slave named Bob to William in his will).

To son Cullin, who seems to be the favored son, William bequeathed:
1. "the manner [manor] Plantation wheron I now live." together with the remaining acres of the tract from which Benjamin had been given 120 acres, the tract totaling 240 acres
2. a ridge of land lying on the south side of Devil's Gut with "all the Low ground land that is between the Ridge and the Gutt and Creek"
3. 50 acres of land on the north side of Devil's Gut
4. one-half of "my Negro Bob"
5. a horse called Darby [may be Daisy]
6. a desk and a feather bed and furniture (a bed and furniture were common bequests of the period and probably meant the feather mattress and a bed frame).

Along with Cullin's bequests came the admonition from William that he was "not to interrupt your mother but let her enjoy the benefit of the house and Plantation with all the improvements thereon which is my Desire."

A joint bequest to Benjamin and Cullin is somewhat confusing, but seems to indicate that their father left them two-thirds of the saw and grist mills with 225 acres of land in the Narrow Mouth Neck Island, which they might use to pay William's debts "if they think fit."

To his one unmarried daughter, Mary, William left a slave girl, Rose, to be hers after her mother's death. To each of his three married daughters, Elizabeth Everitt, Hannah Gardner, and Sarah Blount, he willed one cow and calf or 5 pounds to be paid out of the estate within three years.

While William's brother Benjamin had named him, along with wife Elizabeth and friend John Stewart, as executors, William named his two sons, Benjamin and Cullin. Brother John witnessed the will and William signed with an "X."

As noted earlier, no will has been found for John, the third of the eldest John's sons, to whom he had left his plantation in his will of 1778. Both the younger John, who became John, Sr. after his father's death, and his son John, called John, Jr. in some of the records of the late eighteenth century, appear in a number of deeds of Martin County through the early nineteenth century.[36] Both are found in the Federal Census listings for Martin County through 1810 (Martin County is missing from the Federal Census of 1820). Their deeds cover transactions for land, slaves, and livestock. John, Jr. had nine slaves, the highest number of any of the Hardisons in the 1800 census enumeration. Apparently the two Johns were relatively prosperous in the post-Revolutionary days and were well enough satisfied to remain in the Hardison homeland in the Albemarle.

If life on the plantation and work in the family milling businesses were not sufficiently fulfilling or profitable for Benjamin's and William's sons, apparently town life or at least speculation in town property offered a challenge. In 1790 a group of trustees laid out the town of Plymouth on the banks of the Roanoke River, just to the east of the Hardisons' Martin County lands. Within the next two decades the names of all the sons of Benjamin and William appear on deeds

IV. THE CLOSE OF THE EIGHTEENTH CENTURY, 1785-1800   105

for the purchase and sale of town lots. The town had been started in the 1780s by Arthur Rhodes from a portion of his plantation, Brick House Plantation. The location had long been a shipping point for the planters along the southern banks of the Roanoke because of its proximity to the entry of the river into Albemarle Sound. It was called Plymouth by the many New Englanders who had settled in the area. The Rhodes family, like the Hardisons, had lived in the vicinity since the early eighteenth century and they are believed to have migrated from Massachusetts. Arthur's wife was named Milly and was probably one of the daughters of Joseph Hardison named in his will of 1788, Millicent Rhodes. Arthur was among the executors of Joseph's will. He began laying out the town of Plymouth and selling lots in the 1780s and then turned the project over to a group of trustees in 1790. Until 1799 the town was in Tyrrell County and then in Washington County, after its formation from the western portion of Tyrrell. It was located just east of Welches Creek, the boundary between Martin and Washington counties, in an area long familiar to the Hardisons. It became one of the major ports of North Carolina in the nineteenth century, with schooners sailing in from Albemarle Sound to load lumber, naval stores, tobacco, and other products of the tidewater. Its importance in the ante-bellum era brought about its near destruction during the Civil War, when several naval battles reduced it to eleven battle-scarred buildings. The most memorable battle occurred in 1864 when the Confederate iron-clad ram Albemarle was torpedoed in the river. Today it is a sleepy, graceful old river town which cherishes its history.[37]

Joseph Hardison apparently purchased two town lots from Arthur Rhodes and he left them to his sons William and Wiggins in his will. They sold one of the lots in 1801.[38] Benjamin (presumed to be the brother of Cullen and son of William, whose will was discussed above) made a substantial investment in Plymouth in the 1790s, purchasing four lots and a house, which was described as being opposite a tavern which he owned.[39]

In the first decade of the nineteenth century, the names of all the elder Benjamin's sons—John, William, Ezekiel, Seth, Hardy, Thomas, and Samuel—and one daughter, Elizabeth, with her husband Elijah Etheridge, appear in the deed records of Washington

County for the purchase and sale of town lots in Plymouth.[40] Judging from the number of entries for Ezekiel, whom the deed records identify as a carpenter, he was speculating in town real estate, apparently with something like the zeal with which his grandfather John had purchased tracts of forest land in North Carolina's colonial era. Since he was in the building trades, the new town offered an outlet for his skills and for the output of the family lumber mills.

Records of the Plymouth purchase by one of Ezekiel's brothers, Seth, provide knowledge of the make-up of the elder Benjamin's family as it existed in the early years of the nineteenth century and a key to the identity of the two Hardisons who migrated to Georgia at the turn of the century. Seth purchased a one-half acre lot, number forty-eight, in 1800 for 20 pounds and apparently died, unmarried, soon afterward, leaving his property to be divided among members of his family. Between 1804 and 1807 five of his brothers, Hardy, Samuel, William, John, and Thomas; a sister, Elizabeth and her husband Elijah Etheridge; his mother, now Elizabeth Collins; and a cousin, Benjamin, sold their shares in Seth's lot to Ezekiel. Each of the sellers was paid 5 pounds for his share except John and Thomas, who were paid $10.00 each. The two prices give some idea of equivalent values of pounds and dollars at this time of transition in currency. The place of residence of each of the sellers was noted in the deeds, with Hardy, Samuel, the Etheridges, and Benjamin in Washington County; William in Beaufort; Elizabeth Collins in Martin; and John and Thomas in Georgia. The last two were identified as "John Hardison and Thomas Hardison both of the state of Georgia," who were exercising their right of inheritance in the property of "Seth Hardison Dec'd their Brother." The year of their deed, 1805, helps to fix the approximate time of their settlement in Georgia.[41]

The Washington County deeds of 1800-1810 also contain a number of items for three other family members who are known to have migrated to Georgia—Frederick, Cullen, and Elijah Etheridge.[42] As noted earlier, Elijah, who is identified in the deeds as a "house carpenter," was the husband of Elizabeth Hardison, one of the daughters of Benjamin, who died before Elijah's departure for Georgia. Cullen was the son of the William Hardison who wrote his will in 1797. The Frederick of Washington County, referred to as "planter," was a son

IV. THE CLOSE OF THE EIGHTEENTH CENTURY, 1785-1800

of Jasper (probably Jasper, Jr.), as indicated by his participation in the division of Jasper's homeplace in 1807, and was most likely the Frederick who migrated to Georgia, first to Washington County and later to Crawford County. The other two known Frederick Hardisons were a son of Jasper, Sr. and a son of Richard.

The founding of a new town might open windows of opportunity for young families, but the outlook for North Carolina and particularly for the old counties of the Albemarle was not bright as the new century began. By 1800 the state was entering a period of stagnation which caused it to be called "the Ireland of America" and "the Rip Van Winkle state." It suffered from a variety of ailments, including a poorly designed system of government complicated by one-party politics and bitter sectionalism, primitive agricultural methods and wasteful use of land, and the on-going problem of transportation for its produce resulting from the nature of its coastline and its lack of roads. Plymouth might seem to hold promise as a port but its potential was limited, for to reach it ships must come in through one of the Outer Bank inlets, up Albemarle Sound, and into the Roanoke River.

In the years following the American Revolution, many North Carolinians began to look to the west and the south for the opportunities offered by cheap, new lands in Tennessee and Georgia. The fever of immigration developed into an epidemic in the early decades of the nineteenth century. Alabama and Indiana were added as the most popular destinations, with so many people leaving the state that North Carolina dropped in population from fourth in the nation in 1790 to fifth in 1820 and twelfth by 1860. Many counties, including Martin, actually declined in population, with the highest rate of migration from the state going from the eastern counties. While there had been twenty-eight Hardison households in the federal enumeration for North Carolina in 1800, there were twenty-one in 1810.[43] The migrating Hardisons joined a flood of men, women, and children on the move, sweeping the native Indian population to the west and eventually to reservations. The thirteen original colonies became a dynamic, diverse, and by mid-century a very troubled nation headed toward tragedy.

And how did the Hardisons fare in their new homes—their "brave new world"? The narrative which follows will chronicle the lives of those who left for Georgia early in the nineteenth century, focusing on the family of sons and daughters believed to be the children of John Hardison—son of Benjamin, grandson of John, great-grandson of Jasper.

NOTES

1. Background information on North Carolina's post-Revolutionary era has been drawn from Lefler and Newsome, *North Carolina, the History of a Southern State*, chaps.16-20.
2. See the sections on each of Jasper's sons and daughters in Chapter 2.
3. Martin County Will Book 1, pp.143-44; for an analysis of the Hardisons listed in the Martin County Tax List of 1779, see Chapter 2.
4. Martin County Deed Book B, p.13.
5. Researchers who use census records have access to an invaluable source of family and demographic data, but need to be aware that the great variations in the spelling of names make it difficult to find all the members of a given family. All possible variations should be checked. Also researchers using printed copies of the original manuscript records and the indexes to census records should note that there have been numerous errors in transcribing names from the often difficult-to-read manuscript originals and that there have been omissions in some of the indexes. If more than one index exists for a particular Federal Census, each should be consulted.
6. Alvaretta Kenan Register, editor, *State Census of North Carolina, 1784-1787*, second edition revised (Baltimore: Genealogical Publishing Company, 1987), pp.10-11, 73, 94-96, 117.
7. Identities of the Hardisons in the census records are based on the wills and deeds previously cited and on data in Hawkins and Gilliam, *op. cit.*, chaps.1-3, with the chart of Jasper's descendants on p.23 being particularly useful. This chart has been reproduced in Chapter 2.
8. *Heads of Families at the First Census of the United States, Taken in the Year 1790* (Baltimore: Genealogical Publishing Company, 1966), pp.33, 66-67, 133, 136, 139, 147, and 195.
9. Lefler and Newsome, *op. cit.*, p.715, population figures for North Carolina from its beginning as a colony.
10. Carolina Population Center, University of North Carolina and Statistical Services Center, Budget Division, Department of Administration, *State of North Carolina, County Population Trends, North Carolina, 1790-1960*, North Carolina Population Data Series No.1, March 1969, p.64.
11. Ronald Vern Jackson and G. R. Teeples, editors, *North Carolina 1800 Census* (Provo: Accelerated Indexing Systems, 1974), pp.388-89, lists 26 Hardison families, leaving out David of Martin County and Isaac of Hyde County; Elizabeth Petty Bently, compiler, *Index to the 1800 Census of North Carolina* (Baltimore: Genealogical Publishing Company, 1977), pp.100-01, lists the same families plus David and Isaac, p.40 (Carkeete), and p.234 (Suttons).
12. Lefler and Newsome, *op. cit.*, p.715; *County Population Trends*, p.64.
13. Martin County Deed Book D, p.40; Washington County Deed Book B, p.260.
14. Hawkins and Gilliam, *op. cit.*, p. 23 (list of Jasper, Jr.'s sons) and pp.42-43.
15. Martin County Will Book 1, pp.143-44 (Joseph) and pp.326-28 (William).

IV. THE CLOSE OF THE EIGHTEENTH CENTURY, 1785-1800   109

16. *County Population Trends*, p.64.
17. See Chapter 1 for discussion of Jasper.
18. See Chapter 2 for discussion of Jasper's sons and daughters.
19. *State Records*, vol.22, p.270.
20. *State Records*, vol.14, pp.838-39.
21. See Chapter 3 for Hardisons in the Revolutionary War.
22. Fifth Federal Census, 1830, Florida, Jefferson County, p.163.
23. Hughes, *Martin County Heritage*, p.163 (article #176); Hawkins and Gilliam, *op. cit.*, p.30.
24. Martin County Deed Book A, pp.39, 84, 414, and 538.
25. Tyrrell County Deed Book 4, vol.1, pp.360-61; Tyrrell County Marriage Bonds Index, p.55.
26. Tyrrell County Deed Book 4, vol.2, p.221; most if not all of the eighteenth century records available to the public in Tyrrell and other North Carolina counties are copies of the originals and they contain a number of errors in transcription, including dates and the spelling of proper names, making it possible that this purchase was made in 1765, rather than 1756.
27. Martin County Deed Book A, p.17.
28. See Chapter 2 for an analysis of the Martin County Tax List of 1779, including listings for all the Hardisons; see Chapter 3 for the bequests in John's will of 1778. As noted, the tract given to Benjamin and William may have been a Granville grant of 1761 to John which mentioned Narrow Mouth Neck (Tyrrell County Deed Book 4, vol.1, p.115).
29. Martin County Deed Book A, p.340.
30. Martin County Deed Book A, p.234.
31. Martin County Deed Book C, p.29.
32. Manning and Booker, *Martin County History*, vol.1, pp.103-20 (Jamesville), pp.60-103 (Williamston), pp.120-22 (Blountsville).
33. Martin County Will Book 1, pp.118-19.
34. Martin County Deed Book A, p.538.
35. Martin County Will Book 1, pp.326-28.
36. Martin County Deed Books A-E.
37. Washington County Historical Society, *Historic Washington County*, second printing (Plymouth: Washington County Historical Society, n.d.,), pp.4-5; Blackwell P. Robinson, editor, *The North Carolina Guide* (Chapel Hill: University of North Carolina Press, 1955), pp.436-37.
38. Martin County Will Book 1, pp.143-44; Washington County Deed Book B, p.380.
39. Tyrrell County Deed Book 11, pp.180-81 and Book 12, p.35 (purchase of Plymouth lots); Tyrrell Deed Book 12, p.64 (purchase of house); Washington County Deed Book B, pp.141 and 327 (sale of Plymouth lots).
40. Washington County Deed Book s A and B.
41. Washington County Deed Book A, p.52 (Seth); Book B, p.227 (Hardy); Book B, p.237 (William); Book B, p.251 (Samuel, the Etheridges, and Elizabeth Collins); Book B, p.260 (John and Thomas); Book B, p.449 (Benjamin).
42. Washington County Deed Book B, p.396 (Cullen and Tempy of Beaufort County selling Plymouth lot); Book A, p.83, Book B, pp.251 and 397, and Book C, p.104 (Elijah and Elizabeth Etheridge); Book B, pp.140, 420, 422, and 435, and Book C, pp.40 and 104 (Frederick Hardison).
43. Elizabeth Petty Bentley, compiler, *Index to the 1810 Census of North Carolina* (Baltimore: Genealogical Publishing Company, 1978), p.105. Hardison listings:

Martin County—Benjamin, Cullin, David, Edward, James, John, John, Joshua, Luke; Beaufort—Eliza; Duplin—William; Edgecombe—Harman; Hyde—Joseph; Onslow—Charles, Jesse, Lemuel; Washington—Asa, Ezekiel (Esquire), Frederic, Nancy, Samuel. There are numerous Sutton listings, but none for Bertie County, and no listings for Carkeet/Karkeet. The Martin County data is missing from the Federal Census of 1820.

THE ODYSSEY
⌘ Part 2 ⌘

*Georgia and Florida
1800-1857*

V

From the Albemarle to the Land of Cotton Washington County, 1800-1828

As Jasper Hardison had been drawn to North Carolina in the early years of the eighteenth century by its abundant lands, so were his great-grandsons John, Thomas, Frederick, and Cullen Hardison attracted to Georgia in the opening decades of the nineteenth century. In the post-Revolutionary era, Georgia set about driving the native population from the state's vast interior and making the land available for white settlement. In its colonial era most of Georgia's small population lived on farms and in scattered settlements along the Savannah River and on the islands and mainland paralleling the Atlantic Ocean. The Creek Indians were the dominant peoples of the interior, with the Cherokees occupying a relatively small area in the hill country of the northwest. As cotton culture began to dominate the state's economy in the nineteenth century, the Creeks' lands were coveted by the white population. Georgia, the youngest of the original thirteen colonies, began to attract a flood of newcomers as the Creeks were pushed to the west and their lands opened to settlement.

Georgia in the Eighteenth Century

Georgia, named for King George II, was founded in 1733 as a buffer

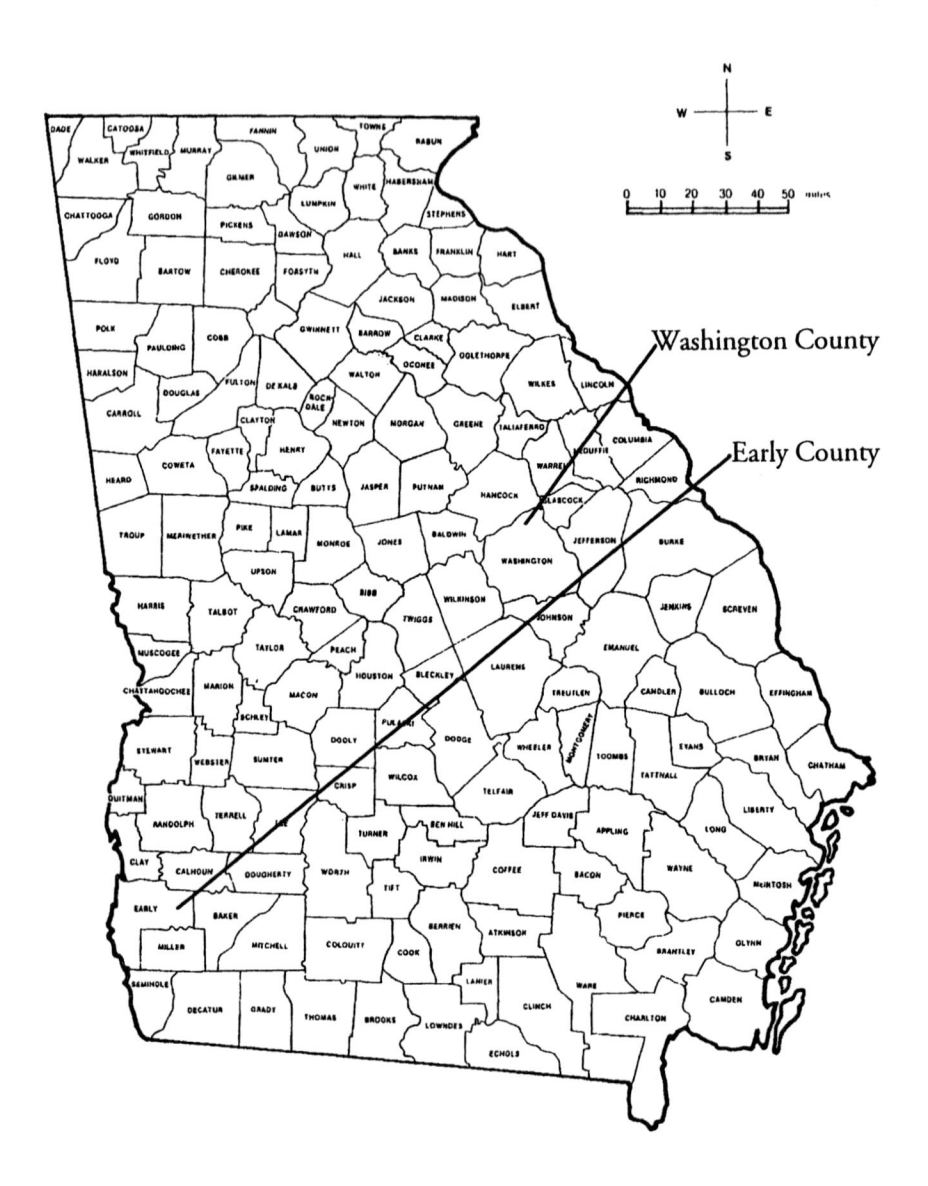

GEORGIA

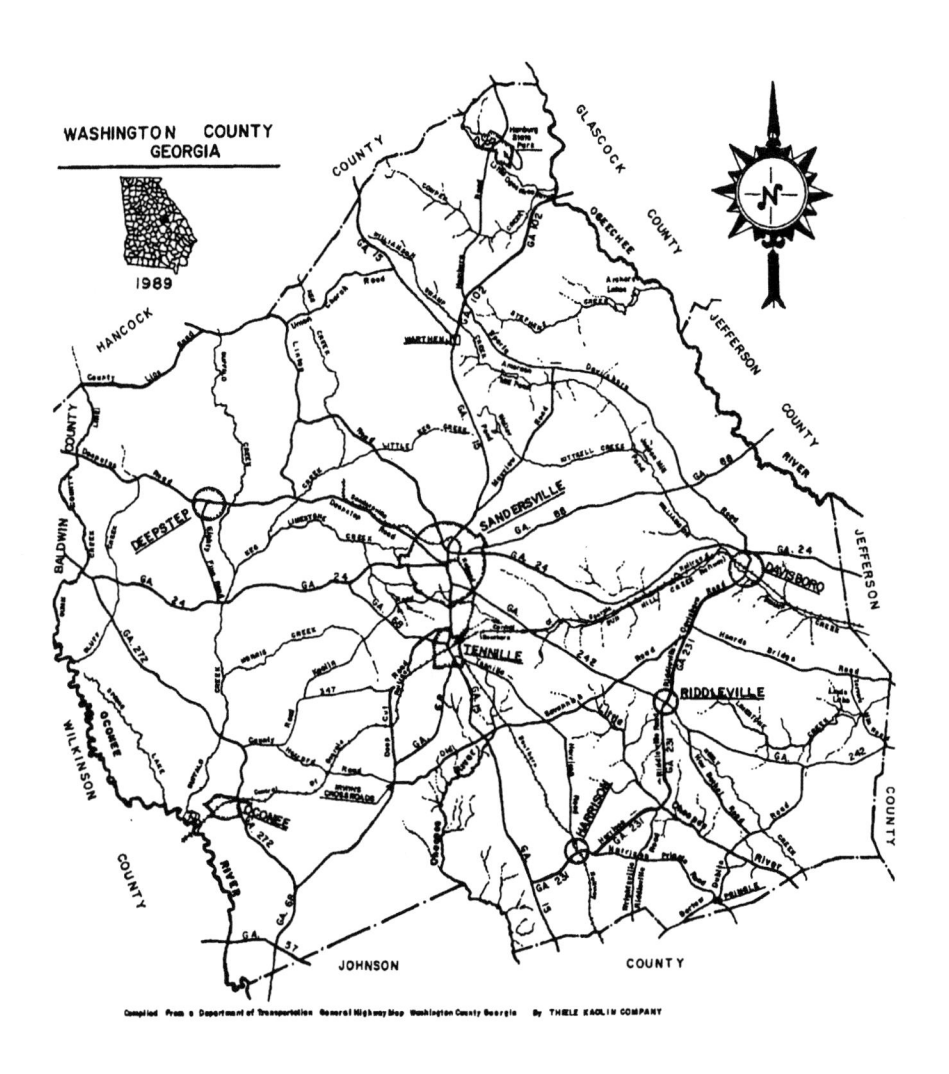

WASHINGTON COUNTY, GEORGIA

Mary Alice Jordan, editor, *Cotton to Kaolin, a History of Washington County, Georgia 1784-1989*
Used by permission of Washington County Historical Society

between Spanish Florida and the Carolinas, a challenge to French claims to lands east of the Mississippi River, and a social experiment conceived by General James Oglethorpe.[1] Spain was a constant threat to the British settlements along the southern Atlantic and, as an officer of high rank in Britain's military establishment, General Oglethorpe was able to join practical considerations with his concern for a significant segment of the nation's prison population. His idealistic scheme was to create a colony which would provide a new start in life for a portion of the thousands of citizens who were incarcerated as debtors. In addition to linking his plan to Britain's military concerns, he was able to build support among politicians and monied interests by advertising the potential of the area as a producer of wine, silk, and olives and as a new market for British goods.

In 1732 King George II gave a charter to Oglethorpe and a group of colleagues with whom he formed a board of Trustees. They were granted land in the southern portion of the original Carolina colony. The area for settlement lay between the Savannah and Altamaha rivers, but the western boundary of the grant was vague, leading to later claims westward to the Mississippi River. Oglethorpe sailed with his first band of approximately 125 settlers on the ship "Anne" in late 1732 and arrived in Charleston, South Carolina in January, 1733. He was careful to build good relations with the Creeks and he negotiated a transfer of land which included Yamacraw Bluff, the site on the Savannah River which he had chosen for the colony's first settlement. In February Oglethorpe and his settlers began work on the village which was to become the city of Savannah, following his plan for the broad streets and open squares which today characterize that gracious city. Since he hoped that the temperate southern climate would produce plants which could not be grown in England, a major part of his plan was the creation of a public garden. It included mulberry trees (for silk worms), grape vines, and olive trees, as well as numerous English plants.

Oglethorpe was equally industrious in developing the colony as a deterrent to Spain's territorial ambitions. He built of series of forts from the south on St. Simons Island to a location on the Savannah River which was named Fort Augusta. He was unsuccessful in his attempts to capture the Spanish fort at St. Augustine, Florida, which was a constant menace to the colony, but dealt a decisive blow to a large force of invading Spaniards in the Battle of Bloody Marsh on St. Simons Island in 1742. This battle, which was an event in what the colonists called the War of Jenkins' Ear, was part of the ongoing struggle among Spain, France, and England for mastery of North America.

Oglethorpe personally supervised the colony in its first ten years and its reputation for good management, tolerance, and abundant opportunity drew an interesting variety of settlers in addition to the inmates from debtors prisons for whom it had originally been intended. Among those who came during the first ten years were parties of Salzbergers, German Protestants escaping persecution; a group of forty Jews; a small party of Moravians and Swiss; and a contingent of Scotch Highlanders. In the next decade a community of Puritans from Massachusetts, which had first moved to South Carolina, established the settlement of Midway. Three of the most interesting individuals from England who were drawn to participate in Oglethorpe's experiment were the religious reformers John and Charles Wesley, whose movement led to the formation of the Methodist Church, and George Whitefield, who founded in Georgia the first orphanage in America. Approximately 5,500 colonists came to Georgia during the twenty years of the Trustees' administration. Of these almost 3,500 came at their own expense, soon outnumbering the Trustee sponsored debtors.

Since the original focus of Oglethorpe's efforts was the creation of a colony for new beginnings for unfortunates who had become mired in debt, he and his fellow Trustees formulated a plan which they hoped would achieve their goal. The heart of the plan was embodied in three major restrictions. The first was a limit of 50 acres of land to each family whose transportation was paid for by the Trustees. Those who paid their own way might receive larger grants, but none of the settlers had full title to their land. They might hold it for life and pass it on to their sons, but they were not allowed to sell or mortgage it, the concern being that they would lose it and again become debtors. The second rule was a prohibition against slavery, with the goal of creating a society of small yeoman farmers dependent on their own labor. The third was to make illegal the importation of hard liquor, fearing the role it had played in the economic ruin of many Englishmen. Land, rum, and slaves were integral parts of the way of life in other Southern colonies and, with the absence of restrictions in these colonies, many original settlers left Georgia in disgust. Gradually the Trustees modified the original prohibitions and they were no longer in force after the Trustees surrendered their charter in 1752 and Georgia became a royal colony. While approximately 5,500 settlers had come to Georgia during its first twenty years, the colony's population in 1752 was estimated at 3,000, of whom about 800 were Negro slaves who had been brought in after the prohibition against slavery was dropped in 1750. Oglethorpe's idealist scheme for a colony of self-sufficient small farmers was as unworkable as the Carolina Lords Proprietors' dreams of great feudal estates worked by loyal serfs. There was simply too much land for the taking and too many land-hungry immigrants. Proprietors and royal authorities in Britain were too far away and too ignorant of the dynamics of the New World to force the colonies into the molds they fashioned on paper.

Georgia prospered under the royal authorities and had better relations with its governors than most of the older colonies. Its major crops, rice, indigo, furs, and lumber (plans for silk, wine, and olives were a failure) found ready markets in Britain, Europe, and the West Indies; however in the 1760s, as Britain attempted to force all colonial trade into her markets and to collect increased revenues, loyalty to the mother country eroded. As in North Carolina, there was an element of civil conflict among the population as the Revolution began and progressed in the 1770s, with bitter division between the Patriots and the many who remained loyal to Britain. Georgia became a major area of combat during the Revolution, as the British attempted to capture and control the Southern colonies after their failure to defeat Washington's forces in the North. Many Georgians fled and the state's population suffered a decline. Savannah was occupied in 1778 and was not surrendered by the British until 1782.

After the Revolution was officially ended by the Treaty of Paris in 1783, one of Georgia's major concerns was the development of plans to draw back the many citizens who had fled during the British occupation and to attract new settlers. The state's main attraction was the thousands of acres of fertile land in the interior. In the closing years of the colonial era, the British authorities had discouraged new settlements which would create hostility among the native population throughout the colonies. With colonial restraints removed, Georgia acted to claim all its lands for white settlers. Only a small fraction of the lands within the present boundaries of the state had been settled in the colonial period and, in addition to these, Georgia claimed the land west of her present boundary to the Mississippi River, basing her claim on her colonial charter.

In 1777, as the transition from colony to state was made during the Revolution, the areas of colonial settlement paralleling the Savannah River and the Atlantic Ocean were organized into eight counties. Two new counties, Washington and Franklin, were established in 1784, to the west of the older counties, on lands occupied by the Creek Indians. These and, in subsequent years, all their other lands were ceded by the Creeks in a series of treaties of questionable legality, beginning with the Treaty of Augusta in 1783. The process of acquisition from the Indians had begun in the colonial era with the Treaty of Savannah, negotiated by General Oglethorpe in 1733, the year of Georgia's founding.[2] In the two new counties liberal land grants were made through a bounty system to military veterans and to civilians who had remained loyal to the revolutionary cause. Also, the headrights system of the royal era of the colonial period was continued, with modifications which allowed up to a thousand acres for a family. Through manipulation of the system of distribution, a few individuals were able to secure grants of several thousand acres. Waste, inefficiency, and disregard for unresolved Indian claims marked the operation of these plans. The problem was exacerbated by the continued use of the metes and bounds system of survey of the colonial era, which was based on such transitory features as trees, trails, and streams. As migrants from the states to the north poured into Georgia in the decades following the end of the Revolution, chaos reigned in the distribution system. James C. Bonner in *A History of Georgia Agriculture* has pointed out, "Including its western lands, to which Indian claims had not yet been extinguished, over ninety-five percent of the Georgia area was classified as public domain. Because of this fact land policy became the primary political concern of Georgians for half a century after the Revolution, helping to explain the highly transitory nature of its agricultural population throughout most of the nineteenth century."[3]

In 1795 the volatile blend of vast public domain, scheming land speculators, eager buyers, and greedy politicians led to the climax in Georgia's land craze, the Legislature's passage of the Yazoo Act. The law allowed 35,000,000 acres of land in present Alabama and Mississippi to be sold to a group of speculators for a cent and a half an acre. Accusations of fraud and bribery abounded and led to the election of a new body of legislators and a new governor, Jared Irwin of Washington County, who had opposed the sale. The act was repealed in 1796 and, with great ceremony, the pages on which it was written were burned before the new state capitol in Louisville, using fire called down from heaven with the aid of a magnifying glass.

The temptation of the lands to the west of Georgia's present boundaries was removed soon after the opening of the nineteenth century. Throughout the decade of the 1790s the federal government had denied the state's claim to lands west of the Chattahoochee River and in 1802 Georgia abandoned the claim in exchange for the government's promise to force the removal of the Creek and Cherokee Indians. Over 31,000,000 acres of public land remained and the state was challenged to develop an orderly means of distribution amidst the conflicting interests of large and small land owners and the land speculators. Several of the state's governors, Jared Irwin, John Milledge, and Josiah Tattnall, championed the yeoman farmer over the large land holder and supported a new law in 1803 which "represented the triumph of a liberal policy of free land and equal grants in farm-sized lots."[4] The law called for a survey of the land to the west of Washington and Franklin counties and for organization into counties before it was granted. Distribution was to be carried out through a series of lotteries. In the first drawing, which took place in 1805, every free white male of 21 years or older who was a citizen of the United States and a resident of Georgia for a year was entitled to one draw or to two if he had a wife or a child. Minor orphans were entitled to one draw and widows with minor children to two. The only charge was a recording fee, which was originally $4.00 per hundred acres. The size of the grant varied over the six distributions from 1805 to 1832, based on estimates of the land's value in the different areas of the state. The range was from 40 acres for the "gold lots," in the area of north Georgia where gold had been discovered, which were distributed in 1832, to 490 acres in the "pine barrens" of south Georgia. Georgia's liberal policy lured thousands of settlers from other states and also tempted Georgians to use their land wastefully, knowing there was always more to the west.

The three decades following the initiation of the lottery system were marked by the tenacious but vain struggle of the Indians to retain their lands and the relentless movement of white settlers into those lands. One Hardison, at least, was to lose his life in the ongoing bloodshed of the Indian wars. In the 1830s the final resistance of the Creeks and Cherokees was broken and they were forcibly removed from Georgia. The lands watered by the rivers with the lilting Indian names—Altamaha, Chattahoochee, Oconee, Ogeechee, Satilla—now belonged to the white man, with his ever-growing body of black laborers.

Washington County

A search of the records of North Carolina and Georgia indicates that four Hardison family members, Benjamin's sons John and Thomas and their cousins Frederick and Cullen, settled in Georgia in the first two decades of the nineteenth century, the first three in Washington County and Cullen in nearby Jones County. By the time of the Hardisons' arrival in Washington County, it was making a transition from the frontier conditions of its first two decades to a more settled agricultural economy and society. In the county's early years at the close of the eighteenth century, the settlers who preceded the Hardisons had journeyed overland on the long established Indian trails through the Carolinas and then on the hunting and trading paths of the Creek Indians, after crossing the Savannah River into Georgia. The name Creek was applied to the various tribes and sub-tribes of indigenous peoples who occupied central and western Georgia. They were hunters and fishers and some were farmers and keepers of livestock. They had traded with the white man since colonial times and their trading paths not only provided entry for the new settlers who appropriated their lands, but served later as the routes for most of the roads built in the nineteenth and twentieth centuries.[5]

Washington County historian Elizabeth P. Newsom has described the early settlers:

> The first white settlers came on horseback and in oxcarts bringing sheep, cattle, horses and pigs. Generally they came in family groups from the same community and settled together along the water courses. By this arrangement the families were company for each other and were mutually helpful and protective. The wilderness and canebrakes furnished bounteous pasture. The woods and waters supplied wild game to supplement their food supply. Rude shelter was thrown up and small plots of land cleared for seed they had brought for garden and crops. The domestic animals adapted well to the frontier life and furnished the additional advantage of being able to transport themselves to market. There were no markets closer than Augusta, 70 miles, and Savannah, 130 miles. Flatboats were used as far up the Oconee River as Rock Landing, and perhaps produce was floated down the Ogeechee. Life for the pioneer was primitive and remote.
>
> For some twenty years after the settlement of Washington County, there was little to attract settlement by people of wealth; primarily the rough country attracted those Americans who had few goods but hoped to gain something through their own hard work. The land was rich; those who came remained independent, and their flocks and herds thrived. Livestock was the major early industry, and after two decades of settlement there was little land in cultivation, although more was worked after the invention of the cotton gin in 1793.[6]

For two decades after the Treaty of Augusta of 1783, numerous Creeks contested the loss of their lands, insisting that only a minority of the tribe had consented to the cession. Scalpings, burning of homes, and raids on livestock were frequent events. Forts were built at strategic locations, particularly on the rivers, and the settlers organized to defend themselves. The frontier conditions and the sense of urgency of the whites is illustrated by a letter of 1786 from a group of Washington County residents to the governor:

> Whereas a Number of our back inhabitants is under a great disadvantag at this time by being Drove by the indins from their several Settlements and habitations and we have now a mind to Mak a Stand through the assistance of your honors the governor and Council in furnishing ous

your petitioners with ammonition to the amount of eight pounds of powder and sixteen pounds of bu and flints for the want of wihitch we shall be obligd to break but we hope your honours will grant our Requists.[7]

Such requests were dramatized by depositions from individual citizens:

Elijah Blackshear and Isom Carter before David Blackshear swore they went to house of Reuben Wilkinson and found house burnt and part of carcases of three people supposed to be Wilkinson, wife and a negro. 30 Nov. 1795[8]

As the eighteenth century ended, the hazard of Indian retaliations lessened with the steady push of the Creeks to the west. The acreage of land cleared for farming increased and the transition from subsistence farming to an increasing cultivation of cotton as a money crop had begun. Two villages, Warthen, in the northeast, and Sandersville, which became the county seat because of its central location, were founded. A few Methodist and Baptist churches, served by itinerant ministers, were formed. Education was haphazard at best and many children, particularly girls, received no formal schooling.[9] Most people lived in crude log cabins, which soon evolved into the familiar dogtrot house with an open passage and one or two rooms on each side. The name dogtrot was well chosen, for dogs, chickens, and children roamed through the passage. Many prosperous farmers continued to live in such houses throughout the ante-bellum period, while others built plantation houses both plain and elegant. These houses might boast porches—back and front, two stories, and fine materials and appointments, but they kept the basic plan of the dogtrot, with the open passage becoming a center hall.[10]

Members of the Hardison family were among the new influx of settlers who came into Washington County in the early nineteenth century, as the transition from frontier conditions was beginning. They and many other farmers were drawn from states to the north, particularly North Carolina, where conditions for large scale cotton farming were not as favorable as in central Georgia. The growing popularity of cotton as a money crop led to an increase in the county's population and in the proportion of blacks to whites, as slaves were brought in to cultivate the crop. In 1790 the total population was 4,550 with 3,856 whites and 694 blacks. By 1830 the total was 9,820 with 5,795 whites, 4,009 slaves, and 16 free blacks.[11] As the population within the original boundaries grew, the county was divided to form new counties. Seventeen counties or parts of counties were carved from the original which had been created in 1784 and by 1825 Washington County was close to its present size. As comprised today, the county is 674 square miles in size. The imaginary demarcation known as the Fall Line, which separates the harder, rockier soils of the Piedmont of Georgia from the softer clays and sands of the Coastal Plain, runs across the northern portion of the county. The level lands of the southern part were better suited to large scale agriculture, but farming was conducted throughout the county in the nineteenth century.[12]

It was to lands in Washington County, within its present limits, that the Hardisons migrated from North Carolina during the first two decades of the 1800s. The researcher who attempts to document the lives of these and other early settlers of the county has a double dose of frustration. Not only have the three earliest Federal Census population enumerations for Georgia, 1790, 1800, and 1810, been lost, but nearly all the official records of Washington County were destroyed by courthouse fires in 1855 and 1864, the latter courtesy of General Sherman. Fortunately enough Georgians have cared about salvaging the remaining county records and assembling a body of information from a variety of official and unofficial sources to make possible the writing of a history of the county and of the individuals who settled it. Most prominent among them is the previously mentioned Elizabeth P. Newsom, who has devoted many years to gathering and making available this information. She has pointed out the significance of the county's records beyond the interests of genealogists and local historians, noting the role of Washington County in the larger picture of southern and southwestern migration in the years between the Revolutionary War and the Civil War: "Since the migration trails from Maryland, Pennsylvania, Virginia, and the Carolinas passed through Washington County, many early Georgia settlers lived in this county for a time before continuing their westward trek to Alabama, Mississippi, Louisiana, Arkansas, Missouri, Texas, and all points west and northwest."[13] As the following account will indicate, some of the

Hardisons remained in Washington County, others settled throughout Georgia, and still others moved on to northern Florida and east Texas, which were the southern and western boundaries of the Cotton Kingdom.

The Hardisons in Washington County

The origin of this study of the Hardison family was knowledge, acquired from their descendants, of four Hardison siblings with North Carolina roots who lived in Washington County, Georgia in the early nineteenth century.[14] They were two brothers, William Lanier and Seth, and their sisters, Temperance and Winnifred, who were married to brothers Enos and Joel Davis. The names of their parents had been guessed at from available data, primarily the Hardison heads of household in the earliest existing Federal Census population enumeration for Georgia—1820, but not documented. The search for their ancestry and for the history of the Hardison family in North Carolina led to the research which is reflected in the preceding four chapters.

The links which joined the North Carolina and Georgia Hardisons were the wills which proved the descent from Jasper, founder of the North Carolina family, through son John and John's son, Benjamin, and the Washington County, North Carolina deed of 1805 which identified John and Thomas "both of the State of Georgia" as members of Benjamin's family. As noted in the previous chapter, the deed was one of several in which the brothers, sister, and mother of Seth Hardison, deceased, sold to Ezekiel Hardison their shares in a town lot in Plymouth, North Carolina, which had belonged to Seth. In their 1805 deed, John and Thomas were identified as brothers of Seth. These three and the other brothers involved in the transfer of ownership of Seth's property, including Ezekiel, were listed as sons of Benjamin Hardison in his will of 1785.[15] This information led to the tentative conclusion that the Seth of Washington County, Georgia was a nephew of the deceased Seth of Washington County, North Carolina, and that he and his brother William Lanier and sisters Temperance and Winnifred were children of either John or Thomas.

The motivation for John's and Thomas' departure from their home in the Albemarle and their migration to Georgia probably lay in the lack of expectations for future prosperity offered by their father's meager bequests and the depressed state of North Carolina's economy. Judging from his age in the last Federal Census in which he appeared, 1830, John was born in the decade between 1760 and 1770.[16] Little is known of his life in North Carolina other than his identity as a son of Benjamin. He may have been the grandson John who was mentioned in the will of 1778 of the eldest John and to whom a small bequest of livestock was made. Possibly he was one of the three John Hardisons included in the main body of the 1779 Martin County Tax List or perhaps the John among the men "in the Service," whose names appear at the end of the list. The first bequests in the will of Benjamin, written in 1785, were to sons John and William, followed by provisions for wife Elizabeth, obviously a second wife, and the five sons, including Thomas, and two daughters of that marriage. The name of John's mother has not been discovered. John and William were given joint ownership of four slaves, a woman named Phibb and her children, Charity, Simon, and Easter, and each was given a feather bed and a cow and calf. As noted in the discussion of Benjamin's will in the preceding chapter, he did not itemize his lands and other possessions, but left all except the bequests to John and William to be used by Elizabeth for a period of eight years for the rearing of her children. After this time the property was to be divided, with Elizabeth to receive one-third of the mills and the plantation and the remainder to be divided among her children. Even though Benjamin was among the most prosperous men of Martin County, as noted by his property valuation in the county's tax list of 1779, the division of his possessions among so many heirs did not provide a generous start in life for any of them.[17] Elizabeth married John Collins after Benjamin's death and, having been given full possession of one-third of Benjamin's mills and plantation, rather than merely the use of them during her lifetime, she may have passed them on to her children or to her new husband.

Since neither John nor younger half-brother Thomas had high expectations in North Carolina, the Georgia land craze had the power to attract. They both probably sold whatever possessions might help pay for their new start, including their share in brother Seth's town lot in Plymouth. The four slaves which were left to John and his brother William had considerable value. Phibb already had the three children who were part of the bequest and might be expected to have more if young enough. It is possible that the slave woman Phibea who is mentioned in the will of 1797 of John and William's uncle, William Hardison, was the same person as Phibb and that John had sold his share in her before leaving North Carolina. A Martin County deed of 1802 records the sale of a plantation on Roses Creek by a Thomas Hardison, but this was more likely Thomas' great-uncle, a very long-lived son of Jasper, or another relative of that name.[18] Probably he was the same Thomas Hardison who acted as agent for John and Thomas in the sale of their share in brother Seth's Plymouth lot. The name John Hardison appears in several Martin County deeds of the 1780s and 1790s, but these appear to involve either the eldest John's son John or his son John. Thomas Hardison and two John Hardisons are listed in the North Carolina State Census of 1784-1787 and the Federal Census enumerations of 1790 and 1800. This Thomas is more likely the son of the eldest Jasper and the Johns, the eldest John's son and his son.[19]

After establishing the identity of John and Thomas of Georgia, the next consideration was to determine their relationship to the Hardison brothers and sisters of Georgia's Washington County. Although John's and Thomas' cousins Cullen and Frederick were listed in the 1820 Georgia census records, they did not leave North Carolina until the 1810s, as indicated by their appearance in the Federal Census enumerations of 1810 for Martin (Cullen—spelled Cullin) and Washington (Frederick) counties and the deed records of those counties.[20] The loss of the pre-Civil War deed records of Washington County, Georgia is a great hindrance to research but other sources exist from which the lives of early settlers in the county may be reconstructed. These will be noted in the history of the Hardisons during the first three decades of the nineteenth century. They include the listing of Thomas Hardison of Washington County as a participant in the land lottery of 1805 and a legal notice in a newspaper of 1811 which places John in the western portion of Washington County. Although no will or other document which provides proof has been found, either John or Thomas seems most likely as the father of the Hardison brothers and sisters of Washington County, with John the better choice as the discussion below will indicate.

John had a large family by the time the Federal Census enumeration was made in 1820, while Thomas' name does not appear in the listings for Georgia in that year. It is possible that Thomas had died and that some of the children in John's household were his. Unfortunately the names of family members other than the head of household were not recorded in the census records until 1850; however a search of the Federal Census enumeration for that year yielded information about three of the four Hardison brothers and sisters believed to be children of John, which helps to establish the time of the family's settlement in Georgia.[21] This information includes William L.'s age as 51, giving him a birth year of 1799, and place of birth as North Carolina; Seth's age as 46, making a birth year of 1804, and place of birth Georgia; and Winnifred (listed in husband Joel Davis' household) as 38, making a birth year of 1812, and place of birth Georgia. Temperance was deceased before 1850. Their ages and states of birth place their arrival at some time between William's birth in North Carolina in 1799 and Seth's in Georgia in approximately 1804 (his age listings in subsequent census records make this time vary by one or two years). The bestowing of the name Seth on the first of the children born in Georgia was evidently a tribute to the brother Seth, who had died recently in North Carolina. Subsequent research on the Hardisons in Georgia and Florida added the names Elizabeth, Nancy, and John M. as members of the same generation and most likely siblings of William L., Seth, Temperance, and Winnifred.[22] Documents pertaining to the disposal of the property of John Hardison in Jefferson County, Florida in 1832 provided the name of his wife, spelled Winaford in these documents.[23] Her maiden name has not been discovered. If the eldest son, William, were her child, she may have been a Lanier, for that was his middle name and most records pertaining to him include the initial "L." The Laniers were a large and prominent family who were neighbors of the Hardisons in Martin County, North Carolina.

The earliest Georgia record for John or Thomas is the listing of the latter as a participant in the land lottery of 1805, the first of the six lotteries, 1805 to 1832, authorized by the Land Lottery Act of 1803. The act represented an attempt to establish a fair and orderly system for distributing Georgia's vast public domain west of Washington

V. TO THE LAND OF COTTON, 1800-1828

County. It abandoned the old metes and bounds system for determining boundaries and called for accurate surveys, organization of counties prior to settlement, and distribution of the former Creek Indian lands by a series of lotteries. The first lottery was held in 1805 and was the only drawing in which the names of all the participants were recorded, whether or not they won land. The list serves as a substitute for Georgia's lost records of the Federal Census of 1800. Participants had to be citizens of the United States and residents of the state for one year. Unmarried males 21 years and older and widows were entitled to one draw, while married men and widows with children were entitled to two. "P," for prize, beside the name indicated a successful draw, while "B," for blank, indicated failure. Thomas Hardison of Washington County was the only Hardison in the list for the 1805 drawing.[24] The one "B" beside his name indicates that he had only one draw, thus was not married, and that he won no land. This data makes brother John the likely choice for the father of William L., Seth, Temperance, and Winnifred. John's failure to participate in the 1805 lottery may have resulted from his presence in North Carolina to carry out the land sale in Plymouth (he and another Thomas Hardison, acting as agent, signed the deed while brother Thomas did not) or might have resulted from an inability to meet the one year residence requirement.

In the absence of Washington County's pre-Civil War land records, it is difficult to know in which portion of the large county the Hardisons first settled. Land in the county was acquired originally through bounty and headrights grants from the colony and state and then through purchase from those who held the original grants. The land lotteries of 1805 through 1832 applied to the lands west of Washington County. Since no Hardisons appear in the various listings for all of Georgia and for Washington County for bounty and headrights grants, the assumption may be made that John and Thomas acquired land by purchase from earlier settlers, as was generally the case for those who arrived in the county after 1800.[25] One of the few sources to provide information on the location of their lands before the Georgia Tax Digest of 1825, the earliest in existence which includes Washington County, were the legal notices in local newspapers.[26] The county's notices were carried first in the newspapers of

Louisville, for the few years it was the capital of Georgia, and then after 1808 in the papers of the new capital, Milledgeville, until the county had its first paper in the 1830s. In 1811 and again in 1815, there were notices in the *Georgia Journal* that 100 acres of pine land on Buffalo Creek belonging to John Hardison were to be sold to satisfy judgments against him, in 1811 by the administrator of the estate of F. Lewis, deceased, and in 1815 by John Crowell.[27] This information places John's land on the western side of the county, Buffalo Creek being a tributary of the Oconee River. These notices mark the beginning of a sad and often repeated theme of acquisition followed by loss, which was sounded throughout the nineteenth century history of the Hardisons.

Military preparedness as well as acquisition of land was a constant concern on the Georgia frontier and militia records provide additional information about the Hardisons. Each county was divided into militia districts which were to contain about one hundred men available for military service. All adult white males were eligible for service. The state assigned numbers to the districts as they were created, for Washington County 88 through 100 and the additional number 136, but the districts in the older counties were generally called by the names of their captains.[28] Following the example of their North Carolina ancestors, two of the Hardisons found places of leadership in the militia. The state archives of Georgia include records of the commissioning of "Thomas Hardeson, Gentl." as an ensign of the 136th District Company of Militia in 1814 and "William L. Hardeson, Gentl." as an ensign of the 98th District Company in 1817. William L. was to rise in rank in the next decade and to remain active in the militia.[29]

By the time the 1820 Federal Census was taken, there were five Hardison households in the state—one in Jones County, to the west of Washington County, and four in Washington. Cullen, who headed the family in Jones, was a son of William Hardison of Martin County, North Carolina, the brother of the Benjamin who was the father of Thomas and John. Cullen and the one other member of his household, a female who was probably his wife, were in the 45 years or older age category.[30] Four years before, in the 1816 Georgia Tax Digest, both Cullen and a Benjamin Hardison, presumed to be Cullen's brother of that name, were listed for Jones County.[31] Benjamin does not appear as a head of household in the 1820 Federal Census enumeration for Georgia or in subsequent Georgia enumerations. A Benjamin Hardison of Morgan County, who may be Cullen's brother, won land in Carroll County in the land lottery of 1827.[32]

The four Washington County Hardison families in the 1820 Federal Census were headed by three males, Frederick, John, and William, and one female, Elizabeth.[33] The make-up of these families may be seen in the following chart:

1820 Federal Census Georgia Washington County

Name of Head of Family	Under 10 yrs. of age	10 and under 16	Between 16 and 18 yrs.	Between 18 and 26 yrs.	Between 26 and 45 yrs.	Of 45 yrs. and upwards	Under 10 yrs. of age	10 and under 16	Between 16 and 26 yrs.	Between 26 and 45 yrs.	Of 45 yrs. and upwards	Foreigners not naturalized	Persons engagd in agriculture	Persons engaged in commerce	Persons engaged in manufacturing	Slaves
Elizabeth			1							1			1			4
Frederick	1	1			1	2	2		1	1			1			
John	1	1	1			1	2	2	3		1		1			1
William	2			1			1		1				1			6

Frederick was a descendant, probably a great-grandson, of the original Jasper of North Carolina, through his son Jasper.[34] Since there were three adult males of various ages in his family and the census records do not specify which was the head of household, it is difficult to know Frederick's age; however later census listings for him make it evident he was the youngest and was about 40 years old in 1820.[35] The female between the ages 26 and 45 was most likely his wife. Four children under 16 years and a female between the ages of 16 and 26 completed the family. Frederick had no slaves.

John, who was in the 45 years or older category, had the largest family of the Hardisons in Georgia in 1820, with a female in the same age group, who was probably his wife, six children under 16, one male between 16 and 18, and three females between 16 and 26. One male slave completed his household. The size of his family and the fact that he and Seth were listed together in the next Federal Census, living in Jefferson County, Florida, reinforces his designation as the father of the Hardison siblings who are named at the beginning of this Washington County narrative—William L., Seth, Temperance, Winnifred, and the younger Hardisons of their generation, Nancy, Elizabeth, and John M. As noted earlier, it is possible that some members of John's household might be children of his half-brother Thomas, whose name does not appear in the 1820 listing.

William, a young man in the 18 to 26 year group, may be William L., the eldest of the Hardison siblings, who was born in 1799. Family records indicate that he married a widow, Mrs. Sarah Lewis, who had at least one child.[36] If this is his family, she is the female between 16 and 26 and one or more of the children under 10 were hers by her former marriage. The six slaves might have come in part from her former husband's estate. It is possible that the William in the 1820 enumeration is another, who moved from Washington County in the 1820s.

The one female Hardison heading a household was Elizabeth, 45 years or older, and she had only one family member, a male between 16 and 18. She was probably a widow with one son and her absence from any subsequent census listings may indicate that she became a part of his household after he reached maturity. She owned one male and three female slaves. Her relationship with the other Hardison families in Georgia has not been discovered.

The absence of Thomas from the list of Hardisons in Georgia in 1820 seems to indicate that he had died by the time the census was taken or had moved from Georgia. It is possible, but not likely due to her age, that Elizabeth was his widow. Not until the 1850 Federal Census enumeration does a Thomas Hardison appear as a head of household in the indexes to the Georgia census records. He is Thomas of Houston County, who was born in North Carolina and was 38 years old in 1850, giving him a birth year of 1812.[37] The presence in his household of a son named Frederick makes it likely that this Thomas was a son of the Frederick who was living in Washington County in 1820 and in Crawford County in 1830.

The Hardisons and Cotton

The story of the Hardisons and their contemporaries in Georgia is inextricably linked with the history of cotton cultivation in the South. The vast majority of Georgians depended on farming for their livelihood and, as James C. Bonner has written in his history of ante-bellum agriculture, "The most significant feature of Georgia agriculture in the half century following the Revolution was the development of cotton as the principal staple crop."[38] In the 1700s the cultivation of long staple "Sea Island" cotton had played an important part in the economy of the coastal areas, where soil and climate allowed it be grown. The short staple variety was well suited to nearly all of the upland area of central Georgia, but the fact that an entire day's labor was required to pick one pound of lint from the seeds made its cultivation as a money crop impossible. Eli Whitney's invention of the cotton gin in 1793 removed this obstacle. Whitney, a recent graduate of Yale College, was a tutor on the plantation of Nathanael Greene, near Savannah, where he had undoubtedly observed the time-consuming process of removing seeds from cotton.

In the decades which followed Whitney's invention, there was a gradual transition in central Georgia from subsistence agriculture to a dependence on cotton as the major money crop. Food and manufactured goods, which had previously been produced at home, or done without, began to be purchased and farmers borrowed to buy more land for cotton and more slaves to cultivate it. According to James C. Bonner, "Middle Georgia was firmly established as a cotton-growing area by 1830, at which time Georgia had taken the lead from South Carolina as the principal producer of the staple."[39] The Georgia land lotteries continued in the 1820s, with drawings in 1820, 1821, and 1827 for lands extending to the Alabama and Florida borders, making thousands of acres of virtually free land available for extending cotton culture to the west and the south. There was a growing demand for Negro slaves to provide an adequate labor force, as the size and number of farms and plantations grew. The institution of slavery was firmly fixed on a state whose colonial charter had expressly forbidden it a century earlier.

The Hardisons were caught up in the race for the acquisition of land and several of them were successful participants in the lotteries of the 1820s. Cullen, of Jones County, won land in Irwin County in south-central Georgia, in 1820; Frederick and William L., of Washington County, in Henry County, in central Georgia, in 1821; Seth, of Washington County, in Muscogee County, on the Alabama border, in 1827; and Benjamin (probably Cullen's brother), of Morgan County, in Carroll County, on the Alabama border, in 1827.[40] As noted earlier, the size of the grants was based on the supposed value of the land for agriculture, with the largest, 490 acres, being in the pine land areas, thought to be poor for farming. Lands which were covered by hardwood forests were considered more fertile and better suited to cotton culture. Cullen's grant in Irwin County in the south Georgia pine lands was 490 acres, while the lots won by the other Hardisons, in that broad band across central Georgia which came to be called the Cotton Belt, were 202½ acres.[41] This rather odd size resulted from the use of the English system of surveying squares of forty-five chains, which produced parcels of this size.[42] The total cost of a lot was a fee of $18.00 in 1820 and 1827 and $19.00 in 1821. The residence requirement for lottery participants had been increased from one to three years by 1820, but the age limit for white males had been dropped from 21 to 18. Winners in one lottery were not allowed to participate in subsequent drawings. The land did not have to be occupied by the winners, but might be sold to other settlers. The 1830-1860 Federal Census records, in giving the county of residence of the Hardisons, do not show that any who drew land in the lotteries of the 1820's became residents of the counties of their winnings.

With the abundance of cheap land in Georgia, farmers were careless in their use of it and the intensive cultivation of cotton depleted the soil. By the 1830s the older areas of central Georgia were suffering the consequences of these factors and the lotteries were seen by some citizens as less of a blessing, if not a curse. James C. Bonner sums up the dilemma, "Before the last land lottery was completed in 1832, many Georgians were realizing that the lotteries and the abundance of cheap land had brought a serious deterioration of agricultural and social conditions in the older counties of the state. A citizen of Sparta called the land lotteries 'the most unjust, unequal, and immoral' of all methods ever employed for distributing public land. The effect of the abundance and cheapness of land, said he, was that it 'begat a careless, slovenly, skimming habit of farming'."[43]

Throughout the ante-bellum decades, migration continued from Washington and other central Georgia counties to the newly opened lands of Georgia and Florida and westward from Alabama through east Texas. By the end of the 1820s, Frederick, John, and Seth had left the county—and possibly Thomas and Elizabeth. In the Washington County listings in the 1825 Georgia Tax Digest, the earliest extant tax records of Washington County, John and William L. are the only Hardisons included. Frederick is listed in Crawford County in the 1830 Federal Census and apparently moved there before the 1825 tax list was compiled. In the 1825 list, John had no property and the only record for him was a poll tax of thirty-one cents and two and a half mills. William L.'s taxable property consisted of the lot in Henry County he had won in the 1821 lottery and 227 acres of pine land in Washington County. The practice of indicating the location of land in the latter county by listing the "water course" which drained it, in William L.'s case Williamson Swamp Creek which flows into the Ogeechee River, helps to place him on the eastern side of the county. His property included only one slave, leaving a question of what had transpired since the 1820 Federal Census listing of six slaves. His total tax was $1.30.[44]

John had evidently not prospered in Washington County and the facts behind his lack of property in 1825 are revealed in part by legal notices in the newspapers of Milledgeville, the *Georgia Journal* and the *Southern Recorder*, which record a continuation of his legal woes of the previous decade. In 1823 he, with William L. Hardison, Theophilus Hardy, and Foreman Hodges, was an unsuccessful participant in a lawsuit which led to a forced sale of land. In 1824 his "Negro girl named Phoebe" was sold to satisfy a debt to John Crowell and in 1825 "three beds, bedsteads and furniture ... property pointed out by said [John] Hardison" were sold to satisfy a judgment in favor of Morgan Brown.[45] It is not surprising that John shook the dust of Washington County from his feet and moved off to the territory of Florida for a new start. The 1830 Federal Census records list him, followed by Seth, in Jefferson County, just south of the Georgia boundary. As previously noted, that county's archives provided records which include the name of John's wife. Spelled Winaford in these documents, it became a popular name among her descendants, with a variety of spellings eventually becoming Winifred or Winnifred.[46] Seth, who had been listed as "defunct" in the Washington County tax record of 1828, had apparently decided that his future lay elsewhere and, for the next thirty years, he and his family lived in northern Florida and southwest Georgia.[47]

As John and Seth set off for Florida, William L. and his sisters Temperance and Winnifred, settled down to farm and raise families in Washington County, where they remained the rest of their lives. As noted earlier, William L. was already married by the time the 1820 census was taken. His sisters married brothers Enos and Joel Davis, of Robeson County, North Carolina, in the 1820s. Enos, born in 1798, and Joel, 1803, first appear in the records of Washington County in the county's listings in the 1825 Georgia Tax Digest and they probably came to the state in the decade of the 1820s. According to one of the Davis family chroniclers, James Porter Davis, a grandson of Joel, they were sons of John Davis and Elizabeth Adams, for whom there are records in the New Bern area of North Carolina. He points out that thousands of Davises from England and Wales came to America and that Davis is the seventh most common surname in the United States, making it difficult to trace family roots. He counted 330 heads of family named Davis in the 1790 Federal census listings for North Carolina, a number of whom were named John Davis. Numerous Davises appear in the bounty, headrights, and lottery records of Georgia and in the 1820 Federal Census there were twelve Davis households in Washington County, three headed by a John Davis. The histories of the Joel and Enos Davis families give no indication that one of these was their father and it is likely that the brothers came to Georgia on their own as adults. According to family tradition they were saddlemakers.[48]

Enos and Joel and a number of other Davises settled on the eastern side of Washington County and their name was given to the town which grew up around early settlements near the Ogeechee River. According to James Porter Davis. the town was named for Enos and Joel. Another Davis is given the honor in the history of the county, *Cotton to Kaolin*, produced by its historical society in 1989, "In 1827, Diocletian Davis, a blacksmith, rode across the river with a knapsack containing his hammer and anvil tied to his horse and decided to settle, establishing the first business in the community. The settlement became known as Davisborough in his honor. The spelling was later changed to Davisboro."[49] Diocletian was from North Carolina and was possibly related to Joel and Enos.[50]

The data for Enos Davis in the 1825 Georgia Tax Digest places his holdings of 142 acres of oak and hickory land on the eastern side of the county, drained by the same water course mentioned for William L.'s land, Williamson Swamp Creek. He had no slaves. Joel was listed as administrator of an estate, with holdings of 380 acres of pine land on the western side of the county, drained by Gum Creek, a tributary of the Oconee River, and 202½ acres each in Houston and Henry counties.[51] The latter holdings were obviously lottery winnings, but since neither Joel's nor Enos' name appears in the list of lottery winners in the 1820s, there is a question as to whose land Joel was administering. One slave is listed with his taxable property. At some time after 1825, he and wife Winnifred acquired land on the eastern side of the county and in 1844 they purchased property between the towns of Davisboro and Tennille which came to be known as Elm Hill. There they established a home, where several generations of Davises were reared, and a farm of approximately 300 acres, which continued to be operated by their descendants well into the twentieth century. In his remembrances of Elm Hill, James Porter Davis has written a poignant account of life as he knew it as a boy, "Here in the nineties of the last century was a small but complete and self-contained unit of southern country life as it had gone on almost unchanged from the days of the colonies. This was not a vast estate with tall white columns, magnolias and slave quarters, nor was it Tobacco Road. It was a farm with a home, work and food for those who lived there, a farm like hundreds of thousands of others. These farms, far more than the great plantations, always were the core of the real South."[52]

By the time the 1830 Federal Census was taken, Enos and Temperance, the older of the Davis brothers and Hardison sisters, were well on their way to the nine children they would have before their deaths in the late 1840s.[53] This census places both of them between the ages of 20 and 30, with four sons and a daughter under the age of 10.

They had two female slaves. Joel, between the ages of 20 and 30, and Winnifred, between 15 and 20, had no children and no slaves.[54] Within the next two and a half decades, they had twelve children.

In the 1830s the Davis families and William L. Hardison's family lived in close proximity on the eastern side of the county. William L.'s and Sarah's family had grown from the three children under 10 years of the 1820 census to a total of seven under the age of 15 and a male between the ages of 20 and 30, who was probably either a relative or a hired hand. Their household was completed by three male and six female slaves, making an interesting comparison with the one declared in the 1825 Tax Digest.[55]

There is no evidence of involvement of the Hardisons in public affairs in ante-bellum Georgia comparable to that of their ancestor John in North Carolina; however William L. continued in a role of leadership in the militia of Washington County which had begun with his commissioning as ensign in 1817. In the 1820s, he was commissioned as lieutenant and then captain of the 94th District Company of Militia.[56] Captain W. L. Hardison's toast at the Fourth of July celebration of 1832 was reported, among those of prominent citizens of the Davisboro community, in a front page article in Milledgeville's *Southern Recorder*.[57] The dinner which was the occasion of the toasts was held at the Davisboro Academy and was provided by William P. Hardwick, a large land holder of the area, into whose family one of the Davis daughters later married.[58] William L.'s toast reflects local sentiments about the tariff issue, which was raging in Congress and prompting secession threats in the South, "May the Congress of the United States learn to be guided by honest and impartial principles. If they understand the theory, they have neglected the practice." It is an interesting commentary on the divisive issue which had prompted the famous exchange of toasts of 1830 between President Andrew Jackson and his Vice-President, John C. Calhoun of South Carolina. Jackson's toast was "Our Union—it must be preserved!" and Calhoun's rejoinder, "The Union—next to our liberty, the most dear."

It may be that William L.'s sense of injury was based on personal distress as well as general Southern outrage over the tariff issue. As the industrial interests of the North had pushed Congress to place taxes on imported manufactured goods to encourage the growth of factories in the United States, Southern agricultural interests had become incensed, since they sold their crops on an unprotected market and increasingly purchased manufactured goods produced outside the South. The years of furor over this issue, from the passage of "the tariff of abominations" in 1828 to the lowering of rates in Henry Clay's tariff bill of 1833, coincided with Georgia's first real agricultural depression. Falling cotton prices in the mid-1820's (they went from twenty-one cents a pound to twelve between 1824 and 1825) came at a time when farmers were increasingly turning to one-crop farming. This blow was followed by a drought which lasted from 1827 through 1832, bringing destitution to many families in the Cotton Belt. Several counties formed relief committees and small and large landowners alike looked for explanations of their misery. In the 1820s some objective citizens had criticized Georgia's growing reliance on agriculture, to the exclusion of investment in manufacturing; increasing indebtedness for land and slaves; and the trend toward a one-crop system, which exhausted the soil and left the farmer at the mercy of fluctuating world market prices. However, as the tariff issue and the crop failures coincided in the late 1820s and early 1830s, the blame was increasingly placed on the tariffs, which raised the price of the manufactured goods the agricultural South must buy from others. As the rates were lowered and favorable crop years followed, this particular North-South issue faded, but the seeds of dissent had been planted and were to grow as Southern states became outnumbered in representation in the Congress with the creation of new states in the West and faster growth of population in the North.[59]

William L.'s losses, which may have resulted from the depression of the 1827-1832 period, were recorded in a legal notice in the February 12, 1834 issue of the *Federal Union*, a Milledgeville newspaper. The notice called for the sale of "one tract of land adjoining William Cowart, Cordell Francis and others, levied on as the property of William L. Hardison to satisfy a mortgage *fi fa* in favor of David McDaniel, for the use of Bias Alford . . . ." Later in the same year the sale of 100 acres of land owned by John Hardison, to satisfy Morgan Brown, was announced.[60] Possibly the departure of John and Seth for Florida in the late 1820s had resulted from disappointments developing in the early days of the depression and in the 1830s William L.

suffered from the depression's ongoing consequences.

In spite of the distance which separated the branches of the family in Florida and Georgia, the ties of kinship remained strong. The brothers and sisters named children for each other and each named a son John. The name of the elder John's wife had been passed on to one of her daughters and was repeated as a name for Temperance's daughter. Seth's son, John Randolph Hardison, was to double the kinship by marrying his first cousin, Winnifred Cornelia Davis, daughter of Temperance and Enos. Even though John Randolph grew up in Florida and southwest Georgia, he obviously had a great love for Washington County, to which he referred affectionately in his letters of the 1860s and 1870s as "Old Washington" and from which he took two brides to Texas.

NOTES

References to the Federal Census records are to the original manuscripts of the population enumerations, unless otherwise indicated. In some cases two numbers appear on one page of the records, the original hand-written number and another printed as the records were edited. The records are available on microfilm in many libraries and record depositories. In this study the collection in the Clayton Library, Center for Genealogical Research, Houston Public Library, Houston, Texas was used.

1. Kenneth Coleman, editor, *A History of Georgia* (Athens: University of Georgia Press, 1977), chaps.1-6, Colonial Period, and chaps.7-10, 1775-1820.
2. James C. Bonner, *Atlas for Georgia History* (Milledgeville: Georgia College, 1969), pp.30-35; Elizabeth Pritchard Newsom, *Washington County, Georgia Tombstone Inscriptions* (Sandersville: published by author, 1967), pp.vii-viii.
3. James C. Bonner, *A History of Georgia Agriculture, 1732-1860* (Athens: University of Georgia Press, 1964), p.11.
4. *Ibid.*, p.38; in chap.3, The Passing of the Frontier, pp.32-46, Bonner describes the interrelation of land politics and the development of agriculture in Georgia.
5. Elizabeth Pritchard Newsom, editor, *Washington County, Georgia 1825 Tax Digest* (Sandersville, published by editor, 1968), pp.xvii-xviii; Mary Alice Jordan, editor, *Cotton to Kaolin, a History of Washington County, Georgia 1784-1989* (Sandersville: Washington County Historical Society, 1989), pp.5-7.
6. Newsom, *Washington County, Georgia 1825 Tax Digest*, pp.xvi-xvii.
7. Frances Wynd, editor, *Washington County, Georgia Records* (Albany: privately printed, n.d.), p.108.
8. *Ibid.*, p.108.
9. Jordan, *Cotton to Kaolin*, pp.9-11; Newsom, *Washington County, Georgia 1825 Tax Digest*, pp.xviii-xx.
10. John Linley, *Architecture of Middle Georgia: the Oconee Area* (Athens: University of Georgia Press, 1972), pp.21-34.
11. Population summaries of First Federal Census, 1790, Georgia, Washington County (this information has survived although the population enumeration has been lost)

and Fifth Federal Census, 1830, Georgia, Washington County.
12. Jordan, *op. cit.*, pp.1-4.
13. Newsom, *Washington County, Georgia 1825 Tax Digest*, p.ix.
14. Cain Family Genealogical Collection, privately held by Cain family members who are descendants of Seth Hardison through his son John Randolph Hardison and John's first wife, Winnifred Cornelia Davis, the daughter of Enos and Temperance Hardison Davis. The collection includes letters and genealogical data on the Hardison, Davis, Wood, and Cain families of Georgia. Additional information on Enos and Joel Davis and their descendants is found in James Porter Davis, *Elm Hill and Its People* (privately published, n.d.). and Sara Jane Overstreet and Barbara Davis-Stovall, *A Davis Family Record* (privately published, 1984). Copies of the latter two sources are in the library of the Washington County Historical Society in Sandersville, Georgia.
15. See Chapter 4 for a discussion of the will of John's and Thomas' father, Benjamin Hardison (Martin County, North Carolina Will Book 1, p.118-19), and the deeds of Washington County, North Carolina pertaining to the property of Seth Hardison.
16. Fifth Federal Census, 1830. Florida, Jefferson County, p.163.
17. "Martin County: 1779 Tax List," *Journal of North Carolina Genealogy*, vol.11, no.2, pp.146-68.
18. Martin County Deed Book D, p.40.
19. Martin County Deed Books C-E; see also discussion of the John Hardison listings in the North Carolina state census of 1784-87 and federal censuses of 1790 and 1800 in Chapter 4.
20. Elizabeth Petty Bentley, compiler, *Index to the 1810 Census of North Carolina* (Baltimore: Genealogical Publishing Company, 1978), p.105; both Cullen and Frederick appear in the deed records of Washington County, North Carolina in the first decade of the 1800s (Books A-C) and Cullen sold 160 acres of land in Martin County in 1814 (Deed Book F, p.367).
21. Seventh Federal Census, 1850, Florida, Gadsden County, p.196 (mss p. 377), Seth Hardison; Seventh Federal Census, 1850, Georgia, Washington County, p.228, William L. Hardison and p.248, Winafred [Hardison] Davis.
22. Mrs. Alma Walker Jackson, interviews, 1990-91, Houston, Texas. Mrs. Jackson's husband, Andrew Talley Jackson, is a descendant of Elizabeth Hardison and Abner Jackson through their son Theophilus Hardee Jackson. Mrs. Jackson has collected extensive genealogical data on the Hardison, Jackson, and related families, which she has shared for this study. Records pertaining to Nancy, John M., and the Jacksons appear in the Jefferson County, Florida and Early County, Georgia archives and will be noted in later chapters.
23. Jefferson County, Florida, Land and Property Book A, pp.395-98.
24. Virginia S. Wood and Ralph V. Wood, editors, *1805 Georgia Land Lottery* (Cambridge: The Greenwood Press, 1964), p.144.
25. Silas Emmett Lucas, Jr., editor, *Index to the Headright and Bounty Grants of Georgia, 1756-1909* (Vidalia: Georgia Genealogical Reprints, 1970); Frances Wynd, *Washington County, Georgia Records*. Lucas' and Wynd's compilations include no headright or bounty listings for the Hardisons.
26. Elizabeth Pritchard Newsom, editor, *Washington County, Georgia Estate Papers* (Sandersville: Washington County Historical Society, 1982). The introduction, pp.ix-xix, provides data on the newspapers which published Washington County's legal notices before the county had a newspaper. On p.xiii Mrs. Newsom states,

"Probably the first Sandersville newspaper was the *Southern Advocate*, advertised for sale February 1839 in the *Southern Recorder* in Milledgeville." She conducted an extensive search for names of Washington County residents in the Milledgeville publications, which began covering the county in 1808. Since her death in 1993 her files have been in the possession of the Washington County Historical Society, which is preparing them for public use. Microfilms of existing copies of the Milledgeville papers are located at the University of Georgia, Athens. Georgia College, Milledgeville, has a collection of both microfilm and originals of issues of some of these papers, dating from 1808. The citations below are based on Mrs. Newsom's files and a search of the Georgia College collection.

27. *Georgia Journal*, Milledgeville, Georgia, January 30 and April 3, 1811; October 11, 1815.
28. Newsom, *Washington County, Georgia 1825 Tax Digest*, pp.ix-x; Bonner, *Atlas for Georgia History*, pp.5-6.
29. Georgia Department of Archives and History, Atlanta, Adjutant General Military Commissions, 1812-15, p.623; 1815-18, p.656.
30. Martin County Will Book 1, pp.326-28, will of William Hardison; Fourth Federal Census, 1820, Georgia, Jones County, p.115.
31. R. J. Taylor, Jr., Foundation, *Index to Georgia Tax Digests* (Spartanburg, South Carolina: The Reprint Company, 1986), 5 vols. These volumes, which cover the period from 1789 to 1817, have no listings for Washington County. The only Hardisons listed are Cullen and Benjamin (spelled Hardenson) in Jones County in 1816, vol.5, p.39, and a Harry Hardinson in Pulaski County for the same year, vol.5, p.39.
32. Martha Lou Houston, compiler, *Reprint of Official Register of Land Lottery of Georgia*, 1827 (Columbus: published by compiler, 1928), p.115.
33. Fourth Federal Census, 1820, Georgia, Washington County, p.128, Frederick; p.133, William; p.144, Elizabeth; and p.146, John.
34. Washington County, North Carolina, Deed Book B, p.435. In this record Frederick is among three persons receiving land in the division of the estate of Jasper Hardison (most likely the third Jasper, a grandson of the founder of the North Carolina family through his son Jasper); information on this branch of the family may be found in Martha Mewborn Marble, "Hardisons of Lenoir County," North Carolina (unpublished manuscript in North Carolina State Library, Raleigh, 1986), pp.3-4.
35. Fifth Federal Census, 1830, Georgia, Crawford County, p.403, lists Frederick Hardison as between ages 40 and 50; Seventh Federal Census, 1850, Georgia, Crawford County, p.428, lists F. Hardison, age 70, birthplace North Carolina.
36. Cain Family Genealogical Collection, in listing the spouses of Hardison siblings, identifies the wife of William L. as Mrs. Sarah Lewis, a widow; several Lewis households are listed in Washington County in the 1820 census; Seventh Federal Census, 1850, Georgia, Washington County, p.228, gives Sarah's age as 53 and birthplace Georgia, while William L.'s age was 51.
37. Seventh Federal Census, 1850, Georgia, Houston County, p.314; in addition to Thomas there are three other Hardison households listed for Houston County in 1850, headed by Henry, p.314, age 22 and born in Georgia, James W., p.314, age 42 and born in North Carolina, and Thomas, Jr., p.316, age 20 and born in Georgia. Marriage records for Crawford County include both Thomas and James W., making it likely they were part of Frederick's family.
38. Bonner, *A History of Georgia Agriculture*, p.51. Chap.4 of Bonner's study, The Rise of Upland Cotton, pp.47-60, gives the background for Georgia's development as a

major cotton producer.
39. *Ibid.*, p.56.
40. Silas Emmett Lucas, Jr., compiler, *The Third or 1820 Land Lottery of Georgia* (Easley, South Carolina: Southern Historical Press, 1986), p.141, Cullin; Lucas, *The Fourth or 1821 Land Lottery of Georgia* (Easley: Southern Historical Press, 1986). p.98, Frederick and William L.; Houston, *Reprint of Official Register of Land Lottery of Georgia*, 1827, p.115, Benjamin and p.161, Seth.
41. Bonner, *Atlas of Georgia History*, pp.55-57.
42. Bonner, *A History of Georgia Agriculture*, p.39.
43. *Ibid.*, p.60.
44. Newsom, *Washington County, Georgia 1825 Tax Digest*, p.30, William L. and p.116, John.
45. *Georgia Journal*, Milledgeville, Georgia, August 12 and December 2, 1823; *Southern Recorder*, Milledgeville, January 27, 1824 and January 25, 1825.
46. Fifth Federal Census, 1830, Florida, Jefferson County, p.163; Jefferson County Land and Property Book A, pp.395-98.
47. Washington County, Georgia, 1828 Tax Digest, microfilm in Washington County Historical Collection, Sandersville, p.117.
48. Data on the Davis brothers and the families they created with Winnifred and Temperance Hardison has been drawn from the previously cited *Elm Hill and Its People* by James Porter Davis and *A Davis Family Record* by Sara Jane Overstreet and Barbara Davis-Stovall, unless otherwise indicated.
49. Jordan, *Cotton to Kaolin*, p.163.
50. A sampler created in 1833 by a descendant of Diocletian has been donated to the Washington County Historical Society. It lists the children of Diocletian (spelled Dioclisian) and gives his life span as 1754-1830.
51. Newsom, *Washington County, Georgia 1825 Tax Digest*, p.37, Enos and p.124, Joel.
52. Davis, *Elm Hill*, p.1.
53. *Ibid.*, p.40.
54. Fifth Federal Census, 1830, Georgia, Washington County, p.248, Joel and p.272, Enos.
55. *Ibid.*, p.248, William L.
56. Georgia Department of Archives and History, Atlanta, Adjutant General Military Commissions, 1820-22, p.163; 1827-29, p.87.
57. *Southern Recorder*, Milledgeville, Georgia, July 19, 1832.
58. Jordan, *Cotton to Kaolin*, p.424, notes the marriage of William P. Hardwick's son, Thomas William, to Mary Elizabeth Davis, daughter of Enos and Temperance Davis, in 1848. A grandson of this marriage, Thomas William Hardwick, born in 1872, was Governor of Georgia, 1921-23, Congressman, and U.S.Senator.
59. Bonner, *A History of Georgia Agriculture*, p.56-60.
60. *Federal Union*, Milledgeville, Georgia, February 12 and December 3, 1834.

VI

A Sojourn in Florida Jefferson County, 1828-1835

The Hardisons' Southern odyssey took John and a portion of his family to the Territory of Florida almost thirty years after his departure from North Carolina. In leaving Washington County, Georgia, he once again parted with family, friends, and familiar places, but in choosing Jefferson County he settled in an area similar to the Georgia Piedmont which he was leaving and among North Carolina and Georgia families. Jefferson County is one of the five counties paralleling the Georgia border which made up the ante-bellum cotton belt of Florida. The unique physical nature of this section was noted by nineteenth century travelers, including the Georgia poet Sidney Lanier, and its pre-Civil War history has been the subject of a recent study by Clifton Paisley, *The Red Hills of Florida, 1528-1865*.[1] The area's rolling hills, red clay soil, and hardwood trees present a dramatic contrast to the flat coastal plains of southern Georgia and the pine forests of northern Florida. Lanier, comparing it to his native land in central Georgia, called it "Piedmont Florida" and included a description in his *Florida, Its Scenery, Climate, and History*, published in 1875.

This southernmost Piedmont stretches about 150 miles along the Alabama and Georgia border, from Jackson County eastward through

Gadsden County
Jefferson County

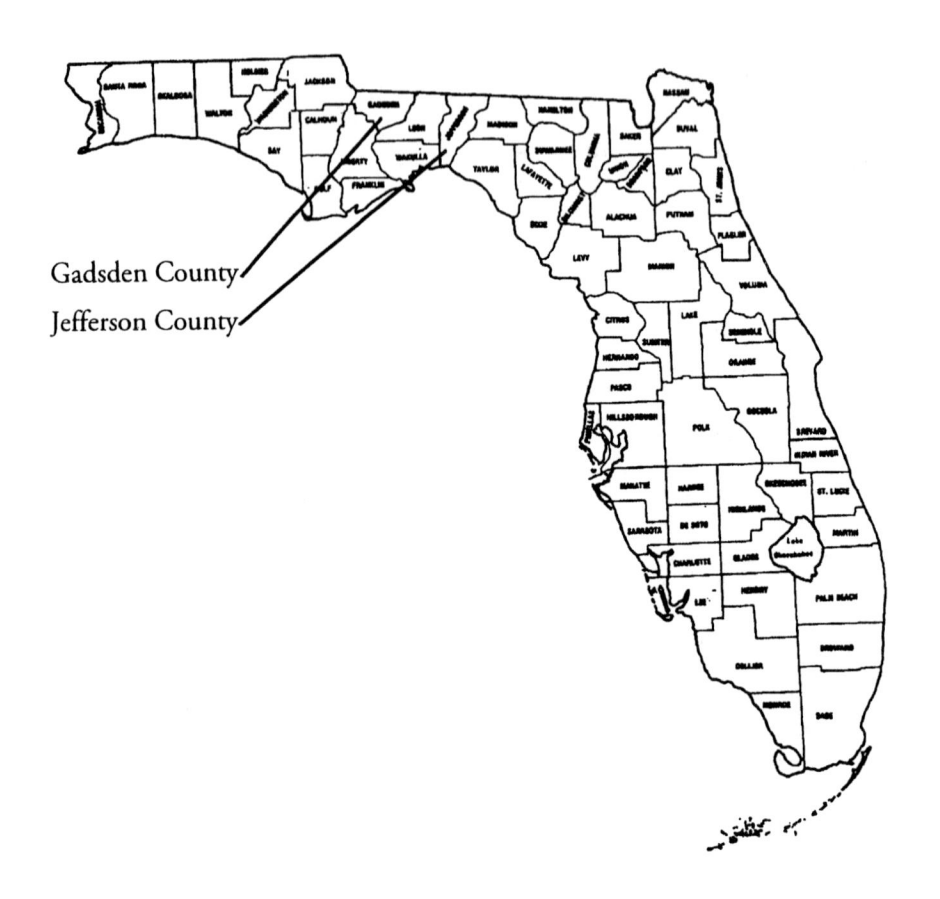

FLORIDA

Gadsden, Leon, Jefferson, and Madison counties. It is at most twenty-five miles deep from north to south. Below the hills are the sandy soils and pine forests typical of northern Florida, which begin south of what geologists call the Cody Scarp. The unique composition of the hills resulted from an accumulation of clays, sands, and rock fragments washed down from the Appalachian Mountains and deposited on a limestone bed millions of years ago, with the deposits gradually being cut into hills and valleys by the heavy rains of Florida. Paisley has noted, "This hilly region clinging to the Georgia line for most of its length, seems more like a southern intrusion of the Peach State than a part of the Sunshine State. But although its five Florida counties resemble their neighbors just across the line, they seem even more akin to the Georgia of the Piedmont or to the Red Hills of Georgia that extend from the area of Houston County to Stewart County and then southward along the Chattahoochee River to Early County, Georgia."[2] The farmers who migrated to Georgia and Florida in the early nineteenth century looked on the rolling, hardwood-forested lands of each of these areas as ideal for cotton culture. These were the lands where various members of the Hardison family settled between the 1820s and 1850s after having passed through Washington County, Georgia.[3]

Early Florida History

The events which preceded Florida's status as a territory of the United States occurred over a period of almost three hundred years, from the discovery and exploration by the Spaniards Panfilo de Narvaez and Hernando de Soto in the early 1500s to the acquisition of Florida from Spain in 1821. During this long history Florida was a prize defended by Spain and coveted by Great Britain and, in the years following independence, the United States. The fate of its native population was a repetition, with unique variations, of the tragic native American themes of destruction, dislocation, and removal. The natives whom the Spanish found living in the "Red Hills" area of northern Florida in the 1500s were known as the Apalachees. They were a settled people who had a highly structured society ruled by chiefs and nobles. They built towns and carried on extensive agriculture. At the time of the Spanish settlement of Florida there were about 25,000 to 30,000 Apalachees, living chiefly in the areas which are today Jefferson and Leon counties. In the 1600s Franciscan friars built a series of missions in the Apalachee lands and among other Indian tribes to the east. Toward the end of this century, in the "Golden Age" of the Florida mission development, two-thirds of the 13,152 Christian Indians in Florida were Apalachees. Along with religious conversion went the harsh treatment of the native populations typical of Spanish colonization. This abuse was heightened as the Spanish became increasingly pressed by English expansion southward from South Carolina and the newly formed colony of Georgia. Indians were used as forced labor in building fortifications and as soldiers in military service. The native populations of both the English and Spanish colonies were caught up in the rivalry between these two great colonial powers in the eighteenth century and in the territorial ambitions of the newly formed United States in the late 1700s and early 1800s.

The various adversities of the Apalachees led to a drastic reduction of their population and the destruction of their culture. Many were killed and others fled, leaving behind abandoned fields and ruined towns and missions. As the 1700s progressed, the Apalachee lands were occupied by a group of Creek Indians, the major group of native Americans in Georgia and Alabama, who came to be known as the Seminoles. The name derived from the Spanish word Cimarrones, meaning "wild ones," for the tribe had broken away from the Creek Confederation. Their two principal towns were Tallahassa, located on one of the hilltops of today's Tallahassee, in Leon County, and Mikasuki, near Lake Miccosukee, to the east of Tallahassee in Jefferson County.

Throughout the 1700s Florida continued to be a coveted prize in the imperial struggle among Spain, England, and the emerging United States. A series of adventurers, military men of each nationality, Indian chiefs, and profit-grasping agents in the Indian trade sought to manipulate the changing conditions to their advantage. England won Florida in 1763 in the treaty ending the Seven Years War (French and Indian War), but lost it to Spain twenty years later at the end of the American Revolution. As Spain's grasp on her American possessions weakened in the late 1700s, the United States became increasingly aggressive in pushing her southern boundaries to the Gulf of Mexico and the tip of the Florida peninsula. While the Spanish had looked on the natives as candidates for conversion to Catholicism and as manpower for their military ventures, the citizens of the United States coveted their land and desired their removal. Florida's native populations were victims of both courses of empire and the half century which followed the end of the American Revolution was a period of intermittent warfare against the Indians of both Georgia and Florida, culminating in the 1830s in the removal of the survivors to reservations.

In the years following the Revolution, the English encouraged the Seminoles and also the large numbers of runaway slaves who lived in northern Florida to resist the movement of the Americans toward Spanish Florida. Many refugee Creeks lent willing ears to this encouragement after their defeat by General Andrew Jackson at Horseshoe Bend in 1814. They were incensed over the Treaty of Fort Jackson which had been dictated to a small band of captives, who did not represent the majority of the Creeks involved in the cession of about 20,000,000 acres of land in eastern Alabama and southern Georgia. As this land began to be settled by American farmers, the Creeks retaliated by raids on their homesteads. When evidence was found to support the accusation of British encouragement of the raids, Andrew Jackson was ordered to end the threat to the nation's southern frontier and little effort was made to conceal the desire of the United States to acquire Florida. The one-sided campaign of 1818, known at the First Seminole War, pitted Jackson's forces of over 3,000, made up of volunteers from Kentucky and Tennessee, Georgia militia, and their Creek allies, against about 1,200 Seminole warriors of northern Florida. Jackson's victory was a prelude to Spain's cession of Florida to the United States, which was formalized by treaty in 1821.

The men in the invading army of Americans had noted the beauty and the agricultural potential of the "Red Hills" area. Captain Hugh Young, the topographical engineer on Jackson's staff, wrote in his "Topographical Memoir" of the close proximity to a shipping outlet for potential crops through the old Spanish port of St. Marks on the Gulf of Mexico. The finalization of the acquisition of Florida in 1821 marked the opening to white settlers of a vast new area of public lands. The first American settlers spilled over from Alabama into the westernmost "Red Hills" county, Jackson, and were followed by Georgians in both Jackson and Gadsden counties. Subsistence agriculture soon gave way to cotton culture, with an increasing number of slaves being brought in to cultivate the money crop. As with Georgia, a large number of the first settlers were from the Carolinas, many of whom came to Florida after a generation in Georgia.

The richest agricultural lands lay to the east of Gadsden County, in what became Leon County in 1824 and Jefferson County, created from Leon in 1827. The Hardisons eventually settled in Gadsden County, but it was to Jefferson that John brought his family when he left Washington County, Georgia in the late 1820s. The lure of rich lands which could produce cotton, added to the proximity to the port of St. Marks, from which it could be shipped to foreign and domestic markets, was irresistible to John Hardison and other farmers as cotton began to dominate the Southern economy. But one obstacle remained, the existing occupants who claimed the land as their own. As noted earlier, a branch of the Creeks, the Seminoles, had replaced the former occupants, the Apalachees. It was their leader, the wily Neamathla, with whom Andrew Jackson, as governor of the Territory of Florida, and subsequent American officials attempted to negotiate the removal of the Seminoles to a reservation in central Florida. Neamathla and fellow chieftains forced a compromise whereby they were given additional small personal reservations in the northern counties. The agreement was formalized in the Treaty of Moultrie Creek in 1823. There was considerable resistance to removal to the reservation since its soil was so inferior to that of the "Red Hills" area, but a show of force by the new territorial governor, William P. DuVal, settled the issue and the Seminoles complied. Neamathla refused to join in the retreat and became the leader of a group of rebellious Creeks. The last chapter of his and their struggle brought tragedy to the Hardison family in the next decade.

The Hardisons in Jefferson County 1828-1835

The Hardisons' move to Florida took them to an area which was far less advanced in white settlement than the land they left behind in

Georgia. Although Washington County had only recently been opened for settlement when John arrived about 1800 and still experienced Indian raids, Georgia had been a state since the Revolution, after fifty years as an English colony. As noted earlier, her history had been marked since its founding by efforts to deal peacefully, though often deviously, with the native population. Florida in the 1820s had only recently been acquired from Spain and remained a territory until 1845. The northern hill country, which had been the scene of armed warfare in the decade preceding the acquisition, was temporarily peaceful during the 1820s and early 1830s, as the Seminoles withdrew to their reservation, and it was in this period that the Hardisons made their move to Jefferson County.

The county was created in 1827 from lands in the eastern portion of Leon County. Today it is a 598 square mile wedge-shaped strip of northern Florida about midway across the state, stretching from the Georgia boundary southwestward to the Gulf of Mexico. Because of its shape and location, it has been referred to as the Keystone County. The northern two-thirds, where Lake Miccosukee is located, has the characteristic rolling hills and fertile lands of the "Red Hills" counties and the southern third is similar to the pine barrens of southern Georgia. The rich farm lands of the northern portion had supported the Apalachees and the Seminoles and in the 1820s they were surveyed and granted to land-hungry white settlers like the Hardisons.[4]

As noted in the preceding chapter, John Hardison had apparently not prospered in Georgia. The Washington County tax list for 1825 did not record any land in his possession and the only data for son Seth in a subsequent list of 1828 was the notation "defunct."[5] Probably both John and Seth had already left Georgia by the latter year, in ample time to appear in the first Federal Census population enumeration to include Florida. The 1830 enumeration for Jefferson County lists adjacent households headed by John and Seth. John, whose age fell in the 60 to 70 year category (giving him a birth year between 1760 and 1770), had a family consisting of a female between 50 and 60 years, most likely his wife, Winnifred (various spellings), and two minors, a male between 15 and 20 and a female between 10 and 15, probably son John M. and daughter Elizabeth, who are known to have come of age in the next decade. The data for Seth placed him in the 20 to 30 year grouping (giving him a birth year between 1800 and 1810), with a household consisting of an adult male and adult female between 30 and 40 years of age and two young females under 10. Neither Seth nor John had any slaves.[6]

The marriage records of Florida reveal that Seth took a wife soon after his move from Georgia. The records of Leon County list him as the groom of Mary Blanford [Blandford], the marriage being performed on May 31, 1829 by the Rev. Theophilus Hardie.[7] The one Blandford family in Leon County in the 1830 Federal Census was headed by Clark Blandford and there are records of Clark Blandford, Jr. living in Warren County, Georgia in the 1820s. Clark of Georgia was guardian of Champ [Champion?] Blandford in the 1820s. In the 1850 Federal Census Champ appears as a member of Seth Hardison's household and is listed as "insane."[8] An interpretation of these data yields an identification of Mary as the probable daughter of Clark, Sr. and sister of Clark, Jr. and Champ, with the latter possibly the male between 30 and 40 who was part of Seth's household as early as 1830.

The presence in Seth and Mary's family of two little girls under the age of 10 only one year after their marriage suggests that either one or both had been married previously. Later records of the family indicate that the two eldest children in Seth's household were daughters, Mary Ann and Nancy, who were born in the 1820s.[9] Hardison family records in the Cain Family Genealogical Collection list the name of Seth's first wife as Mary Barfield and it is likely that they were married while he lived in Washington County, Georgia. The presence of Barfields in the county is documented by data for 1830 on the estate of William Barefield (a frequent spelling of the name), deceased.[10] The name Barfield/Barefield appears frequently in the eighteenth century records of the counties of eastern North Carolina where the Hardisons lived and members of the two families may have migrated to Georgia together. Mary Blandford was possibly the mother of the younger of Seth's two daughters, Nancy, and was certainly the mother of the four sons, Thomas, John, and twins William and Clark, all of whom were born in the 1830s.[11]

The family to which Seth's marriage of 1829 joined him had embarked on a Southern odyssey as varied as that of the Hardisons. As with them, Clark Blandford, Sr.'s origins lay outside the South, as revealed by his application for a pension for his service in the American Revolution. In 1838, at the age of 84, while living in Early County, Georgia, he took advantage of a veterans aid bill of 1832 and submitted a petition for a pension to the federal government. He stated that his military service had begun with enlistment in New Jersey in 1775 and participation in Benedict Arnold's ill-fated siege of Quebec, where he was captured. After parole, he returned to New Jersey, enlisted in the militia, and served until the end of the Revolution. He participated in a number of the battles of the northeast, including the Battle of Monmouth, and "received three wounds, which can show for themselves." He explained his loss of discharge records as a consequence of his frequent relocations since the end of the war, "To wit from New Jersey to the state of Virginia, from thence to the state of Georgia, from thence to the Territory of Florida, from thence returned to the state of Georgia as aforesaid and now a resident of the County of Early."[12]

Soon after Seth Hardison's marriage to Mary Blandford, his sister Nancy married E.[Emerald] Brigham in Jefferson County on March 18, 1830.[13] As with Seth, the ceremony was performed by the Rev. Theophilus Hardie. Emerald was a veteran of the War of 1812 and Nancy's application for a widow's pension provides considerable information on him and on the movements of the Brigham family. According to Nancy's information, Emerald was born May 7, 1794 (Federal Census, Randolph County, Georgia, gives his birthplace as Georgia), enlisted as a private in a militia company at St. Mary's River, Florida in 1813, and was married first to Martha Mott, who died in July, 1829. She described Emerald as "about 5 ft. 9 in. tall, fair complexion, dark blue eyes, brown hair inclined to be curly, very high forehead, and by occupation a farmer and mechanic." She stated that their family lived in Florida until July, 1839, in Early and Randolph counties, Georgia until 1850, in Lowndes County, Alabama until 1853, in Matagorda and DeWitt counties, Texas until 1868, and finally in Blanco County, Texas. Emerald died in DeWitt County on March 15, 1865 (may be 1863). Nancy's birth date is given as March 17, 1806.[14]

The Hardie (also spelled Hardy and Hardee) family of which Rev. Hardie was a member were fellow migrants with the Hardisons from

Washington County, Georgia and probably also from North Carolina, where their names appear in the eighteenth century records of several of the counties of the northeastern area. There is a strong likelihood that the families were related, for there were at least two men named Hardy Hardison in North Carolina in the late 1700s, including one who died in the American Revolution and a half brother of John Hardison.[15] The name Theophilus Hardy appears also in the early eighteenth century records of York County, Maine, where the Stephen Hardison family lived, and in an adjacent area of New Hampshire, so the relationship between the families may have had a long history.[16] The Jefferson County, Florida records include considerable data on Theophilus and William Hardie and William's household was adjacent to those of John and Seth Hardison in the 1830 Federal Census enumeration. Seth's youngest sister, Elizabeth, who married Abner Jackson, named her son Theophilus Hardee Jackson.[17]

The attraction which drew the Hardisons, Hardies, and Blandfords to Florida, along with thousands of other settlers from Georgia and states to the north, was the newly available lands suitable for growing cotton. Since Florida had the status of a territory, following its acquisition from Spain in 1821, its system of land survey and distribution was determined by the federal government. The first land office was established in Tallahassee, ironically one of the former centers of the recently dispossessed Indian population, and in 1825 it began the sale of parcels based on the rectangular system of survey. The surveyor general's office established a principal meridian and base line surveyed at six mile intervals to create townships of thirty-six sections, each a mile square. Townships were grouped in a range, a row of townships lying between two successive meridian lines six miles apart. Records pertaining to the original grants are on file in the Florida State Archives, the Eastern States Office of the Federal Bureau of Land Management, and the National Archives. Subsequent deeds covering sale of the land by original grantees included the descriptions derived from the rectangular system of survey, noting the acreage of the parcel and the range, township, and section in which it was located. The deeds were recorded in the counties in which the land is located.[18]

A search of the early deed records of Jefferson County and the

VI. A SOJOURN IN FLORIDA, 1828-1835   155

printed records of the Tallahassee Land Office did not provide documentation of the Hardisons' earliest acquisitions of land in the county, but the tax list of 1831 includes a listing for Seth, as the owner of 80 acres of land in section 33, township 3, range 4. Theophilus Hardie and Emerald Brigham are also included in the 1831 list. Both Theophilus and Seth were signers in 1832 of a petition to Congress by inhabitants of the Aucilla River vicinity, asking for funds to clear obstructions from the river so as to make it navigable to the Georgia boundary and thus render the area more attractive to new settlers. The river was the eastern boundary of Jefferson County.[19] Patents for land acquired by Allen Hardie (spelled Hardy) in Leon County in 1826 and by Theophilus and Thomas Hardie (spelled Hardy) in Jefferson County in 1827 are listed in the records of the Florida Land Office in Tallahassee, showing this family to be early arrivals in the territory.[20] John Hardison and his family probably shared the land held by Seth, but in November of 1831, John added to the family's holdings with the purchase of a town lot, number 79, in the new county seat, Monticello, the town named for the home of Thomas Jefferson. The purchase was made for the sum of $30.00 paid to its former owner, John G. Robison.[21]

Various aspects of the Hardisons' and the Hardies' lives are revealed in the deed and probate records of the county. In September 1832 Seth appeared as a county official, a role he was to play over several decades in other counties, posting a $500.00 dollar bond to the governor of the Territory of Florida for the performance of the duties of constable in Jefferson County.[22] The early probate records of the county are an assortment of loose records which document the settling of estates, with the first bound book of probate proceedings beginning in 1838. The names of Seth and his younger brother John M. are included in the records of Benjamin Manning's estate in 1832, both owing small debts to Manning and John M. purchasing three cows and calves for $36.25. Theophilus Hardie also appeared in the Manning records in his dual role as farmer and minister, purchasing some cattle and also books of sermons.[23] The Mannings were a North Carolina family and deeds of the 1780s in Martin County document land transactions involving them with both the Hardies and the Hardisons.[24] A third Hardison's name appears in the loose probate papers and raises the question of his identity. A William Hardison was listed in the estate records of James Brooks as owing $10.00, due December 1, 1831. Possibly he was a North Carolina Hardison who had joined the family in Florida and was one of the elderly males included in Seth's household as it was enumerated in the 1840 Federal Census.[25]

John Hardison's role in the family's Southern odyssey came to an end in Jefferson County early in the decade of the 1830s. At some time between his purchase of the town lot in Monticello in November, 1831 and December, 1832, John died. Two documents in the Jefferson County deed records of December, 1832 detail the proceedings whereby "Winaford Hardison widow and relict of John Hardison deceased" lost both lot number 79 and a second lot, number 65, as settlement of debts owed by John. She received $5.00 as the balance of the sale price of the lots after the debts and court costs were paid.[26] Apparently she was undaunted by her losses, for the Florida Land Office in Tallahassee recorded that on January 31, 1833 she purchased 40 acres of land in township 3 north, range 4 east, in Jefferson County. The purchase price was $50.25.[27]

Perhaps Winaford saw her future in Jefferson County, but Seth, his brother John M., and sisters Nancy and Elizabeth did not. In the 1830s they returned to Georgia and made a new start in one of the westernmost counties, Early, where the prospects of bountiful crops of cotton from recently opened lands were promising. Their friend and neighbor Theophilus Hardie also sought a better life, or possibly a more challenging ministry, in Stewart County, Georgia, to the north of Early County. Theophilus sold his land in Jefferson County, first 80 acres to William Hardie in 1828 and an additional 80 to Aaron Pritchet in 1832.[28] A history of Stewart County records that Theophilus was the first pastor called to the Lumpkin Baptist Church. His tenure was brief, however, for he died in 1833 and was the first person buried in the church's cemetery. Other Hardies mentioned in this history are Mary, his daughter, and William, probably his son.[29]

In the 1840s and 1850s Jefferson was to become one of the major cotton producing counties in Florida, with its economic and social life dominated by a small number of planters with large holdings of land and slaves.[30] Just as the Hardisons were leaving, the first banks in Florida were chartered, the most significant institution being the planter-dominated Union Bank which opened in 1835. The major stockholders lived in the "Red Hills" counties and Jefferson County families controlled a majority of the subscriptions to the early stock issues.[31] Although the prospects for this agricultural society looked bright as the decade of the 1830s opened, both planters and yeoman farmers like the Hardisons, with small land holdings and few or no slaves, were suffering by mid-decade. The Hardisons' decision to leave Florida may have been influenced by a severe freeze in 1835, which brought financial distress to many of the newly arrived settlers, and the eruption of new Indian warfare. As historian Kathryn T. Abbey has stated, "Planters who had possessed valid security for their [bank] stock purchases saw it swept away by the frost and the tomahawk. Many left the new country in discouragement and a very effective check was put to further immigration."[32] The nationwide Panic of 1837 and the chaotic banking situation in both the nation and the territory were to have on-going effects on the farmers of Florida and the nation.

The short respite in the Seminole problem ended as the white settlers continued to encroach on their lands and a proposal was made for their total removal from Florida to the western reservations of the Creeks. In 1835, as forced removal was attempted, the Second Seminole War began. Clifton Paisley has compared this struggle to events of our recent past: "Like the Viet Nam War much later, the Seminole War of 1835-1842 troubled the American conscience, was extremely costly in American lives and wealth, and ended inconclusively."[33] Throughout the war years, raids against settlements in the lower edge of the "Red Hills" area, particularly in the eastern counties, Jefferson and Madison, were carried out. The familiar stories of mutilated bodies of adults and children, livestock stolen or killed, and burned homes circulated throughout Jefferson County. Federal troops, local militia, and enraged settlers resolved to eliminate the Seminole menace and in 1837 the charismatic leader Osceola was captured and imprisoned. It was the often repeated story of the struggle between the dispossessed and the new possessors and its predictable end was the removal of the Seminoles from their homeland. But they did not go easily and the struggle dragged on, with the natives escaping into the swamps or woods after their raids. The majority were eventually rounded up and deported to the reservations, but a remnant remained and their descendants are still present in central Florida.

John Hardison had initiated his family's migration from North Carolina shortly after the beginning of the nineteenth century at the mid-point in his own life. As noted previously, the Federal Census of 1830 listed his age as between 60 and 70, far beyond the average life-expectancy of the time, placing his birth between 1760 and 1770. As his native state settled into an era of economic and political stagnation following the American Revolution and his scanty inheritance from his father Benjamin gave little personal promise, he had taken his growing family to lands of opportunity to the south. With the loss to fire of Washington County's land records, the scarcity of early Jefferson County records, and the lack of family letters or other contemporary personal documents, it is impossible to know the full story of John's striving after land and prosperity. The narrative presented in this and the preceding chapter indicates a high degree of disappointment, probably due in part to personal failings and also to economic conditions beyond his control. His legacy to his family was not a great estate but rather his faith in the future and in the potential of the nation's seemingly boundless supply of land. While son William L. and daughters Temperance and Winnifred remained in Washington County, Georgia, sons Seth and John M. and daughters Nancy and Elizabeth continued the Hardisons' odyssey within the South, northward from Florida, later southward again, and finally westward.

NOTES

The Jefferson County records used in this chapter are located in the Florida State Archives, Tallahassee. The deed, will, and marriage records have been microfilmed by the Genealogical Society of the Church of the Latter Day Saints, Salt Lake City, Utah. The citations for both these and the Leon County marriage records are from the microfilms, referred to as L.D.S. film, with appropriate number. A large quantity of the original early Jefferson County records, including probate and court records, were unprocessed at the time I worked in the Archives (1991). The original manuscripts of the tax lists of 1829 and 1831 are located in the Archives.
1. Clifton Paisley, *The Red Hills of Florida, 1528-1865* (Tuscaloosa: University of Alabama Press, 1989), chaps.1-7 present a history of northern Florida from discovery by Spain through acquisition by the United States.
2. *Ibid.*, p.8.

3. See Appendices for list of Hardison heads of household and their counties of residence in Georgia as recorded in the Federal Census population enumerations of 1820-60.
4. Jerrell H. Shofner, *History of Jefferson County* (Tallahassee: Sentry Press, 1976), p.vii.
5. Elizabeth Pritchard Newsom, *Washington County, Georgia 1825 Tax Digest*, p.116 (John); Washington County, Georgia 1828 Tax Digest, microfilm in Washington County Historical Society Collection, p.117 (Seth).
6. Fifth Federal Census, 1830, Florida, Jefferson County, p.163, households nos.324 and 325.
7. Leon County Marriage Records, Register of Marriages, 1829, entry no.45, L.D.S. microfilm #0983459.
8. Fifth Federal Census, 1830, Florida, Leon County, p.127, Clark Blandford's household consisted of a male between 60 and 70 years and a female between 40 and 50; Fred R. Hartz and Emilie K. Hartz, abstracters and compilers, *Genealogical Abstracts from the Georgia Journal (Milledgeville) Newspaper, 1809-1840* (Vidalia: privately published, 1994), vol.3, p.837, Clark Blanford as guardian; R. J. Taylor, Jr. Foundation, *An Index to Georgia Tax Digests* (Spartanburg, S.C.: Reprint Company, 1986), vol.5, p.9, Champ and Clark Blandford listed as taxpayers in Warren County in 1817; Seventh Federal Census, 1850, Florida, Gadsden County, mss. pp.376-77, printed p.196, Champ Blanford, aged 55 years; Federal Census records of Georgia, Warren (1820, p.274), Harris (1830, p.176), Jones (1840, p.136 and 1850, p.217), and Marion (1850, p.301 and 1860, p.266) counties provide data on Clark, Jr. and his descendants; Nettie Powell, *History of Marion County, Georgia* (Columbus: Historical Publishing Company, 1931) includes a biographical sketch of Mark Hardin Blanford, identified as a son of Charles, which should probably read Clark, who was a veteran of the Mexican War and the Civil War and Associate Justice of the Georgia Supreme Court from 1883-1890.
9. Seventh Federal Census, 1850, Florida, Gadsden County, p.219, mss. p.422, Mary (in household of husband John Grey), age 26, birthplace Georgia, and p.216, mss.p.416, Nancy (in household of husband James H. Rives), age 21, birthplace Florida; Eighth Federal Census, 1860, Texas, Polk County, p.18, Mary, age 30, birthplace Georgia, and p.18, Nancy, age 28, birthplace Georgia. Such discrepancies in data in the census records are common, for often ages and other information were furnished by whomever the census-taker found at home and were not always accurate.
10. Elizabeth Pritchard Newsom, *Washington County, Georgia Estate Records* (Sandersville: Washington County Historical Society, 1982), p.84, Jesse Barefield and James Jones as executors of will of William Barefield, May 3, 1830; Federal Census, 1820, Georgia, Jones County, pp.144 and 146, lists 4 Barefield households, headed by John (2), Sampson, and William. See also Taylor, *An Index to Georgia Tax Digests*, vol.1, p.4, Barfields in Hancock and Warren counties (1790s); vol.3, p.5, Hancock County (1804); vol.4, p.5, Jefferson County (1810); vol.5, p.6, Jones, Montgomery, and Warren counties (1816 and 1817).
11. Seventh Federal Census, 1850, Florida, Gadsden County, mss. pp.376-77, printed p.196, lists sons Thomas, age 18 and born in Florida, John, age 16 and born in Georgia, and twins William and Clarke, age 14 and born in Georgia.
12. National Archives, Washington, D.C., Pension application of Clark Blandford, Sr., #R927, Sept. 10, 1838; Taylor, *op. cit.*, vol.2, p.8, Clark was in Georgia at least by 1801 when his name appeared in the Warren County tax list.
13. Jefferson County Marriage Records, Loose Licenses and Marriage Bonds,

1829-1836, L.D.S. film #0927269 (listed in Florida State Archives as microfilm reel #2 of marriage records of Jefferson County), license of "E. Brigham & Miss Nancy Hardyson," March 18, 1830.
14. Federal Archives, Washington, D.C., pension application #43568, Aug. 12, 1884, by Nancy Brigham, widow of Emerald Brigham, veteran of War of 1812; Fifth Federal Census, 1830, Florida, Jefferson County, p.159; Sixth Federal Census, 1840, Georgia, Early County, p.127; Seventh Federal Census, 1850, Georgia, Randolph County, p.397.
15. Fourth Federal Census, 1820, Georgia, Washington County, p.127 (Theophilus); see Chapter 3 for discussion of Hardy Hardison's role in the American Revolution; Martin County (N.C.) Will Book 1, pp.118-19, will of Benjamin Hardison listing Hardy as a son by second wife.
16. Noyes, Libby, and Davis, *Genealogical Dictionary of Maine and New Hampshire*, p.309, includes several Hardy family members who lived in Maine and New Hampshire in the late 1600s and early 1700s, including Theophilus of Exeter, whose baptismal record was dated 1691; the marriage of a later Theophilus, to Mary Sullivan in 1768, is recorded in Town of Berwick (Maine), Record of Marriages, Book 1, p.118.
17. Mrs. Alma Walker Jackson of Houston, Texas, letter of July 27, 1991, concerning her communication with a descendant of the Hardie family who identified William and Theophilus Hardie as brothers, with Allen Hardie of Martin County, North Carolina their father, and the probability that Allen's wife Martha was the sister of Elizabeth Duggan, the second wife of Benjamin Hardison, who was John's father. Mrs. Jackson's husband, Andrew Talley Jackson, is a grandson of Theophilus Hardee Jackson.
18. Arlene Eakle and Johni Cerny, *The Source, a Guidebook of American Genealogy* (Salt Lake City: Ancestry Publishing Company, 1984), pp.224-25 provides an explanation of the rectangular survey system and p.240, the land policies of the Territory of Florida.
19. Jefferson County, Tax Lists of 1829 and 1831, manuscript in Florida State Archives, no page numbers; Clarence Edwin Carter, editor, *The Territorial Papers of the United States* (Washington: National Archives, 1959), vol.24, pp.698-99.
20. Alvie L. Davidson, compiler, *Florida Land: Records of the Tallahassee and Newnanville General Land Office, 1825-1892* (Bowie, Md.: Heritage Books, 1989), p.123.
21. Jefferson County Deed Book A, 1827-1834, p.157, L.D.S. film #927898, microfilm reel #5 of Jefferson County Deed Records, Florida State Archives. (The original manuscript Tract Book covering land grants in the county for 1825-71, arranged by township and range and not indexed by name, is located in the Jefferson County Courthouse.)
22. *Ibid.*, p.362.
23. Jefferson County Loose Probate File, reel #19 of Jefferson County Probate Records, Benjamin Manning Estate, Florida State Archives. Jefferson County's court records for 1828-1890 currently (1991) consist of thirty-five boxes of unprocessed documents in the Florida State Archives.
24. Martin County, N.C., Deed Book A, pp.502 and 538.
25. Sixth Federal Census, 1840, Georgia, Early County, p.127; Seth's father John had a brother named William.
26. Jefferson County Deed Book A, pp.395-97.
27. Davidson, *op. cit.*, p.123.

28. Jefferson County Deed Book A, pp.358 and 511.
29. Helen Eliza Terrill, *History of Stewart County, Georgia* (Columbus: Columbus Office Supply Company, 1958), section one, p.147, pp.154-55, and p.448.
30. Paisley, *op. cit.*, chap.13, Jefferson County as part of the "Cotton Kingdom."
31. Kathryn T. Abbey, "The Union Bank of Tallahassee, an Experiment in Territorial Finance," *Florida Historical Quarterly*, April 1937, vol.15, no.4, pp.207-31.
32. *Ibid.*, p.213.
33. Paisley, *op. cit.*, p.197.

VII

A Return to Georgia Early County, 1835-1845

With the death of John Hardison in Jefferson County, Florida in the early 1830s, the focus of this study becomes the generation of Hardisons who are believed to be his sons and daughters. There will be particular emphasis on Seth and his son John Randolph Hardison, the latter with his wives Winnifred Davis and Mary Northington being the author of a number of letters of 1857-1882 which will be included. While Seth's older brother, William L., and two sisters, Temperance and Winnifred, remained in Washington County, Georgia, Seth with sisters Nancy and Elizabeth and brother John M. moved first to Florida with John in the late 1820s and then, in less than ten years, returned to Georgia and established residence in Early County. Records of the elder John's wife, Winnifred, appear in both Florida and Georgia in the decade of the 1830s. The place of her final residence is not known, but she probably moved to Georgia with the other family members. Her name does not appear in the Federal Census records of 1840 of either Florida or Georgia. Seth and Nancy had married during the family's stay in Florida and, as will be noted, Elizabeth and John M. married soon after the move to Early County.

Inventory and appraisement of Jno M Hardison dec'd
amt bot up

1 Sorrel Mare 300 1 Saddle and bridle 400	7 00
1 Set of ~~~	8 8~
1 Bureau 50¢ 3 Chairs 2.00 1 Trunk 300	5 50
1 Table 300 1 Cradle 1.25 1 box 25	4 50
Gin cotton pr lb yellow at 6½ cts	
Blowing horn 12½ 3 head of Geese 2.25	2 37½
1 Holy Bible 3.50 1 Rifle Gun and Shot bag 20.00	23 50
8 Ducks and 1 pr Guinea fowls	1 25
1 Lot Corn merchantable at 75 cts pr bushel	
1 Lot Short Corn at 37½ cts pr bushel	
1 Lot fodder pr hundred pounds at 1.00	
1 Gourblings &c	1 10

We do certify upon oath that as far as has produced to us by the administrator the above and foregoing contains a true appraisement of the estate of John M Hardison deceased to the best of our Judgement and understanding this the 14th of September 1836.

Matthew Fain
Silas Lee
Jesse Tull
Needham McLendon
Elam F Lee

I do hereby certify that the above appraisers were sworn to perform their duty as such appraisers according to Law this 14th Sept 1836

John M Cogdell J.P.

Recorded Jany 5th 1837
Jno W Perry clk

Inventory of the Estate of John M. Hardison, Deceased, September 14, 1836
Early County, Georgia, Probate Records, Book A, pages 257-258

The area which the Hardisons chose for their new home was located in a recently created county in southwest Georgia. It shared aspects of their former places of residence, both northern Florida and central Georgia, each being a battleground between invading whites and native peoples and prime lands for the cultivation of cotton. Early County, as created by the Georgia Legislature in 1818, covered a huge area of 3,750 square miles in the southwest corner of Georgia, with its western boundary, the Chattahoochee River, separating it from Alabama. It was named for a recent governor, Peter Early. The gently undulating pine-clad lands within its bounds had long been the hunting and fishing grounds of the Apalachee and Creek Indians. They had been wrested from the Lower Creek Indians in the military campaigns of Andrew Jackson and most Creeks refused to view their cession in the Treaty of Fort Jackson of 1814 as valid. The Creeks continued to dispute the white man's claim throughout the next two decades and as the Hardisons arrived, they were preparing for a last stand. The land, particularly along the Chattahoochee River, was seen as prime cotton land, with the additional advantage of being close to a means of cheap transportation to market. The county was surveyed in 250 acre lots, except for partial lots along the river, and distributed in the Georgia Land Lottery of 1820. Eventually the original county was broken up to create seven additional counties and parts of four others, leaving Early with 524.32 square miles.[1]

The county was close to its present size by the time the Hardisons arrived. During the 1820s and 1830s settlers had poured into southwest Georgia from other southern states and from older areas of Georgia where they had worn out their lands or failed to fulfill their expectations. The area was a raw frontier, with few roads and towns. The village of Blakely became Early's county seat after the eastern portion of the original county was organized as Baker County in 1825. The most important settlement in the county was Fort Gaines, later in Clayton County after its creation in 1854, which represented the citizens' preparedness for further warfare with the Creeks. Joel W. Perry, an early settler and the county's first historian, wrote of the roughness of life in the first years of settlement:

Our Fathers Drank Booze and Fought
Upon public days, in 1828 and 1829, the writer has frequently seen a

considerable number of people come riding into town [Blakely], perhaps one-half of them with a woman behind them. When within a few hundred yards of town they would bring a whoop or two and come into town at a gallop and pass nearly across the square, wheel and gallop back in front of the little store, halt, and call for a half pint of whiskey (no selling by drinks in that day), and all take something to drink. By the middle of the afternoon the most of them would be quite happy, and after several couples stripped for a fight, many of them with a woman holding on to them to prevent it. There was very little damage ever done in such rows in those days. No knives or pistols were ever used.[2]

A decade later public drunkenness, along with "profamation of the Sabbath Day" and the selling of whiskey to the slave population were the subjects of a petition of grievance presented to the county's Superior Court in its August Term of 1838. The petition called for the civil magistrates to be more vigilant.[3]

Given later evidence of the Hardisons' active participation in the Baptist Church and the roles they played in the public life of the various communities in which they lived, it is likely that they were repelled by the rough life of their new home, while being drawn to the area by its economic opportunities. Fortunately for this study many incidents of their personal lives and their participation in the affairs of Early County are well documented in the county's archives, which have escaped the courthouse fires which have destroyed so many antebellum records. The listing of John M. Hardison among the jurors chosen for the Inferior Count for the January, 1834 term indicates both that he had attained the age of twenty-one and had lived in the county long enough to establish residence as a citizen of the state and the county.[4] On August 21 of that year, John M. married Mary Fain of Early County, member of a family which had previously lived in Gadsden County, Florida.[5] As will be noted, later records indicate that they had a daughter, Annabella, by 1836. Seth's presence in the county is verified by an entry in the Marks and Brands Book in which he and John M. registered their cattle brands in January, 1836.[6] At various times during his decade of residence in the county, Seth served as justice of the peace, member of a road commission, and tax collector.[7]

Deed and court records indicate that both John M. and Seth acquired land soon after their arrival in the county, as did Abner Jackson, who became the husband of their sister Elizabeth at some time in the early 1830s. John M. owned half of one the original 250 acre lots into which the lands of Early County were surveyed, Seth acquired at least 585 acres, and Abner at least 375 acres. John M.'s and Seth's lands were primarily in the area designated as the Fifth District, in the northwestern portion of the county bordering on the Chattahoochee River and including Fort Gaines, portions of which later became part of Clayton County.ABner's and other members of the Jackson family's were located in the Fourth District, the northeastern portion of the county. A discussion of the role which these acquisitions played in their lives, particularly those of Seth and the Jackson family, is placed at the end of the chapter.

The Hardison brothers and sisters shared the hopes of other migrating Americans that a new location would bring the financial success which the family had so far failed to realize. The year 1836 probably began with bright expectations as the families grew and settled into their new home, but the creation of this new homeland for white settlers had dislodged its native population and in July tragedy struck the Hardison family, as the rumblings of discontent among the Creeks erupted into warfare. The *Columbus* [Georgia] *Sentinel* issue of July 22, 1836 reported the following news:

> Died at his residence in Early County, on the 5th instant, Mr. John M. Hardison, aged 26 years. The deceased died of a wound received in the battle of Chickasawhatchy Swamp, in Baker County, on the 2d. He had been attached to the army throughout all the Indian disturbances. He was wounded after the Indians had been driven by a charge of bayonet from the camp.[8]

This battle was part of the last desperate effort of the Creek Indians along the Alabama-Georgia boundary to prevent the loss of their remaining lands and deportation to the western reservations. The warfare, which had gone on throughout the early months of 1836, consisted of battles between the Creeks and a force of combined federal troops and local militia units in the swamps of the tributary branches of the Chattahoochee River. The Creeks' destruction of the town of Roanoke in Stewart County, to the north of Early, had led to a final determined effort to drive them from southwest Georgia forever and to capture or destroy them before they could disappear into the swamps or flee into Florida. In late June, with a force of 500 men, Colonel Thomas Beall pursued them on the Georgia side of the Chattahoochee River south into Chickasawhatchy Swamp in Baker County, directly east of Early. On an island in the center of the swamp, the Indians had established a camp which was well supplied with stolen arms and food. The white soldiers had to wade several miles through mud and sometimes waist deep water to do battle with their elusive enemy. The Indians finally fled after a fierce but futile defense and John M. Hardison was among the wounded Georgians, dying a few days after the battle. The fallen red men and white alike were casualties of the relentless drive toward America's "Manifest Destiny," her growing determination to conquer and possess the lands from the Atlantic to the Pacific.[9] Remnants of the Creeks escaped to join the Seminoles in Florida and a few managed to hide in the swamps, but the majority were herded together in Alabama and sent on a long journey by boat and forced march to the reservations in Oklahoma. Some were chained to fellow prisoners as they were marched to the gathering point in Montgomery, Alabama, among them the proud and fierce Neamathla of Florida, who at age eighty-four had a leading role in the rebellion. According to an eye witness of his captivity, he appeared to be a brave and distinguished man and never uttered a complaint.[10] The name given to the last campaign to crush the Creek resistance is the "Creek War" of 1836, hardly a war when the opposing forces were so mismatched. The inaccuracy of the name is recognized by the fact that it is usually written with quotation marks.[11]

The task of settling John M. Hardison's affairs fell to Seth, who applied to the Early County Court of Ordinary to be the administrator of his estate in September 1836.[12] Matthew Fain, probably father or brother of John M.'s wife Mary Fain, was appointed guardian of "Anabella Hardison orphan of John M. Hardison" by the same court.[13] The term orphan seems to indicate that Annabella's mother was also dead, but this was not necessarily the case since the term was sometimes used when only the father was deceased. John M.'s early death dramatizes the fact that brief lives and widowhood and orphanhood were common facts of life on the American frontier.

An inventory of John M.'s personal property was made in September, 1836 and a subsequent document recorded the items sold, their prices, and their purchasers. These records were presented to the Clerk of the Court of Ordinary in January 1837.[14] A few months later Seth applied to the Court for permission to sell John M.'s real estate, consisting of the south half (125 acres) of lot number 57 in the Fifth District of Early County.[15] The catalog of John M.'s possessions provides an insight into the goods which a young frontier family might have owned. The inventory and the report of the sale of his goods indicate that his household furnishings consisted of "1 bed, bedstead, and furniture," valued at $35.00 and selling for $50.00; "sundry bed clothes," valued at $26.00, which are more specifically mentioned individually, in the list of articles sold, as a "counterpen," quilt, and "coverled;" a table and three chairs; cradle; spinning wheel and cards; trunk; bread tray; knives and forks; a spider; coffee mill; and miscellaneous pails, crockery, pots, pans, barrels, buckets, jugs, and bottles. Personal possessions were few—a saddle and bridle, pocket pistol, rifle and shot bag, a "blowing Horn," a bolt of calico, spectacles, and a Holy Bible (listed on the same line as the rifle). Agricultural equipment was similarly scanty, being the bare essentials for clearing land and cultivating it—a weeding hoe and a grubbing hoe, ploughs and accompanying equipment for mule or horse, axes, and an iron wedge. John M.'s agricultural pursuits are reflected in the inventory's listings of lots of sugar cane, corn, yellow cotton (long staple), and fodder, along with a potato patch and five bee stands. Livestock seems to have been more of an interest than cultivation of the land for, in addition to a bay mare and two colts, there are seven head of cattle and seventy head of hogs (the original inventory listed only twenty-two, while the record of sales included seventy). The sale of John M.'s possessions brought $521.84, with Seth purchasing a cow and calf, mare and colt, saddle and bridle, quilt, miscellaneous household items, fodder, corn, and potatoes for a total of $137.63.

Subsequent records of Seth's administration of John M.'s estate provide information on other members of the family. In listing disbursements from the proceeds of the sale of John M.'s possessions in a report of September 5, 1839, he noted payments to a number of creditors, including Winnifred (this is the first document in which the name is given this spelling) Hardison and Abner Jackson.[16] It is possible that Winnifred had moved from Jefferson County, Florida by this date, but her inclusion in this list does not make it certain.

John M. and Mary (Fain) Hardison's daughter Annabella continued under the guardianship of Matthew Fain in the 1830s and a report which he filed on January 7, 1839 showed that Seth owed her $380.87 from her father's estate.[17] Since the 1840 Federal Census does not list names of any member of a household except the head, it is difficult to know which family had custody of Annabella, but in the 1850 enumeration, she is listed by name, age 15, in the household of Charles and Julia Applewhite in Stewart County.[18] The Applewhites' relationship to her is not known, but it probably came through the Fain family.

For a little less than a decade after John M.'s death, the three Hardisons of his generation, Seth, Nancy, and Elizabeth, with their growing families continued to live in Early County. In the 1840 Federal Census enumeration the family of Seth and wife Mary Blandford, who had married in 1829, was as follows:[19]

2 males under 5 years (twin sons William and Clark)
2 males between 5 and 10 (sons Thomas and John)
1 male between 30 and 40 (Seth)
1 male between 40 and 50 (probably wife Mary's brother Champ)
1 male between 70 and 80 (identity not known)
1 male between 80 and 90 (probably Mary's father Clark)
1 female between 10 and 15 (daughter Nancy)
1 female between 15 and 20 (daughter Mary Ann)
1 female between 30 and 40 (wife Mary Blandford)

The names which Seth and Mary gave to their children reflect both families. Mary and Nancy were among the most popular girl's names of the period and probably honored members of both families. Later records pertaining to Clark indicate that his middle name began with "B," possibly indicating that he was named Clark Blandford for Mary's father. William, Thomas, and John were among the most popular names in the Hardison family of North Carolina. William's and Thomas' second names are not known. John's middle name, which appears in most later records pertaining to him, was Randolph. There is no evidence of a relationship between the Hardison and Randolph families, but it is most likely that John was named in honor of the brilliant and eccentric John Randolph of Virginia (1773-1833). Randolph's national and local popularity waxed and waned during his long service as a Congressman from Virginia. Throughout his political career he remained an ardent believer in states' rights and in a strict interpretation of the Constitution. A county in Georgia was named for him in 1807, partly because of his fight against the Yazoo land fraud, but the name was changed to Jasper County when his views, particularly his opposition to the War of 1812, became unpopular in Georgia. Again, in 1828, the state named a county in his honor, as his popularity revived with his support of President Andrew Jackson, who championed a policy of Indian removal from Georgia. Randolph further endeared himself to Georgians by speaking out against Jackson in the states' rights issues which grew out of the tariff controversy in the early 1830s. This was one of the last stands of Randolph, who died in 1833, and probably the one which led Seth to name his son in honor of the outspoken Virginian.[20]

Seth's large family grew soon after the 1840 enumeration when his eldest child, Mary Ann, married John Gray in 1842. John was possibly a member of the Gray family who were living in Jefferson County, Florida at the time the Hardisons were there. Seth officiated at the wedding in his capacity as a justice of the peace.[21]

Nancy Hardison and Emerald Brigham, who had married in Jefferson County, Florida in 1830, had a family, including children by his former marriage, which by 1840 consisted of one son under age 5 years and another between ages 10 and 15, a daughter under the age 5, two between the ages 5 and 10, and one between 15 and 20 years. By 1850 the Brighams were living in Randolph County, and listed their children as sons W. L., age 14, John, age 7, and Benjamin, age 7 and daughters M. A., age 11, and N. T., age 4.[22] The Randolph County marriage records of the 1840s include the names of several Brigham children, Seth, Elizabeth, and Wineford.

Elizabeth Hardison probably married after the family's move from Florida to Georgia, but a search of the records of both states has so far yielded no record of her marriage to Abner Jackson. Abner was the son of Clark Jackson of Early County, who had previously lived in Florida and in Wilkinson County, Georgia. According to Jackson family lore, Elizabeth and Abner met when he came to Florida with two of his brothers to participate in one of the military campaigns against the Seminoles. By the time of the 1840 Federal Census enumeration they had three children under the age of 5, one son and two daughters. The son was their eldest child, Theophilus Hardee Jackson, born in 1836 in Early County, and their other children, Winnifred, Sarah, Elizabeth Saphronia, and Mary Ann, were born in the years before Elizabeth's death in the late 1840s after Abner had moved the family to Gadsden County, Florida. In 1851 he married Sarah Holland, with whom he soon migrated to Catahoula Parish, Louisiana.[23]

In addition to the large gathering of Hardison kin in Early County there were also present at least two members of the Barfield (Barefield) family, James and Jesse, who were most likely in-laws of Seth through his first marriage. In his capacity as a justice of the peace, Seth officiated at the marriage of James to Sarah Conyers and Jesse to Mary Riley in 1842.[24] James later joined Seth's family in their move to Gadsden County, Florida and his kinship with the Hardisons is implied in a letter of November 30, 1857 written from Florida by Seth's daughter-in-law Winnifred (Davis) Hardison in which she mentioned "Uncle Barefield and Aunt Sallie."[25]

The lure which drew all of these families to Early County was the lands which had been wrested from the Creek Indians and the hope that they would yield bountiful crops of cotton. By the 1830s the economy of Georgia was based primarily on the cultivation of cotton and both yeoman farmers and planters borrowed heavily to acquire the land and the slaves necessary to produce a profitable crop. The acquisition of land was undoubtedly a primary concern of the Hardisons in making their move from Florida to Georgia and the Early County records include a number of entries concerning Seth's transactions. His slave holdings are a matter of question. The entries in the 1840 Federal Census for slaves is confusing, but the data on the household headed by Seth seems to indicate that it included six slaves. Seth may have acquired them or they may have come into the family through the Blandfords, his wife Mary's family. As will be seen in the

VII. A RETURN TO GEORGIA, 1835-1845 173

following chapter, Seth listed no slaves of his own in the Gadsden County tax records, but entered them in the name of Champ Blandford, presumed to be his brother-in-law, until they became Mary's property in the mid-1850s. Abner Jackson and Emerald Brigham appear to have owned no slaves at the time the 1840 Federal Census was taken.

It is difficult to find evidence of all the purchases of land by members of the family since the deed records of Early County are indexed by grantor (seller) only; however a search of these records and of the court records pertaining to the settlement of John M.'s affairs and to litigation involving Seth's and Abner Jackson's land made possible at least a partial reconstruction of their acquisitions. At the time of his death John M. owned 125 acres, the southern half of lot number 57 in the Fifth District. Records of Seth's earliest purchase have not been found, but possibly it was the 250 acres, lot number 51 in the Fifth District, which he sold in 1840 to John Davis for $1,500.00.[26] He acquired two additional parcels in 1838, the first being "the undivided half" of lot number 202 in the Fourth District which he purchased from the estate of William Phillips for $50.00, to be paid the following year.[27] The second consisted of 210 acres, part of lot number 92 in the Fifth District, which was purchased from Warren Sutton for $1,800.00.[28] As noted earlier, at the time of the Georgia Land Lottery of 1820 the land of Early County had been divided into lots of 250 acres, except partial lots along the Chattahoochee River, and the only cost to the lottery winners was a registration fee of $18.00. Its value as cotton land was reflected in the price it brought at a later date. Partial evidence of Abner Jackson's lands is found in records pertaining to sales to other members of the Jackson family, Ira and Clark, of lot number 403 for $450.00 and half of lot number 400 for $400.00, both in the Fourth District, in 1837 and 1839.[29]

Land in newly opened areas like Early County might be easily acquired because of the large acreages available and the easy credit offered by lenders, but forces leading to financial calamity were building in the 1830s—in Early County, in Georgia, and throughout the nation. The Hardisons and thousands of their fellow citizens found themselves mired in debt and litigation as the national crisis known as the Panic of 1837 spread into the economy of their area. The Panic's roots, though complex, lay immediately in the nation's land boom and the fiscal policies of President Andrew Jackson. As vast numbers of Americans moved westward into newly acquired lands, there was widespread speculation in land. Individual settlers and speculators borrowed heavily to purchase land, entrepreneurs borrowed to finance manufacturing and transportation ventures, and state and local governments incurred debts to build roads and canals. The banks which financed these investments were primarily state chartered banks, many of which were undercapitalized and engaged in a variety of unsound practices. They had thrived in the financial climate created by Jackson's destruction of the national banking institution, the Bank of the United States. Jackson's hostility to the Bank's conservative fiscal practices led him to withdraw federal funds and to place them in selected state banks. While these state institutions were generally reasonably sound, the death of the national bank and the dispersal of its funds led to the chartering of numerous local banks and a proliferation of easy credit. Between 1829 and 1837 the number of banks increased from 329 to 788, while the total capitalization increased only from $110,000,000 to $290,000,000. Jackson became alarmed over the excesses in borrowing and land speculation and in 1836 he issued the Specie Circular, which ordered the land offices in the federal territories to accept nothing but gold and silver currency. The nation's financial "house of cards" began to collapse and Jackson's presidential successor, Martin Van Buren, fell heir to the Panic of 1837, whose effects lasted well into the 1840s.[30]

Apparently Seth was not sufficiently alarmed by the first manifestations of the Panic to prevent his 1838 purchases on credit of the 210 acre plot from Warren Sutton and the half of lot number 202 from the William Phillips estate, but soon he and his in-laws the Jacksons were mired in debt and litigation for lands and goods bought on credit. Their plight was exacerbated by a drop in the price of cotton from twenty cents to ten cents a pound. In describing the ongoing effects of the financial crisis in their area, Early County historian Joel W. Perry wrote, "During the years 1836, 1837, 1838, and 1839, the Central Bank of Georgia commenced suit against many of the citizens of this county. Every note had two or three indorsers, which of course, involved many parties, a large majority of which lived about

Fort Gaines, which was then the business center of the county."[31]

By 1840 Seth was making the previously mentioned sale of 250 acres to John Davis and mortaging his 1838 acquisition of 210 acres from Warren Sutton. Records pertaining to the Sutton purchase illustrate Perry's statement about the multiple parties involved in many of the land negotiations. The deed from Sutton stated the purchase price as $1,800.00, but did not specify the terms of purchase. Probably the land was to be paid for in three $600.00 installments, due in January of each year following the purchase, for a deed of August 1840 between Seth and Henry Cravy of Baker County, which was in effect a mortgage on the land, refers to payments of this amount due on January 1 of 1840 and 1841. Apparently Cravy had served as security for Seth in his debt to Sutton and as Seth was having difficulty in meeting his obligation he mortgaged the land to Cravy for $1,200.00. The mortgage was to be void "if the said Seth Hardison shall pay off & satisfy to him the said Warren Sutton or bearer of said notes the principal & interest due on said two promissory notes when due or keep harmless the said Henry Cravy from the payment of the same."[32] Probably in an effort to meet his obligations to Sutton and Cravy, Seth sold his 250 acre tract, lot number 51 in the Fifth District, to John Davis for $1,500.00 in January, 1840, but undoubtedly this transaction also involved credit and possibly default in payments to Seth.[33] Whatever the circumstances, Seth was unable to meet his obligations to Sutton and Cravy. Superior Court records of 1841-1843 of litigation between Seth and Sutton and Seth and Cravy indicate that he defaulted in his payments to Sutton, that Cravy was compelled to sell some of his own property to pay a portion of the debt, and that Seth failed to meet the court's order to pay the principal and interest and court costs. The court then issued a "Rule Absolute for foreclosure of Mortgage on real estate," barring equity of redemption.[34] With the loss of the land he had attempted to purchase from Sutton and the sale of lot number 51 to John Davis, Seth may well have been left landless in Early County. No deed records for his disposal of the land he purchased from the William Phillips estate in 1838 were found and possibly this purchase was not finalized since it too involved a payment in 1839.[35]

In addition to his woes over indebtedness for land, Seth was plagued by debts incurred for goods, probably household supplies and farming equipment. In these debts he was involved with the Jackson family who, like Seth, were selling portions of their lands.[36] The affairs of Seth and brother-in-law Abner Jackson were intertwined, with Seth serving as security for Abner in several loans. Both were involved in a series of law suits of 1838-1847 brought by creditors for what seem small sums today, $34.50 to $210.00, but were significant debts in terms of the contemporary value of the dollar and the shortage of gold and silver currency.[37]

These misfortunes undoubtedly raised doubts among members of the Hardison and Jackson families about their future in Early county and created friction between the families. Court documents in a lawsuit involving Abner Jackson's father, Clark, and another Early County resident, Stephen Blocker, contain evidence of the personal consequences of the hard times of the 1830s and 1840s. In December of 1842, Blocker petitioned the Superior Court to take testimony from Seth as a material witness in support of his case against Jackson, saying that Seth "was about removing beyond the jurisdiction of this state." Blocker maintained that Seth would testify that he had heard Jackson say that unless he could borrow the money to pay an old indebtedness to Blocker he would lose his claim to the land they were disputing. The court ordered that testimony be taken from Seth "at his own place of abode" on December 10.[38] In April of 1843 the court handed down a decision calling for Jackson to pay Blocker $70.93 with interest from January 1, 1840 and to give up monetary claims he held against Blocker. Blocker was in turn ordered to make title to Jackson for the land in dispute, the southwest half of lot number 387 in the Fourth District, and to pay costs of the suit.[39]

Tempers were soured and hopes were dashed by the fall-out from the Panic of 1837 and, given the Hardisons' penchant for fresh starts on greener acres, it is not surprising that Seth and sisters Elizabeth and Nancy looked elsewhere for a prosperous future. Seth, was indeed "about removing beyond the jurisdiction" of both Early County and Georgia and by the mid-1840s he, with wife Mary and all of their children, was in Florida, living just to the south of the Georgia border in Gadsden County. They were joined there by the family of Elizabeth and Abner Jackson and James Barfield and his family. Nancy and her husband Emerald Brigham settled for a few years in Randolph County, to the north of Early County in Georgia, before moving briefly to Alabama and then to Texas in the 1850s.

NOTES

The account of the Hardisons' decade in Early County is based primarily on the official records of the county. Originals of the deed, will, and marriage records and Court of the Ordinary Minute Book A, 1820-1849, were searched in a visit to the courthouse in Blakely in 1991. I am indebted to Mrs. Alma Walker Jackson for her research in the county's probate and court records as they have been filmed by the Church of the Latter Day Saints' Genealogical Society of Salt Lake City, Utah. The films will be referred to by their designation as L.D.S. film with appropriate number.

1. Mary Grist Whitehead, editor, *Collections of Early County Historical Society*, 1979, (Blakely: Early County Historical Society, 1980), vol.2, pp.1-4.
2. Robert P. Dews, author-editor, *Early Joel* (Chicago: Adams Press, 1976), pp.134-35.
3. Early County Superior Court Records, 1820-1839, Minutes of August Term, 1838, L.D.S. film #164080, pages not numbered.
4. Early County Inferior Court Records, Minute Book B, 1821-1851, L.D.S. film #164118.
5. Early County Marriage Book 2, 1834-1853, p.6.
6. Early County Marks and Brands Book, p.34.
7. Early County Marriage Book 2, pp.6, 64, 66, and 67 (Seth as justice of the peace); Inferior Court Minute Book B, p.125, L.D.S. film #164118 (Seth as a member of a commission to investigate the building of a new road); and Superior Court Records, 1820-1839, Minutes of August Term, 1838, L.D.S. film #164080 (Seth as tax collector in 1836).
8. *Columbus Sentinel*, Columbus, Georgia, July 22, 1836; George White. *Historical Collections of Georgia* (New York: Pudney and Russell, 1854, as reprinted by Heritage Press, Danielsville, 1968), pp.262-64, a report on the Battle of Chickasawhachee including a quotation from an article in the *Columbus Sentinel* mentioning the death of John Hardison.
9. Mark E. Fretwell, *This So Remote Frontier: the Chattahoochee Country of Alabama and Georgia* (Tallahassee: Historic Chattahoochee Commission, 1980), pp.243-44.
10. Clifton Paisley, *The Red Hills of Florida*, 1528-1865, pp.80-1.
11. Fretwell, *op.cit.*, p.245.
12. Early County Court of Ordinary Minute Book A, 1820-1849, p.117.
13. *Ibid.*, p.117; Miles Kenan Womack, Jr., *Gadsden, a Florida County in Word and Picture* (Quincy: Gadsden County Bicentennial Committee, 1976), pp.293 and 295, Matthew and Thomas Fain among the early settlers in Gadsden County, Florida in the 1820s, before their move to Early County.
14. Early County Probate Records, Book A, pp.257-60, L.D.S. film #164098.
15. Early County Court of Ordinary Minute Book A, pp.122-3, 167.
16. Early County Probate Records, Book A, p.312, L.D.S. film #164098.
17. *Ibid.*, p.311.
18. Seventh Federal Census, 1850, Georgia, Stewart County, p.64; Sara Robertson Dixon, *History of Stewart* County (Waycross: A. H. Clark), vol.2, p.137, in abstracts from Bond Book B of Stewart County, Charles Applewhite is listed as guardian for

Christopher and John T. P. Fain, orphans of Reuben Fain, with a bond of $2,400.00.
19. Sixth Federal Census, 1840, Georgia, Early County, p.127; Seventh Federal Census, 1850, Florida, Gadsden County, p.196 (mss.pp.376-77), lists the Hardison children's names and ages and provides the basis for establishing their identity in the previous census; see Chapter 6 on the Hardisons in Jefferson County, Florida for information on Champ and Clark Blandford, presumed to be the brother and father of Seth's wife Mary.
20. James C. Bonner, *Atlas for Georgia History*, p.4.
21. Early County Marriage Book 2, p.66.
22. Sixth Federal Census, 1840, Georgia, Early County, p.127; Seventh Federal Census, 1850, Georgia, Randolph County, p.397.
23. Sixth Federal Census, 1840, Georgia, Early County, p.125; Seventh Federal Census, 1850, Florida, Gadsden County, p.219 (mss.p.422); information in the death certificate of Theophilus Hardee Jackson (1836-1917), Florida State Board of Health, Bureau of Vital Statistics, establishes the identity of Elizabeth Hardison as the wife of Abner Jackson and their identity as the parents of Theophilus, their eldest child, who was born on Oct. 28, 1836 in Early County; Alma Walker Jackson Genealogical Collection, information on second marriage and family of Abner.
24. Early County Marriage Book 2, p.64 (James) and p.67 (Jesse).
25. Cain Family Genealogical Collection, letter of Winnifred (Davis) Hardison, Nov. 30, 1857, to her brother Edwin Davis.
26. Early County Deed Book E, pp.540-41.
27. Early County Probate Records, Book A, p.[311?], L.D.S. film #164098, statement of Mary C. Phillips concerning the estate of William Phillips, deceased, April 3, 1838, recorded Jan. 31, 1839.
28. Early County Deed Book E, p.134.
29. *Ibid.*, pp.406-7.
30. Ralph Volney Harlow, *The United States: from Wilderness to World Power* (New York: Henry Holt and Company, 1949), pp.260-61.
31. Dews, *op. cit.*, p.132.
32. Early County Deed Book E, p.569 (Cravy); p.134 (original deed from Sutton).
33. See footnote #26.
34. Early County Superior Court Records, 1839-47, entries for August, 1842 Adjourned Term and February 1843 Term, L.D.S. film #164083.
35. See footnote #27.
36. Early County Deed Book E, pp.406-7 and 437-38.
37. Early County Superior Court Records, 1831-1841, L.D.S. film #164081, and 1839-1847, L.D.S. film #164083.
38. *Ibid.*, L.D.S. film #164083, entries of Dec., 1842 in minutes of August Adjourned Term of 1842.
39. *Ibid.*, entry of April 28, 1843.

VIII

Back to Florida
Gadsden County, 1845-1857

𝒲ithin little more than ten years after the Hardisons left Florida for their decade in Early County, they were settling into new homes in Gadsden County, one of the five northern "Red Hills" counties which were Florida's cotton belt.[1] Their first stay in Florida had begun in Jefferson, another of these counties, in the late 1820s, only a few years after Spain had transferred possession of Florida to the United States in 1821. Their return took place just as the transition from territorial status to statehood occurred in 1845. During Florida's two and a half decades as a territory, the unique terrain of the "Red Hills" counties, Jackson, Gadsden, Leon, Jefferson, and Madison, with its fertile, rolling lands, so different from the sandy, flat lands to the east and the west, had attracted thousands of settlers from Georgia, the Carolinas, Maryland, and Virginia. Whether yeoman farmer or planter they shared common goals, for as historian James C. Bonner pointed out in his study of agriculture in ante-bellum Georgia, "Man seldom changes his place of abode except in the hope of improving his economic welfare."[2] As agricultural prosperity recovered from the disastrous times following the Panic of 1837, the lure of the successful cultivation of cotton, and also tobacco, drew the

State of Georgia,
WASHINGTON COUNTY.

TO ANY MINISTER OF THE GOSPEL, JUDGE, JUSTICE OF THE INFERIOR COURT, OR JUSTICE OF THE PEACE:

You are hereby authorized to join *John R. Hardison* and *Winifred C. Davis* in the Holy State of Matrimony, according to the CONSTITUTION AND LAWS, of this State: and for so doing this shall be your sufficient LICENSE.

Given under my Hand and Seal, This 25th day of November 1857

Haywood Brookins ORDINARY.

Georgia, *Washington* County.

I do certify, that *John R. Hardison* and *Winifred C. Davis* were duly joined in Matrimony by me, the 26th day of November 1857

Recorded this

L. J. Myrick, a Gospel Minister

Marriage License of Winnifred Cornelia Davis
and John Randolph Hardison, 1857

Washington County, Georgia, Marriage Record Book B, page 304

Hardisons, the Jacksons, and the Barfields to Gadsden County.

Gadsden County, situated between the Apalachicola and the Ocklockonee rivers, just below the Georgia border, was about fifty miles south of Early County. It had been created from the eastern portion of Jackson County in 1823. The county's name reflected its early nineteenth century role in Andrew Jackson's Indian campaigns. The man whom it honored was Lt. James Gadsden, Jackson's aide-de-camp and engineer. During Jackson's 1818 campaign, Gadsden had been responsible for building a fort on the east side of the Apalachicola River on the site of Prospect Bluff, a trading post which had played a significant part in the struggles for empire in Florida. One of the trading companies of the Spanish era, Forbes and Company, had been granted 1,500,000 acres of land by Spain as recompense for losses in the Indian hostilities in the area. The so-called Forbes Purchase covered portions of several present-day Florida counties, including the southern one-third of Gadsden County. This area and much of the western portion of the county lay outside the "Red Hills" section and were generally of poor quality for agriculture. The majority of the settlers, including the Hardisons, chose the eastern side in the vicinity of the Ocklockonee River and its tributary, the Little River. The heaviest settlement was around the village of Quincy, the county seat, where there were stores, churches, and several schools, including the outstanding Quincy Academy, by the time the Hardisons arrived.

Gadsden's settlers experimented with sugar cane, rice, cotton, and tobacco, finding the latter two most profitable as money crops. The plantation system with its large holdings of land and slaves became well established in the county's first two decades, but as elsewhere in the South the majority of settlers, like the Hardisons, had small acreages and few or no slaves. Gadsden became one of Florida's major cotton producing counties along with the other four "Red Hills" counties, which produced 40,952 of the 45,131 bales of cotton grown in Florida in 1850. In that year Gadsden produced 5,609 bales, which at 400 pounds to the bale and ten cents to the pound were worth $224,360.00. Tobacco was the second most valuable crop for the county, with its total market value in 1850 about one-half that of the cotton crop.[3] Cotton cultivation was dominated by the big planters, with the thirty-seven planters who produced fifty or more bales being responsible for sixty-one per cent of the Gadsden crop of 1850. However, these planters were less dominant in tobacco production and tobacco was a significant money crop for a number of the smaller farmers in the 1840s and 1850s. Clifton Paisley has noted in his study of the "Red Hills" counties the importance of tobacco in the county's economy, quoting one of its outstanding citizens:

> After the Civil War, Judge C. H. DuPont, who did not grow one leaf of tobacco on his Mt. Pleasant plantation in 1850, credited the "cash surplus" from tobacco with having elevated the income primarily of small planters and farmers and "the moral and intellectual status" of the people of Gadsden County. There may have been some truth in this assertion for the agricultural census shows that 324 of the 482 farms in Gadsden County grew some tobacco in 1850, while 259 grew some cotton, and the smaller farms grew at least half of the tobacco.[4]

This thriving county, located in the southernmost extension of the ante-bellum Cotton Kingdom was the Hardisons' last home before their migration to Texas on the eve of the Civil War. Gadsden's tax and deed records provide evidence of a considerable degree of prosperity for the family as compared with their former years in Jefferson and Early counties. Seth's land holdings increased from 260 acres in 1845 to 500 acres in 1855 and he possessed a "pleasure carriage" and considerable household furnishings. The family lived in the eastern area of the county in the vicinity of the village of China Hill, about ten miles east of the town of Quincy. They were probably part of that group of farmers whom Clifton Paisley described as growing some cotton and some tobacco, which yielded sufficient cash surplus to allow for more comfortable living than in their frontier years and for the education of their children.

The county was fortunate in having attracted a number of families, particularly the Yonge family, who were interested in establishing schools. In an analysis based on Federal Census records, county historian Miles Kenan Womack, Jr. has pointed out that there were eight academies and grammar schools (probably most were private schools) with 336 students in Gadsden County in 1840 and that by 1850 there were six public schools with six teachers and 300 pupils and three academies with nine teachers and 180 pupils. The most outstanding of the schools was the Quincy Academy, which was organized by the local Masonic Lodge and chartered by the Florida Legislature in the early 1830s. By the 1840s the Academy included a female department.[5] The opportunities offered by these institutions were in dramatic contrast to the shortage of educational facilities in Early County, whose historian Joel W. Perry, a contemporary of the Hardisons, stated that in the years of their residence there was no public education and the few private academies which were chartered encountered financial difficulties and the problem of attracting teachers. Perry wrote that a female "college" was envisioned in the 1830s and a building begun at Fort Gaines, but that the school had a brief life and "stood many years the abode for owls and bats."[6] It is not surprising that Seth's eldest daughter, Mary Ann, signed the Gadsden County deeds which bear her name with an "X," as did Seth's wife Mary Blandford. Women's education received little attention from families or public authorities in Georgia in the early decades of the nineteenth century. Obviously Seth and Mary were ambitious for their sons, for the Federal Census of 1850 records that all four attended school in that year and other records indicate that they were trained for professions while living in Florida. William and Thomas qualified as physicians by attending medical school in Savannah, John became a lawyer, and Clark a bookkeeper.[7] Their cousin Theophilus Hardee Jackson also received a medical education in Savannah. It is possible that they had first attended the Quincy Academy, which enrolled both local and boarding students and offered an ambitious curriculum, including the basics in reading, writing, arithmetic, history, and geography plus "the highest branches of an English education, embracing Natural and Moral Philosophy, Rhetoric, Botany, Chemistry, Geology, Mineralogy, Bookkeeping, etc."[8] Education for the professions was not nearly as rigorous as it is today and at most involved a few years of study after the completion of what is now known as high school.

In addition to the opportunities which the town of Quincy offered to the Hardisons, their proximity to Tallahassee in adjoining Leon County was also a factor in their lives. Although little more than a village, it was the social and political capital of Florida, with a group of about a hundred planter families furnishing the leadership.[9] A number of these families built fine homes and entertained lavishly. Included in their parties during Florida's years as a territory was Achille Murat, a nephew of Napoleon, who owned a plantation in Jefferson County. It is possible that John Randolph Hardison received his professional education in Tallahassee by "reading law" with one of its lawyers. Family lore includes the statement that he was admitted to the bar in Tallahassee and a story that, while in the Confederate Army, he was entertained at the Governor's Mansion by a daughter of the governor.

By the time the 1850 census was taken, both of Seth's daughters were married, leaving a family consisting of Seth and wife Mary and their four sons. As noted, the Federal Census of this year was the first to list the names of all members of the household and to give their age and place of birth. In this enumeration Seth's and Mary's ages were listed as 46 and 50, both born in Georgia. Their four sons were Thomas, age 18 and born in Florida, John, age 16 and born in Georgia, and twins Clarke (usually spelled Clark) and William, age 14 and born in Georgia. Seth and the two elder sons were listed as farmers. Also in the household was Champ Blandford, assumed to be Mary's brother, age 55, born in Georgia, and stated to be "insane."[10] As noted earlier, an adult male had been listed in both the 1830 and 1840 enumerations as a part of Mary and Seth's family; the 1850 enumeration provides his name. He was obviously mentally incompetent and was a ward of the family. The two elderly men included in Seth's household in the Early County enumeration of 1840 were not listed in 1850. Possibly the elder of the two, whose age was between 80 and 90, was Mary's father, Clark Blandford Sr., who had probably died since 1840.[11]

Mary Ann Hardison is listed in the household of husband John Gray (spelled Grey), whom she had married in 1842 in Early County. Their ages were 26 and 35 and both were born in Georgia. Their children were David, age 5 and born in Georgia; John, age 3, born in Florida; and Mary, age 1, born in Florida. John Gray's profession was listed as farmer.[12] By the time of the 1850 enumeration, Mary Ann's sister Nancy was married to Dr. James Harvey Reeves and living in Gadsden County. Their marriage is not recorded in the archives of either Early or Gadsden County, but probably took place in the latter, most of whose records were destroyed in a courthouse fire of 1849. Book A of Gadsden's marriage records dates from that year. Nancy's age in the census records for 1850 was 21 and her birthplace Florida, while Dr. Reeves' (spelled Rives) age and birthplace were listed as 38 and Georgia. They had one child, Mary, age 1 and born in Florida.[13] The Gadsden County archives include records of several Reeves families, all probably related. Seth, acting as justice of the peace, performed the wedding ceremony for John W. Reeves in 1852.[14]

Other members of the Early County contingent in Gadsden were the Barfields and the Jacksons. James and Sarah Conyers Barfield, at whose wedding Seth had officiated in Early in 1842, were listed in the 1850 census enumeration aged 38 and 37, both born in North Carolina. Their household included four girls, Catherine, Nancy, Rachel, and Sarah between the ages 19 and 10, who were probably their nieces, and three boys, James, John, and Thomas, ages 4, 2, and 1.[15] By the time the 1850 enumeration was made, Seth's sister Elizabeth (Hardison) Jackson was deceased and her husband Abner, aged 34 and born in Georgia, was living in Gadsden County with their children, Theophilus, 13 years old; Winnifred, age 11; Sarah, age 8; Sephronia, age 6; and Mary Ann, age 5. All the children were born in Georgia. Abner's profession was listed as blacksmith.[16]

Not only did the Federal Census of 1850 initiate the gathering of more complete information on the make-up of the nation's citizenry, it also called for a separate listing of the slaves held by each owner. This enumeration, repeated in 1860, has been referred to as a Slave Census, although in most cases the slaves' names are missing, with only the owner's name and the number of slaves of each sex and their ages recorded. These records, made at a time when the slavery issue was becoming increasingly divisive, represent an effort at an official count of the enslaved men, women, and children who made up half and sometimes more of the population of the cotton and rice producing areas of the South. As has been noted in the previous chapters, the Hardison families of North Carolina, Georgia, and Florida owned few or no slaves. None were listed for Seth or his father John in the 1830 Federal Census enumeration, but the 1840 census records for Early County, Georgia may be interpreted to indicate that Seth had six in that year. Possibly these were slaves belonging to Champ Blandford, for in the Gadsden County tax records of the 1840s and early 1850s Seth entered slaves in Champ's name but not in his own. However in the Federal Slave Census of 1850 he declared eleven in his own name—six females aged 55, 30, 27, 22, 19, and 3, and five males, aged 25, 8, 5, 2, and 1.[17] He continued entering the slaves in the Gadsden County tax records under Champ's name until the data indicate that Champ was deceased by the mid-1850s. Undoubtedly he had access to their labor throughout the years in Gadsden County.[18]

The land on which Seth and his family settled lay in the eastern portion of the county, which as noted was considered the county's best for agriculture. Evidence of a portion of the family's holdings is found in the Gadsden County deeds and tax records and the Florida Land Office records. An extensive search was made for data concerning Seth's lands in all three sources, but was unsuccessful in locating the original deeds for their acquisition, except the Florida Land Office purchase, probably due to the loss of the courthouse archives in the fire of 1849. Partial compensation for this loss was made by the presence in the county's archives of several deeds covering the transfer by Seth of 250 acres of his holdings, along with ten slaves, to his son John Randolph in 1857, a deed of the same year in which Mary Ann and John Gray transferred to John land which Seth had given them, and deeds growing out of sheriff's sales of these lands in 1858 and 1859. The descriptions in these deeds provide a key to the location of at least half of the 500 acres which Seth declared in his tax returns at the end of his stay in Florida.[19]

Seth's gradual accumulation of land is documented in his tax returns during the twelve years of his residence in Gadsden County. According to the records for 1845 and 1846, he first acquired 130 acres of second rate and 130 acres of third rate land. During the next three years, he declared 210 acres—105 acres each of second and third rate land. By 1851 his acreage had increased to 320 acres of third rate, having been augmented by the purchase in January, 1851 of land from the Florida Land Office.[20] In 1854 his holdings reached 500 acres, classified as second rate and the following year as third rate. Just as in Georgia, the value of the land was determined by whether it had a preponderance of hardwood trees, thought to be the best land for farming, or pines, which grew primarily in sandy soil. During the 1845-1855 period the land was taxed at eleven mills per acre for first rate, eight and a fourth for second, and four and an eighth for third. In 1856 the tax system was altered and, in place of a tax per acre, a dollar value was placed on each holding, with a tax of sixteen and a half cents per hundred dollars of value. In 1856 Seth's land was valued at $600.00 and in 1857, after he had begun to dispose of it in preparation for his move to Texas, $440.00. These figures indicate that in ten years of residence in Gadsden County, he had almost doubled his holdings of land—from 260 to 500 acres.

In addition to providing a record of Seth's land holdings, the tax records include information on his family's other possessions and give some indication of their standard of living. New categories of taxable property, which indicate the growing affluence of the area, were added by the county from year to year. By 1855 they included such items as pleasure carriages—as contrasted to farm vehicles, gold and silver watches, and billiard tables. In several returns Seth paid tax on a vehicle in the pleasure carriage category and in 1856 he valued his household furnishings at $500.00 and his livestock at the same amount. Data concerning the payment of a poll tax by male residents helps to determine age, for the tax was assessed only for males aged 21 through 50. Seth paid the tax until 1854, while his eldest son, Thomas, first paid in 1855 and next eldest, John Randolph, in 1857 (Federal Census records indicate that his birth year was either 1834 or 1835).

A significant source of the county's revenue was a tax on slaves. Throughout the years 1845-1854, Seth did not declare any slaves, but each year he made a return for "C. Blanford," whose number of slaves increased, probably by birth, from eight to twelve. In 1855 Mary Hardison appeared in the tax rolls for the first time, declaring twelve slaves. The obvious conclusion is that her brother Champ had died in 1854 or 1855 and the slaves had become her property. In the 1856 returns, "Seth Hardison trustee" declared the slaves, whose worth was given as $6,000.00. This sum makes an interesting comparison with the $600.00 value placed on his 500 acres of land. The tax rate in that year was sixteen and a half cents per $100.00 of value for both land and slaves. As noted earlier in Seth's listing of Champ's slaves in the

1850 Federal Slave Census, the majority were women and children, with only one adult male. In the late 1850s an able-bodied male "field hand" sold for $1,000.00 or more dollars. A comparison of these values highlights the cheapness of land, based on its ongoing availability, and the contrasting investment represented by enslaved human labor. The economic calamity which abolition represented to the slave holder is obvious. The Hardisons and thousands of other Southern farmers and planters were soon to experience that calamity.

The tax records shed light on the circumstances of the extended family of the Hardisons as well as on Seth's immediate family. His son-in-law John Gray declared one slave and no land in 1845 and 1846, but in the latter year Seth gave 62 acres to John and Mary Ann and this land and the one slave were declared in 1847, along with an entry of $165.00 under the heading "money loaned at interest." John's acreage varied over the years of his residence in Gadsden County in the late 1840s and early 1850s, but the highest was 182 acres and he never declared more than one slave. This slave was valued at $1,000.00 in 1856. John was typical of the Southern yeoman farmer, with his small holdings in both land and slaves. Seth's other son-in-law, Dr. James H. Reeves, was first listed in the Gadsden County tax rolls in 1848. Throughout the 1848-1856 period in which he was included, his major income was derived from the practice of medicine, ranging from $300.00 to $2,000.00. His land holdings were small, at most 60 acres, and in only one year did he declare any slaves—two in 1852. In listing his personal possessions, a vehicle in the pleasure carriage category, probably his means of transportation in making his house calls, and a silver watch are most frequently mentioned. The Texas records of Dr. Reeves indicate that he was a lay minister in the Baptist Church, later serving in several Texas churches. The highest value on household furnishings set by either the Grays or Reeves was $150.00.

Dr. Reeves' profession was one chosen by an unusual number of the young men among the sons of Seth and his sisters. Those known to have studied medicine include Seth's sons Thomas and William, Elizabeth (Hardison) and Abner Jackson's son Theophilus Hardee Jackson, and Winnifred (Hardison) and Joel Davis' sons Enos A., Charles I., and James P.[21] The last three, who were natives of Washington County, Georgia, attended medical school in Atlanta, while the Florida cousins studied in Savannah. A possible influence on the young men in Gadsden County may have been Malcolm Nicholson, who is identified as the "father of medicine in Florida" on a marker in the Nicholson-Freeman Cemetery near the village of China Hill. A letter of 1857 written by Theophilus to his father Abner Jackson while he was completing his studies at Oglethorpe Medical College is evidence of the ambitions and also of the financial sacrifices of the families:[22]

Savannah, Georgia
February 17, 1857

Dear Pa,

It is now Wednesday night bedtime. The whole world seems to be locked into a death-like quietness. It is indeed a true picture of the hour for sleep, with nothing save the occasional howl of a watchdog or the heavy tread of the policeman's horse to indicate the existence of life, yet I do not feel disposed to sleep. My thoughts were never more wakeful than now. They lead me homewards and to future life. What success I will have, time only can tell, but it is a subject that I spend many serious thoughts upon. I am anxious to know what will be my fate. But of this I will say no more at present. The time for me to leave Savannah is growing short and you will want to know what I expect to do. I think now that I will stay here till the end of the course, which will be two weeks from today. And as to money, Pa, I believe that I have told you all that is necessary. I told you what I was due the faculty and then $25 to carry me home and other little matters for books. It will have to be governed by the quantity received. Send me what money you can without too great a sacrifice and, if that won't pay me through, I can take out as many tickets as I pay for and let the balance remain till I get the money.

T. H. Jackson

Probably the fate which Theophilus was contemplating in 1857 did not include any forebodings of the civil strife which in just four years would engulf his homeland and bring to an end the South's way of life. In that year his Hardison cousins were preparing for their migration from Florida to Texas and Seth's two older sons were married. Thomas' bride is identified in family records as Mrs. Ann Walker, a widow from Alabama who was several years his senior, and John Randolph married his first cousin, Winnifred Cornelia Davis of Washington County, Georgia. Winnifred was the daughter of Temperance (Hardison) and Enos Davis, who were parents of at least nine children.[23] She had been orphaned when both Temperance and Enos died in the late 1840s, possibly of typhoid fever which led to the deaths of three of their sons in young adulthood, James, Benjamin, and John. Enos did not leave a will and Washington County documents of 1848-1851 record the settlement of his estate.[24] His brother Joel was made administrator and their nephew Owen C. Pope (son of their sister Selah) was appointed guardian to Enos' four minor children, Winnifred Cornelia, Sarah Ann, Joel A., and Edwin T. In 1851 Thomas W. Hardwick, the husband of the eldest daughter, Mary Elizabeth, was appointed guardian of Winnifred and Sarah, while Thomas L. Davis, Enos' eldest living son, became Edwin's guardian and administrator for his now deceased brother Joel. Enos' sixteen slaves were probably the most valuable inheritance of his children, being valued at $7,000.00, and in 1849 the slaves were divided among them, with Winnifred receiving two males, Harry and Leroy, valued at $700.00 and $300.00.

In the years after their parents' deaths, Winnifred and her younger sister Sarah and brothers Joel and Edwin lived with various members of their family in Georgia. On November 26, 1857, Winnifred married John Randolph Hardison at the home of her brother Thomas L. Davis in Washington County.[25] As will be seen from Winnifred's letter of November 30, 1857, with which this chapter closes, the couple journeyed to John's home in Gadsden County immediately after the wedding and prepared to emigrate to Texas with his family.

Preparations for a Move to Texas

Like the younger generation of his family, the ever-optimistic Seth apparently had no thought of an end to the Cotton Kingdom, but only of its perpetuation in a new Eden where land was cheap, plentiful, and fertile. The Hardisons were rather late among their contemporaries in succumbing to "Texas fever," possibly because of their relative prosperity in Florida, but by the end of the 1850s they were fully infected. In 1857 as the family prepared to migrate from Florida to

Texas, both Seth and son-in-law John Gray transferred portions of their property to Seth's son John Randolph. In a series of four deeds drawn up in Gadsden County on January 10, 1857, John Gray and wife Mary Ann transferred land and Seth Hardison and wife Mary transferred both land and slaves to John Randolph.[26] The Grays sold two tracts totaling 62 acres for $150.00, the deed noting that this land had previously been conveyed to them by Seth in a deed dated November 14, 1846. Two deeds from Seth and Mary to John Randolph covered the sale of one tract of 42 acres for $55.00 and three others totaling 208 acres for $500.00. A hint of complications to come lay in the proviso, in the deed transferring Seth's three tracts, that the title was clear "excepting the claims of the Union Bank of Florida." This bank had been founded by a group of planters in the "Red Hills" counties and was the center of much controversy after it failed in the wake of the Panic of 1837.[27]

In addition to the land transfers of January, 1857, Seth and Mary sold ten slaves, three adults and seven children, to John Randolph for $5,000.00. As noted earlier, the Hardisons had recently inherited the twelve slaves of Champ Blandford. The deed for the slaves lists them by name and sex: "Henry a man about thirty years old, Mary a woman and her three children Penney, Poldo, and Anthony, and Milley a woman and her four children Joe, Benjamin, Ann, and Kate." The eleven slaves whom Seth had declared in the Slave Census of 1850, presumably those belonging to Champ, had included five adult females, one adult male, and five children under ten years. Obviously Seth had either retained or sold three of the adult females to someone other than his son. The number of children had probably grown by natural increase from the five of 1850 to the seven in the deed of 1857. By the time the 1860 Slave Census was taken, the Hardisons were living in Polk County, Texas. All of the slaves belonging to the family except those of the Grays and Ann Hardison, the wife of Thomas, who had died in 1859, were recorded under John Randolph's name.[28] He listed fourteen slaves including four adult males, probably a combination of the slaves inherited from Champ Blandford and those brought from Georgia by Winnifred, as mentioned in her letter of November, 1857.

The 1857 county tax returns of Seth and John Randolph shed

light on the role which Seth's transfers of property played in the management of their property. In these returns Seth declared as property only real estate, stating its worth as $440.00, while John, who was listed in the tax records for the first time, declared land worth $200.00. As noted earlier, Seth had declared 500 acres in his 1855 returns but had transferred only 250 acres to John in the 1857 deeds. A search of Gadsden County's deed records has not revealed his disposal of the other half of his land. In addition to real estate, John's returns included "notes and obligations" worth $400.00, slaves valued at $4,000.00, a vehicle at $200.00, livestock at $500.00, household furnishings at $200.00, and a watch at $50.00. Probably much of this personal property was left in his care by his father. John was listed as "J.R. Hardison, trustee," possibly indicating that the probate procedure for the Blandford slaves was not complete.

Obviously the Hardisons were attempting to set their affairs in order and to realize as much as possible from the disposal of their property before leaving Florida. Winnifred's letter of November 30, 1857 stated that Seth and John's brother Thomas were already in Texas "making every necessary preparation for all." Seth and the Grays had transferred title to at least a portion of their land to John and it was his responsibility to dispose of it as favorably as possible. Winnifred wrote that "John thinks he cannot get off before the 29th of Dec. at which time we will certainly leave. Their sale will come off here on Fryday next." The nature of this sale is not indicated, but sheriff's sales of 1858 and 1859 must have made a considerable dent in the proceeds which the family had hoped to gain from the disposal of their property. In 1858 the four tracts of land, totaling 250 acres, which Seth had transferred to John the previous year, were levied upon by the county sheriff to satisfy a writ against Seth dating from 1852 for a debt of $26.30 to Boling H. Robinson. The total from the sale was $137.50. In the following year the same procedure for a writ against Seth for a debt of $117.26, dating from 1848, led to the sale of the land which he had previously given to daughter Mary Ann and her husband John Gray. Everitt Wilcox became the new owner of the lands in both sales.[29] No mention is made in the deed to Wilcox of the claims of the Union Bank of Florida which had been noted in the 1857 deed of transfer from Seth to son John. Possibly Seth's creditors had been stockholders in the defunct bank. If the transfers of the property to John had been attempts to avoid their loss, the procedure was unsuccessful. Possibly Seth had raised money for resettlement in Texas by disposing of other portions of his land before his departure from Florida in 1857.

Whatever the outcome of the Hardisons' efforts to profit from their years in Gadsden County, they were determined to seek a new level of prosperity in fabled Texas, the ultimate Promised Land for land hungry Southerners. Winnifred's letter is an appropriate ending to the portion of this study which tells of the strivings in Georgia and Florida of John Hardison and his sons and daughters. While three of his children, William L., Temperance, and Winnifred, lived out their lives in Washington County, Georgia, which had been his first destination after leaving North Carolina about 1800, two of the four who had accompanied him to Jefferson County, Florida in the late 1820s, Seth and Nancy, migrated to Texas in the 1850s. The other two were deceased, John M. in the Indian hostilities of 1836 and Elizabeth in the late 1840s, after her move to Gadsden County with husband Abner Jackson. Abner joined the family's westward trek in the 1850s, settling in Catahoula Parish, Louisiana. His son Theophilus apparently preferred Florida and settled in Liberty County.

The marriage of Seth's son John Randolph Hardison to Temperance and Enos Davis' daughter Winnifred Cornelia Davis not only joined first cousins but it strengthened the ties between the western and eastern branches of the family. The major portion of the letters of the 1860s and 1870s included in this study were written from Texas to the family back home in Georgia, a number of them urging the family's younger members to join the flood of migrants from the older southern states to the west. Winnifred, known as Winnie, wrote the earliest letter in the collection to her younger brother, Edwin Davis, a few days after her marriage to John.[30]

There are a number of individuals named in Winnifred's letter and a brief identification of those who are known will add to its interest. Enos was Winnifred's cousin, the son of Joel and Winnifred Davis, and Thomas was her brother. Liz and Mr. Hardwick were her sister Elizabeth and her husband Thomas William Hardwick. Apparently Winnie's brother Edd [Edwin], to whom she wrote the letter, was living with the Hardwicks. Their place of residence at the time the letter was written is not indicated. The younger Liz and Tempy were probably Uncle Joel's teenage daughters, Elizabeth and Temperance, who were among his ten children listed in the 1850 Federal Census. Thomas Davis' wife was also named Temperance. As noted previously, Uncle Barefield and Aunt Sally were James Barfield and his wife Sarah Conyers, living in Gadsden County, and Aunt Nancy was Seth's sister who had married Emerald Brigham and was living in Texas.[31] The Tom who was in Texas was Seth's son Thomas. Harry, Lim, and "the others" were most likely slaves whom Winnie had inherited in the division of her father's estate.

China Hill, Nov. 30th, 1857

My Dear Little Edd,

'Tis with no little happiness that I embrace the pleasing privaledge of addressing you; in reply to your very welcomed and interesting letter, which was received in due time. Edd I would have replied sooner, but thought that I would wait until I arrived here.

We were married on last Thur. at 11 o'clock. Their were but few guests present, Uncle Joel's family and Miss Oswall's Aunt Susan, and Aunt Penny M. with two or three others were all. We took our leave of Washington [County] at nine o'clock of the same day, came to Albany [Georgia] the same hour next day, and there we took passage next morning (traveled all night). The trip was quite pleasant with the exception of being badly crowded in the stage as the weather was quite warm for the season.

We reached this place in time for dinner on Saturday, finding most of the relatives here. Yes, Eddy, I was met with a warm and welcome greeting by all, which makes me feel very happy. I could not wish for more than I now realize. All are so kind to me "that it serves to disperse the gloom (in part) that would inevatibly arise from my being separated from you all." Though I will not dwell upon that, as I hope ere a great length of time has sped, we will meet. I was so sorry that you all were not with us at Tennille [Georgia] last Thursday. Enos, Thos, and the girls went to the depot with us, and guess they came near freezing before they got home for certainly it was as cold a night as I ever felt. But it is like a summer day this morning, unpleasant in the sun. Harry came willingly, in fact he said he had rather come with me than to remain with his wife. Lim and the others are in high glee. They did not get here untill yesterday evening. Uncle Barefield met us in Albany with a waggon for them and baggage.

Edd, John received a letter from Uncle Seth. He has arrived in Texas, was much pleased with the country, found Tom enjoying life with his new wife. He states that Tom is building, and making every necessary preparation for all. John thinks he cannot get off before the 29th of Dec. at which time we will certainly leave. Their sale will come off here on Fryday next. Uncle Barefield's family will not go this winter from the fact that he cannot sell his land. He says that he is determined on going next fall. Aunt Sally received a letter from Aunt Nancy, yesterday. She gives a glowing account of the country. She is living in South West Texas. Says the country is suitable for any class of people, and good society and schools.

Edd, I received a letter from Mr. Hardwick just before I left. I should have thought that you all were home by now if he had not have written me differently. I am glad that you all are becoming better pleased with the country, hope you will still become more so, as you are staying. I was delighted to learn that Liz was better. I certainly hope that she will realize a lasting improvement, though I do not think, from what I can glean from the letters which I have received, that you all are pleased with the country, consequently you will not remain long. Uncle Joel's and Tom's folks are highly delighted at the thought of your return. They will be so lonely. Tempy says she misses you so much, is anxious to see you. Tom received your letter. Enos's school was up Fryday before I came off. He will teach at Newsome's next year, and in the winter go to Texas. The family are still speaking of immigrating either their or to Arcansas. I think Uncle J. prefers the latter.

O! Edd, Kegler is taking on considerably at Joel's. He was there every Sunday that I was up there except one. I imagine tis Liz and if so, it will take very well. It would amuse you to see Aunt Win flying around. Ed what think you—a man the name of Fountain was at Tom's on Thursday, and after all were gone but him he went in the room where we were and pulled a bottle of Cologne from his pocket asking us to smell it. After that Liz came in, and all were sitting still when to my astonishment he ask her to give him her [Remainder of letter missing.]

Unfortunately the closing portion of the letter is missing, but its contents tell much of the families and individuals involved. Winnie appears to have been a lively, articulate Southern belle, interested in a bit of gossip about her cousins and friends and happy over her marriage. Though excited about the imminent departure for Texas, she was already a bit homesick for her extensive circle of friends and kin in Georgia. The restlessness reflected in her talk about migration plans of various members of the family was common among Southerners of the period, who were anxious to extend the geographic limits of the Cotton Kingdom and to lay claim to a personal share of the lands of Arkansas and Texas. Winnie had cast her lot with the branch of her mother's family most willing to seek its fortune in new lands and in 1858 she and John Randolph joined the family in Polk County, one of the eastern Texas counties where the plantation system of the Old South was being established.

NOTES

Research in the official records of Gadsden County was done in both the courthouse in Quincy and in the Florida State Archives, Tallahassee. The Archives' holdings are primarily L.D.S. microfilms of the originals, as in the case of the Jefferson County records referred to previously. The deed records in Books A and B available to the public in the courthouse archives are typescripts of the originals, which are now virtually illegible. The deed records are available also on microfilm in the Archives.

1. Clifton Paisley, *The Red Hills of Florida*, 1528-1865, chaps.6 and 11; Miles Kenan Womack, Jr., *Gadsden, a Florida County in Word and Picture*. These previously cited works provide background information on Gadsden County.
2. James C. Bonner, *A History of Georgia Agriculture*, 1732-1860, p.61.
3. Paisley, *op. cit.*, p.119.
4. *Ibid.*, p.130.
5. Womack, *op. cit.*, pp.38-40, Quincy schools; p.21, China Hill, located a few miles east of Quincy, post office established in 1836, discontinued in 1867.
6. Robert P. Dews, *Early Joel*, p.73.
7. Cain Family Genealogical Collection provides some data on the education of Seth's sons and Eighth Federal Census, 1860, Texas, Polk County, p.43, lists the professions of John (lawyer), William (physician), and Clark (bookkeeper). Thomas died in 1859, shortly after the family moved to Texas.
8. Womack, *op. cit.*, p.40.
9. Paisley, *op. cit.*, chaps.8 and 12 provide information on Leon County and Tallahassee.
10. Seventh Federal Census, 1850, Florida, Gadsden County, p.196 (mss.pp.376-77). By 1850 the accepted spelling of Blandford seems to have been Blanford.
11. Sixth Federal Census, 1840, Georgia, Early County, p.127.
12. Seventh Federal Census, 1850, Florida, Gadsden County, p.219 (mss.p.422).
13. *Ibid.*, p.216 (mss.p.416).
14. Gadsden County Marriage Records, Book A, p.46.

15. Seventh Federal Census, 1850, Florida, Gadsden County, p.215 (mss.p.414); Gadsden County Probate Records, 1852-88, p.65, L.D.S. film #915821, record of a $400.00 bond for James Barfield as guardian for minors Nancy, Rachel, and Sarah W. Conyers, co-signed by Seth Hardison and James H. Reeves.
16. Seventh Federal Census, 1850, Florida, Gadsden County, p.219 (mss.p.422).
17. Sixth Federal Census, 1840, Georgia, Early County, p.127; Seventh Federal Census, 1850, Slave Population, Florida, Gadsden County, p.241 (Hardison), p.263 (Reeves).
18. Gadsden County Tax Records, 1845-60, microfilm in Florida State Archives, Tallahassee.
19. Gadsden County Deed Book A, 4 deeds dated January 10, 1857—p.545, deed from Mary Ann and John Gray to John R. Hardison for 2 tracts, 20 acres, north end of S.W. quarter of S.W. quarter of Section 4, Township 2 N., Range 2 W. and for 42 and 42\100 acres, S.E. quarter of Section 4, Township 2, Range 2 N. and W., $150; p.546, deed from Mary and Seth Hardison to John R. Hardison for 10 slaves, $5,000; pp.546-47, deed from Mary and Seth to John for 42 and 42/100 acres, N.E. quarter of S.E. quarter of Section 4, Township 2, Range 2 N. and W., $55, and p.578, deed from Mary and Seth to John for 3 tracts, 84 and 84/100 acres, W. half of S.E. quarter of Section 4, Township 2 N., Range 2 W., 42 and 42/100 acres, S.E. quarter of S.W. quarter, Section 4, Township 2 N., Range 2 W., and 80 acres, part of S.E. quarter, Section 5, Township 2, Range 2 N. and W., $500; Gadsden County Deed Book B, p.9, March 1, 1858, deed from Sheriff James M. Smith to Everitt Wilcox for the 4 tracts which Seth and Mary had sold to John, and p.10, March 7, 1859, deed from Sheriff Smith to Wilcox for the 2 tracts which the Grays had sold to John.
20. State of Florida, Tract Book, vol.1, 1N-1W to 7N-8W, p.38, deed #10131, purchase by Seth Hardison of the N.E. ¼ of the S.E. ½ of Section 4, Township 2 N., Range 2 W., purchase made January 1, 1851, deed dated September 1, 1852; U.S. Field Notes: Florida, vol.28, p.115 indicate the land was third rate pine. I am indebted to Dr. Joe Knetsch of the Florida Department of Natural Resources for this information (1991).
21. James Porter Davis, *Elm Hill and Its People*, pp.36-40, data on the family of Winnifred and Joel Davis.
22. Alma Walker Jackson Genealogical Collection includes a typescript of Theophilus' letter and data on his career as a physician in the Confederate Army and his post-Civil War life in Liberty County, Florida, where he served as chairman of the Board of Education. He was married to Nancy Talley in 1862, applied to the State of Florida for a Confederate soldier's pension in 1909, and died in Liberty County in 1917. Nancy applied for a widow's pension in 1918.
23. Cain Collection provided information on the wife of Thomas Hardison. See also data on Ann in Chapter 9. Data on members of the Temperance (Hardison) and Enos Davis and Winnifred (Hardison) and Joel Davis families is based on the previously cited *Elm Hill and Its People* by James Porter Davis (pp.36-40 includes lists of the children in the two families) and *A Davis Family Record* by Sara Jane Overstreet and Barbara Davis-Stovall (privately published works, copies of which are available in the collection of the Washington County Historical Society, Sandersville); Federal Census records for Washington County for 1830 and 1840 include Enos' family and 1830-60 Joel's family; Davis family data is also found in *Cotton to Kaolin: a History of Washington County, Georgia, 1784-1989*, edited by Mary Alice Jordan.

24. Washington County Letters Testamentary, Administrative, Guardianship, and Apprenticeship, Book A, 1829-1876, pp.364-65, 397, 468-69, and 473; Division of Estates, Book A, 1829-1871, pp.102-03 and 112.
25. Washington County, Georgia, Marriage Records, Book B, p.304; *Central Georgian*, Sandersville, Georgia, December 3, 1857, an announcement of the marriage using the date of the license, November 25, rather than the date of the marriage.
26. Gadsden County Deed Book A, pp.545-47 and 578 (see footnote #19 for descriptions of tracts).
27. Paisley, *op. cit.*, pp.94 and 99-102; Kathryn T. Abbey, "The Union Bank of Tallahassee, an Experiment in Territorial Finance," *Florida Historical Quarterly*, April, 1937, vol.15, no.4, pp.207-31.
28. Eighth Federal Census, 1860, Slave Population, Texas, Polk County, p.7-8.
29. Gadsden County Deed Book B, pp.9-10.
30. Cain Collection, typescript of letter of November, 30, 1857, in the handwriting of Winnifred Cornelia (Davis) Hardison; location of the original is not known, but possibly is in the possession of the heirs of Edwin T. Davis, who died in 1879 and was buried in the place of his residence, Thomasville, Georgia. As in all letters which will be reproduced in this study, the spelling, punctuation, and capitalizations of the originals (or the available typescripts) will be reproduced. Identities of persons mentioned in the letter are based on the previously listed sources on the Davis families.
31. United States Archives, Washington, D. C., pension application, #43568, Aug. 12, 1884, by Nancy (Hardison) Brigham for a widow's pension based on the service of her husband Emerald Brigham (died 1863) in the War of 1812. Nancy stated that the family had lived in Early County and Randolph County, Georgia, from 1839-50, in Lowndes County, Alabama until 1853, in Matagorda County and De Witt County, Texas from 1853 until 1868, and finally in Blanco County, Texas. The family was listed in De Witt County in the 1860 Federal Census.

THE ODYSSEY

❧ Part 3 ❧

*Texas and the Confederacy
1857-1875*

IX

On to Texas
Polk County and Liberty County, 1857-1862

*T*exas captured the imagination of the Hardisons and thousands of other Southerners as cotton cultivation moved steadily westward in the first half of the nineteenth century. Its vast untilled lands, which seemed to stretch endlessly to the west, held the promise of prosperity. Its recent history of rebellion against Mexico and a decade of independence as a republic added luster to its appeal. It was a lure both to the ambitious and to the previously unsuccessful, who believed it would fulfill their dreams.

Texas from Colony to State

Like Florida, Texas had been explored and claimed by Spain in the 1500s and had remained a part of the Spanish empire until the early nineteenth century. It was like Florida also in its failure to yield the gold and silver treasure which the early explorers frantically sought. Its vast lands, from French Louisiana on the east to an undefined point west of its current boundaries; its fierce Indians; and its failure to yield ready riches made its administration both difficult and less a matter of concern than such profitable areas as Mexico and Peru.

Limestone County
Polk County
Liberty County

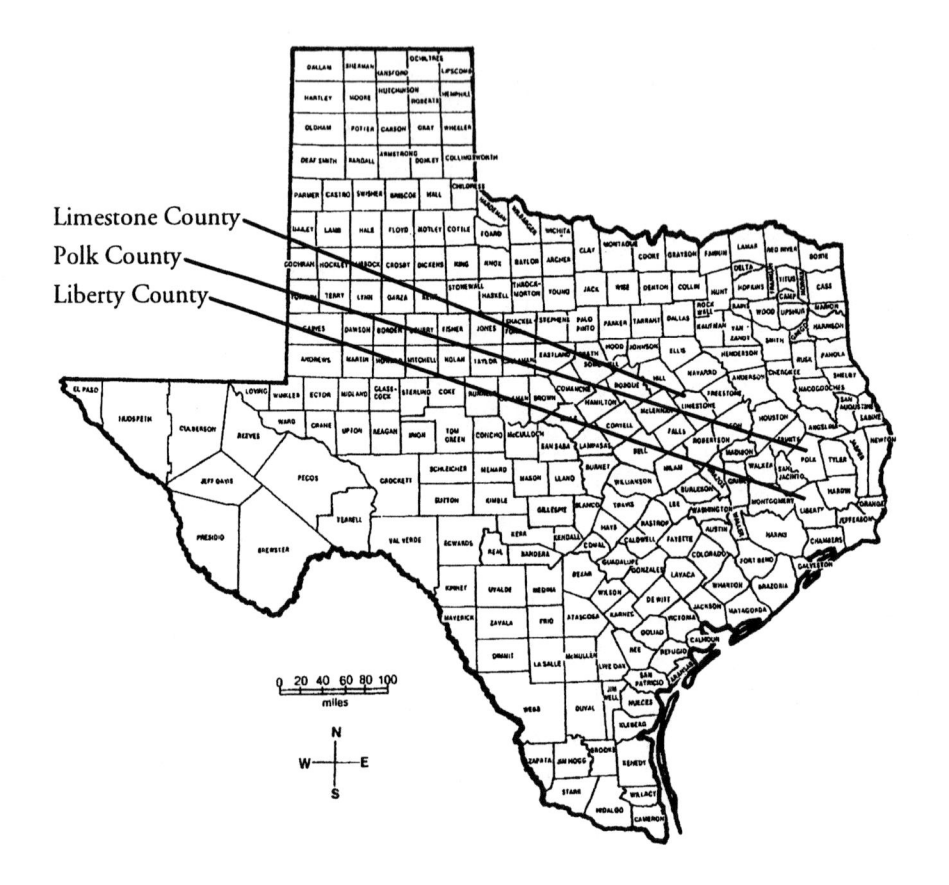

TEXAS

Catholic missionaries, more interested in souls than gold, began to establish a chain of missions in the late seventeenth century and by 1731 there were twelve missions scattered over the vast area. The settlement which grew up around the most famous of them, San Antonio, became the center of government, with the eastern outpost for the province in Nacogdoches. As Spain's American empire crumbled, Florida was ceded to the United States and Mexico won its independence in 1821, taking Texas as part of its territory.[1]

Eager to populate Texas, Mexico initiated a plan to attract settlers from the United States. The ever restless and land-hungry farmers of the South were eager to move into fresh new lands, having already populated Alabama, Mississippi, and Louisiana in the early decades of the nineteenth century. Wishing to have control over the process of settlement, Mexico established the *empresario* system whereby vast tracts of land were granted to selected individuals who were responsible for recruiting a specified number of settlers of good character. The first and most famous of the *empresarios* was Stephen F. Austin, a native of Connecticut, who recruited the original "Old Three Hundred" families between 1821 and 1824. They settled on his grant in south-central Texas in the valleys of the Brazos and Colorado rivers. Other *empresarios* received grants between the Guadaloupe and Trinity rivers.

Unauthorized groups and individuals came across the Sabine River, the eastern boundary between Louisiana and Texas. Some settled in the southeast in the vicinity of the present town of Liberty, which became known as the Atascocita District, and others to the north around the old Spanish towns of Nacogdoches and San Augustine. Many applied for land grants from the Mexican government and others were squatters. Another strain of migration, which had begun before Mexico achieved her independence, was the continuing settlement in the valley of the Red River on the northeast border by families from Tennessee, Kentucky, and the mountain areas of North Carolina and Virginia. Among these immigrants was John Hardison of Kentucky, probably a member of one of the North Carolina Hardison families who had moved to Tennessee early in the nineteenth century. He was granted land in what is now Grayson County, bordering the Red River, by the Mexican government in 1835.[2]

During the period of Mexican control the white population grew from approximately 3,000 to about 30,000, most of whom were former citizens of the United States. Mexico's official policy was that all settlers must become members of the Roman Catholic Church and citizens of Mexico and that none should own slaves. While those who had official status as a member of one of the colonies founded by the *empresarios* or were recipients of land grants might go through the motions of accepting these requirements, there is little doubt that few of them or the thousands of "unofficial" immigrants had any intention of allegiance to the Catholic Church or the Mexican government.

Too late Mexico became alarmed over the growing tide of settlers. Fearing a rebellion which would lead to attempts at annexation to the United States, Mexico began to issue onerous regulations, including the disarming of all colonists except those in the militia. These measures were accelerated when Santa Anna became president of Mexico in 1833 and the armed conflict which led to the formation of the Lone Star Republic in 1836 was inevitable. The fight-to-the-death at the Alamo in San Antonio and the massacre of Texans at Goliad, capped by the remarkable victory over Santa Anna's army by Sam Houston's greatly outnumbered "Texians," welded the scattered settlements into a tenacious new political entity. Over the next nine years the Republic's officials sought annexation by the United States, but their efforts were stalled by the increasingly heated debate over the extension of slavery into the western territories. The earliest settlers had been small farmers from the upper South, with few or no slaves, but increasingly the new arrivals were from the lower South and they saw Texas as a logical extension of the Cotton Kingdom. Political leaders such as Henry Clay and Martin Van Buren, who opposed annexation out of fear of undoing the delicate balance between slave and free states, were rejected when the nation elected pro-annexation Democrat James K. Polk as president in 1844. Great Britain's imperial ambitions and her growing interest in Texas, as the producer of cotton needed for its textile industry, helped to build additional support for annexation. In 1845 Texas became a state after the passage of a joint resolution of Congress. It was granted immediate statehood rather than having to go through a period as a territory and was allowed to retain all its public lands and to have the right to divide its vast area into as many as five states.

IX. ON TO TEXAS, 1857-1862

Mexico had threatened to declare war on the United States if it annexed Texas. Actions of American armed forces in the border areas soon provoked hostilities and the Mexican War ensued in 1846. Mexico's defeat was followed by the Treaty of Guadaloupe Hidalgo in 1848, with the United States not only keeping Texas but receiving all the land Mexico claimed from the Rio Grande to the Pacific Ocean. The western boundary of Texas was ill-defined and the state tried to claim portions of the newly ceded lands, including parts of New Mexico, Oklahoma, Kansas, Wyoming, and Colorado. The United States paid Texas $10,000,000 to surrender its claim and the state's western boundaries were set much as they are today.

The public lands of Texas amounted to approximately 181,965,332 acres, as it assumed the boundaries of statehood. The General Land Office, created in 1836, was responsible for disposing of the land in a way to attract settlers and to create revenue for the state. It also had to deal with the grants made by the Spanish, Mexicans, and Lone Star Republic and with the numerous claims of settlers who had dubious or non-existent titles. The Republic had made special grants to men who rendered service to the Texas Revolution and to the Republic and also headrights grants to heads of families and single men who settled in Texas during the period of the Republic. The headrights grants varied according to the time of arrival, with the largest being one league (4,428.4 acres) plus one labor (177.1 acres) for a married man who had arrived in the Republic prior to the founding date, March 2, 1836, and the smallest, 320 acres for a single man who had arrived between 1840 and 1842. Preemption grants, which covered homestead and settler's claims, were given to individuals who actually resided on a tract of no more than 320 acres for at least three consecutive years dating from January 22, 1845. In 1854 this acreage was changed to 160 acres and the preemption program ended in 1899.[3] By the time the Hardisons arrived, acquisition by purchase from the original owner was frequently the means of securing land in the most desirable areas. Both Seth and his son John purchased land which had been carved out of the headrights league of John Burgess, an earlier settler in Polk County.

The Western Extension of the Cotton Kingdom

Prior to the Revolution, the immigrants had come primarily from the upper South—Kentucky, Tennessee, and the mountain regions of North Carolina and Virginia. Most were slaveless small farmers, along with a contingent of adventurers and men escaping debt and the law. As historian Terry G. Jordan has pointed out in his study of migration to Texas, the Texas Revolution was essentially a contest "between the poorly led peasant-soldiers of Mexico and sharpshooting backwoodsmen of the Upper South, led by Tennesseans such as Sam Houston and David Crockett."[4] In the two decades between the Revolution and the arrival of the Hardisons in the late 1850s, these early settlers were joined by a great wave of migration from the lower South. The newcomers were drawn by the plentiful, cheap, and fertile land, which was well suited to cotton cultivation, and by the elimination of Mexico's prohibition of slavery. The population of Texas, which had been estimated as 30,000 in 1836, had grown to 212,000 by 1850 and 604,000 by 1860.

Already citizens from the older states along the Atlantic seaboard had claimed the best lands of Alabama, Mississippi, and Louisiana, always pushing the Indian population farther to the west. The opening of Texas to settlement was welcomed by both planters and small farmers who hoped to achieve planter status. The primary destination of the settlers from the lower South was that distinctive area known as East Texas, the lands lying along the Trinity River eastward to the border with Louisiana and from the Red River on the north to the Gulf of Mexico in the south. It was an area in which they felt at home, for its climate, fertile soil, and thick forests of pines and hardwoods duplicated the lands they were leaving behind. They began to dominate East Texas in the 1850s and, although small farmers by far exceeded the number of planters, they established the distinctive way of life of the Cotton Kingdom, complete with plantations, cotton, sugar cane, and slavery.

Migration from the upper South continued but increasingly these families settled farther west to the interior, especially the rich lands of the Blackland Prairie, stretching from the area around the present city of Dallas southward to Austin, and the Hill Country, west of Austin. They were generally small farmers with few or no slaves. The differences between the two groups were soon to be dramatized as the issue of secession polarized the population on the eve of the Civil War. Governor Sam Houston, reflecting the views of many of his fellow immigrants from the upper South, opposed secession and was forced out of office by a legislature dominated by settlers from the lower South.[5]

The Hardisons in Polk County

The Hardison family contributed to both the upper South and lower South contingents in Texas. As noted John Hardison of Kentucky received a land grant in what is now Grayson County, in north Texas along the Red River, in 1835. His application for land stated that he had been in Texas since 1830, had a family consisting of two persons, and was industrious and of good moral character. It is possible that the Hardison families of Lamar and Harrison counties, in the northeastern area, who are listed in the 1860 Federal Census, were his descendants or members of Hardison families who had first migrated from North Carolina to Tennessee in the early 1800s.[6] The Seth Hardison family was typical of the lower Southerners in their ongoing migrations, dating from the late 1700s, from North Carolina to Georgia and westward through the Gulf coast states to East Texas. Seth's sister Nancy, with her husband Emerald Brigham, had preceded him in Texas by several years. While Seth lived in Florida, they spent a few years in Alabama and then migrated in 1853 to Texas. They first settled in Matagorda County on the Gulf coast and then moved inland to the northwest to DeWitt County, where they were living at the time the 1860 Federal Census was taken. In 1868 the family moved once again, to Blanco County in the Hill Country west of Austin.[7]

The destination of Seth and his family in their 1857-1858 migration was Polk County, located in the southern portion of East Texas, where bottom lands along the Trinity River were considered prime lands for cotton cultivation. The river flows through the western portion of the county on its way to the Gulf of Mexico and farms and plantations clustered along the many creeks and streams which drained into the river. In the ante-bellum years water transportation was as important to the farmers of the area as it had been in the Hardisons' early eighteenth century years in North Carolina, since the roads were few and poor and the railroad had not yet reached this new frontier. Steamboats and smaller vessels plied the Trinity, subject to its whims of flood and drought, and docked at river towns to load cotton and cattle.

Polk County was formed in 1846 and named for President James K. Polk, in recognition of his support of Texas' entry into the United States. Its county seat was Livingston, named in honor of the Tennessee home town of Moses L. Choate, the settler who donated the land on which it was located. The county's population grew rapidly in the years following Texas statehood, drawing settlers primarily from the states of the lower South.

The Hardisons were attracted to the rich lands along the Trinity River and settled in the vicinity of Colita. This village in western Polk County had first been called the Louisiana Settlement for its early residents, a few families who migrated from Louisiana in the 1840s. As its population grew to several hundred, a post office was established in 1853 and the town was named in honor of Colita, the chieftain of the Coushatti Indians. He had earned the gratitude of Texans for his services during the struggle with Mexico and was a friend to General Sam Houston, who had respect for the Indians and was an adopted son of the Cherokees. Through Houston's insistence a reservation was established in Polk County for Colita's people, along with the remnant of a Creek tribe known as the Alabamas. The Alabamas and the Coushatti were among the native peoples, including the Cherokees, Seminoles, and Kickapoos, who had been driven west from their original homes in the southeastern states. Most had been forced from the lands where they attempted to settle in Texas, but through Houston's insistence Colita's people were given a home in Polk County in the area known as the Big Thicket. It continues to be the home of their descendants.

The primary concern of every immigrant family on its arrival in Texas was the acquisition of land. A number of the new settlers were trained in the professions, as were Thomas and William in medicine and John in the law, but the ownership of land was what gave status and the promise of wealth. As the first of the Seth Hardison family to arrive, the eldest son, Thomas, made the family's initial purchase in

August, 1857. Polk County's deed records document a transaction between Thomas G. Hardison and William B. Hardin for 640 acres located "3 or 4 miles East of the Trinity River" for $3,200.00, yielding a price of $5.00 per acre.[8] The land was to be paid for in three installments, $1,000.00 by January 1, 1859, $1,000.00 by January 1, 1860, and $1,200.00 by January 1, 1861, with ten percent interest from date of maturity. Texas used the old metes and bounds system of survey, with descriptions based on natural features and boundaries of abutting land. For Thomas' acquisition, the deed began "at the most westerly corner of a survey made for C. Devore at a stake from which a pine 30 inches in diameter [is] marked . . . ." Apparently there was some question as to Hardin's title, for he guaranteed the purchase up to $5.00 an acre in case his title should fail.

An additional Polk County deed entry pertaining to Thomas' family is the record of the purchase by his wife, Ann M. Hardison, of a female slave in February, 1858 from C. L. McCarty, a slave dealer in Galveston.[9] The girl, named Louisa, was described as "of black complexion and aged about sixteen years." Ann paid the very large sum of $1,150.00 for Louisa, undoubtedly with the idea that she would produce a number of children as future slaves.

Probably all the Hardison family lived together in the first months of their Texas residence on the land which Thomas had purchased, for the earliest records of purchases by Seth, son John, and son-in-law John Gray are dated October and December, 1858. A letter written by John's wife Winnifred to her brother Edwin Davis of Georgia in June of that year describes the family's expectations, as well as revealing a touch of homesickness. Winnifred wrote from Livingston, the county seat of Polk County.[10] Of the family members whom she mentioned, Uncle Joel was her father's brother, Enos was his son, and Thomas, Liz, and Sal [Sarah] were her brother and sisters. Old Washington and Washington refer to the county in Georgia from which she had come. Her articulate use of language reflects the family's concern for educating its daughters and indicates a significant advance beyond the opportunities of the previous generation.

Livingston, June 10th, 1858

My Dear Little Buddy,

We have just received a letter from Enos, telling of the times and doings of Old Washington, which caused me for a few moments to think myself among you. How sad were my feelings, when I awoke from my dream of revery, "to find that my fancied pleasures were wafted away by that destroyer of happiness (disappointment)." Eddy, while in this mood, I thought that time could not be successfully killed than by pening you some of my stray thoughts. Thus I find my pen glyding o're these pure pages. Ed if it were not for writing and receiving others from you all absence would be as death, "and space as a grave." Surely tis disagreable to be separated from "those loved and cherished friends." But let us not dwell on that theme. Hoping that e're we have gulled the flowers of many summers, "there will be a general meeting with absent ones." 'Twould be a pleasure undescribable to be with you all, if but a short time, Still I know that will have no affect [on] it, so I bear it patiently.

Well Edd another 24 hours have become things that were, "and the sable mantle of night is thrown o'er us, reminding us of the close of life." Edd what changes will be wrought throughout the land, "e're bright Aurora begins its dayly test?" Many "will go to the bourn from which no traveler ever returns, and many will be loaded down with grief. The others will be as happy as the sportive lamb." Thus it is and will be until time shall be no more.

Edd while I am pening these lines, John is lying on the bed sick. He was taken with a chill this morning, has spent a pretty sick day. I think he has no fever now, is complaining of a headache. He will exspose hisself too much hunting etc.

And Susy Dudly is no more, "has commited suicide." I see the matrimonial ball moves occasionally in Washing[ton]. I dreamed last night that Lill was married or I was at her wedding. I guess Enos thinks he had better keep aloof from the snares of love, Susy used to give him fits I opine, though that flaim had long since perished. Who is his bright particular one now? He writes me he is out of the ring until he comes to Texas — good idea that! Enos writes that the dye is cast as regards his coming to Texas. Also his family if Uncle can find sail for his land. I look forward with much pleasure to that time. O! that you could be one of the party. But it won't be long afore you will come, will it? I think Uncle Joel's family will be pleased, and I am confident 'twill be better for them after they get here, But if they can do that and get them land, all will be well. Land of the best quality can be had at $1.50 to $2 per Acre, unimproved, then improved at $5—as much land as he could cultivate would be all that he would ever want as land never wears out, the most improves, and manure is used only on poor sandy land, this we needn't have. There is one man offering 3,000 Acres at $1 with your own time to pay in by paying interest yearly. I mean he will sell any quantity of it—it will bring 60 bush. of corn per Acre. Gray speaks of buying from him. Provision will certainly be cheap next year, 'tis thought by many that corn won't be more than 25 to 30 cts. Some farmers are trying to engage their crop at 40. Our crop is promising. We have splendid season [?] when needed, have one field in roasting years [corn]. I received a letter from Mrs. H [Hardwick?], and one from Liz this week. She says her health is not good, I am sorry to hear she does not improve there. They are not atal pleased with Fla. Liz said tis worse than Geo[rgia]. and the Land is as poor they thought of returning to Washington soon, a good idea I guess. I was fearful it would be sickly. Liz makes many inquiries about Texas, says she intends coming to look at the country, and thinks it probable they will one day move here. Won't that be nice, then you and Thos. must come to complete my happiness. Tell Thos. John is wondering why he don't write, sais he will write when he finds anything to interest him. I would write to him but John writes all and then 'tis a task for me to write. Sal hasn't written to me yeat—I will pay her. Liz writes me that she was quite a Belle at the Springs, has many suitors, said I would be amused to see her flying around.

About your little sweet heart, I will certainly try and select you one to your taste. I have not yet seen any. But will before you get here. I do not know that I can please your refined taste, will do my best. Give my love to Thos, Tempy & children, also Uncle Joel's family. All are up this morning seeming to enjoy life and health. I hope you are likewise blessed. Write often Edd, tell me all the news.

Your devoted sister,
Win Hard-

The purchases of land which Winnifred anticipated took place a few months after her letter was written. John acquired his first tract on October 18, 1858 in a purchase of 270 acres for $2,700.00 from Angus McLeod.[11] The land was located in western Polk County on the east side of the Trinity River, lying between two of its tributaries,

Kickapoo Creek and Sandy Creek. It had been acquired previously, in 1855, by McLeod from the league of land belonging to John Burgess. McLeod's terms to John were $200.00 to be paid by January, 1859 and two payments of $1,250.00, in January, 1860 and January, 1861. The original deed included a record of the $200.00 initial payment on January 19, 1859. According to Winnifred's generalizations concerning the price of land in her letter of June, 1858, John had paid a high price for his tract, probably because it was improved land and rich bottom land with a potential for high crop yields. Later records pertaining to the land indicate that it became known as "the John Hardison place." A feature identified as Hardison Slough on a recent map of Lake Livingston, the lake created in Polk County by the damming of the Trinity River, probably marks the location of the land.[12] The area is now under the waters of the lake, to the south of the Kickapoo and Sandy Creek marinas, and just to the west of Highway 190. Apparently John intended the land to be used for raising cattle as well as farming for in July, 1860 he purchased from McLeod for $20.00 the cattle brand which the latter had registered in the Polk County Book of Marks and Brands in 1855. It was described as "mark crop and half crop in each year [ear]—Brand thus -5-."[13]

A puzzling paragraph in the deed from McLeod to John precedes the terms of the land sale. It relates to an agreement between the two concerning the sum of $5,000.00. It is difficult to determine from the wording of the document whether McLeod owed the sum to John or John to McLeod. The deed records of Polk County do not include any other references to dealings between them.

Shortly after his purchase from McLeod, John, his father Seth, and his brother-in-law John Gray contracted for another tract from the John Burgess league, this time dealing directly with Burgess. Together they acquired a parcel of 496 acres for $1,488.00, yielding a price of $3.00 per acre. It adjoined the land recently purchased by John and lay on the east side of Kickapoo Creek and northern side of Sandy Creek. It was to be paid for in equal installments of $496.00 in January of 1860, 1861, and 1862.[14]

Nothing is known of the houses in which the family lived in their years in Texas. Probably they were very simple structures of the sort described by Emma Haynes in her history of Polk County. She based

IX. ON TO TEXAS, 1857-1862

her descriptions on recollections of elderly residents of the county, who recalled that most of the houses were built of logs from the abundant forests and were often of the plan called the double-pen house, with a center hall extending from the front to the back and a wide gallery on the front. Others consisted of one large room with smaller rooms attached on three sides. Most of the houses had a separate structure for the kitchen and sometimes the dining room. As the area developed and saw mills were built, the use of dressed lumber both on the inside and outside of the houses increased. The more affluent settlers brought furniture with them but in general the furnishings were sturdy home-made pieces.[15]

While the acquisition of land was the family's major concern after arriving in Texas, church membership was also of primary importance for at least Seth and daughter Nancy and her husband, Dr. James Harvey Reeves. The church which they joined was Bethel Baptist Church founded in 1849 on the western side of Polk County.[16] It had both white and black members but services for each were held separately, the white in the morning and black in the afternoon. Church business was conducted after the morning preaching and strict decorum for these "Conference" meetings was called for in Bethel's by-laws. The church's records indicate that membership was not easily acquired or lightly considered and that a major concern was "unchristian" conduct, with strong emphasis on the sins of drinking and dancing. Members were "labored" with in attempts at correction, but if repentance and correction did not result, the sinner was dropped from membership. One high-spirited member's experience is recorded in the Conference minutes of June 30, 1866:

> Bethel Church met and after preaching conference was opened for business. The committee reported that Sister Dunnam had confessed having danced again and that she would not promise not to dance any more, because she did not believe she should abstain from dancing when ever she was where fidling and dancing was going on. She talked as though it would be impossible for her to resist the temptation. She said she would rather stay in the Church, but she knew she could not stay in the Church and follow dancing, therefore the Church would have do as they thought best with her. By unanimous consent, all members voted to withdraw fellowship from Sister Maggie Dunnam.

The participation of Seth Hardison and the Reeves family in Bethel Church dates from July 3, 1859, when the Conference minutes record that "Bro James H. Reeves came forward and stated to the Church that he wished to join by letter but had left his letter but would present it next meeting. He was received on that condition provided his letter was in order." The letter referred to was one of dismissal from the church in which he had previously held membership, stating that he was in good standing at the time of his departure. Later records indicate that Dr. Reeves became a lay minister in at least two Texas churches and in Bethel Church his leadership potential was soon recognized as he was called on to preach and was chosen as a representative to the denominational organization known as the Tryon Association. His wife, "Sister Nancy Reeves," was received by letter in September, 1859. The previous month, Seth Hardison presented himself for membership by transfer of letter, when opportunity for membership was offered after preaching, "but his letter being out of order he withdrew his application until next meeting." Possibly this opportunity had been offered only to new members on profession of faith and Seth was not turned away, although the records show that he did not become a member until August, 1862, when he was received by application. Soon after being received, he was chosen as a delegate to the Tryon Association and apparently remained a resident of Polk County and member of the church until 1869. In May of that year "a letter of dismission was granted to Bro. Seth Hardison as he had moved away from this Church & wished to join a Church near where he is living."

As the family's first year in Texas drew to a close, their future seemed to hold the promise which had drawn them westward. Within the time between their arrival and the recording of their family members in the Federal Census of 1860, their numbers increased with the birth of three children—Lilly Mary to John and Winnifred, Thomas to Thomas and Ann, and Willie to Nancy and James H. Reeves. But death was to stalk the family almost from the beginning of its Texas sojourn. By April of 1859 Thomas, Seth's eldest son, was dead and the man who had sold him land in 1857, William B. Hardin, had received a judgment in the Spring Term of the Polk County District Court against his wife Ann for non-payment of the outstanding indebtedness. The judgment was for $1,027.15 and court costs and called for foreclosure and sale by the county sheriff to the highest bidder. In July Hardin purchased for $900.00 the tract of 640 acres which he had so recently deeded to Thomas.[17]

The births and death above noted are reflected in the make-up of the Hardison-Gray-Reeves families as recorded in the population enumeration of the Federal Census of 1860.[18] The ages of some of the family members are at variance by several years from previous census records and family records and the time of birth of John and Winnifred's daughter Lilly is incorrect. According to John, Lilly's birthdate was January 13, 1859, although the census record of 1860, taken in July, gave her an age of only one month.[19] Another obvious error is the age of Mary Ann Gray, given as 26 in Gadsden County, Florida in 1850 and 30 in 1860. As previously noted in the chapter on Jefferson County, Florida, Mary Ann was the eldest daughter of Seth, probably born to his brief marriage to his first wife in the mid-1820s, making her about 35 years old in 1860. The age of the second daughter, Nancy Reeves, varies less, being listed as 21 in 1850 (Gadsden County), 28 in 1860 (Polk County), and 40 in 1870 (Limestone County, Texas). She was probably about 30 in 1860, having been born to Seth and his second wife, Mary Blandford, who were married in 1829. According to the 1850 census she was born in Florida, while her place of birth in the 1860 census is listed as Georgia. As stated earlier in relation to federal census records, ages and spelling of names often varied from year to year, depending on who gave the information to the agent at the time he called and the vagaries of his and family members' spelling abilities.

1860 Federal Census
Texas
Polk County

Order of visit to family	Name of each resident in household	Age	Sex	Occupation	Value of real estate	Value of personal estate	Place of birth
113	F. Anderson	23	M	Farmer			Fla.
	J. R. Hardison	26	M	Lawyer	$2,000	$10,000	Ga.
	W. C. Hardison	26	F				Ga.
	Lilly Hardison	1/12	F				Tex.
114	Seth Hardison	57	M				Ga.
	Mary Hardison	65	F				Ga.
	W. F. Hardison	23	M	M. D.			Ga.
	C. B. Hardison	23	M	Bookkeeper			Ga.
	Reuben Roach	21	M	Farm Laborer			
115	A. Hardison	37	F				Ala.
	T. Walker	20	F	Farmer			Fla.
	Emily Jackson	15	F				Ala.
	J. Jackson	8	M				Fla.
	Jane Jackson	6	F				Fla.
	Thomas Hardison	9/12	M				Tex.
	David Halston	17	M	Laborer			Ala.
116	John Gray	42	M	Farmer			Ga.
	Mary Gray	30	F				Ga.
	D. L. Gray	16	M	Laborer			Fla.
	Mary A. Gray	12	F				Fla.
	J. H. Gray	10	M				Fla.
	Sarah Gray	6	F				Fla.
117	James H. Reeves	45	M	M. D.			Ga.
	Nancy H. Reeves	28	F				Ga.
	Carrie Reeves	10	F				Fla.
	Sarah Clark Reeves	5	F				Fla.
	Willie Reeves	1	M				Tex.

The data on Seth and Mary and on their sons and daughters reflects previously cited records, excepting the noted variations in age and the addition of children since the 1850 enumeration. Information on the make-up of the family of Thomas' widow Ann helps to piece together her history prior to her marriage to Thomas. Born in Alabama, she was apparently first married to a Mr. Walker and then to a Mr. Jackson and lived with them in Florida. In the 1850 Federal Census Ann M. Jackson, age 29 and born in Alabama, is listed in the household of Isaac Jackson, age 46 and born in North Carolina, along with a child named Florida Walker, age 10 and born in Florida, and another named Emily Jackson, age 5 and born in Florida.[20] In the 1860 enumeration T. (possibly F.) Walker and Emily Jackson correspond with the 1850 data. In addition to Emily, Ann's household of 1860 included two other Jackson children, J. (possibly I., for Isaac, whose name appears in the 1870 census with Ann) and Jane, ages 8 and 6 and born in Florida. This information indicates that after her marriage to Thomas Hardison in the late 1850s, Ann's children by previous marriages became part of their newly established household in Texas. The records show that she was several years older than Thomas, with her age in the 1860 enumeration being listed as 37 while Thomas would have been 28, if the age of 18 listed for him in Gadsden County, Florida in 1850 was correct. Their son Thomas, not quite a year old when the census was taken in July, 1860, was obviously born after his father's death, since the elder Thomas had died by the time his land was foreclosed on in 1859. Apparently the infant Thomas did not survive childhood, for he is not listed in Ann's household in 1870, by which time she was living in adjoining Liberty County with her older children.[21]

The three non-family males, F. Anderson, Reuben Roach, and David Halston, who are listed in the households of John, Seth, and Ann were possibly young men who had migrated with them from Florida or were living with the families as farm laborers.

While the above data from the Federal Census population enumerations reveals the make-up of the Hardison and related families, the Federal Slave Census of 1860 gives information on the black members of their households.[22] All of the slaves belonging to the Hardisons, except for Ann, were recorded under John's name. Their sex, age, color (mulatto or black), and the number of houses in which they lived were recorded, but not their names. Fourteen slaves were listed for John and they probably account for the major portion of the $10,000.00 in personal property listed for him in the 1860 census record. They included four adult males, ages between 18 and 35, one adult female age 28, four females between 6 and 16 years, and five males between 5 months and 12 years, living in three slave houses. Eight were described as black and six as mulatto. The slaves listed by John were probably a combination of those inherited from his mother's brother, Champ Blandford, and from Winnifred's father, Enos Davis, as described in the preceding chapter. Obviously some sales and trades had been made since the 1850 Slave Census, when Seth listed eleven—five adult females, one adult male, and five children under 10 years. Ann Hardison's slaves were a black male of 65 years, a mulatto female of 20 years (probably Louisa, whom she had purchased in 1858), and a mulatto male of 6 months. Ann had one slave house. The Grays owned two slaves, a black female of 25 years and a black male of 7, but had no slave house. There is no listing for the Reeves in either Polk or Liberty County.

With land and slaves, the major components of large scale agriculture in the ante-bellum South, the Hardisons had high expectations as a new decade opened in 1860. What they lacked was other capital which could see them through the early years of their new venture, for like most Southern farmers and planters they were heavily in debt and faced ruin if the crops of one year failed or the price of cotton dropped. These were calculated risks which the family had dealt with in the past years of their Southern pilgrimage, but the 1860s brought family deaths, drought, and national calamity which were disheartening and ruinous.

The stress of the indebtedness which had been incurred, coupled with the first death, that of Thomas in 1859, has already been noted in connection with the foreclosure on the land for which he had contracted in 1857. The deed records of Polk County indicate early troubles for John, as in March of 1860 he mortgaged one of his slaves, Harry (possibly Henry), described as being about 35 years old. Money was needed to cover a debt of $567.65, the note for which was in the hands of a third party for collection.[23] In March of the following year, John, Seth, and John Gray sold back to John Burgess for $1,600.00 the tract of 496 acres which they had contracted to purchase from Burgess for $1,488.00 in 1858. Possibly they had been able to meet the first payment which was due in January of 1860, but were unable to meet the 1861 payment.[24] Drought may have been a factor in their decision to give up the land, for the history of a Liberty

County church speaks of the "intolerable drouth" which Texas suffered in the early 1860s.[25]

Two more family deaths occurred in the first years of the 1860s, Seth's wife, Mary (Blandford) Hardison, and one of their twin sons, Clark B. (B. probably for Blandford).[26] Clark was listed as age 23, with the profession of bookkeeper, in the 1860 census. Mary died at some time between her signing of the deed returning the land to Burgess in March, 1861 and November 30, 1862 when Seth married Sarah Tipton in Polk County. A daughter, Lula, was born to this marriage in 1864, but Sarah did not live long after her birth.[27] On January 31, 1865, Seth took another wife in Polk County, Martha Johnson, the ceremony being performed by his son-in-law, Dr. James H. Reeves. In 1866 Martha bore a child, James Harvey, undoubtedly named for Dr. Reeves, and died soon after.[28] Undeterred by the loss of three wives within five years and needing someone to care for his two young children, Seth, now nearly 70 years old, married once more, on June 16, 1867.[29] His fifth wife was Mrs. Mary Anne Dowden of Polk County, a widow with two young children. They had no children and she survived him.[30]

Another wedding in the early years of the 1860s completed the marriages of Seth and Mary (Blandford) Hardison's children. William, the twin brother of Clark, married Josephine Elkins of Savannah, Georgia on December 12, 1860.[31] According to family data, Josephine's mother kept a boarding house in Savannah and probably William had met her during his medical training in that city in the late 1850s.[32]

War Years and a Move to Liberty County

State and national crises were added to the personal woes of the Hardison family, as the opening shots of the Civil War were fired in 1861 and Texas was plunged into its own civil strife. As noted in the introductory portion of this chapter, the population of the state had been drawn from two very different elements of the South. The bitter controversy over the issue of secession from the United States and participation in the Confederate States reflected the opposing views of these elements. Governor Sam Houston, who had migrated from Tennessee, had been a pivotal leader in the Texas Revolution and a strong advocate of the annexation of Texas to the United States. He represented the sentiments of many of the settlers from the upper South, mostly small farmers with few or no slaves, who believed that the state's best interests lay with remaining in the Union. In the controversy which erupted he was defeated by the pro-secession forces, primarily settlers who had migrated from the lower South, and was forced from the governorship. Texas entered the Confederacy and soon its young men were headed for the battlefields in the older states, from which they or their parents had recently emigrated.

In the midst of the crises of the opening year of the Civil War, the Hardison family's major concern seems to have been an effort to rectify errors they felt had been made in settling near the Trinity River in Polk County. Although fertile, such river valley lands were often unhealthy places to live. Three family members, Seth's sons Thomas and Clark and his wife Mary, had died within the first five years of their residence in Texas, possibly from yellow fever. The family's new destination was the northwest portion of adjoining Liberty County, where they settled in the community of Tarkington Prairie, a few miles from the present town of Cleveland. Unfortunately the early deed records of Liberty County have been lost in a courthouse fire, but the tax records indicate that in the early 1860s all the family members except Seth settled in the county.[33] Apparently the Reeves were the first to go, for they appear in the 1861 records with a small holding of 31 acres of land and two slaves. Dr. Reeves continued his participation in the Baptist Church, joining the Oak Shade Baptist Church and serving as its pastor in 1863.[34] He disappeared from the tax records after 1863 and probably moved to Limestone County at that time.

In 1862 the other Hardison son-in-law, John Gray, and John Hardison were listed in the Liberty County tax records. During most of the decade John Gray entered 92 acres and, through 1865, two slaves. In the records for several years, Mary Ann Gray had a separate listing, with personal property of varying value, up to a few hundred dollars. John remained on the tax rolls through 1868, but Mary Ann's name does not appear after 1867. According to a letter written by John Hardison in 1873, Mary Ann died soon after the end of the Civil War.[35]

John Hardison's entry in the 1862 tax records of Liberty County was 107 acres of land valued at $331.00 and two slaves at $1650.00. Although he moved his residence from Polk County, the tax records of that county indicate that he retained the land which he had purchased from Angus McLeod in 1858 and left most of his slaves under the supervision of his father, presumably to continue cultivation of the land. The number of his slaves in the Polk County tax records went from a high of twelve in 1860 to eight in 1862.[36] Of course the use of their labor was lost as the result of emancipation at the close of the Civil War. The deed and court records of Polk indicate that throughout the 1860s John struggled to keep title to his land in that county, but was unable to meet his obligations for mortgage payment and by 1871 he lost possession.[37] He lived only briefly on his recently acquired Liberty County land before volunteering for the Confederate Army in 1862, but returned there, rather than to Polk County, after the Civil War. He remained on the Liberty County tax rolls through 1866 and then moved to Limestone County.

The youngest of Seth's sons, William, first appeared on the tax rolls of Liberty County in 1865, with only two horses listed as his property. In 1866 and 1867 he declared 150 acres and references to him and his wife Josephine in family correspondence indicate that they were living in the county at that time. At the end of the decade he moved to Freestone County, to the northwest of Liberty and Polk and near the family members who had relocated in Limestone County.

Ann, the widow of Thomas Hardison, also left Polk County in the 1860s. Judging from her listing with the children of her first two marriages, Florida Walker (married to Gustavus Garvey) and the Jackson children, in the 1870 Federal Census for Liberty County, they shared a household. Her name does not appear in the Liberty County tax rolls, indicating that if she had any property she had turned it over to her Jackson sons. As noted previously, the infant son of Ann and Thomas who was listed in the 1860 Polk County census does not appear in Ann's household in 1870 and presumably did not survive early childhood. The family was living in the Tarkington Prairie community when the census was taken in 1870, but data on the Jacksons in Emma Haynes' *History of Polk County* places them in the Colita community of Polk County and Bethel Baptist Church after their marriages in the 1870s. Isaac Jackson, who was eighteen years old in 1870, developed an interest in cotton gins and grist mills and established a small general store in Polk County as well as engaging in farming.[38]

Tarkington Prairie, the Liberty County community around which the Reeves, Grays, and John, William, and Ann Hardison gathered, was named for Burton B. Tarkington. He was a pioneer settler from Indiana who migrated to Texas with his wife Sarah Berry in the 1820s. Searching for land suitable for raising cattle, he came into the area which became Liberty County and found the prairie he considered ideal on the western side of the Trinity River. Its vast grass lands were a cattle raiser's paradise and its fine, sandy soil well suited to growing corn and feed crops as well as cotton and sugar cane. He received grants for the land and soon attracted other settlers. By the time the Hardison family arrived, there were many farms clustering around a village with its own post office and school. In 1857 the Oak Shade Baptist Church was founded and during his brief residence in the community Dr. James Harvey Reeves served as its minister. The area is still identified by the name Tarkington Prairie, but no longer has a post office, having been replaced as the major settlement in northwestern Liberty County by the town of Cleveland, five miles to the north of the Tarkington home site.[39]

On March 16, 1862 John Hardison wrote a letter from Tarkington Prairie which is an appropriate ending to the narrative of his family's first five years in Texas. It is a dramatic contrast to the letter which his bride, Winnifred Davis, wrote from Florida on November 30, 1857 on the eve of their departure for Texas. The great expectations which she had communicated to her brother Edwin were now replaced by John's news of her death and the looming dislocations of war. However, in spite of the deep grief which John expressed and his concern over his two motherless daughters, his letter reveals the buoyant, optimistic personality and the faith in Texas which enabled him to cope with the hardships of the Civil War and the bitter years of Reconstruction. Edwin was already in the Confederate Army at the time John wrote.[40]

IX. ON TO TEXAS, 1857-1862

Tarkington's Prairie Texas
Sunday Eve Mch 16th [18]62

My Dear Edwin,

What must be my feelings now I have seated myself for the purpose of answering your last kind letter addressed to my poor dear Win, and dated at your Camp, 4th Feby! when first I have to tell you of her recent sad and lamented death? Yes Edwin my dear wife is gone from me now, leaving me lonely and desolate and almost broken hearted. On the very morning after your kind and brotherly letter was received—on Thursday the 12th inst. ½ past 10 o'clock am [A.M.] she breathed her last and her pure spirit took its flight to mansions above. Oh Edwin my heart grows cold when I reflect that she is gone from me never to return. Notwithstanding I am convinced as fully as I am of my own existance that her guileless soul is at this very moment basking in all the transplendant glory of High Heaven and when I look over the lines just written they all fall far short of expressing the feelings of my bosom. But if you will bear with me my dear Brother I will tell you all, that the stroke may if possible be mitigated and yourself and dear Thomas may be enabled to bear the sad fate with fortitude and Christian resignation and to pray for me in my bereavement, and that we may all join her in that Happy Home in peace when we are called hence. Just 5 weeks before her death while sitting by my side at the dinner table, she complained a little of a sore throat, and being quite hungry and the best of health she ate very hearty, thus it passed without further notice for the 2 hours I remained at the house, when I returned to my school (for I was teaching). When I came home at night I found her in bed with a high fever and the affection of the glands increased pain and difficulty of swallowing. To arrest this we applied the usual remedies in such cases and relief was the result, but the desease seated first in the right eye and then the right lobe of the brain and then spreading to the other side of the head. It was very painful until it broke when it drained both at the nostrils and left ear. The discharges were very large and continued for several days. In the meantime she was alternately better & worse, part of the time sitting up and once or twice she walked out into the garden. In this way things went on until some days before her death, when she was taken again with pain severe in the head which was undoubtedly caused by an accumulation of matter upon the brain, but we succeeded in getting it to run again when she was again better. By this time the period of her deliverance arrived and on Tuesday night last at 10 o'clock she was delivered of a pretty little girl babe, after which she revived & was quite cheerful and took every necessary nourishment, sit up in the bed and gave her lady friends some directions about some little matters and expressed great hope of getting well, Now that the trial she so much dreaded had passed all was cheerful, and her lady friends who had been in long and patient attendance were led to hope for her recovery and restoration to their society. But we were doomed to a different fate. On Wednesday noon she became again restless complaining of a heavy pain in the head, which was soon followed by speechlessness and insensibility and general paralisis of the intire system in which state she existed until Thursday when she breathed her last at the hour mentioned.

It was the accumulation of matter upon the brain in her weak state of health that caused her death. Her constitution was good and no symptoms of desease elsewhere. She passed away without leaving any requests as to anything. Her funeral was preached at the Baptist church near my residence today. There was a large concourse of people in attendance and I have everything that fellow mortals can do to console me in my deprecations and especially am I indebted to the kind and noble ladies of the community for their constant kindness & attention and many expressions of sympathy. I have given my little babe the full name of its mother and tho quite small it is very well thus far and seems to be doing as well as I could desire. I have it in the care of a kind foster mother who lives only about 300 yards from my door & has a child herself she has sucked for it. My dear Lilly is still in the bloom of health and grows more & more interesting every day. She makes many serious inquiries about her Ma since her death but takes everything much better than I could have looked for. My sister Mary Ann has her most of the time, but she will come to see her Pa almost every day. Sister Mary lives only 1½ miles off. I hope & trust I may be permitted to live and raise my 2 sweet babes fit mementos as they are of their mother. They are all I have to live for now and I am determined to stay with them as long as I can.

I have a good school here in Liberty County and I think this a more healthy country than where we lived in Polk. I live in a large prairie immediately on the main road leading from the up country to the coast.

The prairie is only about 4 or 5 miles wide here, making it about 2 miles on either side of me to the main timber. However I live on a narrow strip of timber, say about ½ mile in width, and have some as good land as I want, such as will bring 40 bbls. [bushels] corn per acre with 2 plowings. The prairie below me stretches out to one vast plain interspersed at intervals with islands of timber until it reaches the coast about 40 to 50 miles south of me. I live on the upland between the Trinity and Sanjacinto Rivers, west of the former and east of the latter. The land is generally good and the timber, but the open prairie is naturally poor in most places, but numbers of acres of it have been made rich by the immense numbers of cattle raised here for years past. The range for cattle is failing, but for hogs & sheep I never saw better. I saw a one year old hog killed a few days ago which netted 190 lbs. fatted entirely on the mash. Pork is worth 4 to 5 cts. here, and has sold as high as 5 ½ to 7 on credit til the war breaks. Corn is in abundance and can be had for 40 c cash and 50 to 75 on time. We have had plenty of Texas flour brought to us at 6 c per lbs.—so you can see times are easy here yet a while. Well we have war times here too. Our Governor has called for 15,000 men, by the 29th inst. and great efforts are making throughout the State to have them ready to keep off a draft. We have us one company of cavalry in this prairie which will report next Saturday. 3 companies are ready in the County, and I learned last night from one of my Polk County neighbors that 4 companies were ready from Polk Co. Dr. Wm. L. [John's brother] was fixing off. I am anxious to go but it has been decided by our meetings that I be one to stay to see to the destitute women & children left behind—besides I have a mail contract and am bound for the transportation of the mail which would stop were I to leave, and my bond forfeited. I am giving every dollar I possess and whatelse I can do in the way of procuring horses, guns & other equipment for those who are going.

Well Edwin I have written a long letter and think I had better now quit. I wish you to write to Liz & Sarah giving the particulars of Win's illness and death and also the birth of her child its sex and name & when you can, send me the date of Win's birth tho I believe she was born in March of the same year I was but don't remember the day. Win wrote you a long letter just before she was taken sick, and I sent it to the care of Uncle Joel with instructions to forward to you. Tender my warmest love

to Thomas, and be assured of the same good feeling for yourself.
Direct to   Your sad Bro
Tarkington's Prairie   Jno. R. Hardison   Liberty Co.
(P.S. I can't tell what will be my address now, will write you again soon.)
Excuse my bad writing for I am very nervous.
Hope to hear from you before I leave the State.

  Well Edwin this is the 28th March and my letter still here, but I will mail this morning. I have volunteered in the C[onfederate] Service for 3 years or the war. We have a fine company of Cavalry made up from the neighborhood. I have the office of Orderly Sergeant which you know is a very laborious one. We join Col. Carter's Reg. Texas Lancers, & will leave for Hempstead next Tuesday for drill & our destination in the service will be Arkansas. I leave my dear little children quite well and provided with everything they need. My babe grows f[?].

The death of Winnifred, following so soon after the decease of John's brothers Thomas and Clark and his mother, seems a fulfillment of the words in her letter of June 10, 1858 to Edwin, "Edd what changes will be wrought throughout the land, e're bright Aurora begins its dayly test? Many will go to the bourn from which no traveler ever returns, and many will be loaded down with grief . . . ." Deaths such as those in the Hardison family and the previously cited losses in Winnifred's family in Georgia were frequently experienced griefs in nineteenth century America, before the advances of modern medicine moderated or eliminated many scourges. Winnifred probably died of an acute infection which antibiotics might have halted. Her death occurred at the end of the first year of the Civil War and before the war ended three years later her brother Thomas and cousin Enos Davis were dead, along with many thousands of young men of the Union and the Confederacy.

  In April, 1862 John left his daughters Lilly and Winnifred in Liberty County with his sister Mary Ann Gray, as he departed for service with the cavalry company made up of men from his neighborhood. Although Texas did not become a major battlefield, the hardships of war soon became evident as the Union blockade of the Gulf ports shut out the manufactured goods on which the agricultural economy depended. Agriculture itself was hampered as thousands of young men departed for the eastern states, leaving many fields unplanted and untended. A history of the Oak Shade Baptist Church of Tarkington Prairie includes examples of the shortages and hardships of the war years. The preacher assisting Dr. Reeves, in his role as pastor of Oak Shade, in a revival meeting in 1863 wore a coat made of blue bed-ticking. Homespun clothing dyed with the extract of black walnut bark, wild indigo, swamp maple, or elderberries was worn by everyone. Confederate money was plentiful but almost worthless, with $40.00 required to buy a spool of thread, $150.00 for a ham, $75.00 a pound for sugar, and $1,200.00 for a barrel of flour. "Almost all men were in the army and many of them filled a soldier's grave. Want, distress, anguish reigned everywhere. The country was literally in mourning."[41]

NOTES

The early records of Polk County have escaped the fires which have destroyed so many eighteenth and nineteenth county archives and they have been well preserved. The deed, marriage, and court records provide much useful information on the Hardisons' first years in Texas. The deed records are well indexed, but the court records are not and time did not allow the search needed to gain a full account of John R. Hardison's litigation in regard to his land in the 1860s and early 1870s. Information from the Polk County archives has been augmented by local histories, which are available in the Murphy Memorial Library in Livingston, the county seat. Additional material on both Polk and Liberty counties is found in the Sam Houston Regional Library and Research Center in the town of Liberty. The deed records of Liberty County for the 1860s were destroyed in a courthouse fire, but the tax records of the 1860s document the family's presence and the extent and location of their holdings. These records and the Polk County tax records are available on microfilm in the Texas Collection of the Houston Public Library.

1. Background history of the development of Texas in the decades preceding the Hardisons' arrival is found in Terry G. Jordan, *Immigration to Texas* (Boston: American Press, 1981) and Barnes F. Lathrop, *Migration into East Texas, 1835-1860* (Austin: Texas State Historical Association, 1949).
2. State of Texas, General Land Office, Austin, original title in the Spanish Collection, Box 80, Folder 40.
3. Arlene Eakle and Johni Cerny, *The Source*, p.250.
4. Jordan, *op. cit.*, p.11..
5. *Ibid.*, pp.12-13.
6. Eighth Federal Census, 1860, Texas, Lamar County, p.77, and Harrison County, p.464; see also Ninth Federal Census, 1870, Texas, for Hardison families in Lamar County, p.328, and Bosque County, p.426.
7. United States Archives, Washington, D.C., pension application #43568, Aug. 12, 1884, by Nancy (Hardison) Brigham of Blanco County for a widow's pension based on the service of her husband Emerald Brigham (died 1863) in the War of 1812.
8. Polk County Deed Book G, pp.223-24.
9. *Ibid.*, pp.221-22.

10. Cain Family Genealogical Collection, typescript of a letter from Winnifred (Davis) Hardison to her brother Edwin Davis, probably copied from the original of the letter in the possession of descendants of Edwin, who lived in Thomasville, Georgia after the Civil War. Spelling, punctuation, and capitalizations of this typescript and of the typescript of the letter of March 16, 1862 of John R. Hardison to Edwin have been retained.
11. Polk County Deed Book G, pp.485-86.
12. *Map of Livingston Reservoir* (Dallas: A.I.D. Associates, 1972).
13. Polk County Deed Book H, p.645; the original registration by McLeod is found in Marks and Brands Book A, p.49.
14. Polk County Deed Book G, pp.473-74.
15. Emma Haynes, *The History of Polk County* (typescript, 1937, in Sam Houston Library and Research Center, Liberty), p.114.
16. Talmadge L. Buller, compiler, *Records of Bethel Baptist Church of Polk County, Texas* (typescript in Murphy Memorial Library, Livingston). vol.1, pp.46, 62-63, and 97.
17. Polk County District Court, Civil Minutes, Book C, pp.228-29; Polk County Deed Book H, pp.187-89.
18. Eighth Federal Census, 1860, Texas, Polk County, mss. p.18, printed p.43.
19. Cain Collection, letter of June 1, 1873 from John R. Hardison to his sister-in-law Mary Elizabeth (Davis) Hardwick of Georgia, noting that Lilly (in this case spelled Lily) was 14 years old on January 13, 1873.
20. Seventh Federal Census, 1850, Florida, Calhoun County, p.39.
21. Ninth Federal Census, 1870, Texas, Liberty County, p.8; Emma Haynes, *History of Polk County* (Livingston: Keen Printing Co., 1968),vol.1, pp.104-05 (information on the Jacksons and Hardisons, some of which is inaccurate, including the identification of Ann's husband as Dr.Seth Hardison).
22. Eighth Federal Census, 1860, Slave Population, Texas, Polk County, pp.7-8; Seventh Federal Census, 1850, Slave Population, Florida, Gadsden County, p.241.
23. Polk County Deed Book H, pp.463-64.
24. Polk County Deed Book I, pp.195-96.
25. Dora Johnson, *History of Oak Shade Baptist Church, 1857-1970* (unpublished mss., 1971), p.2; a copy of the history was given to me by the pastor in 1986.
26. Cain Collection, John R. Hardison's letter of June 1, 1873 stated that "Bro Thos & Clark & Mother died before the war & Sister Mary just after."
27. Polk County Marriage Record, vol.B-2, p.97; Lula's gravestone in the Lost Prairie Cemetery in Limestone County gives her dates as 1864-1916. She married J. W. Sandifer (1863-1919), who is buried beside her. Lula may have been a nickname, for she is referred to as Sallie in the 1870 Federal Census, Limestone County, listing for Seth's family and may have been named for her mother, the former Sarah Tipton. Her marriage record of 1885 lists her as S. T. (possibly L.) Hardison, data from Limestone County Marriage Book C, p.403, as listed in *Limestone County, Texas Marriage Index, 1874-1900* (Buffalo, Texas: Four Scribes, n.d.).
28. Polk County Marriage Record, vol.B-2, p.126; James Harvey Hardison's gravestone in the Lost Prairie Cemetery gives his dates as 1866-1943.
29. Polk County Marriage Record, vol.B-2, p,210.
30. Ninth Federal Census, 1870, Texas, Limestone County, p.244, following Seth, Mary A. Hardison is listed, age 30, born in Alabama, with two Dowden children, ages 11 and 9, both born in Texas; Seth's children by the two previous marriages are included also, with the daughter listed as Sallie.
31. Chatham County, Georgia, Marriage Records, 1860.

32. Cain Collection, data from May (Wood) Cain.
33. Liberty County Tax Records, 1860-1870 (microfilm in Texas Collection of Houston Public Library).
34. Johnson, *op. cit.*, pp.2-3.
35. Cain Collection, see quote from John R. Hardison letter of June 1, 1873 in footnote #26. Mary Ann's husband may be the John W. Gray listed in the Limestone County Tax Records for 1867. He was taxed for two horses but no land.
36. Polk County Tax Records, 1858-1865 (microfilm in Texas Collection of Houston Public Library).
37. Polk County Deed Book K, pp.226-28; Book N, pp.234-36 and pp.566-71. The litigation reflected in these deeds will be discussed in the chapter covering John's affairs after the Civil War.
38. See sources for Ann and her children in footnote #21.
39. Leota Carrol and Leila Mae Catchings, *Burton B. Tarkington, Founder of Tarkington Prairie* (mss. in Sam Houston Regional Library and Research Center, Liberty, n.d.).
40. Cain Collection, typescript of letter of March 16, 1862 from John R. Hardison to his brother-in-law Edwin Davis. As noted in regard to the previously cited typescript of Winnifred's letter of June 10, 1858, this copy was probably made from the original belonging to descendants of Edwin Davis. It is most likely that the funeral of Winnifred was held at the Oak Shade Baptist Church and that the preacher was John's brother-in-law, Dr. Reeves. The cemetery was greatly damaged by a hurricane and I was unable to find a stone for her when I visited the church in 1986.
41. Johnson, *op. cit.*, p.3.

X

*The South at War
John Hardison's Service in the
Confederate Army, 1862-1863*

On March 20, 1862 John Randolph Hardison volunteered for a three year term of service in the Confederate Army. He enlisted in a company formed in Liberty County, Texas, which soon became a part of the Third Regiment of Carter's Brigade of Texas Lancers. Following a series of reorganizations, the company was designated Company G, Twenty-fifth Regiment, Texas Cavalry (dismounted), and in 1863 it became a component of the Texas Brigade, which served in the Army of Tennessee until the end of the war.[1] John was joined in Confederate service by his brother, Dr. William L. Hardison, and at least seven sons of his father's sisters, including Benjamin Brigham of Texas (son of Nancy and Emerald Brigham); Dr. Theophilus H. Jackson of Florida (son of Elizabeth and Abner Jackson); Thomas L. and Edwin T. Davis of Georgia (sons of Temperance and Enos Davis); Enos, Lawson, and William Davis of Georgia (sons of Winnifred and Joel Davis).[2]

At the time of John's enlistment in 1862, the Civil War had been in progress for almost a year, dating from April 12, 1861, when Fort Sumter in the harbor at Charleston was fired on by Confederate

May thy life be free from cares, May the bright and happy sunshine of true friendship ever attend thee and dispel and dissipate the dark shadows from thy pathway through life— May you find a noble true and loving heart—beating always in unison with thine own, that you may not in truth exclaim, as I can—

"Alone I'm floating down the tide
With naught to guide my barque.
No love light gleams upon my sky
The clouds are drear and dark."

May Heaven's best blessings always attend you May you live a long life of happiness and love, And when thou art wearied with time and earthly things be assured that—

"There is a home of joy and bliss
Where skies are clear and bright
Where fragrant flowers are clustering round
The throne of life and light
And would'st thou learn the name which God
That beauteous land hath given?
Bow down thine ear—I'll whisper soft
Dost hear me Mary?— 'tis Heaven."

Bay Spring Ga—
Saturday Eve. Jany 1864—

J. Randolph H.
25th Texas Cavalry

John Randolph Hardison to Mary Fletcher Northington
in Her Autograph Book, 1864

Slaughter Collection

X. THE SOUTH AT WAR, 1862-1863

forces. President Lincoln had refused to recognize the right of South Carolina to the federal fortifications in the harbor and announced his intention to re-provision Fort Sumter. Refusing also to recognize the right of the Southern states to withdraw from the Union and form a separate nation, Lincoln saw the struggle as a civil conflict, while the seceding states saw it as a contest between two separate nations which were made up of sovereign states. Many Southerners objected to the designation "Civil War" for the conflict and insisted instead on calling it the "War between the States" or the "War for Southern Independence." In the few surviving writings of John Hardison for the war years, he spoke of the Union troops as invaders and championed the cause for Southern independence. The states' rights sentiments of his father's generation, which had inspired his parents to give him the name of one of the leading supporters of those sentiments, John Randolph of Virginia, gave meaning to the sacrifices which he and the other young men of the South were willing to make.

The role of the slavery controversy, which many historians have considered the major cause of the war, needs to be seen in the context of the conflict over the nature of the Union and the rights of the states within the Union. These had been divisive issues at various times ever since the beginning of the nation's existence. In the years preceding the Civil War the South had come to believe that the political and economic policies of the federal government were detrimental to its interests as an agricultural society with a heavy dependence on slave labor. Increasingly these policies were being determined by a Congress in which Southerners were outnumbered by representatives of the more populous states of the North and the growing number of western states. With the victory of Abraham Lincoln and the newly formed Republican Party in the presidential election of 1860, the South looked upon the entire federal establishment as hostile to its interests. Its more radical element successfully pushed for secession and the formation of a separate nation. Lincoln refused to heed the advice to "let the erring sisters go in peace" and, with his decision to deny South Carolina's claim to sovereignty over the federal fort at Fort Sumter, the powder keg of festering hostilities was ignited.

Initially the Confederacy, under the leadership of President Jefferson Davis, rejected proposals to invade the North and concentrated its efforts on preparing to protect the boundaries of the newly formed nation. Lincoln feared the build-up of military forces in Virginia as a threat to the Union capital in Washington and the first major battle was fought at Bull Run on July 21, 1861 in an effort to strike a blow at those forces. The decisive Confederate victory was a shock to the North and a cause for jubilation in the South. The celebration was short lived, however, as Lincoln and the Union military establishment prepared a comprehensive strategy to put down what was considered a rebellion and to crush the military and civilian resistance. The major components of their strategy were to blockade or conquer the port cities of the South in order to cut off access to arms and goods from abroad, to capture the Confederate capital of Richmond and defeat the armed forces in Virginia which threatened Washington, to gain control of the Mississippi River and its tributaries in order to cut off supplies from the Trans-Mississippi states, to gain control of the rivers of Tennessee and the rail and supply center at Chattanooga, and to occupy the lower South, particularly Georgia which was a major source of food for General Robert E. Lee's forces in Virginia. For four years the conflict raged as the South countered the North's efforts and occasionally made forays into Union territory. John Hardison began his military service in his adopted state of Texas and by a circuitous route became one of the defenders of his native state of Georgia.

Enlistment in Texas and Service in Arkansas

John began his service a year after the war began. During that year the expectations of the South for a short and successful encounter with Union forces, which would lead to recognition of the independence of the Confederate States of America, had been disappointed. In the spring of 1862 the South was on the defensive on all fronts, with the loss of New Orleans, the advances of General George B. McClelland on Richmond, and the likelihood of the loss of the Mississippi River valley after the defeats at Fort Henry, Fort Donelson, and Shiloh. The early enthusiasm for volunteering which had marked the first months of the war in 1861 was dampened as the realities of a long struggle were recognized. As John noted in his letter of March 16, 1862 to his brother-in-law Edwin Davis, there was talk of a draft in Texas. This rumor became reality in April when the Confederate Congress passed a conscription act which applied to men of ages eighteen to thirty-five. It included a highly criticized provision which exempted men who owned twenty or more slaves, leading to the often-voiced complaint that the conflict was "a rich man's war and a poor man's fight." John had been reluctant to volunteer because of the recent illness and death of his wife Winnifred and his concern over the welfare of his two young daughters. However, soon after beginning his letter, in which he informed Edwin of Winnifred's death, he volunteered "for 3 years or the war," as he noted in a postscript dated March 28.[3]

Like the majority of Texas volunteers, John joined a company of cavalry, for Texans never walked when they could ride. Eventually many of the cavalry units, including John's, were dispossessed of their horses as the Confederacy had a far greater need for infantry and also lacked the means of feeding so many horses. The company which John joined was formed in his neighborhood in Liberty County and, as the men chose their officers, he was given the office of first sergeant, with W. D. Davis as captain. John's brother Dr. William L. Hardison enlisted in the company as a private, but was discharged in June because of illness. He was again on the company's rolls from September through December and in 1865, with several entries on the rolls indicating incapacity to serve due to illness.[4]

John's company was one of a number of volunteer units formed in Texas in the spring of 1862. In April it became part of an organization known as the Texas Lancers, which the Reverend George W. Carter had been given permission by the Confederate government to form in the spring of 1861. Carter was a Methodist minister, who had been president of Soule University, a small college in the little town of Chappell Hill, to the north of Houston. The romanticism which characterized a number of Southerners in the early days of the war had led him to call "To the Chivalry of Texas" for the creation of the Texas Lancers. Since a sufficient supply of cavalry sabers was not available, the men were to be equipped with lances which would be manufactured in Texas. Since the lances did not materialize and the regiments were "dismounted" within a few months, it was fortunate that the recruits had been advised to bring their shot-guns, revolvers, and bowie knives. They and other Texas recruits were armed with whatever guns they had possessed as civilians and the great variety created a problem of supplying adequate ammunition. Another problem in the Texas units was the egalitarianism and individualism which life on the frontier had fostered. The men chose their own officers at the company level, based more on popularity than military ability, and they had little respect for military discipline or rank.

By the spring of 1862 Carter had enough recruits to form thirty companies and he was commissioned as a colonel and given permission to divide the men into three regiments, the First, Second, and Third Texas Lancers. Officially these units were designated the Twenty-first, Twenty-fourth, and the Twenty-fifth Texas Cavalry Regiments. John's company was assigned to the Twenty-fifth Regiment and designated as Company G, in which he was elected first sergeant. Carter was appointed as brigade commander and also commander of the Twenty-first Regiment, while two other Methodist clergymen, Colonel Franklin C. Wilkes and Colonel Clayton C. Gillespie, led the Twenty-fourth and Twenty-fifth. The brigade gathered in Hempstead, a short distance to the north of Houston, and in the summer was ordered to Arkansas to join other Confederate forces in preventing invasion and occupation of the state by Union forces.

As the brigade made its way through Texas and Louisiana, the men disgraced themselves by pillaging the countryside for fodder for their mounts—and for themselves as well, as they raided smokehouses and farm yards. The outrage of the farmers coupled with the growing realization of the greater need for infantry than cavalry led to the decision on July 29 to relieve two of the regiments, the Twenty-fourth and Twenty-fifth, of their horses. These units were thereafter known as dismounted cavalry regiments. The Twenty-first kept its horses and joined a cavalry brigade led by Colonel William H. Parsons. The Twenty-fourth and Twenty-fifth, along with the Sixth Texas Infantry, were assigned to a new brigade headed by Colonel Robert R. Garland.

In September, 1862, Colonel Garland was ordered to assemble his command at Fort Hindman on the Arkansas River as part of an effort to prevent enemy forces from using the river, a major tributary of the Mississippi River, in an invasion of Arkansas. A concerted assault by a large concentration of Union forces was in the making, as they determined to eliminate all resistance to control of the Mississippi. These forces included the command of Major General William T. Sherman, with whom the Texans were to become well acquainted during the course of the war. Close to 5,000 Confederate troops, belonging primarily to units from Texas along with several from Arkansas and Louisiana, were gathered at a place known as Arkansas Post, about twenty-five miles west of the confluence of the Arkansas and the Mississippi rivers. A fort had been hastily constructed by slave labor at the site of an abandoned settlement which had been at various times a French trading post, a Spanish fort, and an early capital of the Arkansas Territory. The unhealthy climate of the swampy area had caused it be abandoned as a habitation, but it was valuable as the location for a fort which could prevent Union naval forces from using the Arkansas River as an invasion route to the state. The fort was named for Major General Thomas C. Hindman, the commander of the Trans-Mississippi Department of the Confederacy. It was a crude square structure about 300 feet on each side, constructed of logs and earthworks. It was armed with one eight-inch and two nine-inch guns, which had come from the Confederate Navy ram *Pontchartrain*, plus several light field guns. A series of outlying works, including piles driven into the riverbed and connected with heavy chains, were constructed, along with log huts for barracks.[5]

The men were eager for a confrontation with the enemy and feared the war would end before they had an opportunity for combat. Within a few months they were to learn that war was harsh and deadly, not a glorious adventure, but in the meantime their suffering had already begun as the combination of unhealthy location and winter cold took a heavy toll of the poorly housed men. At times funerals for the victims went on through the day and into the night. Christmas passed with considerable complaints about the lack of the bountiful and festive food of past years, with the absence of egg-nog particularly regretted. As the new year opened the inaction of the past four months was soon to end. Captain Samuel T. Foster of the Twenty-fourth Texas Regiment wrote in his diary in early January, 1863, "We enjoy our Christmas as well as we know how in camp, having no Egg-nog— New Year comes in and all goes on quiet enough until Jan 8th [January 9, 1863] when we are ordered to fall in for a fight this time sure enough."[6]

The Battle of Arkansas Post was about to begin, as a Union force of approximately 30,000 men, under the command of Major General John A. McClernand, set out to destroy Fort Hindman and prepare the way for the conquest of Arkansas and control of the Mississippi River. Serving under McClernand were Brigadier General George W. Morgan with the Thirteenth Army Corps, Major General William T. Sherman with the Fifteenth Army Corps, and Admiral David D. Porter with a fleet of gunboats. The Union infantry, artillery, and navy were deployed for several days in early January and the Confederate troops prepared for attack. Some of the men were curious as well as anxious as their first combat drew near and were almost killed when they were fired upon while peering from the river banks at the novelty of a Yankee ironclad gunboat. Bravado and curiosity were soon replaced by desperate fighting as the battle began at mid-day on January 11.

The brigade to which John Hardison belonged was assigned to a portion of the outer defenses extending from the fort toward a bayou. As the large Union infantry force moved in toward the fort, the brigade had to change its position and was forced to crawl on hands and knees through the trenches to avoid being shot. The big guns of the fort fired on the gunboats and the artillery and infantry used all arms at their disposal to drive off the enemy, but the troops were greatly outnumbered and the fort was gradually pounded to pieces. All the surrounding buildings caught fire, mingling with the gunsmoke to create a hellish scene. The fort commander, Brigadier General Thomas J. Churchill, had been ordered "to hold out till help arrived or until all dead," but by four o'clock in the afternoon a white flag was raised on the flag staff of the fort and soon white handkerchiefs and shirt tails were hoisted on ramrods in the area held by the Twenty-fourth Texas Cavalry Regiment. General Churchill was furious and accused Colonel Garland, the commander of the brigade which included the Twenty-fourth as well as John's regiment, the Twenty-fifth, of making the decision to surrender. Garland maintained that he had been ordered to surrender by a member of Churchill's staff, which Churchill denied. Since the Confederate forces were so completely outnumbered and outgunned, they could not have won the battle, but the surrender gave an unsavory reputation to the whole force at Fort Hindman and especially Colonel Garland.

The casualties were relatively light. For the Union they were 134 killed, 898 wounded, and 29 missing, while for the Confederates approximately 60 dead and 75 to 80 wounded. But for the 4,791 men taken prisoner the loss of life was just beginning. The men were put on boats and taken up the Mississippi River to prison camps, the officers to Camp Chase, Ohio, and the enlisted men to Camp Douglas at Chicago and Camp Butler near Springfield, Illinois. John Hardison, listed as a private in the muster roll of Company G, Twenty-fifth Texas Cavalry, was imprisoned at Camp Butler. The men's clothing, housing, food, and medical care were totally inadequate and approximately thirty percent of them died during their incarceration. A few of the prisoners escaped and some took the oath of allegiance to the Union and were released, but most relied on the hope for a prisoner exchange. Their hope was rewarded in early April when the first contingent was ordered to board trains for Virginia. After a long and circuitous journey they arrived at City Point, Virginia on the James River. They were followed during April by the other survivors of the Battle of Arkansas Post.

John, like many of the men, was ill as a consequence of prison life and was admitted on April 15 to the Episcopal Church Hospital in Williamsburg. He was later sent to a hospital in Petersburg where he was issued clothing on May 18. The muster roll for his company which covers the first half of 1863 indicates that he remained in the hospital through June and was furloughed on July 6. The muster roll for July and August records that he was due pay for use of a horse for one month, possibly indicating that he used his furlough time for a visit with his relatives in Georgia. Later records show that he rejoined his regiment in time for participation in the Battle of Chickamauga in September.

Beginning of Service in the Texas Brigade

While John was recuperating from the effects of his imprisonment, those among his fellow soldiers from Arkansas Post who were fit for service were divided into companies of one hundred men and put up in a camp of tents in Virginia. They were briefly pressed into service in a defensive force protecting Richmond at the time of the Battle of

Chancellorsville at the end of April. In May they were ordered to join General Joseph E. Johnston's Division of the West in Mississippi, service they welcomed as bringing them closer to home, but their orders were changed as they made their way through Tennessee by train. They were assigned instead to the Army of Tennessee, commanded by General Braxton Bragg, and sent to Tullahoma, Tennessee. Knowledge of their surrender at Arkansas Post led the soldiers whom they joined to taunt them with remarks like "We don't want you if you can't see a Yank without holding up your shirt to him." They were consolidated into a single brigade and placed in the division of Major General Patrick Cleburne, who was rumored to be the only division officer who would take them into his command. His faith in them was justified and he would eventually have cause to call them a "band of heroes." Cleburne's division belonged to the corps commanded by Lieutenant General William J. Hardee.

The Texans' new organization was known as the Texas Brigade and eventually Granbury's Texas Brigade, for Hiram B. Granbury, the most popular of their several commanders. They were commanded briefly by their Arkansas Post commander, Brigadier General Thomas J. Churchill, and then by Brigadier General James Deshler. The brigade consisted of two regiments, the first made up of the Sixth and Tenth Texas Infantry and the Fifteenth Texas Cavalry (dismounted) and the second formed from the Seventeenth, Eighteenth, Twenty-fourth, and Twenty-fifth Texas Cavalry (dismounted). The several independent cavalry companies led by Captains Nutt, Richardson, Johnson, and Denson, which had served at Arkansas Post, were combined as Company L of the first of these regiments. The Arkansas troops who had served with the Texans, the Nineteenth and Twenty-fourth Arkansas Infantry, were consolidated into the Arkansas Battalion. The officer who had been blamed for the surrender at Arkansas Post, Colonel Garland, was passed over when commands were assigned. The regiment to which John Hardison's Twenty-fifth Texas Cavalry was assigned was put under the command first of Colonel Clayton C. Gillespie and then Colonel Franklin C. Wilkes, two of the Methodist clergymen from Texas who had helped form the Texas Lancers in 1861. The men from Arkansas Post, who had come into service wearing whatever uniforms could be assembled at home in the first year of the war, were now clothed in Confederate gray. Along with the new clothing came military discipline and drill from General Cleburne, a native of Ireland who had been trained in the British army. The Texas Brigade soon became a tenacious fighting force which earned his gratitude and praise.

As the Texans prepared to go into service with the Army of Tennessee in the summer of 1863, the South was about to suffer two major defeats. Victories in the latter part of 1862 had bolstered the hope of the Confederacy that its independence might be recognized and the hostilities ended, but the course of the war went against the South as 1863 progressed. July was a fateful month as Lee's invasion of Pennsylvania culminated in the disaster at Gettysburg and Grant's conquest of Vicksburg gave the Union control of the Mississippi valley and cut the Confederacy in half. From that time the Confederacy was fighting a losing battle, but the war dragged on for nearly two more years. Lee's Army of Northern Virginia had yet to be defeated in its defense of Richmond and the state of Virginia. The rail center at Chattanooga and the state of Georgia, which was a major source of food for Lee's forces, were unconquered. John Hardison's remaining time of service was in the Army of Tennessee as it attempted to prevent, and then to contain, the invasion of the lower South by the Union forces gathered in Tennessee.

John Hardison was on medical leave during the summer of 1863 as the Texas Brigade began its service in the Army of Tennessee. His former comrades saw limited action during General Bragg's unsuccessful attempt to hold central Tennessee and prevent the capture of Chattanooga. Union General William S. Rosecrans took Chattanooga on September 9 and drove the Confederates into northwest Georgia. John had returned to active service by September, in time to join his brigade in their first major battle, as they turned on the invaders in a maneuver which led to the Battle of Chickamauga on September 19-20. The opposing forces faced each other on either side of Chickamauga Creek in Georgia, a short distance from the Tennessee border. When the battle began on September 19, the lines see-sawed back and forth across the creek, with successive charges and countercharges. The Texas Brigade, now commanded by Brigadier General James Deshler, was sent into action in the afternoon. Soon they were splashing through waist-deep water across the creek and fighting in a large open field where the trees and dead grass had been ignited by the constant firing. They must have been reminded of the similar conditions under which they had fought at Arkansas Post, but this encounter was of far greater duration and ferocity and was to have a very different ending. A fellow member of John Hardison's regiment, Captain Samuel T. Foster of the Twenty-fourth Texas Cavalry, said it "made Ark. Post appear as childs play to it."[7] The Texans broke into a gap in the Union forces and captured a number of prisoners and battle flags, undoubtedly with a great sense of satisfaction as they recalled their own experience as captives.

When night fell the battle was temporarily suspended and both sides prepared to resume the next day. Both the wounded and the still active men suffered greatly from an early frost. Miscommunication within the Confederate command led to a delay in the start of the battle in the morning and the Confederate offensive did not get under way until after nine. James M. McCaffrey in his history of the Texas Brigade, *This Band of Heroes*, has described the opening of the second day: "The Federal works bristled with muskets and cannons as Deshler's brigade began its advance about 10.00 A.M. As the Confederates moved into the open they were met by a tremendous artillery and small arms fire. They halfheartednly cracked jokes to relieve the tension and they pulled the brims of their hats down low as they leaned forward into the fury of lead as if it were a rainstorm."[8] As the battle continued the brigade was ordered to a position on the crest of a small hill where the men were told to lie down and commence firing. The enemy was protected by breastworks they had hastily thrown up during the night and they poured fire on the Confederates throughout the afternoon, causing heavy casualties. When the Union line began to bend back upon itself after a heavy assault by men led by Lieutenant General James Longstreet, whom General Lee had sent from Virginia to bolster Bragg's army, Deshler's brigade and the brigade commanded by Brigadier General Lucius Polk were ordered forward. Late in the afternoon part of Union General Rosecrans' forces fled the battlefield, while the determined stand of General George H. Thomas won him the name the "Rock of Chickamauga," but even Thomas was forced to admit defeat. The Union troops retreated toward the town of Rossville as darkness settled over the field of battle, now a scene of carnage.

The contest was a Confederate victory, but it was a Pyrrhic victory when the heavy casualties were considered. The Union casualties totaled about 16,000 and the Confederate 18,000. On September 19 Cleburne's division had numbered 5,115 and during the two days of battle it lost 204 killed, 1,539 wounded, and 6 missing, making a rate of a little over thirty-four percent casualties. The Texas Brigade had begun the battle with 1,783 men and lost 52 killed and 366 wounded. John Hardison was among the wounded on the second day, September 20, as was his regiment's commander, Colonel Franklin C. Wilkes. The brigade's commander, General Deshler, had been killed instantly when struck in the chest by an artillery projectile. Command now passed to Colonel Roger Q. Mills.

The nature of John's wound is not indicated in the company muster record for September and October, which noted that he was in the hospital due to wounds received on September 20, nor is it known by his descendants. Obviously it was severe for he was on medical leave the remainder of 1863. Care of the wounded was of the most primitive nature both on the battlefield and in hospitals. The men often had to lie untended and underfoot as a battle progressed and in hospitals shattered limbs were amputated with little or no anesthesia or attention to infection. John was spared the maiming of amputation and also a long stay in a crude military hospital. He was fortunate in being close to his Hardison and Davis relatives in Washington County and he took advantage of his opportunity for a visit with them when he was able to travel. He did not return to active service until sometime early in 1864. As John was furloughed to recuperate, his fellow members of the Texas Brigade were ordered to Tennessee as the Confederates attempted to prevent the consolidation of the Union forces preparing for an assault on Georgia. Once again they were to face troops led by General William T. Sherman, as well as the formidable Ulysses S. Grant and George H. Thomas. Much to the dismay of his growing body of critics, General Bragg had chosen to rest and recuperate after the Battle of Chickamauga, rather than immediately pursue the enemy. By the time he moved toward Chattanooga, the Union forces were well entrenched. In the spectacular battles on the mountain heights around Chattanooga the Texans fought valiantly, with particular distinction at Missionary Ridge, but the Confederates were unable to dislodge the enemy. At the end of November Bragg was forced to retreat back into Georgia, as the victorious enemy shouted "Remember Chickamauga." Although defeated, General Cleburne again had cause for pride in the men from Arkansas Post whom he had given a chance to regain their military reputation under his command. In making his report of the service of the Texas Brigade, he wrote, "Sadly, but not fearfully, this band of heroes left the hill they had held so well and followed the army across the Chickamauga."[9]

As the Union army pursued General Bragg's retreating Army of Tennessee, the Texas Brigade served as the rear guard for Cleburne's division. At Ringgold Gap, in northwest Georgia, it again fought with distinction as it helped to hold off a much larger force of Union troops and prevent an attack on the main body of Bragg's army. The enemy, led by General Joseph Hooker, suffered heavy losses and turned around and headed for Chattanooga without further pursuit. Bragg, who had become increasingly unpopular with his men and with the Confederate leadership and citizenry for his repeated failure to take advantage of opportunities to pursue the invaders, resigned and was replaced by General Joseph E. Johnston.

In December, 1863, Johnston was received with great enthusiasm by the Army of Tennessee. As he assumed leadership of its approximately 36,000 men, it was estimated that about 6,000 of them had no arms and an equal number were without shoes or adequate clothing and blankets. Morale was poor and a number of the Texans had simply walked away and returned home. Johnston acted to restore the men's enthusiasm for the Confederate cause and urged those whose three year enlistments had expired to re-enlist. Most of the men in the Texas Brigade responded and morale among them rose after Colonel Hiram B. Granbury of Texas was promoted to the rank of brigadier general in March, 1864 and given command of the brigade.

As General Johnston took his new command, the Army of Tennessee went into winter quarters, from December, 1863 until the spring of 1864, in the vicinity of Dalton, Georgia. The Union troops settled in at Chattanooga. Each army was gathering strength for the great contest for control of the rail and supply center at Atlanta and for the state of Georgia. During the winter liberal furloughs were allowed by Johnston and John's was particularly generous, lasting from late fall of 1863 until January, 1864. He appeared on the muster records of his regiment as being in the hospital in September and October and absent with leave in November and December. A pay record dated January 14, 1864 states that J.R. Hardison, First Sergeant of Company G, Twenty-fifth Regiment, Texas Cavalry, was paid $40.00 at Savannah, Georgia for May and June of the previous year, at the rate of $20.00 per month. The record bears the notation that he was absent on furlough of sixty days granted by the Examining Board of Lake City, Florida. The last of these entries in his service record seems to indicate that he used part of his furlough for a visit to the northern area of Florida. Family lore includes the story of a visit to Tallahassee, close to his former home in Gadsden County, where he was entertained by a daughter of Governor John Milton of Florida. A poem which he later wrote concerning Union invasions of the Jacksonville area was probably inspired by his Florida visit. It was published in a Washington County, Georgia newspaper, the *Central Georgian*, on May 25, 1864 and will be quoted in the following chapter.

A Romantic Interlude

When John had recovered sufficiently from his wounds to leave the hospital in the fall of 1863, he went to Washington County, in central Georgia, to visit his numerous kinsmen. These relatives were his uncle, William L. Hardison, and his family; his aunt, Winnifred (Hardison), and her husband, Joel Davis, with their children; and brothers and sisters of his deceased wife, Winnifred (Davis), who were also his cousins through Winnifred's mother, Temperance (Hardison) Davis, wife of Enos Davis. Both Temperance and Enos were deceased by this time. The Hardisons lived near Oconee, a village in the southwestern corner of the county which had grown up around Station Fourteen on the recently built Central of Georgia Railroad, and the Davis families at Davisboro on the eastern side of the county.

A family anecdote relates that John, while still recuperating from his wounds, came to his Uncle William's home at Oconee, walked down the steep hill at the back of the house, and drank from the creek as he held to a tree at the foot of the hill.[10] In a letter written after the war to one of his Davis sisters-in-law, he asked especially about "Aunt Lucy," possibly a former slave, many of whom were referred to as "aunt" and "uncle" by their white owners, saying, "Oh Is dear good old Aunt Lucy still alive? If so god bless her old soul—give her my best love. If she's dead I know she's gone straight to Heaven just for her good to you and to me when I was wounded."[11] The loving care of returning servicemen was a common occurrence for Washington County residents, who claimed the distinction of sending a higher percentage of their men into service than any other county in the Confederacy.[12] Among these men were the previously cited members of the Davis families, Edwin and Thomas, sons of Temperance and Enos Davis, and Enos, Lawson, and William, sons of Winnifred and Joel Davis. Thomas and Enos died during the war. Enos, a physician, died of typhoid fever while serving in Virginia.

In the letters which John wrote after the war, he often spoke of "Old Washington" and obviously had great affection for the county of his father's birth and of his own memories of visits during his youth. As he recuperated from his wounds and was able to join in the social life of family and friends, he was soon to have further cause for a fondness for the county as he met and courted a young teacher, Mary Fletcher Northington. Mary lived in the Bay Spring community near Oconee.[13] She was probably a member of the gatherings of local young people with the numerous soldiers who were stationed in Georgia in the winter of 1863-64, preparing to defend the state from invasion. Many families of the county had already suffered the loss of husbands, sons, and fathers, but in this period before the county was ravaged during Sherman's March to the Sea, it was able to provide a bountiful welcome to returning soldiers.

Undoubtedly John was received with great hospitality by family and friends and, as a recent widower with a romantic nature, was susceptible to attentive Southern belles. He had courted his recently deceased wife, Winnifred Davis, in Washington County in the previous decade and memories of that happy time must have been in his mind as he turned his attentions to another native of the county. Mary, the daughter of James Foster Northington and his wife Amelia (Fisher), was a mature young lady of twenty-four.[14] She was a teacher in the

Bay Spring Academy, associated with the Bay Spring Methodist Church, for which her maternal grandfather, Metcalf Fisher, a native of Massachusetts, had given the land in 1854.[15] In the few writings of her maiden days which have been preserved by descendants, she appears as a serious, cultivated young woman, with a deeply religious nature. One of her writings of November, 1863 was an essay on the qualities of an educated and cultivated person. With the sentimentality typical of the Victorian era, she stated, "A love of Poetry and Flowers exhibits a refined and cultivated taste in a person." A poem written in the same month evokes the image of a romantic young woman, wondering if the death of so many men of her acquaintance in the war would rob her of a partner in life:[16]

Not Yet
By Mary F. Northington

I have not found him yet -
My soul is yet unwounded,
Though by all beauty and life surrounded;
Though many a glorious prize
Has flashed before my eyes -
Not yet, not yet.

I have not found him yet -
There was one that I cherished,
A creature now of the dim past that hath perished,
But at the gates of wealth
He said, with parting breath,
"Not yet, not yet."

I have not found him yet -
I did not wish one given
Only, to part with at the door of heaven,
While I of love bereft,
To earth and toil be left -
Not yet, not yet.

I have not found him yet -
No angels ever lisp his
Sweet name to me, and add with gentle whisper
"Ere long he shall be thine - "

> *Alas, if love be mine*
> *It is - not yet.*
>
> *I have not found him yet -*
> *Perhaps some day's unsealing*
> *Will bring my heart a wonderful revealing;*
> *My twin soul shall be known,*
> *And I no more alone.*
> *But not - not - yet.*
>
> School Room November 24th 1863

Mary's anxious and lonely heart was soon to encounter another which was equally vulnerable to romance. At some time between her November writings and January of 1864 she met John Hardison, who was a few years her senior at the age of twenty-nine. He too had been a teacher, as well as lawyer and farmer, and they shared a love of language and learning. In a lengthy entry in her autograph book, which is quoted below, he gave full sway to his fondness for literary allusion and extravagant language. The reader may imagine the effects of such an outpouring on Mary and guess that her "Not Yet" changed to at least "Perhaps."[17]

To Miss M. F. Northington
Fair and Gentle One.
   'Tis Evening- the hour of twilight- beautiful- hushed and shadowy. The creeping shadows wave and mingle among the tall trees- No arrowy moonbeam frought with silvery light disturbs the quiet reign of the pensive hour- No star-jewel rests its quivering radience upon her dark yet beautiful brow- Ah! none. Softly- Silently- Calmly with her glow-tinted shades and sweet musings she holds gentle sway o'er her Earthly habitation. Blest hour- Dream loving twilight! How fit a season for the Soul to go out and open a pathway to the well beloved plains of the Past that beautiful shadow-land peopled with Early dreams and loves- dim distant- yet cherished forever- the lost Paradise of life! Happy Hour! Beautiful is it not? And now the shades of darkness grow thicker and hover over the bosom of Earth. Lifting my eyes above I behold the Arch of Heaven bespangled with twinkling worlds that look down upon our Globe in love- and me thinks I hear something whisper- some secret monitor- Angel of peace and love perhaps, which says-

> "Yes, frail mortal there is a home
> Above yon star lit sky-
> Where flowers bloom eternally
> And never droop nor die"

An hour so bright and auspicious to the mortal gaze as this, and so, fit for silent meditation- very naturally reminds me of my promise to pen a "thought" and a "wish" for you in your Album. The "thought" is contained in the foregoing- What think you of it? Do you smile? I'll grant you the privilige- but pray screen it from The Critic's eye- But the "wish"? Ah! the "wish" How shall I express that? What words can fitly tell my heart's best wish for thee? Verse is common and used by the multitude and if I employ prose some may think it strange or an effort to appear different from others- Then it shall be neither the one nor the other but a part of both- May thy life be free from cares, May the bright and happy sunshine of true friendship ever attend thee and dispel and disipate the dark shadows from thy pathway through life- May you find a noble true and loving heart- beating always in unison with thine own, that you may not in truth exclaim- as I can-

> "Alone I'm floating down the tide
> With naught to guide my barque,
> No love light gleams upon my sky
> The clouds are drear and dark."

May Heaven's blessings always attend you May you live a long life of happiness and love, And when thou art wearied with time and earthly things be assured that-

> "There is a home of joy and bliss
> Where skies are clear and bright
> Where fragrant flowers are clustering 'round
> The throne of life and light
> And would'st thou learn the name which God
> That beautious land hath given?
> Bow down thine ear- I'll whisper soft
> Dost hear me Mary?- 'tis Heaven"

Bay Springs Geo=
Saturday Eve- Jany - 1864-   *J. Randolph- H-*
                                                          25th Texas Cavalry

By the time John wrote these words he was probably ready to return to active service and join his fellow Texans in their winter quarters at Dalton, Georgia. The Confederacy had been cut off from its western states, as it lost control of the Mississippi River in 1863, and the major campaigns which were expected to begin in the spring of 1864 were for Georgia and the other southeastern states and for Virginia. Lincoln was determined to bring the war to a successful close and chose two men who had achieved outstanding victories in the western campaigns to deliver the final blows to the Confederacy. Ulysses S. Grant was named general in chief of Union forces in March, 1864 and was also appointed to head the Army of the Potomac, with the assignment of crushing General Robert E. Lee's Army of Northern Virginia. Also in March, General William T. Sherman, who had served under Grant, took Grant's former position as commander of the Military Division of the Mississippi. The armies under Sherman, now in control of Tennessee, were to invade and conquer Georgia.

The various attitudes of Georgians during the uneasy months preceding Sherman's onslaught may be seen in the following letter which was printed on February 3, 1864 in the Washington County newspaper, the *Central Georgian*. It is very likely that the letter was submitted by Mary Fletcher Northington for it was headed "Bay Spring, Ga." and signed "M.F.N." The letter had been written on December 31, 1863 and was addressed to Ivy W. Duggan, an outstanding teacher of the county who had volunteered for service in the Confederate Army in 1861 and was stationed in Virginia. As the letter indicates, he sent reports from the battlefront to his hometown newspaper.[18]

> Mr. Ivy W. Duggin [Duggan]: Respected Sir - Permit me through the Central Georgian to address you these lines, in response to your communication, which I have just read. Pardon me, sir, but I must say that the columns of the Georgian are scanned weekly for your ever interesting letters. We only wish that your facilities for writing were greater, in order that your communications might be more lengthy and appear oftener.
>
> But sir, your last contained a very grave charge against my sex, a charge which I desire to contradict. You say, a young officer recently asserted that all the women at home are whipped. I deny it. There may be and doubtless are, creatures of both sexes at home who were ready to cry "hold enough," at the fire of the first gun. But allow me to say, sir, that

where you find one of that class among females you will find three among men.—I would not be understood as saying there are many among either; but I would hurl back the charge upon this "gallant" young officer, and say "physician heal thy self."

The women whipped? Never, never! We loathe and despise all idea of subjugation, or submission to Yankee rule. Yea, more: we detest the cowardly skulkers, and whining puppies who would force it upon us. The true and the brave are beloved by every woman worthy of the name; but he who would stand by and quietly do nothing, waiting for his neighbors to do all the fighting, undergo all the hardship, is not worthy of the esteem of any. When our independence is achieved I expect some of them will be the first to cry out, "aint we brave?"

I admit we feel depressed in spirits often; but it is when we reflect upon the sufferings of our country, the hardships and dangers to which our brave soldiers are exposed for our defence, Oh! if we could only alleviate their sufferings! but we are deprived of the privilege. It is these sad reflections that cause us to sigh and weep the bitter tears of grief, and not feelings of fear. Believing in the goodness and justice of God, we have every reason to anticipate success. We should then hope for independent peace, pray for independent peace, fight for it, ever remembering that—

"Freedom's battle once begun
Bequeathed from bleeding sire to sun [son].
Though baffled oft, is ever won."

Remembering that if we are but true to ourselves, that if we are worthy of the precious liberty for which we fight, a just and kind Providence will certainly give us the victory.

You desired to know what was going on at home. I will answer for the ladies of this vicinity: we are busily engaged knitting socks for the soldiers, and will be for some time. We are ready and willing at any time to contribute to the comfort of our dear soldiers, who are so nobly defending our homes.

As I am a resident of Georgia, I consider myself a recipient of the compliments you so generously bestowed upon the ladies of our noble old State, and thank you kindly for the honor you bestow. Hoping that you may never have cause to change your good opinion, I will desist lest I weary you.

Respectfully, M.F.N.

Such expressions of support on the home front and an ongoing belief in the cause of Southern independence bolstered the morale of the men in service, as they fought what was increasingly a losing battle. The states of the Confederacy were being drained of their young manhood, while the more populous North was able to provide a seemingly endless supply of men to take the place of the thousands killed or wounded in battle. Food, clothing, and military supplies were in short supply, as the Union's blockade shut out imports from abroad and their victories in the western theater cut off agricultural produce from the states west of the Mississippi. Georgia had been looked to for both food and military supplies and now it was being targeted for a major campaign. Sherman was ordered first to defeat the Army of Tennessee and then to go into Georgia's interior and inflict all possible damage to its war resources. During 1864 John Hardison, as a combatant, and Mary Northington, as a civilian, were to know the wrath which Sherman visited upon Georgia.

NOTES

1. The major sources for the account of the campaigns in which John Hardison and the Texas Brigade participated are *One of Cleburne's Command, the Civil War Reminiscences and Diary of Capt. Samuel T. Foster, Granbury's Texas Brigade, CSA*, edited by Norman D. Brown (Austin: University of Texas Press, 1980); *This Band of Heroes, Granbury's Texas Brigade, C.S.A.*, by James M. McCaffrey (Austin: Eakin Press, 1985); and the Compiled Service Record of John R. Hardison, National Archives, Washington, D.C. Foster served in the Twenty-fourth Regiment, Texas Cavalry (dismounted), which like John Hardison's Twenty-fifth Regiment began its combat service in Arkansas and became a part of the Texas Brigade in 1863. His descriptions of the campaigns in which he participated, augmented by Brown's editorial notes, and McCaffrey's history provide the framework within which John Hardison's service record is set. Both Brown and McCaffrey have made extensive use of *War of the Rebellion: a Compilation of the Official Records of the Union and Confederate Armies*, 128 vols. (Washington, D.C.: Government Printing Office, 1880-1901) and of histories and reminiscences by participants in the campaigns in which the Texas Brigade took part. McCaffrey's history includes a list of all the units which became a part of the Texas Brigade and the names of the men who served in each (pp.175-236). Specific references to John's service are based on his Compiled Service Record, which includes notes of his listing in company muster rolls and pay records and records of his capture, imprisonment, and hospitalizations.

2. Accounts of the Confederate service of Benjamin Brigham and Theophilus Jackson may be found in their applications for pensions, Benjamin's to the State of Texas in 1916 and Theophilus' to Florida in 1909. References to the service of the Davises are included in Elm Hill and Its People, by James Porter Davis (pp.36-38) and A Davis Family Record, by Sarah Jane Overstreet and Barbara Davis-Stovall (pp.5, 14, 18).

X. THE SOUTH AT WAR, 1862-1863

3. Cain Family Genealogical Collection, letter of March 16-28, 1862 from John R. Hardison to Edwin Davis. Text of letter is printed in the previous chapter.
4. Miriam Partlow, *Liberty, Liberty County, and the Atascosito District* (Austin: Pemberton Press, Jenkins Publishing Co., 1974), pp.212-13 (brief history of the company) and pp.344-45 (muster roll). In McCaffrey, *This Band of Heroes*, p.232, the list of the men who served in Company G, Twenty-fifth Regiment, Texas Cavalry, includes four Hardisons—J. L., J. R., William L., and W. M., but J. L. is probably a misreading of J. R., John's usual designation in his Compiled Service Record, and W. M. for his brother William L. William's Compiled Service Record, National Archives, documents his discharge in June, 1862; his return to service in Company G, Twenty-fifth Texas Cavalry from September-December, 1862, during which time there are several notations regarding his illness, including "Left Sick on the march" in September when his company was on its way to Arkansas; and his membership in the portion of Company G which was serving in Louisiana in the Trans-Mississippi Confederate Army in January-March, 1865. When William died in 1873 his brother John referred in a letter of June 1, 1873 to his "old Asthmetic affections."
5. The remains of Fort Hindman are now under the waters of the Arkansas River, which changed its course over the years after the Civil War. The site of the settlement of Arkansas Post has been under the care of the National Park Service since 1964.
6. Norman D. Brown, editor, *One of Cleburne's Command*, p.12.
7. *Ibid.*, p.54.
8. McCaffrey, *op. cit.*, p.75.
9. Brown, *op. cit.*, p.66.
10. Cain Collection, anecdote recorded by John Hardison's granddaughter, May (Wood) Cain, includes a drawing of William L. Hardison's house, a simple wooden structure.
11. Cain Collection, letter of June 1, 1873 from John Hardison to Mary Elizabeth (Davis) Hardwick.
12. Mary Alice Jordan, editor, *Cotton to Kaolin*, pp.23-24.
13. In Mary Northington's writings, the name of the village in which she lived is given as "Bay Spring," while in present usage the spelling is "Bay Springs." It was the home of both her grandfather, Metcalf Fisher (d.1860), a native of Massachusetts, who had been a successful businessman and land owner, and of her parents.
14. Seventh Federal Census, 1850, Georgia, Washington County, p.220, Mary F., age 11, is listed in the household of James F. Northington, age 40 and born in North Carolina, and Milly [Amelia] R. Northington, age 36 and born in Georgia.
15. *Bay Springs United Methodist Church, History, 1852-1955* (unpublished mss. based on material gathered by Catherine Everett Thurston and other church members, n.d.), pp.1-2, deed of Metcalf Fisher, 1854, to the trustees of Bay Spring Church, which included Mary's father, for an acre and three quarters of land for a church building.
16. Nancy Louise Brown Slaughter Collection, poetry and other writings of Mary Fletcher Northington.
17. *Ibid.*, autograph book of Mary Fletcher Northington. The book has black lacquered wooden covers with a painted design inlaid with mother-of-pearl. The entries were written by family and friends, primarily in the early 1860s. Mary was often referred to by the nickname "Mollie." The entry written by Mary's mother, Amelia (Milly), is indicative of her deeply religious nature: "Gods word is the chart by which an

immortal may direct his voyage over the see of life and in to the haven of eternal reste." It is signed, "Your devoted Mother, M. R. Northington."
18. *Central Georgian*, Sandersville, Georgia, February 3, 1864.

XI

The South in Defeat
John Hardison and the Texas Brigade from Georgia to North Carolina, 1864-1865

*T*he winter months of 1864 were a time of waiting and preparation for both the Union and Confederate forces. General Johnston continued his efforts to build morale in the Army of Tennessee and among his actions was the appointment of Colonel Hiram B. Granbury to command the Texas Brigade. Requests for Granbury had come from the officers and men of the brigade and also from the Texas delegation to the Confederate Congress. He was a native of Mississippi who had migrated to Texas as a young man in the 1850s and settled in Waco, where he had begun a career as an attorney. Like the Texans at Arkansas Post he had been a prisoner of war, having been among the men of the Seventh Texas Infantry captured at Fort Donelson, and he had served with distinction at Chickamauga and Missionary Ridge. In March, 1864 he was raised to the rank of brigadier general and given command of the Texas Brigade, which was known thereafter as Granbury's Texas Brigade. In his own effort at morale building, he attempted to reorganize the brigade's units so as to restore as nearly as possible the original regiments which had existed before the consolidation of the Arkansas Post survivors the pre-

Letter of John Randolph Hardison to Mary Fletcher Northington,
August 14, 1864, written after the Battle of Atlanta

Ryan Collection

XI. THE SOUTH IN DEFEAT, 1864-1865

vious year. Losses had been too great to reconstitute all the units and the regiment in which John Hardison served, the Twenty-fifth Texas Cavalry, was now joined with the Twenty-fourth to create one regiment. John was elected second lieutenant by the men of the consolidated regiment on March 9, 1864. He received his first pay as a commissioned officer, at the rate of $90.00 a month, on July 1, 1864.

During the relative leisure of the winter months, John probably continued his visits to Washington County, while other Texans visited their Georgia relatives and found ways to pass the time of waiting. Samuel T. Foster of the Twenty-fourth Texas Cavalry, whose reminiscences and diary have previously been quoted, wrote of camp life in this period, "There are a great many things happens in a large army to keep the camp in something to talk about . . . ." He spoke of such diverse matters as a rumor that General Johnston was going to appoint a board to examine all officers for fitness to serve in their rank, the great number of baptisms which were being performed by Baptist minister General Lowrey in spite of the cold weather, and the ingenuity of a soldier who was bringing whiskey into camp corked up in his gun barrel.[1] John Hardison, with his romantic and literary turn of mind, found time to write a poem, which was dated April 30, 1864 and published in the Children's Column of the *Central Georgian* on May 25. It was inspired by his concern for friends in northeastern Florida, in the area of Jacksonville and the St. John's River, which Union troops had struck several times and permanently occupied in February, 1864. The poem was probably inspired by sights he had witnessed during his visit to northern Florida in his recent furlough.[2]

Our Home in the Land of Flowers
Affectionately dedicated to Misses Mariah, Helen, Maggie, and Florida B..... of White Springs Fla., who were driven by the merciless and cruel foe, from the "Homes of their childhood," near the beautiful and lovely River St. John's in East Florida.

By J. Randolph H.

Our dear old Home in the Orange grove,
   In the land where flowers eternal bloom,
Where the dew falls soft as the breath of love,
   And where we used in delight to roam,
Yea happy Home by the Riverside,

Where Old Ocean's tides alternate flow,
  Where the wild Goose, on the wave doth ride;
    Must we from thy blest endearments go.
Alas! alas! We have said farewell,
  To the old Halls where in Youth we met,
Our stories of mirth and joy to tell,
  And where in our midst our parents sat.
Our steps are turned to the setting sun,
  Homeless and sad we are wandering on,
No cheering words our hearts have won.
  Our thoughts go back to our distant home.

We think of the flowers we planted there,
  Where vandals now in their councils meet,
And we wonder if they'll bloom as fair,
  As once they did our smiles to greet.
Will not the rose but wither and die,
  When touched by the northen demon's hand,
And drop from its stem in the dust to lie
  In our loved home in the Flowery land?

Will not the lilly grow paler still;
  And the Jasmine withhold its perfume,
The orange sweets fail the air to fill,
  And the scene once bright be draped in gloom?
Will the nightengale's notes still be heard,
  And the murmering waters still roll on;
Yes these with the voice of the mocking bird,
  Will ever enchant our happy home.

Though wicked despots may revil now,
  In those grand old Halls once our delight,
"Brave Southerns" will soon force them to bow,
  To the shrine of "Truth, Justice and Rights,"
God hasten the coming of that hour,
  When Liberty's Sun again shall arise,
In glory above vile Tyrant's power,
  Dispeling the gloom 'neath Southern skies.
Then the angel of Peace will hover again,

O'er the Flowery Plains of the Sunny South,
And returning Exiles with joy will exclaim,
"Home again free from Demons of the North;"
With joyful hearts they will gather around,
The dear old fire side,—Oh! happy band,
And music's sweet tones again will resound,
In their dear Old Home in the Southern Land.
Army of Tenn., April 30th 1864

The Atlanta Campaign

By the time John wrote his poem the opportunity for such musings was running out and in early May the Union forces began their drive toward Atlanta. The plight of invasion and exile which he had described was soon to be visited on the residents of Georgia, and the Confederate soldiers were to know harrowing months of hard fighting, marching, and entrenching. Sherman commanded a force of approximately 100,000, including the Army of the Tennessee under James B. McPherson, the Army of the Cumberland under George H. Thomas, and the Army of the Ohio commanded by John M. Schofield.[3] Johnston's Army of Tennessee had been augmented to number about 70,000. It included the infantry corps commanded by John Bell Hood, Leonidas Polk, and William J. Hardee and the cavalry of Joseph E. Wheeler.

For two and a half months, dating from early May, the Union armies moved cautiously but steadily from Chattanooga toward Atlanta, fighting against determined resistance in the mountainous terrain of northwestern Georgia. The Texas Brigade moved up and down the ridges and through the gaps in the mountains, digging in and then moving out as the enemy pushed relentlessly toward Atlanta. Muster rolls and other official records place John Hardison in service with his regiment from March throughout the remainder of 1864 and he may be assumed to have participated in the Texas Brigade's movements throughout the Atlanta campaign. From their winter camp near Dalton the Confederates moved through the villages of Dug Gap, Resaca, Calhoun, Adairsville, Cassville, and Cartersville, expecting battle as the enemy pursued, but in effect retreating steadily toward Atlanta. For a time both generals avoided a major confrontation until late

May, when Johnston decided to take a stand to block the enemy's progress near the town of Dallas. In the ensuing engagement of May 27, known both as the Battle of New Hope Church and the Battle of Pickett's Mill, Granbury's Brigade distinguished itself with its masterful use of rifles, inflicting many casualties on the enemy in point-blank fire, as the Texans fought to hold a ridge. After repulsing the enemy in the afternoon, the Texans were ordered to prepare for another attack in the evening. Screaming what Captain Samuel T. Foster referred to as "a regular Texas Yell, or an Indian Yell, or perhaps both together," they rushed down their ridge and swept it of enemy troops, taking over 200 prisoners.[4] Johnston's men had won the battle but such victories came dear. The Texas Brigade's losses were 33 men killed and 114 wounded.

After the battle there was a lull of several weeks in which both Union and Confederate forces established new positions. Johnston developed a strong defensive position along Lost, Pine, and Brush mountains in the vicinity of Kennesaw Mountain. Sherman had great respect for Johnston's military abilities and, as the Union forces moved farther and farther from their supply base in Tennessee, he had avoided a direct attack against the Confederates. However, on June 27 he changed his tactics and made a head-on assault against Johnston's entrenched position. This move proved to be a mistake and he suffered a defeat in the Battle of Kennesaw Mountain. His casualties were estimated at 3,000 as compared to 750 for the Confederates.

Such victories were welcome to the Confederates, but their cost in the dwindling manpower resources of the South made Johnston reluctant to commit his troops to a major confrontation with a force which greatly outnumbered his own. The people in the North were growing weary of the heavy casualties inflicted by the Confederate forces and were anxious for decisive victories which would bring the war to a close. Lincoln was being challenged in the presidential election campaign of 1864 by Democratic nominee General George B. McClelland, whose party was strongly critical of Lincoln's conduct of the war. By constantly frustrating Sherman's hopes for a knock-out blow against Atlanta, Johnston hoped that Lincoln might be defeated at the polls and the way opened for a negotiated peace which would

XI. THE SOUTH IN DEFEAT, 1864-1865

recognize Southern independence. With this goal in mind, along with the knowledge of Sherman's great superiority in numbers, he kept retreating toward Atlanta. On July 9 The Army of Tennessee crossed the Chattahoochee River, the last major natural barrier between the armies. Captain Samuel T. Foster wrote the following assessment of the Confederate dilemma at this time:[5]

> We have not been driven out of a single position that we have taken since we left Dalton Ga.; but we have had to fall back to keep the Yanks from getting behind us. According to the official reports publised in their own reports the Yanks have just two to our one, and while we are fighting back 40,000 men with our 42,000, they have another 40,000 to flank us. Therefore the difficulty, one half of their army are in front of us while the other half are away to the west of us moving south, and when we stop to fight these that are following us, those that are to the west of us move on to the south.

The crossing of the Chattahoochee provided a brief respite and the Texans enjoyed the opportunity to wash their clothes and bathe in the river, hoping to rid themselves of the ever present lice. They welcomed the addition of Georgia's summer bounty of fruit and vegetables to their scanty and monotonous army rations. However, their relief was soon marred by the announcement on July 17 that President Jefferson Davis was replacing General Johnston with General John Bell Hood. Davis had a personal dislike of Johnston, wanted a decisive defeat of Sherman, and now had the excuse of Johnston's failure to stop the Union advance. The men of the Texas Brigade, along with most of the men in Johnston's command, were incensed and some threatened to desert. They felt that he cared about their welfare and was doing the best he could with the resources he had. Hood had fought with them at Chickamauga, where he had lost his right leg, but they were fearful of his impetuous and aggressive nature. These fears were soon to be realized as his leadership led to defeat in Georgia and slaughter in Tennessee.

During July Sherman's forces followed the Confederates in crossing the Chattahoochee River and prepared to approach Atlanta from the north and the east. The city was protected with a ring of earthworks, which Sherman chose not to attack. Instead he intended to destroy the four rail lines which met in Atlanta, forcing the Confederates to either retreat or come outside their defenses for a battle in the open. Hood did not approve of a waiting game and on July 20 he opened the struggle for possession of Atlanta by a surprise attack on General George Thomas' Army of the Cumberland. Thomas was crossing Peachtree Creek while the other two armies in Sherman's command were farther east destroying the Georgia Railroad. As Thomas had proved at Chickamauga, he was a powerful opponent and the Confederates were defeated with heavy losses.

The Texas Brigade had not participated in the battle, but had marched into Atlanta and then east to a location known as Bald Hill, where during the night they hastily dug trenches and built breastworks. In the morning of July 21 they found themselves in an exposed position and were raked with artillery and infantry fire which caused heavy losses with no gain of ground. John Hardison's regiment, the consolidated Twenty-fourth and Twenty-fifth Texas regiments, was driven from its position by a massive infantry attack, but recovered and drove the enemy back with heavy losses. However, the day was not won and the brigade retreated into Atlanta. There it joined the rest of Hardee's corps, as it prepared to follow Hood's orders for an assault on the rear of Union General McPherson's Army of the Tennessee. The brigade suffered heavy losses, including 47 killed, 120 wounded, and 19 captured.

The engagement known as the Battle of Atlanta began the next day, July 22, as McPherson moved into the recently abandoned Confederate trenches east of Atlanta and Hood launched a surprise attack on the rear of the Union line between Decatur and Atlanta. McPherson was killed when he ran into skirmishers from Cleburne's division, possibly by shots fired by the Texas Brigade. Along with their Arkansas comrades, the Texans moved into close contact with the enemy, sometimes using bayonets and even fists. As the enemy readjusted its lines to meet their attack, the advancing Confederates were ordered to fall back to avoid capture but troops of the Seventeenth and Eighteenth Texas regiments did not move in time and were captured. Portions of the Texas Brigade continued fighting as the men tried to regroup and John Hardison's regiment captured the flag of the Third Iowa.

XI. THE SOUTH IN DEFEAT, 1864-1865

In the meantime, Hood put the second part of his plan into action with a frontal attack, led by General Benjamin F. Cheatham, in the late afternoon of July 22. Although both the frontal and rear assaults met with initial success, the Confederates were unable to win the battle and Hood met with failure in his second effort to deal a decisive blow to Sherman's forces. Confederate casualties were enormous, about 8,000 out of the approximately 36,000 troops involved, while Union losses were almost 4,000 out of 30,000. The Texas Brigade had 311 casualties—19 killed, 107 wounded, 160 captured, and 25 missing. General Hardee, to whose corps the brigade belonged, called the battle "one of the most desperate and bloody of the war." So accustomed had the Texas veterans become to the carnage of battle that Captain Foster wrote only briefly in his diary the day following the battle, including the remark "All quiet this morning, after a terrible day yesterday all along the lines." After telling of the taking of boots, hats, and knives from the enemy dead, he added "We cook and eat, talk and laugh with the enemys dead lying all about us as though they were so many logs."[6]

The Confederate casualties were so great that the divisions had to be reorganized and a brigade of Georgians commanded by Brigadier General Hugh W. Mercer was added to Cleburne's division. John Hardison's brother-in-law, Edwin T. Davis, was an officer in the Fifty-seventh Regiment of Georgia Volunteers, which was a part of Mercer's Brigade, and, along with John, he served in the Army of Tennessee until the end of the war.[7]

In spite of its name, the Battle of Atlanta had not won control of the city for General Sherman. That prize was over a month away and in the meantime the two opposing forces struggled for control of the railroads which were the key to possession of the city. Both armies shifted their lines from the eastern side of Atlanta toward the important rail lines on the west. Sherman's men systematically destroyed the railroads, pulling up and burning the cross ties and heating the rails until they could be twisted around trees, creating what were called "Sherman's neckties." He continually shelled the fortified city of Atlanta where Hood had set up his headquarters. In early August the Texas Brigade was ordered from the east to the north side of the city and then the southwest, moving toward the town of East Point. They were engaged in occasional skirmishing and were exposed to almost constant shelling and picket firing. However, their relative inaction in the latter portion of August allowed sufficient leisure for John Hardison to continue his courting of Mary Northington, as he wrote the following letter:[8]

In Line of Battle
Near Atlanta Ga.
August 14th 1864

Miss M. F. Northington
My Much Esteemed Friend

 The happiness that pening a letter to you would afford me, could I feel assured that it would meet your kind approbation would be altogether indiscribable. The desire however to correspond by letter with a pleasant and intelligent Lady whom I can confide in and claim as "friend" in the true acceptation of the term, and the hope that a letter from [page stained and torn] assurance that honesty of purpose and purity of motive actuates me to write will not offend you at least must be my apology for presuming to address you.

 Just here another (to me) serious difficulty presents itself to view, now that I have made the proposition. It is my fear that anything I may be able to communicate will wholly fail to interest you, or even be worthy of your favourable consideration, while on the other hand I am assured that should I be the fortunate and happy recipient of a letter from under your fair hand it would be all that my most ardent fancy could picture or my heart desire in point of purity of sentiment, beauty of expression — true piety and Christian furvour and genuine female Excellence and loveliness.

 While these convictions of my inability and unworthiness force themselves upon me, and bid me, as it were desist ere I conclude a first letter, I cannot without hope that you will, in view of the unfavorable circumstances which must continue to surround me as long as I remain in the field, pardon and overlook many of the short comings and imperfections which must necessarily characterize this and succeeding letters should I have encouragement to write again.

 From the foregoing I trust that you will be able to discern that my motive in proposing a correspondence with you is a pure one, and I hope too that you will be pleased to accept my proposition as I cannot perceive that there could be any imprudence attached to such a course, — Forcible argument this — Ex partee — all on one side. Perhaps you still think quite differently. We shall see.

How changed the scene since I was with you last! On that beautiful and lovely Sabbath Evening we were strolling along together far far removed from the tumult & confusion which surround me to day. Then we were reviling [revelling] in the silvery flashes of the pale moon beams as they flooded the bosom of Earth with their mellow light and tinged all nature with a heavenly hue, as the expiring day faded from view until lost in the dim distance far o'er the western hills. Then I was realizing the felicity of Woman's Charm and tender smiles, and drinking in the eloquence of her enchanting words. Now I am where the keen crack of the rifle rings out on the air and the deafening roar of artillery comes floating o'er the hills, and where the gallant sons of our loved south are standing as a wall of fire between the heartless invader and our endeared and innocent ones at home. How changed the scene!—Not so with the honest heart. While the present is draped in gloom the heart lives in the bright memory of the past and cherishes a hope of a blissful future—a happy re-union with the loved ones we would die to save. Oh! then the meeting of the faithful one with the object of his hearts pure love will constitute a heaven on Earth. Then the return of the long absent parent and companion to the objects of his devotion will be joy unspeakable. Then the noble Brother and son will receive the warm kiss of his fond Mother and devoted sister. Then the hills will leap for joy and the murmuring streamlet will join in the universal praise of a grateful people to the Giver of all good.

The rose bud that's doomed to blush unseen in the seclusion of the mountain recess and give forth its fragrance in climes where man has scarcely trod, is none the less pure because it chances not to bedeck the swelling bosom of the blushing bride at the hymenial altar, nor is the tear-drop resting on the cheek of the sorrow-stricken maiden any the less beautiful than when it is transformed into the glittering dew-gem dancing in the morning sun light, on the face of the newly opened lilly, or when it falls in the shape of the chrystal rain drop from the silvery summer cloud; neither should the out gushings of the pure and loving heart be any the less cherished because they do not always happen to spring from royal bosoms.

Thus if I am not seriously mistaken (and I know I am not) I have found in you all those agreeable and excellent traits of character which adorn and beautify your sex — which tend so materially to elivate and improve the moral and religious taste of society, and which render Woman invaluable, "a pearl of great price" in the estimation of God as well as of Man. A tear of sympathy for the disconsolate and sorrowful — an encouraging word for the down cast and desponding — (this last is me — Despondency — Oh! thou bane to all my joys! — My soul take courage now Avaunt dull care, — away away) a smile and cheerful greeting for your friends and a "heart" o'er flowing with warm affection for those you love.

I rejoined my command on yesterday Evening and my fellow soldiers were so glad to see me that they very readily excused me for yielding to the irresistible persuasions of a lady to stay away a few days over my time. I am sure I shall never regret having done so, although I was subjecting myself to trial for absence without leave by Court Martial. What would you have thought, and how would you have felt, if I had been placed under arrest upon arriving here, when I assure you that it was your request that influenced me to remain til Monday. How careful we should be in directing our influence when we know we possess it over our friends, particularly when those friends know not how to go adversly to our wishes.

The troops here are in the best health and buoyant spirits — altogether hopeful of ultimate success, though many places in our Brigade and in my own Regiment have been made vacant. Many have fought their last fight and won their last battle, and all of them that is mortal now sleeps in a soldier's grave. I cannot help feeling sad and melancholy when I reflect how many braves have fallen since I was with them before.

It is thought by many here that there will not probably be another general engagement with the Enemy near Atlanta if at all. The flanking movements of Sherman seem to have been effectually stopped and he is reported to be contracting his lines with the view it is supposed of making a retrograde move, i-e [i.e.] to draw off from Atlanta. It is very certain that we have a considerable force of Cavalry in his rear doing great damage to his stores and cutting his line of communication. Time alone can determine what must be the final result as to another general engagement. If it must come I trust and believe that with the help of an all seeing providence we will be successful. There is nothing more doing now than the useless habbit of picket firing in front of our works and occasional shelling of the City & a few other points along our lines.

The weather is oppressively warm with occasional showers — but the troops are bivouacked in the thick timber to screen them from the burning rays of the sun. Since I began to write the Evening has considerably advanced and the firing in our front has become more vigorous, indicating some probability of a demonstration on our lines. I mention this to give you an idea of the uncertainty of things here. Just now we are having comparative quiet but within the next two hours to come we may be in the heat of battle. Such is war. My fate may be sealed and my form cold and inanimate ere this letter reaches you, or even before tomorrow's sun has set.

Pardon me for dwelling so long upon this unpleasant subject — I have had the pleasure of meeting my Brother in law Lieut. Davis. He is sorely grieved at the death of Bro Thomas Davis — Edwin is left alone now, the last Brother and son of his family [sons of Temperance (Hardison) and Enos Davis], but we all have the consolation of feeling that our Brother died triumphing in the Christian faith.

The apple you were so kind as to give me contained four seeds. I wish I knew whether that was a favorable number — It was named — "M-a-r-y" I cannot conclude without again expressing my wishes for your future welfare and prosperity as well as my profound regard for you — May not I hope to be favored with a letter from you very soon, O! Do not quite forget, — May you ever be happy —

Good by -

Your (May I claim the privilige) devoted friend,

J. R. Hardison

P.S. Ha. ha. Do you like postscrips I believe the Ladies always have "something to add" therefore you cannot complain if I do likewise unless you may object to my usurping a privilige which has, from time immemorial, been conseded exclusively to Woman.

You must not expect anything of interest from me in the columns of the *Georgian* very soon though I will try to furnish it a short letter for the next week's issue, that is if we do not have to move in the meantime. O! Do not quite forget———

a friend, Randolph

Gracious! you must really pardon my unaccountable nonchalence in not

having mentioned something about that beautiful Dress before now. I'm sure it was not because I had not thought of it many times-
"Many daughters have done virtuously but thou excellest them all"
"Give her of the fruit of her hands, and let her own works praise her in the gates"   Bible

Lieut J. R. Hardison
Co "G" 25th Texas Cav.
Granbury's Brigade
Cleburne's Division
Army of Tenn.

The period of relative inaction for Granbury's men was about to end as Sherman prepared to seize the prize which he had been working toward since May. In August he ended his bombardment of the Confederate lines and began to close in on Atlanta from the south and southwest. On August 25 he moved toward the town of Jonesboro, twenty-six miles south of Atlanta, with the intention of cutting the Macon and Western Railroad, the last line still in possession of the Confederates. On August 30 Hood ordered General Hardee's corps, including the Texas Brigade, to Jonesboro, to repulse what he thought was an attack by Union raiders. A battle began on the next day and Granbury's men had a major role in the battle plan. John Hardison's regiment was designated the battalion of direction and the entire Confederate battle line was to base its movements on the motion of this regiment. The brigade went into action in mid-afternoon and soon encountered a Union dismounted cavalry force which fled before their fire. Captain Samuel T. Foster in describing the chase, in which his and John Hardison's regiment participated, said "We followed them as long as we could find any to follow, when we went back."[9] Instead of stopping at the Flint River, as they had been instructed, the Tenth Texas pursued the enemy across the river and destroyed an enemy gun battery. At one point in the battle, when Hardee thought that Granbury's men had given way and fallen back, Granbury is said to have remarked to him "General, my men never fall back unless ordered back."[10]

The battle continued on September 1 and Granbury's men repeatedly repulsed efforts to break their portion of the Confederate line, but Hardee's position became increasingly hopeless. He reported to Hood that his corps was completely outnumbered and in risk of being captured. Hood finally realized the gravity of the situation and the possibility that his entire army might be trapped in Atlanta. On the night of September 1 he gave the order to destroy all the military stores in Atlanta that could not be removed and to evacuate the city. The next day the mayor surrendered the city to Sherman and Hood moved his greatly reduced Army of Tennessee to the south. The Texas Brigade with the rest of Hardee's corps moved to Lovejoy's Station and began fortifications in preparation for another battle. However, rather than pursuing Hood, Sherman concentrated his forces in Atlanta and forced all the civilian residents to evacuate. He called for a two day truce to allow them to gather their possessions and arranged for them to be met and escorted to Lovejoy's Station by some of Hood's men. His actions toward the citizens of Atlanta were considered heartless and harsh and drew strong criticism from Hood. They were to be only the beginning of the suffering he visited upon the people of Georgia.

During September Sherman chose not to follow up his advantage against Hood's army. There was some skirmishing around Lovejoy's Station for a few days early in the month but the enemy was repulsed and soon the two armies were at rest a few miles from each other. President Jefferson Davis visited the Army of Tennessee to discuss strategy and check on the morale of its troops, but disregarded the advice of Hood's corps commanders that the general should be replaced. Davis refused requests that he reinstate General Johnston and he replaced General Hardee as commander of the corps in which the Texas Brigade was serving with Lieutenant General Benjamin Cheatham.

With the Atlanta campaign lost, there was great despondency among the surviving troops and deep anxiety and sorrow in the civilian population of Georgia. As Hood contemplated his next move, the men in his command had a short time to recuperate from the terrible sounds and sights they had known since the campaign began in May. Again John Hardison found an opportunity to write to Mary Northington:[11]

"In the Ditches" — Love Joy's Station
Macon and Western Rail Road
Septr 7th 1864

Miss Fletcher

About the 16th of August I presumed so far as to address you a somewhat lengthy and what I supposed to be, friendly letter proposing a social correspondence with you and in which I took occasion to refer to our former—to me—pleasant association, together with other things expressive of my kindly feeling and due appreciation of your moral and intellectual worth and many admirable traits of character etc, but as I have as yet received nothing in reply, I am fearful I have incurred your displeasure. Or it may be that the ruling of the [illegible word] Gods has carried my letter wide of its destination, or if not so, the same inexplicable fate may have attended your response and have borne it far from me.

The belief, and I must add the hope, that this latter supposition may be true, induces me to write you again, not that I would impose a second letter on you, did I know that you had received the first letter and had declined responding to it, but that you, as well as myself may be relieved of some anxiety of feeling, provided you did receive my first letter and replied to it as I believed you would do when I addressed you.

During the recent Evacuation of Atlanta by our forces, the Army Post Office together with its intire contents, was consumed by fire. Consequently thousands of letters for the soldiers were destroyed, and, in all probability your billet to me (if indeed you had written) may have shared that same fate. Under this state of things I deemed it not imprudent to trouble you with this note and I hope you will pardon the intrusion in view of the circumstances which surround me. If on the other hand you have seen proper not to countenance my proposition to correspond with you, and have treated my first letter accordingly—as a piece of worthless trash not entitled to notice or credit—I know not how I shall obtain pardon and forgiveness for a second intrusion. I can only implore your pardon.

Surely you will not deny me the privilege of respecting you if you cannot allow me the pleasure of your friendship.

Military oppositions have been very active in this department since the 30th inst. [August 30]—A series of battles have been fought, some resulting in victories to southern armies and others in partial defeats.

The weather has been very inclement for several days and our troops have suffered materially, but I desist from further comment on this topic for the present for fear I may worry you. A note of explanation from you will greatly relieve my anxiety and is therefore earnestly desired at your earliest convenience.

Be assured that you will ever have my highest esteem.

With feelings of great respect
J. Randolph Hardison
25th Texas Cavalry
Granbury's Brigade
Cleburne's Division
Army of Tennessee.

No letters from Mary to John and no further letters from him written during the Civil War years have been found in the various family collections. Obviously John's letters of August and September, 1864 were received by Mary and treasured by her and her descendants over the years and it is quite likely that she wrote in reply. The lives of the men in the Texas Brigade over the remaining months of the war were so chaotic and violent that it is possible John might not have received her letters or been able to preserve them. Before the end of 1864 Mary had her own encounter with the wrath of Sherman as the Union forces invaded Washington County in their "March to the Sea," destroying the way of life she had known since birth. One can only wish that both John's and Mary's writings for this last phase of the war years had survived, since both were articulate and sensitive authors.

By the autumn of 1864 it was obvious that the Confederate cause was lost. The Union had won significant victories in all theaters of the war except Virginia, where Lee continued to deal punishing blows to Grant's forces. Grant was pressing hard on Lee's Army of Northern Virginia and he put General Philip Sheridan in charge of a campaign to seize the Shenandoah Valley and destroy the food supplies for Lee's troops. Lee fought tenaciously, but, with the manpower of the South depleted and supplies of food and munitions from the southeastern and trans-Mississippi states cut off, he was fighting in vain. Still the war went on until the spring of 1865.

General Hood, in spite of the terrible losses which the Army of Tennessee had suffered in Georgia, refused to concede that he had been beaten by Sherman. In consultation with President Jefferson Davis, a strategy to draw Sherman out of Atlanta and put him on the defensive was agreed to. Hood's plan was to move his army into northwest Georgia, between Atlanta and Chattanooga, where he would cut Sherman's supply lines from Tennessee and force him to do battle at a place of Hood's choosing. If this plan failed, Hood was to turn and pursue Sherman through Georgia.

By the end of September the Army of Tennessee had moved its camp to Palmetto in western Georgia, near the West Point Railroad, and the men rested while Hood developed his new strategy. The feelings of the Texans is probably well represented in the diary entries of Captain Samuel T. Foster, who voiced strong dislike and distrust of both Hood and Davis. As the troops were ordered to move out of Palmetto on September 29, he expressed the opinion, "This army is going to do something wrong—or rather it will undertake something that will not be a success, if the future is to be judged by the past . . . ."[12] How prescient and how understated were his forebodings in light of the subsequent history of the Army of Tennessee!

John Hardison's concerns in late September were probably similar to Foster's and led him to thoughts of the hardships which lay ahead for the men in their regiment and brigade. On September 22 he wrote the following appeal for publication in the *Central Georgian*, the Washington County newspaper for which he had written previously.[13]

For the *Central Georgian*
An Appeal in Behalf of Texans.
Camp Granbury's Brigade
Atlanta and West Point RR.
Sept. 22, 1864

Ladies of Washington County and surrounding vicinity:

I am endeavoring to procure good, substantial, and durable socks for the members of my company and regiment and, if possible for Granbury's entire Brigade of Texans, and I beg permission to appeal to your patriotism in behalf of these brave men who, while they are fighting for your rights and liberties, have been cut off from their homes and abundant resources for almost three long years.

You can readily imagine how much we must suffer from the want of those many comforts with which our mothers, wives, daughters and sisters would bounteously supply us, was there any means of communication open to our homes in Texas.

The government has never succeeded in manufacturing an article of socks of much worth or durability, and only a very limited supply of any quality, hence the soldier must procure them from other sources and from the ladies at home, or else must go without them through the frost and snow and chilling blasts of winter.

Then may we not hope that you who have always done so much, will now make another effort in our behalf. We know that you have been very kind to us in time past, for which we trust we are truly grateful, and it is the belief that you are still ready and willing to do your part nobly in our common cause that induces us to call on you now for help.

To those of you who may respond to this appeal, I would suggest that you form yourselves into societies in your several neighborhoods, in order to have better concert of action, and agree upon some place of deposit for the articles as they may be completed. By this means I hope and believe that you will be able to manufacture and collect together a goodly number of socks without its operating very grievously on any one individual, and I can assure you ladies, that any number you may succeed in preparing be it only a dozen or twenty pairs, will be thankfully received.

The materials should be coarse and strong and, if possible mixed with wool. A very small proportion of wool mixed with cotton will render the socks much more comfortable and pleasant in winter.

After you have resolved yourselves into societies and gotten under way fairly be pleased to write me from each association, stating the number of pairs you think you will be able to have in readiness by the first to the fifteenth November, that I may go myself or send some other trusty person to receive and bring them to our command.

Hoping to have a favorable hearing from you very soon,

I am ladies very respectfully
Your obedient servant, J. Randolph Hardison
Lt. Com'g Co. G, 25th Texas, Granbury's Brigade
Cleburne's Division, Army of Tenn.

The success of this request is not known, but the need was great, as the depletion of Southern resources left the soldiers more and more poorly clothed and supplied. Even though there is no entry in John's service record between August and December, 1864, he presumably participated in the campaign on which Hood was about to embark. The entry for December states simply that he was in the Army of Tennessee. He continued to be recorded in that service from January through March, 1865, the latter month being the last dated entry in his service record. The letter which is printed above ends with his identifying himself as lieutenant commanding his company, obviously a promotion in rank from his election as second lieutenant in March, 1864. The great loss of men in the Atlanta campaign brought raises in rank to many of the survivors and Hood's new campaign was to further increase the burdens of responsibility to the lower ranks of officers. In the post-war years John's wife frequently referred to him as "the Captain," indicating that he achieved that rank before the end of his service. His official service record lists him variously as private, sergeant, second lieutenant, and lieutenant.

At the end of September, 1864 Hood moved his army from Palmetto to a line west of Marietta and then northwest toward Dalton, retracing the path they had taken earlier in the year with Johnston. Sherman pursued them for a few weeks and frustrated their attempts to destroy the rail lines from Tennessee and seize supplies in northern Georgia, but soon turned his attentions to reducing the state of Georgia to total submission. His original instructions from Grant had been to crush the Army of Tennessee, but having defeated them in the Atlanta campaign he allowed them to cross over into northern Alabama. Knowing that Hood now intended to invade Tennessee rather than continue the fight in Georgia, Sherman dispatched a force which more than outnumbered Hood's army to deal with him and the cavalry of Nathan Bedford Forrest in Tennessee. He then turned his attention to Georgia, having convinced Grant that he and his army could best serve the Union cause by bringing total war to the heartland of the Confederacy.

Hood's Tennessee Campaign

Having failed in his attempts to draw Sherman back into Tennessee

XI. THE SOUTH IN DEFEAT, 1864-1865

or destroy his supply lines, Hood developed a daring and desperate plan. In mid-October, while his army camped in northwest Georgia near the site of the September, 1863 Battle of Chickamauga, he conceived the idea of a bold thrust into middle Tennessee, with the expectation of defeating the relatively small enemy forces holding Nashville, to be followed by an invasion of Kentucky and a move toward Cincinnati. At the end of the month he ordered the Army of Tennessee into northeastern Alabama, leaving the cavalry forces under General Joseph Wheeler to follow Sherman's movements in Georgia. The men were told to expect hard marching and fighting, but were promised adequate food and clothing and fighting in places of Hood's choosing against a foe of equal size. On October 18 the army crossed from Georgia into northeastern Alabama where they remained at Tuscumbia for a month, waiting for the rain-swollen Tennessee River to allow passage and for General Nathan Bedford Forrest's cavalry to be in a position to augment Hood's army. Presumably John Hardison was among the troops and observed the sight which his fellow member of the consolidated Twenty-fourth and Twenty-fifth Texas Regiment described in his diary:[14]

> Nov. 15 This morning we leave our camp and march up the river two miles, and cross the Tenn. River on the longest Pontoon bridge I have ever seen. I stoped on a high bluff bank to see the army crossing. Each Brigade had its band playing ahead of it, all marching by fours. The pontoon bridge is flat on the water and one and a half miles long, and at the distance I am, it looks like the men were walking on the water. It is a pretty and at the same time a strange sight, a sight that is not seen more than once in a life time— The town of Florence is just across the river on the north side, and once was a very pretty place, but wars destroying hand has been here and left its mark....

Hood's delay in implementing his plan had allowed Sherman to send forces into Tennessee which were to be more than a match for his manpower. The Army of Tennessee's old foe, General George H. Thomas, was assigned to prepare defenses at Nashville and General John M. Schofield was sent to meet Hood. The latter commanded about 30,000 men, including two infantry corps and a cavalry unit, a force roughly equal in size to Hood's army. There is a question among chroniclers of this phase of the war whether Hood knew about the large force under Thomas, which was being assembled in Nashville, when he made his invasion plans, or whether he anticipated only a confrontation with Schofield's forces. As Hood headed toward Nashville in pursuit of Schofield, their armies met near the town of Spring Hill. After inconclusive fighting on November 29, in which the Confederates failed to take the town, Schofield's men slipped away during the night and marched on north along the road to Franklin. Hood accused his subordinate, General Benjamin H. Cheatham, who was commander of the corps which included the Texas Brigade, of failure to block the road, but Cheatham insisted that he had not been given specific orders for this action.

Once again time was working against Hood as he hastened to catch up with Schofield and attempt to defeat him before he could reach Nashville. The armies met on November 30 in the disastrous Battle of Franklin. A few miles south of the town, on the pike between Columbia and Franklin, the Confederates formed their battle line in the late afternoon and began to advance on the enemy as a military band played *Dixie* and *The Bonnie Blue Flag*. Hood's men moved successfully against the advance outpost, but the Union troops soon recovered and as Cleburne's division, including Granbury's Texas Brigade, went into action on the east side of the pike they were caught in a heavy cross fire. Both Cleburne and Granbury were killed, the latter as he was charging with his Texans. After the war a Union participant said of this phase of the battle, "I never saw men put in such a hellish position as Cleburne's division was in for a few minutes at Franklin. The wonder is that any of them escaped death or capture."[15]

The fighting went on into the night until Hood ended his attack at nine o'clock. Again Schofield slipped away during the night, moving his forces toward Nashville. The Confederate losses were horrendous. Out of Hood's approximately 20,000 to 27,000 men in action, 1,750 were killed, 3,800 wounded, and 702 were missing. Five Confederate generals, including Cleburne and Granbury were killed, and another mortally wounded. Five more were wounded. Having fought from a defensive position, the Union losses were dramatically fewer, 189 killed, 1,033 wounded, and 1,104 missing.

The indictment of General Hood in Captain Samuel T. Foster's

December 1 entry reflects both the anger of his men and a body of opinion in the post-war evaluation of Hood's leadership. After speaking of the ghastly sight which met his eyes on the morning after the battle, Foster wrote:[16]

> Gen. Hood has betrayed us (The Army of Tenn). This is not the kind of fighting he promised us at Tuscumbia and Florence Ala. when we started into Tenn. This was not a "fight with equal numbers and choice of the ground" by no means.
>
> And the wails and cries of widows and orphans made at Franklin Tenn Nov 30th 1864 will heat up the fires of the bottomless pit to burn the soul of Gen J B Hood for Murdering their husbands and fathers at that place that day. It can't be called anything else but cold blooded Murder.
>
> He sacrificed those men to make the name of Hood famous; when if the History of it is ever written it will make him *infamous*.

Regardless of the blood-letting at Franklin, Hood was unwilling to concede defeat. He pushed on toward Nashville in spite of the severely damaged morale of his outnumbered men. They were suffering greatly in the freezing cold due to lack of adequate clothing, particularly shoes. How welcome those socks John Hardison had requested from Washington County would have been! So depleted was the leadership that a captain, E. T. Broughton, was appointed to take General Granbury's place as commander of the Texas Brigade and a captain, John F. Matthews, rather than a major, headed the consolidated Twenty-fourth and Twenty-fifth Regiment.

During the first half of December Hood moved his men to within a few miles of Nashville and ordered them to dig in. He knew that he could not hope to succeed in a direct assault on the city, fully aware now of the presence of General Thomas' large force and the heavy fortification of the city. He hoped instead that a Union force would attack outside the city and that he could defeat it. On December 15 Thomas obliged, as he came forth from the city, and the Battle of Nashville began. The Texas Brigade fought well as they assisted the other troops on Hood's right in holding off the enemy on the first day, but as the fighting resumed on December 16 the superior strength of the enemy, approximately 50,000 against 25,000 Confederates, forced Hood's men to relinquish their positions and retreat.

During the battle the Texans had their first experience of fighting against Negro troops. Hood's losses were disastrous—4,500 captured and about 1,500 killed and wounded, as compared to casualties of about 3,000 for the Union.

With considerable harassment from Union troops, the defeated, bitter, and depleted Army of Tennessee retreated through Tennessee and back into Alabama. During the campaign it had sustained losses of 10,000 men, which added to an equal number of casualties in the Atlanta campaign had reduced it to about the size of a division. Grant's original instructions to Sherman to crush the Army of Tennessee had been accomplished by Schofield and Thomas. Hood's hopes of a decisive blow which might have led the war-weary North to a cessation of hostilities and recognition of Southern independence were completely demolished. Lincoln had been re-elected in November and was pushing Sherman and Grant to bring the war to an end. Sherman was continuing with his harsh punishment of Georgia and Grant was wearing down Lee's masterful defense of Virginia. With the loss of the supplies from Georgia and the Carolinas which had maintained his army, Lee's efforts were soon to be hopeless.

As the defeated Army of Tennessee marched back into Alabama and then to Tupelo, Mississippi, the men were angry and exhausted. Knowing that they had completely lost confidence in him, Hood asked to be relieved of command. He was replaced by Lieutenant General Richard Taylor, son of former President Zachary Taylor. Taylor presided over the dismemberment of the Army, as its units were parceled out to other organizations in the Confederacy's frantic efforts to prevent final defeat. Most of the men, including Granbury's Texas Brigade, were sent to the Carolinas where they made up part of a force still called the Army of Tennessee, headed by the now reinstated General Joseph E. Johnston. Presumably John Hardison was with the brigade as it moved into its last campaign. He is listed in the regimental returns for his unit as being in the Army of Tennessee in the months of December, 1864 and January, February, and March, 1865. A notation dated January 9 at Tupelo, Mississippi indicates that by Special Order Number Four he was "detailed for 20 days." The February and March entries place him "on detached service" in the Army of Tennessee.

At the end of January the Texans traveled by train from Mississippi through Alabama and Georgia on their way to South Carolina. At stops on their journey they disgraced themselves by looting for food and drink, particularly in Montgomery, with their officers unable to restrain them. For many months they had lacked adequate food and clothing—and tobacco and whiskey—and they went wild without the discipline of marching and battle. As they passed through Georgia they learned of the destruction which Sherman had wrought since their departure from the state the previous October. One can imagine the concern which John Hardison felt for Mary Northington and his many relatives and friends in Washington County, which had been in the direct path of Sherman's march. His brigade was transported by train as far as Milledgeville, the state capital, which had miraculously escaped major destruction. The Texans camped there briefly before marching on toward Augusta and the Carolinas and probably John took advantage of this opportunity to make a brief visit to nearby Washington County. He would have found it a pitiful sight, for it lay directly in the Union army's "March to the Sea."

Sherman's Destruction in Georgia

The march took place between November 16 and December 24, 1864, the period in which Hood had invaded Tennessee and been forced to retrace his steps into Alabama. While the Army of Tennessee experienced disastrous defeat, the people of Georgia were subjected to wanton destruction by Sherman's force of 60,000 men. The Confederates could field a force of only a fraction of that number—militia units, military college cadets, the cavalry led by Lieutenant General Joseph Wheeler which Hood had left behind, and a small force under General William J. Hardee in Savannah. As Sherman set out from Atlanta in mid-November, he ordered the destruction of all buildings with any military potential and the fires spread to leave the city a smoking ruin. The army fanned out in a front sixty miles wide moving from Atlanta southeast toward Savannah. The general's orders were for the men to live on the bountiful produce of the countryside and to destroy what they could not eat. His discipline was deliberately lax and he made no attempt to restrain the horde of opportunists and army deserters, known as bummers, who followed the army and preyed on the helpless civilians. There were lawless Southerners as well as Yankees among the bummers. Together the soldiers and their followers engaged in an orgy of destruction, burning houses and public buildings, eating or destroying all the farm animals, emptying the smokehouses and barns, and engaging in malicious acts such as pouring syrup into church pipe organs and chopping up pianos.

As the army approached Milledgeville, about one hundred miles southeast of Atlanta, in late November, Governor Joseph E. Brown fled toward Savannah. He left behind under the command of his adjutant, General Harry Wayne, a token force of a few hundred men and military cadets, augmented by a group of convicts from the state penitentiary. As Sherman's massive force entered Milledgeville on November 22, Wayne took his hopelessly outnumbered little force by train to the nearby town of Gordon. On this bitter cold day the main body of the Union army's left wing fell into line for a march up Greene Street to the capitol, with their flags flying and military band playing *Yankee Doodle*. Sherman took the handsome Palladian style governor's mansion as his headquarters and began to be visited by leading citizens, including representatives from the Masons, who implored the general to spare their beautiful little city from the fate of Atlanta. They were in large part successful and the residences and public buildings, except the state penitentiary and arsenal, were spared. The greatest damage was done in the capitol, where a group of the soldiers held a mock session of the legislature and then proceeded to loot the building, throwing the fine collection of books in its library out the windows and trampling them. With the 30,000 soldiers who swarmed through the town, great damage was done to its churches and to the yards and gardens of its homes, but they were not burned. Perhaps the behavior of the ladies of the town helped to prevent this ultimate destruction. One Union officer observed that most of the women in the town smiled pleasantly even as soldiers ransacked their houses. It was the older women who were defiant, and they were quieted by their daughters. Perhaps such restraint saved them from the fate of one lady of the community who was raped as she lay ill at home.[17]

With great relief the citizens of Milledgeville observed the departure of the ravagers on November 25. It was now the turn of Washington County to host them, as they headed southeast across the Oconee River on their path to Savannah. The county was known for its high level of enthusiasm for the Confederate cause, claiming as noted previously that it had sent a higher percentage of its men into service than any other county of the South. Its people had much to fear as two wings of the army converged on the county, one led by General Slocum marching from Milledgeville toward the centrally located county seat, Sandersville, and the other, under General Howard, moving toward the village of Oconee in the southern portion. The goal of the latter was the destruction of the railroad bridge crossing the Oconee River and it was here that General Wayne and Major F. W. Capers, commandant of the Georgia Military Institute, led their little band of 650 men and boys in an attempt to stop the advance party. A band of Union cavalrymen led by Judson Kilpatrick lost forty-five men to Wayne's men but succeeded in setting fire to the trestle. Wayne's men attempted to beat out the fire, but had to retreat. In the meantime a pontoon bridge had been built over the river and Howard's men swarmed into the swamps which lay to the east. Moving into the hilly country above the river, they headed toward the village of Oconee, the home of John's uncle William L. Hardison and a few miles from the Northingtons' home in Bay Spring. They proceeded to lay waste to the country and tear up the portion of the Central of Georgia Railroad which passed through on its way toward Savannah.

While Howard's men burned and pillaged in the southern portion of the county, Sherman accompanied Slocum's wing to Sandersville. They met with resistance from the small cavalry force under General Joseph Wheeler, which soon had to retreat after driving off the advance skirmishers, and were fired on by men stationed in the county courthouse as they rode into town. Sherman's anger mounted and led him to the decision to burn the town when he learned that a small group of Union prisoners, whom Wheeler had captured and imprisoned overnight, had been murdered by a lynch mob. The town's chief spokesman, Methodist minister J. D. Anthony, pleaded with the general not to burn the town, telling him that the lynchers were not Georgians, much less citizens of Sandersville. Possibly they were some of the Confederate soldiers passing through the county or camp-following stragglers. Reportedly saying that he did not war on women or children, Sherman agreed to burn only the courthouse, a handsome Greek Revival building, and the jail.[18]

Although the homes of the town were not burned, their contents were looted and all food stolen or destroyed. Ella Mitchell, a child at the time of the invasion and later a teacher and county historian, described the reign of terror which left the town a ruin and its citizens destitute:[19]

> From Saturday morning [November 26] until Monday many inhabitants had neither food nor water. It seems beyond belief that not a chicken was left, not a hog, and only a few cows, no meal nor flour, the ground was strewn with food, carpets were drenched with syrup and then covered with meal. Negro soldiers entered private homes and searched for valuables. My mother refused to unlock her bureau drawers, but a soldier placed his bayonet at her back and forced her to march in front of him. Father was helpless from a terrible hemorrhage brought on by excitement, to save him she obeyed the Yankee's command, then he helped himself to all valuables that she had overlooked when hiding some treasures.

Having vented his anger on Sandersville, Sherman moved south three miles toward the county's rail center in Tennille, where his soldiers continued their destruction of the railroads. There the two wings of the army were rejoined and they proceeded eastward across Williamson Swamp Creek, destroying the tracks of the Central of Georgia Railroad as they headed toward its next station in the village of Davisboro. They burned the depot and finally moved out of Washington County on the road to Savannah. In four days they had destroyed what settlers like the Hardisons, Northingtons, and Davises had spent a half century building.

North Carolina and Surrender

If John Hardison had a chance to visit in Washington County, as he passed through Georgia with the Texas Brigade in early February, 1865, he must have begun his last campaign in a state of despondency. Georgia lay in ruins and the Confederate force which the Texans were on their way to join was hopelessly outnumbered by the nearly 100,000 men Sherman would soon concentrate in North

Carolina. As the Texans and other units from the Army of Tennessee made their way from Augusta, Georgia through western South Carolina in early February, Sherman began his march from Savannah toward Columbia. He had arrived in the Savannah area in early December and on Christmas eve sent a telegram to President Lincoln offering him the city as a Christmas gift. After consolidating his gains in January, he was ready to humiliate and devastate the state which he blamed for instigating secession and the war. In February both Columbia and Charleston fell to Union forces and Columbia suffered the fate of Atlanta. The origin of the fire which consumed South Carolina's capital city continues to be debated, but if Sherman did not order it he was certainly not sorry to see the city burn. The homes, gardens, and plantations of Charleston were also laid waste.

Having accomplished his goals in South Carolina, Sherman moved on to North Carolina in March. His plan was to defeat the Confederate units gathering there and then join Grant in forcing Lee to give up his valiant defense of Richmond and the state of Virginia. Once again he was to face General Joseph E. Johnston, who had been called back into service to head the remnants of Hood's command, which included the Texas Brigade, and all the other Confederate troops from Georgia, Florida, and the Carolinas which could be assembled. These forces included the men under General William J. Hardee, who had retreated from Savannah as Sherman entered, and General Braxton Bragg's command, which had defended Wilmington and escaped after the city was captured. The varied remnants of Confederate units, totaling at most 30,000, which Johnston commanded was known as the Army of Tennessee, but it bore no resemblance to the proud army he had commanded in the first half of 1864. The forces which Sherman brought together in North Carolina numbered about 100,000 seasoned and well supplied troops.

Sherman and Johnston had great respect for each other's abilities and Sherman was aware of the blows which the latter's depleted army was still able to inflict. Their commands met in one last battle on March 19 at the village of Bentonville, to the south of Raleigh, as Johnston attacked the advance party of Sherman's main forces, hoping to slow down their march toward Virginia. At first the Confederates met with success as the ragged but determined veterans pushed the enemy back, but when the mass of Union troops arrived they were forced to retreat. Skirmishing continued the next day and on March 21 a combined Confederate infantry and cavalry force met with success in repulsing an attack on Johnston's line. The Texas Brigade was still on its way to join Johnston and did not participate in the battle.

The Battle of Bentonville did nothing to alter the fact that Sherman's massive force could do anything it liked in North Carolina and that Johnston could only hope to slow down its move toward Virginia. Johnston reorganized his meager forces on April 9 and the Texas Brigade ceased to exist as a unit. Its eight regiments were combined to form the First Consolidated Texas Regiment and assigned to General Daniel Govan's brigade, along with combined regiments of Arkansas troops.

On the day when this reorganization was taking place, Lee met with Grant at Appomattox Courthouse and surrendered the Army of Northern Virginia. As the news spread throughout the Confederacy, there were varied reactions—at first disbelief, then grief and disappointment that the long fight had not succeeded in winning Southern independence, and finally relief. Both Johnston and Sherman were anxious to avoid useless bloodshed in North Carolina and began to parley over terms of surrender. Sherman was as generous in his terms as he had been vicious in pursuing the war. He originally called for the men of the Army of Tennessee to disband and go home, taking their weapons to their state arsenals and resuming their civil rights in the United States. However, by the time he asked approval for these terms, Lincoln had been assassinated and the vengefulness which was to mark the Reconstruction period led to their rejection. The terms which Johnston and Sherman eventually agreed upon, on April 26 in the simple farmhouse of the Bennett family near Durham, were relatively lenient. They called for the men to turn in their weapons and to sign paroles in the town of Greensboro, in central North Carolina to the west of Raleigh. The men were allowed to keep any privately owned horses or mules and officers were permitted to keep their side arms. One rifle to every five enlisted men was allowed to enable the men to hunt for food on the way home. The federal government agreed to furnish transportation to their homes whenever possible.

Of the thousands of Texans who had served in Granbury's Texas Brigade only 440 were present to sign paroles in North Carolina. Johnston made a farewell address to his command and on April 28 the men of the Texas Brigade expressed their sentiments to this greatly loved general, saying in part, "We . . . respectfully desire to assure General Johnston of our undiminished confidence and esteem; and fully sympathizing with him in the present issue of our affairs, do most cordially tender him the hospitality of our State and our homes (such as the future may provide for us)."[20]

On May 1 the Texans heard a farewell sermon and on May 2 began to make their way back home. Travel by rail and boat were available for part of the way, but most of the men had to walk hundreds of weary miles through country where destruction had taken a ruinous toll on all means of transportation, including horses and mules. The course of John Hardison is not known.[21] Probably he was torn between his desire to continue his courtship of Mary Northington in Georgia and his concern over the two little daughters whom he had left with his sister three years before in Texas. Whatever journey or journeys he undertook after the surrender, his courtship was successful and it brought him to Washington County in January, 1866, when he and Mary were married. For three years he had fought in defense of his native land and his convictions and now, with the woman he loved, he entered a new phase of life with the buoyancy, enthusiasm, and idealism which characterized him.

NOTES

As in the preceding chapter, the major sources for information on the history of the Texas Brigade are *One of Cleburne's Command, the Civil War Reminiscences and Diary of Capt. Samuel T. Foster, Granbury's Texas Brigade, CSA*, edited by Norman D. Brown, and *This Band of Heroes, Granbury's Texas Brigade, C.S.A.* by James M. McCaffrey. References to the military service of John Randolph Hardison are based on his Compiled Service Record, National Archives.

1. Norman D. Brown, editor, *One of Cleburne's Command*, pp.69-70. As noted, Foster served in the Twenty-fourth Texas Cavalry Regiment (dismounted) which was joined with John Hardison's regiment, the Twenty-fifth, in a consolidated regiment of the Texas Brigade in March, 1864.
2. *Central Georgian*, Sandersville, Georgia, May 25, 1864. There is no evidence that John Hardison ever lived in the area he described. The identity of the girls to whom he dedicated the poem is not known; probably they were relatives or friends whom he had visited in his youth, when living in Gadsden County, Florida. White Springs is a town in Hamilton County, Florida.

3. Union armies were named for rivers, while Confederate armies used the names of states.
4. Brown, *op. cit.*, p.85.
5. *Ibid.*, p.101.
6. *Ibid.*, p.115.
7. Compiled Service Record, National Archives, Edwin T. Davis, Company A, 57th Regiment Georgia Infantry.
8. Elizabeth Shreve Ryan Collection (gift from Nancy Louise Brown Slaughter), letter of Aug. 14, 1864 from John Randolph Hardison to Mary Fletcher Northington.
9. Brown, *op. cit.*, p.126.
10. *Ibid.*, p.128.
11. Ryan Collection, letter of September 7, 1864 from John Randolph Hardison to Mary Fletcher Northington.
12. Brown, *op. cit.*, p.135.
13. Cain Family Genealogical Collection, typescript of a clipping from the *Central Georgian*, Sandersville, Georgia. The date of publication is not included in the typescript.
14. Brown, *op. cit.*, p.144.
15. *Ibid.*, p.148.
16. *Ibid.*, p.151.
17. Burke Davis, *Sherman's March* (New York: Vintage Books, 1988, originally published by Random House, 1980), pp.65-66 (quotation regarding the women of Milledgeville); see pp.58-68 for Sherman's stay in Milledgeville.
18. Davis., *op. cit.*, see pp.69-80 for Sherman in Washington County; see also Mary Alice Jordan, editor, *Cotton to Kaolin*, pp.27-32.
19. Ella Mitchell, *History of Washington County* (Atlanta: Cherokee Publishing Company, 1973, reprint of the original, which was copyrighted in 1924), p.67.
20. James M. McCaffrey, *This Band of Heroes*, p.155.
21. *Ibid.*, in his comprehensive listing of the units and the men who served in Granbury's Texas Brigade (pp.175-236), McCaffrey designated those who received paroles in Greensboro. John Hardison's name (p.232) has not been so designated. The last entry in his Compiled Service Record is for March, 1865, when he was listed as "on detached service in the army of Tenn."

XII

New Beginnings in Texas during Reconstruction Limestone County, 1865-1875

*J*ohn Hardison's war-time courtship of Mary Northington was successful and on January 23, 1866 they were married in Washington County, Georgia.[1] While John's first wife, Winnifred Cornelia Davis, had belonged to one of the several Davis families living on the far eastern side of the county, Mary came from the Bay Spring community in the southwest corner of the county, a few miles south of the Central of Georgia Railroad station in Oconee. Her mother's father, Metcalf Fisher, was one of the early settlers in this area, which lay on the high ground to the east of the Oconee River and its great swamp. As Metcalf's children married, several of them, including his daughter Milly (Amelia) and her husband James Foster Northington, Mary's parents, established their homes and farms in the Bay Spring community. Mary grew up in a large family, which included the children of her aunt Elizabeth, married to William H. Robison, and uncle, John Fisher.

Mary Northington's Family
Both Mary's father and her grandfather Fisher were outstanding and

I, John Randolph Hardison, do solemnly swear that I will faithfully and impartially discharge and perform all the duties incumbent on me as an Attorney and Counsellor at Law, and that I will honestly demean myself in the practice of the Law and discharge my duty to my clients to the best of my ability agreeable to the Constitution and laws of the State of Texas. And I do further solemnly swear that since the adoption of the Constitution of the State of Texas by the Congress of the United States, I being a Citizen of this State, have not fought a duel with deadly weapons within this State nor out of it, nor have I sent or accepted a challenge to fight a duel with deadly weapons, nor have I acted as second in carrying a challenge, or aided, advised or assisted any person thus offending. So help me God.

Sworn to and subscribed
before me this 3rd day
of November A.D. 1866.

J. Randolph Hardison

Wm. A. Wilson
Judge 15th Judicial Dist. Texas

Oath for License to Practice Law in Texas,
John Randolph Hardison, 1866

Slaughter Collection

highly regarded citizens in their immediate neighborhood and in Washington County. Their relative affluence made possible the education she received and her consequent career as a teacher. Both were leaders in the Bay Spring Methodist Church and her mother was noted for her piety and devotion to the church. Metcalf's role in the church, to which he deeded 1¾ acres of land for a building in 1854, is interesting in light of his New England origins.[2] He was born in Massachusetts about 1778, the son of John Fisher and Mehitable Metcalf, descendants of Puritan families who had established the town of Dedham, near Boston, in the 1630s.[3]

Metcalf Fisher, like the first Hardisons in Washington County, had settled in Georgia soon after the establishment of the county in the late eighteenth century. He was lured from his home in Massachusetts by the abundant lands being opened for settlement and cotton cultivation. He is listed in Washington County, with his wife and children, in the earliest existing Federal Census for Georgia, 1820, and was at that time about 42 years old.[4] Data from descendants give his wife's name as Elizabeth Schaffner (various spellings, including Shoffner), a native of South Carolina.[5] In the population enumeration segment of the census, Metcalf is listed as being engaged in agriculture, commerce, and manufacturing, and in the listing of manufacturers he is described as a "cotton machine maker." Land speculation was also an interest, for in the 1828 tax records of Washington County, he listed not only his holdings of 900 acres in the county, but also a total of 2,100 acres in other counties, including Early, Troup, Upson, Irwin, Lee, and Wilkinson.[6] The odd size of several of the acreages, 202½ and 490 acres, indicates that they were land lottery winnings which had resulted either from lucky draws he had made in the Georgia land lotteries of the first third of the century or had bought from other winners. The smaller number of acres was the division made in counties which had hardwood forests, thought to indicate land suitable for cotton cultivation, and the larger in the pine forests of south Georgia, whose sandy soil was considered inferior. In addition to his land holdings he owned ten slaves in 1828.

Metcalf lived a long, useful, and successful life, as indicated by the estate he left at the time of his death and the descriptions of him in the county's newspaper, the *Central Georgian*. In the notice of his death, which occurred in January, 1860, he was referred to as "an old and esteemed citizen of this county" and later in the year as "that excellent man."[7] He and his family played a leading role in the Bay Spring Methodist Church, which with its academy was a focal point of their community. As noted, Metcalf gave a lot for the church building from his land in 1854, and the church's location was moved at that time from its original site a few miles to the south, to take advantage of the road, now Georgia Highway 272, from Milledgeville to the coast, which passed through the southern portion of the county.[8] Mary Northington probably received her education at the Bay Spring Academy and she taught there both before and after her marriage.

Mary's father, James Foster Northington, like the first Hardisons and Davises in Washington County was a native of North Carolina, where he was born in 1809.[9] There are two Northington families listed in the 1820 Federal Census for Georgia, headed by John Northington in Morgan County and James Northington in Oglethorpe County, but none in Washington County until 1830, when the families of William and Jesse Northington first appear.[10] Mary's father James was probably one of the two young adult sons in Jesse's household. Later census listings include Jesse and a son Jesse A. living in the town of Sandersville, while James and his family settled on a farm in the Bay Spring area. Metcalf Fisher's daughter Amelia (Milly) was born in 1814 and married James in 1834. They had four daughters and three sons; from eldest to youngest, with their ages as listed in the 1860 Federal Census, they were Harriet Missouri, called Hattie, age 21; Mary Fletcher, age 20 (she was born in December, 1839 and the census was taken before her birthday); Martha Elizabeth, called Lizzie, age 17; Indiana, age 14; James Fisher, called Jimmie, age 11; Marcellus Addison, age 8; and William Capers, called Capers (named for Methodist Bishop Capers), age 6.[11]

A little over a year before the beginning of the Civil War, Metcalf Fisher died and left his considerable estate to his son John; daughters Amelia (wife of James F. Northington), Elizabeth (wife of William H. Robison), Sarah Ann (wife of James N. Wood); granddaughter Mary Josey (wife of John W. Josey); and the children of his deceased son William.[12] Metcalf's will, which was dated November 4, 1859, included a provision for his second wife, Lavinia, including personal possessions and a trust fund of $2,000.00, but Lavinia died within the month, on November 29, 1859, only a short time before Metcalf's death in the last week of January, 1860.[13]

Metcalf's heirs received substantial benefits in spite of their considerable number. He noted in the will that he had already given each of his children $1,600.00 and he expressed the hope that they would be able to divide the estate among themselves without going through the process of law. Special provisions for the eldest daughter, Elizabeth, who was living with her husband and children on a portion of Metcalf's land (estimated at 374 acres), were made to insure her inheritance for the sole use of herself and her children. She died a few months after her father, and her husband, William H. Robison, member of an old Washington County family, purchased the remainder of Metcalf's plantation, 450 acres, for $3,070.00 from the other heirs in October, 1860.[14] It remained in the Robison family for many years. Metcalf suggested that if his son John desired to have his mill, probably a grist mill, that it be a portion of his share of the estate at the value of $1,000.00.

The will was probated in February, 1860, an inventory of Metcalf's personal property was made and a public sale announced, and his thirteen slaves, valued at almost $12,000.00, divided among his heirs.[15] The inventory of livestock and farming equipment reflected Metcalf's extensive agricultural operations and the list of his household furnishings indicated a comfortable, well furnished home. The latter included a bookcase and books, dining table, twenty chairs, looking glass, clock, lamps and candlesticks, fire-dogs and tongs, chamber pots and bowls, spinning wheel, and a number of beds, including one mahogany bedstead. In addition to farm vehicles such as wagons and oxcarts, he had owned two carriages and a buggy along with several horses, including a pair of black horses.

Metcalf's home was probably the house described by a descendant of Elizabeth (Fisher) Robison, who recalled it from childhood visits, "The old house was the type that had a hall, or I might say an open hall, through the house with the dining room and kitchen built about fifteen feet from the house with a walk way leading from the hall to the dining room. The old house had four bedrooms, two on each side of the open hall and a small guest room built on the front porch."[16]

Such houses were typical of those owned by the planters and prosperous farmers of middle Georgia and the small room at the end of the porch was a common feature. The room was called "the prophets' chamber" because of its frequent use by the circuit-riding ministers who needed overnight accomodations.[17] With their zeal for the Methodist church, both the Fishers and Robisons must have frequently extended hospitality to its clergy. One of Elizabeth and William Robison's seven sons, William, was a Methodist minister.[18]

The inheritance of Metcalf's daughter Amelia, along with success in her husband James Northington's farming operations, is reflected in the difference between the value of James' property as stated in the 1850 Federal Census, $790.00, and the 1860 listing, $5,000.00 for his real estate and $6,100.00 for personal property.[19] The major portion of the value of his personal property was undoubtedly his slaves. In the 1860 Slave Census he listed seven slaves, five females between the ages of 6 and 56 and two males, ages 19 and 3. In the division of Metcalf Fisher's slaves the Northingtons received two males valued at $2,000.00, George and Crum. Their value in the original inventory was given as $1,300.00 for George and $300.00 for Crum.

As the decade of the 1860s opened, the future for the Northingtons and the other families of the Fisher connection must have seemed promising. They had land and laborers to produce the crop for which the textile mills of the North and England had a constant demand and they had families of industrious and ambitious children. But death stalked them as it did the Hardison and Davis families, both from natural causes and the disastrous war which was about to begin. In 1860 Metcalf's daughter Elizabeth Robison died in April, a few months after her father's decease in the first month of the year, and Elizabeth's only daughter, Mary, died in the fall of the year. Five of the Robisons' seven sons served in the Confederate Army and three of them died while in service.[20] In the year after the war John Fisher, Metcalf's surviving son, died.[21] The family circle which had seemed so full as the decade opened was now painfully reduced. To the grief over the loss of loved ones was added the overwhelming reality of the death of the way of life which Southerners had known throughout the century. Truly that life was "gone with the wind," and for every member of society, black or white, dislocations and

XII. NEW BEGINNINGS IN TEXAS, 1865-1875

drastic changes lay ahead. A minority of Southerners, along with a group of enterprising Northerners, managed to reap profits as the conquered states rose from the ashes of defeat, but for the majority the closing decades of the century were a time of struggle and frustration.

In spite of the joy which Mary Northington felt over the survival of John Hardison in the war which had taken the lives of so many young men of her acquaintance, she was sad as she bid farewell to her family and began her journey to Texas after their wedding on January 23, 1866. She was a devoted daughter and sister and had lived her twenty-six years in a community where she and her family were valued and respected members. She had an anxious nature and was concerned as she contemplated the hardships her parents, then in their fifties, faced in devastated Washington County. Her feelings are reflected in a line from the first letter she wrote from Texas, "I never will forget how you looked standing on that old red hill after we left you."[22] John Hardison was a great booster of Texas and he took a second bride from Washington County with high expectations, in spite of the changes which the war and military occupation by the Union army had brought about. Mary's "Not Yet" sentiments of maidenhood and John's years as a widower had passed and they now entered a new relationship and an uncertain future.

Soon after their wedding they journeyed to Texas, first by rail from Georgia to New Orleans, then by steamship from New Orleans to Galveston, and finally by ship to Houston and rail to Liberty County. John returned to the place of residence from which he had entered the Confederate Army and where he had left his daughters Lilly and Winnifred with his sister Mary Ann Gray in 1862, after the death of his first wife. He resumed his teaching and farming pursuits for about a year and then moved to Limestone County, located to the north and west of Liberty, on the western edge of East Texas. The story of John and Mary is best told in their own words as found in the letters they wrote to their relatives in Georgia from 1866 through 1875. These letters and a few written to them will be included in the chapters which follow. A brief account of the rancorous and violent years of Reconstruction in Texas and particularly in Limestone County provides the context in which the letters were written.

Texas in the Years of Reconstruction

The state to which John Hardison brought his new bride in 1866 was a far different place from the land of peace and plenty which he and his family had envisioned when they migrated from Florida in the late 1850s. The political divisions over the secession issue, which had torn Texas asunder at the beginning of the Civil War, were now repeated as the Texans who had supported the Confederate cause struggled for control of the state with those who had remained loyal to the Union. Their strife over the restructuring of the state government and a return to the federal union was made infinitely more challenging and complex by the presence of military occupation forces and the political, social, and economic problems created by the emancipation of the slaves.[23]

In the spring of 1865 as news of the surrenders of Lee's and Johnston's forces in Virginia and North Carolina reached Texas, there was great disappointment over the failure of the Confederacy to achieve independence and apprehension over the future of the South as a conquered land. The survivors of the Texas units which had fought in the eastern states began their long and tortuous journeys back to the homes they had left three or four years before. The major portion of the Texans in the Confederate forces at the end of the war were in the Trans-Mississippi Army, which was headed by General Edmund Kirby Smith. In May he began surrender negotiations with General Philip Sheridan, commander of the Union forces in the area west of the Mississippi, whose headquarters were in New Orleans. The negotiations dragged as Smith tried to get as liberal terms as possible for his men and for the states of Texas and Louisiana. Intending to use Houston as a gathering point for the surrender, he evacuated the Confederate forces which had held the port city of Galveston. This move triggered a complete break-down in military discipline and by the time Smith had worked out a surrender agreement the majority of the men had abandoned all army discipline. They swarmed over Galveston, Houston, Austin, and the smaller towns and countryside, looting state and Confederate supplies of food, clothing, and arms and the state treasury in Austin. Those who bothered to excuse their actions said that they had not been paid or supplied for months and that the goods and monies were rightfully theirs. Texas entered a period of lawlessness and violence, which prevailed in varying degrees well into the next decade. In the wake of the surrender, General Smith and Governor Murrah of Texas fled to Mexico as the army of occupation moved toward the state. With both civil and Confederate military authority in disarray, the situation deteriorated further after newly arrived Union General Gordon Granger read the Emancipation Proclamation to the former slaves on June 19, the day still celebrated by black Texans as "Juneteenth." Thousands of the black people abandoned the fields and houses of their former masters and wandered about the countryside, expecting to be fed and clothed by the Union army and hoping that growing rumors of a land distribution by Christmas of that year were true.

For Texans, whose homeland had escaped the ravages of warfare which the eastern states of the Confederacy had suffered, the nine years of Reconstruction were, except for the cessation of loss of men in battle, more terrible than the war years. For the majority of whites, whether slave holders or not, it was "The World Turned Upside Down," as the blacks became citizens. For the blacks, although freedom was welcomed and celebrated, the disruptions in the state's economy led to want and to strife with the owners of the land, while their entry into the political arena led to manipulation by the radical Republicans and intimidation by ruthless members of the white majority. In many ways Texas had not moved beyond the status of a frontier society and the natural violence of such a society was exacerbated by the breakdown of civil government and its replacement by a military force determined to reform the state's social, political, and economic institutions. The criminal element within the population and the large Indian population of the western frontier took advantage of the situation to rob, murder, and pillage.

Over the nine years from 1865 to 1874, the state went through a series of governors, generals, and forms of government as the federal government attempted to force the state to renounce its right to secede, to recognize the emancipation of the slaves as stated in the Thirteenth Amendment, and to grant political and civil rights to the former slaves as declared in the Fourteenth and Fifteenth Amendments to the federal constitution. Under the liberal reconstruction policies of President Andrew Johnson, Texas was allowed to hold a constitutional convention in 1866 to undo the legislation which had provided for secession from the Union and participation in the Confederacy and to recognize the emancipation of the slaves. A governor, J. W. Throckmorton, was elected to replace the provisional governor, A. J. Hamilton, who had been appointed by the military, and senators and representations were elected to Congress. Both the minority of white Texans who had remained loyal to the Union during the war and the radical Republican Congressmen in Washington were highly suspicious of the new state government. Their hostility grew as the legislature fashioned laws to force the newly freed blacks to enter into work contracts and refused to approve the Fourteenth Amendment. Congress denied seats to the senators and representatives who were elected under the newly constituted state government.

Early in 1867 Congress laid the groundwork for scuttling Johnson's plans and replacing them with a total revamping of the governments of the Southern states. The South was divided into military districts, of which Louisiana and Texas made up the Fifth District, headed by General Sheridan. Sheridan removed Throckmorton as governor, replacing him with E. M. Pease, a pre-war governor who had remained loyal to the Union. With the political foundations of state authority undermined and insufficient military forces to police the vast areas of Texas, lawlessness escalated. To this misery was added a yellow fever epidemic in the southern and southeastern areas of the state.

In June of 1868 a second constitutional convention was called and it labored until January of the next year to fashion a new government which would meet the requirements of the Congress. By the time the convention was called, the Union sympathizers among the white population had formed the Republican Party in Texas. The party worked through the Freedmen's Bureau, an agency set up to watch over the welfare of the former slaves, and the Union League, an organization to bring the blacks into the political system, to gain the support of the newly enfranchised blacks. The whites in the party were far from united in their goals and there was great rancor and distrust between the "radicals" and "conservatives." The majority of the whites in the state united in the Democratic Party. The constitutional convention led to many bitter confrontations and was used as a forum by the various factions, but its final accomplishments were fashioned by a coalition of the conservative Republicans and moderate Democrats. The secession ordinance, the debts incurred by the state during the war, and all acts of the wartime government counter to the Constitution and the laws of the federal government were renounced. The right of the blacks to political and civil rights was recognized, but the convention refused the radicals' demand for disfranchisement of the whites who had fought for the Confederacy or were the largest land and slave holders. Representatives from the radical faction went to Washington to request President Grant and the Congress to refuse to accept the work of the convention, but Grant leaned toward the voices of moderation and in 1870 the new state government went into operation. The radicals did not accept defeat and by rallying the black vote for their candidate, Edmund J. Davis, and gaining the co-operation of the Union military commander in manipulating voter registration, they succeeded in capturing the governorship. Another factor in Davis' success was the lack of participation of a large number of white voters, who feared that if the more moderate candidate won the Grant administration would not allow the reconstruction process to be completed. Davis was a Texan who had remained loyal to the Union during the war and served in its army.

The new governor managed by a series of maneuvers, including the arrest of several state legislators, to gain control of the legislature. He used his influence to push through laws which greatly enlarged his appointive powers and created a police force under his personal control. Some of his goals, such as a statewide public education system for both blacks and whites, the protection of blacks from exploitation and intimidation, the encouragement of railroad building, and the protection of the frontier from outlaw gangs and the Indians, were laudable for both the existing population and the many new settlers who came after the war. However, his harsh and arbitrary use of power and his disdain for the concerns of the white majority, at a time when moderation and the arts of persuasion were sorely needed, made him one of the most hated public figures in Texas history. His administration guaranteed Texas' adherence to the Democratic Party for many years to come. John Hardison's assessment of him may be read in his letter of October 17, 1870 to his brother-in-law, Edwin

Davis of Georgia. As the end of his four year term was approaching, both state and national forces conspired to defeat his re-election. The national leadership, as well as the white citizenry of Texas, was weary of the ongoing rancor of the reconstruction process and the Democrats were able to capture the state government in 1874. Davis tried to have the state courts set aside the election and he appealed to Grant for support, but his efforts failed. The white majority reclaimed the state and the blacks had to wait until the civil rights movement of the 1960s for their cause to once more become a matter of national concern.

Limestone County and the Hardisons During Reconstruction

The original destination of the 1857-1858 Texas migration of Seth and Mary Hardison and their sons and daughters, Thomas, John, Clark, William, Mary Ann, and Nancy, was Polk County, in the southeastern area of the state, but it was their home for only a few years. As noted in the discussion of their stay in Polk County, Seth's wife Mary and sons Thomas and Clark died within the first five years of their residence in Texas and all of the family except Seth moved to adjoining Liberty County early in the 1860s. Within a few years after their move, they began a new migration. Nancy (Hardison) Reeves and husband Dr. James Harvey Reeves were the first to move to Limestone County, in the early 1860s, and John and his family joined them in 1867, after a brief stay in Liberty County following his return after the war. John's sister Mary Ann, with whom he had left his daughters during his service in the Confederate Army, died soon after the war and her husband may be the John Gray who appeared in the Limestone County tax records in 1867. Seth had remained in Polk County during the war years and continued to make tax returns for the 270 acres of land and slaves, varying in number from eight to twelve, which were listed in son John's name, but he too moved to Limestone County after the war. Joining Seth were the third of the three wives he married in the 1860s after the death of Mary, his wife of many years, and the young daughter and son of the first and second of these wives. The last of the family to move was Seth's youngest son, Dr. William L. Hardison, who located in Freestone County,

XII. NEW BEGINNINGS IN TEXAS, 1865-1875

which adjoined Limestone, with his wife Josephine and two young sons. Ann Hardison, the widow of Thomas, the eldest son, was the only family member to remain in Liberty County, where she was listed with the Jackson and Walker children of her former marriages in the Federal Census of 1870. She had managed to retain 185 acres of land in Polk County and continued to pay taxes on it during the 1860s.[24] Seth's sister, Nancy (Hardison) Brigham, and her family lived in Blanco County, in the Hill Country of Texas near Austin, during the Reconstruction era, but the family correspondence makes no mention of contacts between the Hardisons and the Brighams.[25]

John and Mary's letters of 1866-1867 do not indicate why they moved from Liberty County, but possible reasons were the racial tensions which were particularly high in the counties of southeast Texas, which had a large black population, and a yellow fever epidemic which took many lives in that area in 1867. The deed records of this period for both Liberty and Limestone counties have been lost in courthouse fires, making it impossible to know exactly how and when John disposed of his land in Liberty or bought in Limestone. The tax records of Limestone provide information on the size and location of his property, a small farm of about 50 acres in the southeastern area of the county.

Limestone County was created in 1846, soon after Texas became a state.[26] It is located on the western edge of East Texas, about one hundred miles south of Dallas. At the time of its formation, it had only recently been a frontier area and in 1836 it was the scene of a Comanche Indian raid and massacre in which the nine year old daughter of one of the settlers was kidnapped. She was Cynthia Ann Parker, who grew up with the Comanches and was the mother of a son who became Chief Quanah Parker, the last great chief of the Comanches. The town of Springfield, on the banks of the Navasota River, was the county seat until 1873 when it was bypassed by the railroad and was replaced by the new town of Groesbeck. Mexia, in the northeastern portion of the county also became a major town because of its rail connections. The county has had a total of eight courthouses, including three which were lost to fire, two in 1873 and another in 1890. The current building is a handsome brick edifice built in 1924.

Stock raising and agriculture were the chief pursuits of the early settlers of the county, but the plantation system and slavery did not dominate the economy as much as in the southeastern counties. By the time the Hardisons arrived cotton was becoming the dominant crop. The population lived primarily on farms, but there were several small communities scattered over the county in the pre-railroad days. The Hardisons and Reeves were residents of two in the southeastern portion, Personville and Lost Prairie, which were only a few miles apart.

Personville, where John and his family lived, was founded in 1854 by B. D. Person, a native of North Carolina, who had come to Texas by way of Tennessee. A post office was established in 1855 and the settlement gradually grew into a village. According to a marker on the site, at the time Personville was razed by fire in 1916 it had a blacksmith shop, lumber yard, bank, hotel, twelve mercantile establishments, two drugstores, and three doctors. It was partially rebuilt after the fire but by that time its rail connections had been discontinued and it was gradually abandoned by most of its residents. The major portion of John and Mary's letters were written from Personville and they bring to life the personal and public concerns of its residents in the years following the Civil War.

A few miles to the west of Personville was the settlement known as Lost Prairie. The Reeves and the Hardisons were active in both, particularly in the Baptist church in the latter. There are several versions of the origin of the name Lost Prairie, including the one on the historical marker located at the site of its cemetery and church, which states that it was so-named by a pioneer who was lost in the woods and finally stumbled onto a prairie. Before they were cleared for agriculture, there were a number of such prairies in central Texas, which were great open expanses of tall grass frequented by buffalo and a variety of other animals. The appearance of the prairie as the first settlers found it is described in a history of the Lost Prairie Baptist Church: "At that time the natural scenery was most beautiful indeed. By the 20th of February the prairies and open woods presented the appearance of a vast wheat field, interspersed with the most beautiful flowers. Deer, mule-earred rabbits, turkeys, and prairie chickens were abundant."[27]

The Lost Prairie Church is the oldest in Limestone County, having been founded in 1853 as Lake Creek Church. It occupied several sites before the present building and cemetery were established on land now located on the south side of Highway 164, about ten miles east of Groesbeck. As noted previously, the Reeves and Seth Hardison were active in the Baptist denomination in Polk County and the Reeves in Liberty County. A quotation from Lost Prairie Church's history tells of the role played in that church's formative years in the mid-1850s by Seth's daughter Nancy and her husband Dr. Reeves, and incidentally gives useful family data:

> At this juncture, while the little church seemed to be sinking into the "slough of despond," a Baptist minister from Florida, Dr. James H. Reeves, came among us. He called the scattered members together, subsequently united with the church, and brought his family and settled among us. He served the church two years, during which time his labors were signally blessed. He, with the assistance of his wife, organized a Sabbath School, and ... did much toward building up the broken down walls of Zion. Early in the year 1859 he gave up his charge here and moved to Polk county. He afterward returned and united again with this church [1866]; then again took his letter, moved to Leon county, and joined the Concord church; since which time he joined the anti-Missionary Baptists and died a member of that body.[28]

This information indicates that the Reeves preceded the Hardisons in migrating from Florida to Texas and that they came first to Limestone County, before moving to Polk where Seth and the rest of the family settled in 1857-1858. Dr. Reeves had probably been drawn to Limestone because of the presence of other members of the Reeves family, William Jay Reeves, possibly his brother, and his wife, Mary Hawkins of Georgia. William (1825-1907) and Mary (1828-1917) and their family are buried in the Lost Prairie Cemetery in the same long east-west row in the center of the cemetery which is shared by Seth's youngest son James Harvey Hardison (1866-1943), and his family. Two adult size unmarked mounds between the Hardison and Reeves graves may be the graves of John Randolph Hardison and his father Seth. Since Dr. Reeves died in Leon County, he and possibly his wife Nancy are probably buried there.

Limestone County has suffered great losses of its early land records due to the courthouse fires of 1873 and 1890. In the absence of deed records for the years of the Hardison and Reeves residence, the tax returns provide information on the extent, location, and value of their property. John and Seth Hardison first appeared in the Limestone rolls in 1868. They declared no land but each entered one horse, Seth's valued at $75.00 and John's at $50.00, and the latter entered additional property valued at $10.00. By 1869 John had acquired the 50 acre farm on which he lived until he sold it in 1874. Its tax valuation varied from $150.00 in 1869 to $600.00 in 1873 and he stated in a letter of February 24, 1874 that he had sold it for $700.00. The farm was located in the southeastern portion of the county in the former M. R. Palacios land grant, one of several large Spanish grants of 1833 on the eastern side of what later became Limestone County. No land is listed for Seth and he disappeared from the tax rolls after his death in 1871. The only possessions declared by either John or Seth, other than their horses and John's land, were a few cattle and John's personal property, which never exceeded $100.00 in value. The Reeves family held land in the same area as the Hardisons.[29]

While John Hardison struggled to make a living with his small farm in Limestone County, he attempted to salvage some of the property in Polk County for which he had contracted when he first arrived in Texas. As noted previously, John had purchased 270 acres on the east side of the Trinity River in October, 1858 and had joined with his father and his brother-in-law, John Gray, in the purchase of an additional 496 acre tract in the same area in December, 1858. The jointly held land was sold back to its original owner, John Burgess, in March of 1861.[30] While John had joined the Grays and other members of the family in moving to Liberty County in 1861 or 1862 and later to Limestone County, he attempted to retain ownership of his 270 acre tract in Polk. His struggle continued until 1871 when he lost it through forced sale to pay creditors from whom he had borrowed in his effort to retain the land. The deed records of Polk County include references to two loans to John made in 1860, probably to enable him to meet the $1,250.00 notes due on the land in January of 1860 and 1861 or to meet other obligations incurred in his efforts to cultivate the land.[31] In 1866, soon after his return to Texas after the Civil War, John mortgaged the 270 acres to protect the men who had been his sureties in one of the loans of 1860.[32] The terms of the mortgage called for him to redeem the land by March of 1867 or face a sheriff's sale to compensate his creditors. Litigation followed his inability to pay his indebtedness and in September of 1871 the land, which had been divided into one 30 acre and six 40 acre lots, was sold at the courthouse door in Livingston, bringing a total of $504.00.[33] John's frustrations and disappointments over this loss are reflected in the remarks of his letters of the early 1870s on the financial reverses which he was suffering.

The Hardisons and the Reeves came into Limestone County during the forlorn and troubled times of Reconstruction. The county became the scene of great racial tension and violent acts on the part of both blacks and whites. The friction between the white population and the agents of the Freedmen's Bureau, as well as black troops in Union Army units and Governor Davis' special police force, led to animosity toward all blacks and to intimidation and murder. John and Mary Hardison moved to Limestone at about the time Charles E. Culver was appointed in June of 1867 as the county's agent for the Freedmen's Bureau. According to Limestone County historian Ray A. Walter, Culver's policies set the stage for ongoing strife between the races: "Dictatorial prowess being his ambition he issued orders prohibiting any person from carrying firearms and decreed that all firearms in the county must be deposited with him or some member of his 'gallant army.' Such orders antagonized the citizens and they refused to obey. People were treated harshly and even Union men agreed the white people were being punished too severely."[34] Culver was murdered in November, 1867 in a confrontation with a man who had refused to give up his rifle. The resulting tension was acute and continued in varying degrees of intensity throughout the remaining years of Reconstruction.

As Texas went through the various stages of return to self-rule and participation in the federal government, the black population began to exercise its newly gained right to vote and hold office and quite naturally supported Governor Davis and the Republicans. The members of the Democratic party, who were the majority of the white voters, bided their time until they could gain control of the state government and send Democratic representatives to Congress. Racial tensions in Limestone County escalated as the time approached for the election of Congressmen in October, 1871. In September the Democrats in the county distributed circulars urging every member of the party to register to vote, claiming that "The victory is within our grasp." Governor Davis stepped up the presence of his special police force in the county in preparation for the election. In late September a confrontation between four black members of the force and a white man in a saloon in Groesbeck led to the killing of the white man. Armed conflict between the predominantly black police force and the alarmed white citizens was narrowly averted by the efforts of Mayor Adolph Zadek to keep the peace. The black policeman who had fired the shots in the killing was arrested and the legal authorities in the county warned whites to avoid actions which could lead to Governor Davis' intervention.

In this tense atmosphere, the Congressional elections took place in early October. Davis was determined to win victories for the Republican candidates throughout the state and ordered his special police force and armed militiamen to surround the polling places. On election day there was considerable disorder in some of the counties, with the greatest in Limestone and Freestone counties. In spite of Davis' efforts the Democratic candidates were all successful. Fraud was charged in some of the contests, including that of the representative for the congressional district of which Limestone County was a part. Davis' attempts to set aside the election of the Democrat, D. C. Giddings, were defeated, but he struck a retaliatory blow against two of the counties in the district. On October 9, he placed Limestone and Freestone counties under martial law, assessed a penalty of $50,000.00 against the citizens of Limestone, and quartered troops to enforce order. The legislature was not in sympathy with Davis' actions and on November 6 passed a resolution disapproving his orders as excessive and unnecessary. Davis revoked his proclamation ten days later. In 1873 the legislature indemnified the citizens of Limestone County who had been fined, among them John Hardison whose fine had been $7.90.[35]

The bitterness which resulted from Limestone County's experiences led to deep hatred for Governor Davis and the Republican Party and to years of fear and distrust in relations between the races.

Intimidation and murder were used by some of the whites to keep the blacks from realizing their newly won political and civil rights. Ray A. Walter, in his previously cited history of the county, has stated concerning the early 1870s: "No estimated damage has ever been made of the atrocious acts committed during these troublesome times, but it is safe to surmise that literally hundreds of Negroes were murdered. Various groups attempted to destroy records and, evidently, did a good job; few records have been located prior to 1874."[36]

Amidst these traumatic events the Hardisons attempted to salvage whatever they could of their past lives and to create a present and a future which held promise of a measure of security and prosperity for their families. The letters which are presented in the following chapters describe in the words of John and Mary Hardison the joys and sorrows and the hopes and disappointments which they experienced.

NOTES

1. Washington County, Georgia, Marriage Book C, p.132, the license was issued on Jan. 16 and the wedding took place on Jan. 23.
2. Washington County Deed Book O, p.752; original spelling was Bay Spring and later Bay Springs.
3. Ruby Robison Penton and Joel R. Penton, *Samuel Robison of Washington County, Georgia* (Savannah: Tad Evans, 1994), p. 476 (data on Metcalf and his wife based on research of Walter Robison Cox); Philip A. Fisher, *The Fisher Genealogy* (Everett: Massachusetts Publishing Company, 1898), this and other works in the library of the New England Historic Genealogical Society, Boston, provide information on the Fisher and Metcalf families; death notice of Metcalf in *Central Georgian*, Sandersville, Georgia, February 1, 1860, stated that he died in the last week of January in the eighty-second year of his life. See footnote #5.
4. Fourth Federal Census, 1820, Georgia, Washington County, p.143.
5. Seventh Federal Census, 1850, Georgia, Washington County, p.221, the listing for Metcalf and wife Elizabeth gives his birthplace as Massachusetts. and hers as South Carolina and the age of both as 67.
6. 1828 Tax Digest of Washington County, Georgia, Georgia Department of Archives and History (copy in collection of Washington County Historical Society, Sandersville).
7. *Central Georgian*, February 1, 1860 (Metcalf's death notice) and May 9, 1860 (Metcalf mentioned in death notice of daughter Elizabeth Robison who died on April 22).
8. *Bay Springs United Methodist Church, History, 1852-1955* (unpublished mss. based on material gathered by Catherine Everett Thurston and other members of the church, n.d.).
9. *Sandersville Herald*, Sandersville, Georgia, April 6,1893, memorial to James Foster Northington gives his birth and death dates as Nov. 11, 1809 and Jan 31, 1893.
10. Fifth Federal Census, 1830, Georgia, Washington County, p.239 (Jesse) and p.241

(William N.); Seventh Federal Census, 1850, Georgia, Washington County, p.209 (Jesse, age 63, shoemaker) and p.210 (Jesse A., age 27, wheelwright; in the 1860 census, p.181, he is listed as a merchant); Second Federal Census, 1800, North Carolina, Cumberland County, includes a listing for Jesse Northington.

11. Eighth Federal Census, 1860, Georgia, Washington County, p.193 (family of James F. Northington); Elizabeth Shreve Ryan Collection (gift from Nancy Louise Brown Slaughter), clipping without date or source, gives data on Amelia (d. in 1887) in her obituary.
12. Washington County Estate Papers and Wills, Book B, pp.135-37.
13. *Central Georgian*, Dec. 7, 1859.
14. Washington County Deed Book F, pp.603-04
15. Washington County, Court of Ordinary Records, Feb. 1860 (record of probate); Appraisements, Book A (inventory, Feb. 10, 1860); Division of Estates, Book A, Feb. 1861 (record of division of slaves). The value assigned to the slaves differs between the inventory ($9,850) and the record of division ($11,450).
16. Penton, *op. cit.*, p.483.
17. John Linley, *Architecture of Middle Georgia, the Oconee Area* (Athens: University of Georgia Press, 1972), p.22.
18. Penton, *op. cit.*, p.485.
19. Seventh Federal Census, 1850, Georgia, Washington County, p.220; Eighth Federal Census, 1860, Georgia, Washington County, p.193; Eighth Federal Census, 1860, Georgia, Washington County, Slave Population, p.21.
20. Penton, *op. cit.*, pp.484-86.
21. The year of John Fisher's death is based on the date of the inventory of his possessions, April 23, 1866, Washington County Appraisements, Book B, pp.102-03.
22. Nancy Louise Brown Slaughter Collection, letter of Feb. 15, 1866 from Mary (Northington) Hardison to her parents.
23. William Ramsdell, *Reconstruction in Texas* (Austin: University of Texas Press, 1970, paperback edition in the series Texas History Paperbacks; originally published by Columbia University Press, 1910). This study has been used for coverage of the major events in Texas' Reconstruction history.
24. The Ninth Federal Census, 1870, Texas, Limestone County, includes listings for the households of James H. Reeves, John Hardison, and Seth Hardison as follows:
    p.206, James H. Reeves, physician, age 58
     Nancy H., age 40
     Sallie C., age 13
     John W., age 5
     James, age 7
     a male whose name is illegible, age 12
     Carrie E. Person, age 19 (the Reeves' married daughter)
     Lewis R. Person, age 27 (husband of Carrie)
     Lewis L. Person, age 1 (Carrie's son)
    p.206, John R. Hardison, attorney, age 35
     Mary F., age 30
     Emilie [Amelia], age 1
     Lilly, age 11
     Winnie C., age 8
    p.244, Seth Hardison, laborer, age 68
     Mary A., age 30

Sallie, age 6 [usually called Lula]
James, age 5
Caroline Dowden, age 11 (daughter of Mary A.)
Eliza Dowden, age 9 (daughter of Mary A.)
John Gray, listed on p.195, Limestone County, may be the husband of Mary Ann (Hardison) Gray.
Ann Hardison, widow of Thomas Hardison, is listed on p.8 in Ninth Federal Census, 1870, Texas, Liberty County.
William L. Hardison was not found in either the listings for Liberty or Freestone counties. His purchase of 100 acres of land in Freestone County on Jan. 8, 1873 is recorded in Freestone County Deed Book L, p.639.

25. John Stribling Moursund, *Blanco County Families for One Hundred Years* (Burnet, Texas: Nortex Press, 1981), pp.25-26; Blanco County News, *Heritage of Blanco County*, Texas (Dallas: Curtis Media Corp., 1987), pp.372-73. Both sources contain data on the Brigham family's roots and their years in Texas through the twentieth century.
26. Ray A. Walter, *A History of Limestone County* (Austin: Von Boeckmann-Jones, 1959), chaps.4 and 5 cover the history of the county from 1846 through 1875.
27. T. H. Beavers and Cliff Sims, compilers, *Lost Prairie Baptist Church* (compiled in 1959 from church records, including an account of the church's history from its founding to 1886). I am indebted to Mrs. Illa May McCoslin of Limestone County for the use of her copy of the history.
28. *Ibid.*, p.9 (note this portion of the history deals with the period up to 1886, indicating that Dr. Reeves had died by that year).
29. Limestone County Tax Records, 1866-1875 (microfilm in Texas Collection of Houston Public Library). The previously cited tax records for Polk and Liberty counties are also found in this collection.
30. Polk County Deed Book G, pp.473-74, 485-86; Polk County Deed Book I, pp.195-96.
31. Polk County Deed Book H, pp.463-64 (slave Henry or Harry used as security for debt of $567.65); Deed Book K, pp.226-28 (reference to loan of $610.50 in mortgage of 1866).
32. Polk County Deed Book K, pp.226-28.
33. Polk County Deed Book N, pp.234-36, 566-71.
34. Walter, *op. cit.*, p.54.
35. References to events connected with the declaration of martial law in Limestone County are found in Ramsdell, *op. cit.*, pp.310-11; Walter, *op. cit.*, pp.53-62; and H. P. N. Gammel, *The Laws of Texas*, 1822-1897 (Austin: Gammel Book Co., 1898), vol.VII, chap.CCXXXIII, pp.1351-61 (J. R. Hardison and W. J. and J. W. Reeves on p.1354).
36. Walter, *op. cit.*, p.62.

XIII

Family Life in Texas during Reconstruction Letters of John and Mary Hardison Part One, 1866-1870

$\mathcal{T}$he letters which are presented below were written primarily by John and Mary Hardison to their relatives in Washington County, Georgia during the years of their residence in Liberty and Limestone counties. There are a few written to them by family members in Georgia and by John to his daughter Lilly, when she was boarding with the family of her uncle, Dr. William L. Hardison, in Freestone County, while attending a school in adjoining Navarro County. Obviously the letters were cherished by their recipients and they have survived for more than a hundred years because of the value placed on them by descendants. They have been preserved by members of the Cain family, descendants of John and his first wife, Winnifred Cornelia Davis, and by Nancy Louise Brown Slaughter, the daughter of John and Mary's youngest daughter, Annie (Hardison) Brown.

The letters present a poignant account of the daily lives of an Old South family struggling to survive in the hard times of the post-war South. John's dreams of establishing a plantation on the boundless acres of Texas were replaced by the reality of a small farm worked by his own labor. Since coming to Texas, his family circle had been re-

Personville Tenn April 4th 1868

Miss Indiana Northington;

My Dear Sister;

I was the happy recipient of an interesting letter from you a few days ago; and I assure you it met with a every reception indeed. You said something in regard to my not writing to you in sometime; well dear sister you ought not to wait for me to answer every letter. You have but two to write to, and I have a great many. It is a great satisfaction to write to you all, and equally as much so to receive a kind letter from any of you. So please write oftener in future.

Well dear sister Sweet Spring has come at last robed in all her former beauty and loveliness. Yes every thing looks superbly lovely & happy, while I am writing the little songsters are carroling their cheerful little songs in all the trees, just now a dear little mocking bird lit on my house and cheered me with quite a multitude of sweet notes. Well I know you want to hear about my little affairs. I have not much to write now that will interest you. As yet I have not seen much in

Letter of Mary Northington Hardison to Her Sister,
Indiana Northington, April 4, 1868
Slaughter Collection

duced by the death of his older sister, two of his brothers, and his mother. His father, now with two young children from his late marriages, was an old man, listed as a "laborer" in the 1870 Federal Census. But John was an optimistic, buoyant man and, with a new help-mate, he returned to Texas after his Confederate service and directed his energies and considerable abilities to providing for his family. He and Mary lived briefly in his former home in Liberty County, where he conducted a school and in November, 1866 renewed his credentials as an attorney, signing an oath of loyalty to the newly reconstituted Texas state government. After moving to Limestone County in 1867, he pursued a legal career for several years, representing himself on his business card as a "General Land and Claim Agent," practicing in the counties composing the Thirteenth Judicial District. Along with his law practice, he carried on a merchandising business and farmed, but his great love was the land and he increasingly devoted his energies to farming in the 1870s.

Mary's life revolved around her domestic concerns and growing family. She wrote frequently of sewing, which was both a necessity and a pleasure. She was devoted to the family she had left behind in Georgia and was often homesick. The letters indicate that the visit she and John made in the winter of 1868-1869 was the only one she made during her Texas years. Mary's health was delicate and, with frequent child-bearing and hard work, she was often ill. Short lifespans and untimely deaths, particularly among child-bearing women and the very young, made the worries which she frequently expressed real sources of anxiety and grief. She was deeply religious and her faith sustained her through the crises of her life.

Nothing is known of the house in which the family lived, other than Mary's remark in her letter of November 17, 1869 that her dining room was sixteen feet square and that she had her cooking stove in that room. This description referred to the house into which she and John moved earlier in that year, shortly before the birth of their daughter Amelia on April 12. Probably it was a very simple wood frame structure and whatever remained of it after the Hardisons' residence disappeared in the fire which destroyed Personville in 1916.

The letters are both articulate and lively and reflect the education of the authors, which was far beyond the average of their day. However the grammar and spelling are far short of perfection and these imperfections, as well as the random capitalizations, have been left intact so that the reader may see the letters in as near the original form as possible. If words or letters have been needed to make the text more intelligible, the additions have been made in brackets. Punctuation and paragraphing were often random or non-existent, particularly in John's letters, which were frequently written at night when he was weary from farming. Slight alterations in these details have been made to render the letters more readable. An "s" or a "c" at the end of the heading for each letter indicates whether it came from the Slaughter or the Cain collection.

The identities of the persons who are mentioned in Mary and John's letters, other than their children, are as follows:

Mary:
- Mother _____ Amelia (Fisher) Northington—"Milly"
- Father _____ James Foster Northington
- Sisters _____ Harriet Missouri —"Hattie" or Missouri, married to Thomas Mims
  - Martha Elizabeth—"Lizzie," married to Haynes Renfroe
  - Indiana
  - (A sister named Annie is referred to in a few letters, but her identity has not been established; possibly this was another name for Indiana)
- Brothers _____ James Fisher—"Jimmie"
  - Marcellus Addison
  - William Capers
- Husband _____ referred to as "Love" or "the Captain"

Friends and neighbors in Limestone County, particularly "Grandma" Bird (also spelled Byrd), Dr. Glass, the Rambos, and the Mortons; relatives, friends, and Methodist clergy in Georgia.

John:
- Brother _____ Dr. William L.
- Sister _____ Nancy (Hardison) Reeves
- Brother-in-law ___ Dr. James Harvey Reeves
- Half-brother _____ James Harvey—"Jimmie," son of John's father

	Seth, who lived with John and Mary after Seth died in 1871
Sister-in-law	Mary Elizabeth (Davis) Hardwick—"Liz," sister of John's first wife
Brother-in-law	Edwin T. Davis, brother of John's first wife
Wife	referred to as Mary or Fletcher

Friends in Limestone County; friends and relatives in Georgia, including the families of his aunt and uncle, Winnifred and Joel Davis, and sister-in-law Sallie (Sarah Ann Davis) and her husband John West Sheffield, and deceased members of his family—mother, father, brothers Thomas and Clark, and sister Mary Ann, particularly in his letter of June 1, 1873.

The Hardison children were Lilly Mary (b.1859), Winnifred Cornelia (b.1862), John Randolph (b. and d.1867), Amelia Randolph (b.1869), Nancy Missouri (b.1871), and Annie Glass—later changed to Annie Mary (b.1873).

John Randolph Hardison to Mary's Parents, Amelia (Fisher) and James F. Northington, and Her Sister and Brother-in-law, Lizzie (Northington) and Haynes Renfroe s

Galveston Texas
Wednesday Feby 7 1866

Dear Father and Mother—

Without feeling at all like writing, we will tell you today that we are at last on Texas soil. We arrived at Galveston on yesterday morning, after a boisterous voyage at Sea of several days duration. We sailed from New Orleans on board Steam Ship "Texas" Thursday, Feby 1st at 8½ P.M. and made the Port of Galveston in 56 hours, but owing to a rough sea and low water on the Bar we could not come inside our anchorage and had to remain for more than 60 hours outside with a heavy wind and severe rain most of the time. This was indeed a sore trial as we were tossed on the surging billows without cessation. Most of the Passengers were very sick and seemed to have suffered intensely but Mary and myself escaped wonderfully. Were scarcely sick at all. I felt that we were very fortunate in being so slightly sick while on the Gulf and I am gratified to tell you that Mary stood the fatigue of travel much better than I could have hoped for. She is looking quite well today but is at desperate outs with Steam Boats & Steam Ships and with going to Sea, and says she doesn't think she can start on a return trip to Georgia until the Rail Road is complete from Liberty Texas to New Orleans. We go to Houston this Afternoon Per Steamer "Rob Roy," will reach that city by 12 M. tomorrow & Friday will go out to Liberty per Rail Road & will reach our journey's end by Saturday 6 P.M. if not before.

I have no general news of importance to tell you of. Parties from interior of our State inform me that preparations for farming are active, and Merchants and other business men here tell me of a great falling off in trade, this nothing more than I had predicted. In fact it is only "The beginning of the end," for the cotton—"The great ruler of Commerce" is now nearly done coming from the interior and hence forward business in its every feature must be greatly circumscribed. We truly hope that this may find you all quite well and as happy as circumstances will permit you to be. Be assured that all is well with us, and in conclusion please accept further evidences of our grateful remembrance and lasting affection.

Your distant Children
John & Mary

Galveston Feby 7th 1866

Dear Haynes & Lizzie

As we have all our letters to send to you to be forwarded to their destination I will not slight you this time as I did before when I wrote from Sister Hattie's, though I have written all I have to write to Father & Mother on the other pages which you are at liberty to read. You can well imagine our gratitude to a kind Providence for saving us from being sick at sea which nearly every other Passenger on board our vessel was very ill most of the time. Mary has held up under every thing remarkably well and is as cheerful to day as I could expect her to be. We have nothing to dread now in performing the remainder of our journey & will reach home by Saturday if not before. We have been detained as I stated to Father & Mother much longer than there was any use of—you must really pardon this very poor affair of a letter, for my head is so dizzy from being tossed at Sea that it is with difficulty I can write at all. Do write us soon.

Your regarding Bro & obliged friend
J. R. Hardison

XIII. FAMILY LIFE IN TEXAS DURING RECONSTRUCTION

Mary Fletcher (Northington) Hardison to Her Parents s

Liberty Texas Feb 15th 1866

My Dear Father and Mother

I will attempt for the first time since my departure from you to pen you a letter. I arrived at my new home safely after many days wearisome travel—yes we reached home on the night of the 10th inst—about 10 o'clock, and I can assure you I felt gratified when I came to realize that my journey was completed, but I think that I performed it remarkably well, I was a little sick when we crossed the gulf. I did not suffer any inconvenience from cold as I anticipated I should. Well I cannot yet give my opinion of Texas as I have not had sufficient time and opportunity for seeing the country & [page torn and stained] pronounce judgement. I have seen [page torn and stained] very much from our brief acquaintance, he has the apperance of a perfect gentleman [probably refers to John's brother William L. Hardison], I have not seen his wife yet. Well Pa & Ma you must write to me often, for I shall be always anxious to hear from you all, and you may be assured your dear letters will be very interesting to me and most tenderly appreciated. I will conclude for to night, Adieu.

March 16th 1866

Well Dear Parents:

When I began my communication I did not think it would be so long before I would close it, but I saw no chance to have it mailed consequently I did not feel like writing and leting it lie over here. I am yet without any inteligince from you, Oh! I would be so happy to hear from you all. I am very well contented with my new home, get a long pretty well house keeping. I know Ma you would like to know something of my Domestic affairs—well I have some very nice Poultry—Chickens Ducks & Geese, and I am going to have some Guineas & Turkeys, then I will have a pretty variety of fowls. We are going to have a very good garden, we sowed it the 14th of Feb, and now our Peas are running nicely & we have Cabbage and Beet plants large enough to set out, also green Salad to use on the table [page torn] grew in 32 days, we have Beans & Cucumbers up and a variety of other vegetables. I have not done much work since I came, part of the time I have had a very sore finger, I had a rising on the end of my middle finger on my right hand, it was caused from getting a little pine splinter under the nail. Well Ma I am sorry I forgot to make your collar, but I have crotched you one out of number 36 spool thread. I hope it will fit you nicely, I did not make it because you needed it, but because I had nothing else to do and felt like I had rather be doing something for you than not, I hope you will accept it. Well Ma who wove your Jeans for you? how do you get along making cloth?

How is your garden? Have you succeeded in keeping your cook? Tell me the news when you write, Ma you use to say you never intended writing to any of us when we married and left you, but now dear Mother you must be sure to write to me, if you dont wish the Capt. to see your letters I promise you not to show them, but you need not be afraid of him for he is not a misschieveous fellow, he as well as myself would delight to hear from you. Well the Capt & I joined the M.E. church last Sabbath, he on probation I by letter. The Capt was not a member of any church previously. I was much gratified to see him join. I am happy to inform you I am blessed with a pious husband, yes dear Parents he is a good christian, he opens & closes his school with prayer, and also has family prayers regular, he is all that a true and devoted wife could ask for. The Capt is as kind and affectionate to me as it is possible for a husband to be to a wife I think. I have nothing to fear as regards his treatment to-wards me.

Well Pa how are you getting on with your farming works? Did your negroes remain with you? Tell me Pa what kind of a trip you had going from Milledgeville, you were afraid you could not cross the creek.

I never will forget how you looked standing on that old red hill after we left you. My dear Parents I can assure you it was a severe trial to me to part with you, I know children never were blessed with better Parents than we had, and it is always with pleasure I think of you both. And you must remember my Darling husband & I in your pure prayers. Ma I have a very good cook, she is one of the best disposed negroes I ever saw, has one little boy, she seems to think a good deal of me. Well Dr. Hardison's wife has been to visit me four times. She came three times before I returned her calls. Then the Capt & I walk over to see her, and then she soon returned our call. She manifests all the friendship possible, she has tried to do me a good many favors but I have always respectfully declined. I will treat her with respect, but I can never forget how she treated my Darling. The Doctor is a perfect gentleman & treats me like a sister.

Well I must close for this time, for Bro Kemp (that is our circuit preacher) is waiting to take my letters to Liberty to be mailed, this is the first opportunity we have had directly to send any letters. My Dear Parents please write us soon & write often, you don't know how anxious we are to hear from you all. Write soon.

I am as ever your affectionate
Daughter M.F. Hardison

Is Brother Laury your preacher? If so give our kindest Regards to him, also to Dr. Palmer & his wife.

Mary Fletcher (Northington) Hardison to Her Mothers

"At Home" Liberty Texas
July 23rd 1866

My Dear Mother:

I will try and pen you a letter this evening, as the Pen is the only medium through which we can possibly obtain any intelligence from each other. And Oh! what sweet happiness it is to me to receive a precious letter from my darling Relatives far far away—yes it affords me a pure felicity, such as neither tongues can express or [page torn] My dear Mother I prize that brief but kind & affectionate letter of yours that I was the happy recipient of some weeks ago as dearly as it is possible for a devoted child to do. And I hope you will in future write to us more frequent, for in so doing you will my heart fill with pure joy inexpressable. Well Ma why don't Pa write to us? I think surely he has written and we have failed to receive them, but I shall continue to look for some from his interesting pen for I know when they do arrive that it will pay well to read them. We are all quite well and getting along very well, and kind Heaven grant that this may find you all in the enjoyment of perfect health and good spirits and happy. Dear Ma I spend much time in thinking of you all, Oh! how exquisitely happy I would be to see you all now and injoy your sweet & pleasant society. But I sweetly contemplate meetting you all at some future day, Ma wont that be a glorious meetting, I can anticipate all how sweet it will be and weep like a little child—yes dear Ma I hardly think of you and My dear Father without shedding tears, I love you both with the purest and fondest devotion, I know that childrin were never blest with better parents than we were. May Heaven's richest blessing ever rest upon you is my humble prayer always.

When have you heard from Uncle Jimmie Woods family? I wished very much to call and see them as we passed through Notasulga [Alabama] but we did not have time consequently my wish could not be gratified. Ma do you ever hear from Uncle Windfield's family? if so [how] are they getting along since his death. How does Aunt Mary Fisher and her family get along in particular Sallie, has Dewberry ever been heard of since his departure. Well I will dessist from my interogation for a while. I have but little to write to interest you for times here are dull, our school is still progressing. There has been a good deal of sickness in our community but I have been blest with pretty good health, for which I trust I am truly gratful. I have been visiting but little from various causes. I have some very pleasant neighbors which I love very much, two familys I must tell you about—Major More's family and Mr Murphy's family.

Well Sister More (for that is the way we call each other) is one of the best women I think I ever saw, she is a very pious lady and a good neighbor. She visits me frequently, has spent several days with me. She was very kind to me during my sickness last spring, would advise me as tenderly as a sister. I love her very dearly and I have every assureance that my love is fully reciprocated. She always asks me about my Father's family when we are together in particular you, she told me the next time I wrote to you to present her love to you.

Well about Mr Murphy, he is a Mr "Josh Middleton" but a most excellent kind hearted man, he has been very kind and obliging to us ever since our arrival, he is one of the best Patrons the Capt has, he will pay him at the close of his school $110.00 in gold, besides paying me for his two daughters taking lessons in em[broidery?].

[Remainder of letter missing.]

James F. Northington to Mary Fletcher (Northington) Hardison s

Oconee November 25th 1866

Dear Fletcher

I have concluded this evening to write you a few lines. I reckon you remember what a great cross it is for me to write a letter. Hard work makes my fingers that stiff that I can hardly hold a pen therefore you must accept bad writing but I will try and write so that you can read what I write.

Thank the good Lord that this leaves me in very good health. The ballance of the family is all well at present. I have worked very hard this year and in the main enjoyed very good health. I have ploughed more this year than I have in any year in eight or ten years past, and have stood it about as well as any body. Do not know how long I shall be able to continue. I am now in my 58th year. Of course I cannot hold out many more years, but my desire is when I fail to labour that the good Lord may take me to himself.

Your Mother stands it very well too. She complains of pains in her arms and shoulder frequently. But her general health is good. She is in her 53rd year so you see we are getting old. Your mother left home this evening for Sandersville to see Lizzy. Haynes sent for her to go up. Sent us word that Lizzy had a Daughter this morning and was doing very well. Dr. Smith was with her. I was truly glad [to] hear it was over with. I hope she will soon be up. Your [?] will stay with her this week. Missouri wrote her she would come down and stay some days with her.

So you see I have two grand children. Bobby has been with us more or less for the last 2 months. Every time he goes home he gets sick. He left with his grand ma this evening in pretty good health. I expect she will bring him back with her. He is very fond of us and the children. He is a very smart and interesting little fellow and promises to be a noble boy if he is rightly brought up which I hope he will receive from his parents. They have taken a good [deal] of pains with him so far.

Well Fletcher, I will now say something about the boys. Jimmy went to school this year. I think he has improved very much. Any way he is [a] clever boy, and we think he intends to pursue the right way. He says he wants to stay home next year till crops is laid by and help me with the crop. Marcillus went the last term until he was taken sick. He lost 4 or 5 weeks the latter part of the term. He improved very fast while he continued at school and was very intent on learning till was taken sick. Capers went the last term but he was not as studius as the other boys. I think he will do better here after. He [is] young and full of life and don't take the interest the other boys did. Indianna is well and as industrious as ever always busy.

Well about my crop. I have no reason to complain. I did not plant very heavy had but little help. Made good corn cotton and potatoes. My wheat crop was very short—hardly half crop. I commenced sowing last week. Aim to sow pretty largely the present year of wheat and rye. Well about Uncle Norris he is one of the best old negroes in the world honest hard working faithfull old man. Have not been an ill word spoken during year between him and one of the family. He is well satisfied with his years work and is to stay with me another year.

There has been a great deal of sickness through this country this year though not very fatal. Some have died. Moses Joiner lost his child by his last wife, it died of fever. Old Mr. Grayham fell off the bridge and kill himself [page torn] Our old nighbough Mrs. Landingham [page torn] ago. Her husband told me she died in peace [page torn] was prepared for a better world. She was truly [page torn] woman. She has left but one child behind, her oldest daughter Frances. So the world or people go as time [rolls?] on.

You ask about Harris. He is still merchandising at Bay Spring. I reckon doing pretty well. Hugh Lawson has a store at No. 14 [Oconee]. You ask if cars run to 14 yet. They have been running through ever since last June. We have regular Mail [page torn] When you write to us direct your [page torn] Oconee Ga. I will send you two [page torn] in a few days. Perhaps you would [page torn] and see the news of the county. Col. Henry D. Capers of the old twentyth Georgia battalon is now the Editor. The office is owned by him and J.N. Gilmer. He is the son of the venerable Bishop William Capers. I have not seen [him] yet but un[der]stand he is a pius man. I learned that he conducted meeting last Sunday in Sandersville for Bro Anthony and reproved some of the boys sharply for their misbihavour. I hope he will be a benefit to Sandersville for it needs help surely.

I carried your school account to Sandersville but Major Brooking was gone to Burke County. I left it with Mr. [?], he said it was all right, that the ordinary would give a certificate bearing 7 per cent interest and would pay as soon as the county was able. I will attend to it for you. Your account for 1864 [page torn] in confederate and Sherman destroyed all [page torn] When I see Brooking I will ask him about it [page torn]

I am truly glad to hear you speak of your pleasant situation and the kindness of your companion, it gives me great satisfaction to hear of my children being content and happy. I pray that the good lord may bless and protect you and your kind husband through life and bring you at last to his heavenly kingdom where I hope to meet all my dear children. They are all in the church now except Capers. Marcillus [page torn] church two months ago. My desire has [page torn] to raise my children right though I doubtless [page torn] many a time in doing all that I should [page torn] but I trust the good Lord will pardon my failing.

Fletcher I want you to pray for me in my declining years that I may be more devoted to the service of the lord. I try to remember you in all my prayers, and if I should never see you again in this world I shall not have any fears about your christian life. I hold you as dear as any father can hold his child. You have been a dutiful child to me. I am sorry that I was not able to do more for you than I have done but I hope to see you and the Capt at my house some time yet. I think you might find a place some where in this country that would suit you as well perhaps as Texas and be near to us where we could enjoy one anothers society. I should like that my children were near enough to me that I could visit them and they me often. Life is but short abest and it is our privilege to

[Remainder of letter missing.]

John Randolph Hardison to Mary's Parents s

Direct to
Person Ville Lime stone Co Texas

At Home Person Ville Tex
Wednesday Noon, July 10th [18]67

= Good News =

Dear Father & Mother

I write you to day to relieve your anxiety and solicitude with regard to the welfare of your daughter Mary and am happy to inform you and all the family that She has gotten safely through all her dreaded troubles and is now the happy Mother of a fine little boy—she was taken in labor at 10 o clock on yesterday morning just after a fit of vomiting which attacked her just at day light, and she was delivered this morning at about half past 9 oclock. The child is very large and as you see the labor was very tedious and very severe towards the last. Mary was so timid and doubting that she seemed involuntarily to resist the pain until the last hour, which caused much excitement and rigidity of the organs and made it essential for her Physician to use considerable mechanical force, and this caused of necessity material bruise and swelling of the child's forehead, but they both are now entirely easy and as far as human eyes can see are doing altogether well—and I recon we are as happy and grateful to a Merciful Providense as we can well be, and we are assured that you all will rejoice with us when you learn of the happy event.

Mary has dreaded this trial for many long months and has never been hopeful as to her recovery from it, and now that it is all over and she and her babe doing well you can perhaps imagine how much I am relieved. Dr Reeves and Sis Nan were with us all the time and placed us under renewed obligations by their efficient aid and heartfelt sympathy. Mary calls her Boy "John Randolph." I proposed "James" in the place of "John" and then left her to decide, and she concluded to give it my name in full. You all may be well assured that she will lack nothing in the way of medical attention, kindness and good nursing—and with the continuance of God's favor I hope soon to be privileged to inform you of her final recovery and restoration to perfect health and strength.

The best news of a general character I have to tell you is that the labor of the honest farmers in our country has been blessed with abundant crops, I never saw better corn crops in any country. The corn is now made and beginning to ripen. We shall have plenty and much to spare. Farmers are offering to engage now at 40c to be delivered at gathering time but it is supposed that there will be plenty at 30c after the crop is housed. The cotton crops are also fine and well advanced. Our Potatoes are also excellent. The wheat crop is shorter than usual—but a great deal more than will be necessary for home consumption, a great deal of flour is now seeking a market further south. So with these assurances for bread and hundreds of thousands of porkers and the finest beeves you ever saw for meat we can invite with safety any sufferers in the Old States to seek homes among us. To all who want good homes and lands at fair prices in a plentiful Country we say Come! Come!! Come!!! This thus far has been a wet season with us in Texas and in many districts the crops have been seriously injured by the rains. The water courses have been very high & many of the Bottom farms have been destroyed by the overflows. The Trinity River has been several feet higher than ever known before hence all the crops in its bottom are ruined. The freedmen in our State have not done very well as a general thing. Most of them take too much holiday and will not work in wet weather and the consequence is the crops are general poor where their labor has been wholly relied upon. Where the farm work has been done chiefly by white men the case is far otherwise as in this section of the state where white labor prevails almost to the utter exclusion of freedmen and this is one grand reason why our crops are so good. There is a good deal of summer sickness here caused by the very wet season as is generally supposed. The sickness is however of a mild type and yields readily to proper treatment. Well we have had no letters from any of you in a long long time, and cannot divine the cause of your long silence. We have 2 packages of papers from Lizzie & Indiana since any letters. We have never heard whether you received the "Texas Almanac" I sent you in Feby and Mary is anxious to know if the Boys received their presents from her which she sent early last Spring.

We are anxious to hear from you all again, and when you write please tell us about Thomas and Missouri—where they live and how they are doing, for we hear nothing from them only through you.

Sunday July 14th 1867

Today Mary and Little Jimmie are doing as well almost as we could desire and fully as well as we could have expected. Mary is free from soreness pain or fever—Has a good apetite and a good flow of milk—Our Boy sleeps and grows just like a little pig and gets prettier every day so this is the best news I can tell you now.

Do write soon to your unworthy son
J R Hardison

Mary Fletcher (Northington) Hardison to Her Parents s

Personville Texas Jan 22nd 1868

My Dear Father: and,
My Dear Mother:

It is with much pleasure I avail myself of this opportunity for the purpose of communicating to you a little, to let you know how we are progressing generally. Well Dear Parents I heartily wish you and my Loved Brothers & Sisters a "Happy New Year"—yes I fervently pray Heavens richest blessings upon you all. We are quite well and getting along finely, my own health is much better than it has been for months previous. We have a plenty to make us comfortable and contented. Love is doing a pretty good practice and then he is doing very well in his Mercantile business, there is but one draw-back to our happiness, and that is being so far from my dear family. Oh! if we could only be blessed with the sweet privilege of having you all to visit us often! But the stern hand of "Fate" has decreed otherwise, and we will try to be content for a while. I know Love can make more money here and make it faster than he could make there, but he is willing in a few years if we all live to move back to Georgia, so as to place me near my people. I write this because you would like to know our plans. It is Love's greatest wish to take me back to live near you, he knows what a sore trial it is to me & you to be seperated so far. I have allways indulged the fond Hope that sooner or later we would live near each other, and kind Heaven grant it, is my earnest petition.

Well I am now going to make quilts and comforts, I will first make the "Kentucky Star" then finish next a quilt I began last year called "The Rose & Vine" they are both very pretty. "The Rose & Vine" is for my Love, it is a sweet beauty indeed. We have not begun to garden yet, for the weather is too cold, we had the largest snow here Dec 30th & 31st that has ever been seen here by the oldest settlers of the place, it measured 2 feet, since then the weather has been [?] and cold. I think we will begin to plant about the 14th of Feb & that should be soon enough. Well Pa, I have a [?] lot of Hogs my Love bought for me some time ago. I have now a fine chance of young pigs, I feel very proud of my flock. Love bought me a little bunch of cows the other day, paid $2.50 apiece for the milch cows, good ones too. Don't you think that cheap?

Well Ma, a word about Poultry. I have the finest lot I ever saw. I have about 100 laying hens, 44 puddle Ducks, 9 Guineas, 4 Turkies, 1 Gobler, & other beautiful hins. My yard is full of fowls. My Ducks are all colours, and beautiful to behold, whenever I step out they will all flock around me and follow me all over the yard. Love buys a great many fowls, he will ship all we do not want to keep to Bryan City. I don't think I will keep more than 75 laying hens. Love went to Galveston in Dec. to purchase his stock. He bought me two Dresses, a nice lot of fine stockings, a fine cloak and shoes, and other little articles to tedious to mention. I was very lonely during his absence. Now he is obliged to be absent a good deal for he has quite a chance of collecting to do. I wish I could have Indiana to spend a year or two with us or one of the boys. Dont you and ma think you could spare us one. Love needs a cleark very much and would do a good part by one of the boys if he could get one of them to come. I think Marcellous would make a good lawyer with propper teaching, and Love will spare no pains if you let him come home with us when we visit you this coming fall, or let Brother Jimmie come and we will make a merchant of him. People have more Gold & Silver here than they have there, yes I have seen more since I have been here, than I seen in all my life before. I dont see why Bill Barksdale & Bartlett could not make a living. I think they must be in the fault not the country, for this is the best country to make money in I ever saw, and make it with so little labor too. A rich planter from Mississippi told me a few days ago, that he made more corn here last year in 20 acres of land, just him and his little boys and then went a hunting and fishing whenever they pleased, than he made on 50 acres of as good land as there was in most parts of Mississippi with all the labor of his servants. This is good country for farming; if people dont live well it is because they dont half try, for it requires but little labor here to make a fine support.

Dr. Reeves & family have moved to Leon County about 22 miles below here. I regreted very much to give up Sister Nan, but the Dr thought he could do a better practice there. We have some very good neighbors, I find true friends wherever I go. I have an intimate lady friend here, her name is Laura Persons. She is a widow lady about 32 years of age, is a very nice intelligent industrious good tempered lady. We esteem her very highly. Well my Love will start to Bryan City next Saturday morning, it is about 70 miles from this place. He is going to meet some of his goods there, that is the nearest point to any R. Road, he will be gone for 10 days. Oh! I will be so lonely during his absence, how I wish for one of my dear family to stay with me. I grive much about my sweet little Darling Babe. O! if he had lived he would of been so much comfort in my lonely hours, yes he would of been a source of true happiness and delight to me at all times, but he is a sweet little angel now and I know it is wrong to wish him back. Well Pa wont you answer this letter? Please do for you can't imagine what a true happiness it is for me to receive a letter from "Home." Now you must try to spare time enough, but it is not the time you regard, it is because you are out of practice. I know that is it. My Darling regards you with great love and esteem, and often has written to you, but has never received a letter from you. Now Pa please try and write to him. You must tell all about your farming plans for this year. Are you going to send the boys to School any? If you do not try and have them study at home. I feel a great interest in them. I want them to make noble high minded intelligent men, yes men that will be a bright ornament to society, good & great men. Ma, you must write and tell me about your domestic affairs. Have you Liza and her children yet? I have a good old cook, one of the best old negroes I ever saw, she is about 45, never gets mad, and thinks that there is no one like Miss Mary as she calls me. She goes ahead does all my work well. She is now fixing to make me a barrel of soap.

When did you hear from Missouri last? and how is she getting along now? I received a letter from her a week or two ago, but it was written the first of Nov., was a long time coming but I was truly glad to get it. I also received one from Lizzie and Brother Haynes. They were full of news. I never heard of so many marriages before at one time. I was much astonished at Aunt Mary Fishers & Sis Palmers marriages. How come Sis to marry Harris? Do tell me. Tell Sister Indiana not to marry untill she payes me a long visit. Don't let Jimmie think of marrying untill he is a settled man with a good education. I know Jimmie will say "Fletcher is crazy" but I know how it is very frequently. Well Dear Parents I have written a great deal, and trust it will interest you, now I must desist for a while. Tell Brothers and Indiana to write to us and now Pa and Ma please write to me and Love. Give our best and kindest love to all the family and acept the same yourselves. Please write. I will send buddie Cappers a little bow to wear on his sweet neck.

Ever your loving Daughter.
M.F. Hardison

Tell me who your preacher is for this year & please send out the list of appointments if it is not to inconvenient. You must tell us all the news when you write. Have you any School? Well enough at present.

Your, Mary

John Randolph Hardison to Mary Fletcher (Northington) Hardison s

At A M Perry's
Bryan Station
Jany 30th 1868

My Dear Love,

As I may have to be detained here yet a day or two, I will send you a note by Mr Rambo, to let you know that I am quite well and comfortably situated as to the weather, but I should feel much better these cold nights with you in a big warm bed than I do here. I am stopping with my friend Byrd of Cold Springs. We sleep together on a very good matress with plenty of Blankets, etc.

Did you ever see such cold weather, but this Morning it is quite pleasant to what it was yesterday. Owing to the severe Norther I do not look for Jay to night, & in case he dont come I will have to wait still another day or so but dont be uneasy about me for all is well here. Goods are low, Cotton & Hides improving. I sold a load for Jay on yesterday at $10\frac{1}{4}$ cents. The Tax to come out of course. I sold Chickens at $18\frac{3}{4}$ and 20c Egs 25c Hames 4[?]. I have engaged 1000 lbs Hides here to a friend and he advances me $40.00 on them so I will be scouring the Country for Hides when I return but dont mention this to any one, until I come. 10c & 15c is all I can pay for Chickens, Eggs $12\frac{1}{2}$ or maybe 15c. I will be at home by Monday night if possible, if not as soon thereafter as I can make the trip. You know I must try to get my goods forwarded from this point before I leave if there is any chance at all. I can see the Tax man after I go home at some other place. I truly hope that you keep well and cheerful, will bring all the articles you sent for.

Truly Your Devoted, Randolph

Mary Fletcher (Northington) Hardison to Indiana Northington s

Personville Texas April 4th 1868

Miss Indiana Northington:
My Dear Sister,

I was the happy recipient of an interesting letter from your pen a few days ago; and I assure you it met with a warm reception indeed. You said something in regard to my not writing to you in sometime, well dear sister you ought not to wait for me to answer every letter. You have but two to write to, and I have a great many, it is a great satisfaction to write to you all, and equally as much so to receive a kind letter from any of you. Do please write oftener in future.

Well dear sister "Sweet Spring" has come at last robed in all her former beauty and true loveliness. Yes every thing looks superbly lovely & happy, while I am writing the little songsters are carrolling their cheerful little songs in all the trees, just now a dear little mocking bird lit on my house and cheered me with quite a multitude of sweet notes. Well I know you want to hear about my little affairs. I have not much to write now that will interest you. As yet I have not done much in the poultry line, I have some hens sitting—but no young chickens. My Turkeys are laying, my Ducks and guineas are not laying yet. Love is gone down to Leon County to see his sister, I look for him at 2 o clock this evening, Love is kept going most all the time, he gets a great deal to do in way of practice. I am now ingaged in quilting. I got one out of the frames this week, and now have one in, they are plain quilts. I am piecing me some fine ones.

I was sorry to hear of Uncle Billie & his wifes missfortune, I think it sounds very badly. Where did she go to when she left him? Indiana what has become of Amelia Fisher that was? and where does she live? I was proud of Bobbie's sweet little hair, tell him Aunt Mary kissed it, and will keep it to remember him by, kiss him for me & Amelia too, I know they are good & lovely children. I want to see them so much. You all must have your Photographs taken and send them to me. I want them so much. I have a beautiful Photograph Album, Love got for me the last time he was at Bryan

City, it is a beautiful album, it will hold 50 Photographs. Now please send me some of the family. Tell Cousin Wink to send me his & his ladys. I would be happy to place them in my album. Tell me when you write again, who your preacher is this year.

Where does Sallie Dewberry live? and how does she get along now? Where does Harris & Sis live? When you write again write a long letter & tell me all the news. I will write to Bro Jimmie soon and give him a chat about not writing to me more frequently. I hope the Boys will improve their time, I know they have fine minds and can be smart men if they will try. I feel a great interest in their welfare, I want them to be great and good men. Tell them when I come to visit them I want to meet bright & intelligent young men, yes—first class gentlemen. Tell them all to write to us. I will write to Pa & Ma soon. I hope this may find you all well and cheerful and quite happy. Tell Caroline to be a good smart girl & if I come I will bring her some present. Indiana I wish you would decide (if Pa & Ma is willing) to come home with me, if I live to visit you all. You would be such a comfort to me especially when Love would be gone, which is often. I wont insist if it is not agreeable to their feelings, but I truly hope they will spare us you or one of the boys. Well Sister, it is time to close my poor letter. You will please excuse it for times are rather dull here and I have not much to interest you with. Please write soon and Tell Pa & Ma & the Boys to write also.

Give my kindest Love to Pa Ma & the boys and accept the same yourself. Write soon.

I will send you the [belt?] by mail.

As ever your loving sister,
M. F. Hardison

John Randolph Hardison to Edwin T. Davis c

Oconee, Geo[rgia]
Jany 15th, 1869

Dear Edwin,

Your very kind and highly esteemed letter of 11th Inst is now before me, contents duly noted, and while we are delighted to hear from you all again and appreciate your kindness in writing to me so promptly, we are very much grieved to learn that it is impracticable for you to come this far to see us, for under existing circumstances I don't see that it will be possible for us to go on to Thomas Ville to pay you a visit during our stay in Georgia. Mary, though in very good health generally, is not in a condition to travel much without endangering her welfare, and this of itself would make me solicitous for her, but in addition I have business in other parts of Ga. which will consume a good deal of my time, to say nothing of two cases I have in this county which I must pay proper attention to before I return home. I will leave here on Monday next for Barnes Ville Ga. & will be absent a week or ten days perhaps, as I have to contend with an old lady who has in hand some legacies which I am empowered to collect. I have a letter from her stating that she is ready & anxious to settle but at the same time she says that, after consulting council she may decline to do so on certain conditions, but I shall go fully armed and equipped for the contest etc etc. I have a suit pending some where in the Middle Circuit of Florida on a note for $500.00 besides interest. I had judgement just before the war & during the war I was offered Confed. money in payment but declined, know nothing of the case since the War. Have written my lawyer (Wilk Call) since I came here, & am expecting an answer daily. If things do not come up properly before I am ready to return I may need your assistance and will write you giving full particulars.

Yes, I have been to see Sister Liz, found her looking much better every way than I ever saw her before. Bobbie was at home and I was gratified to find in him all the evidences of high moral and intellectual worth. He has returned to Athens. I rode with him from 13 [station 13 on the Central of Georgia Railroad—the town of Tennille] to 14 [Oconee] as he went on. I am sure he will prove an honor and comfort to his Parents in after years. Eddie I found to be a nice sweet little Boy retaining his early favor. I enjoyed my visit very much as you may well know but there was a vacancy there which can never be filled. We talked about Dear Little Trudie and Liz tried to tell me the circumstances of her last illness & death. I saw many of her Books, Toys, and play things of her early youth, and you may be sure I was sad.

In answer to some of your questions, we will leave here on our return by the 10th Feby. I will continue the practice of my profession after I return home and I am gratified to say that it is beginning to be lucrative again in our state. Suffice It to say that I am making some money by the practice of my profession, and it is hard money at that. I am not trading much now, but watch my chances when a good thing comes along. My sweet little children Lilly and Win were very well indeed when we left home and you may be sure I am anxious to see them again. They are interesting as I think and I intend to give them the best of Educational opportunities. I think my reasons for not bringing them now are good. (I mean aside from my duty to keep them within the bosom of their Mother's kindred as much as possible.) They are quite young & would not appreciate a visit now like they will when they grow older. It has ever been my intention to place them in your care and have their education finished in Ga. but they are unwilling to be left here now, but when they grow older they will be delighted to come & then I hope they will be a greater comfort to all of you than they can be now. I hope also to be able then to spend much of my time with them & if I continue to prosper as I have done I shall be. Edwin I can't write the half I wish to now but I will write again before I leave and answer yours more fully. My best love to Mattie & that Beauty of yours & to Sallie & children.

the same devoted
John

Don't fail to write instanter.

Mary Fletcher (Northington) Hardison to Her Father s

Personville Limestone Co Texas
March 28th 1869.

Mr. James F. Northington,
My Dear Father

 It is a very fair pleasant Spring Sabbath Evening, and as everything is quiet and the Capt is busy writing, I have concluded it was a most favorable time for me to pen you a few lines, for we are boarding yet and it is seldom we are alone, (that is without company) we will move to our Home about the first of April, and shall be glad to see the time arrive, for there is no place like home with me now. We are all pretty well at present. I was very sick a few days ago with a spell of cramp colic, but now my health is as good as I could desire. Love has a good deal of business to attend to at present, he will be absent for several days to come at court in Springfield. Well Pa I dont know what to write to interest you for with us times are rather dull. Farmers has thus far done but very little towards planting, for it has been quite cold and rainy up to a few days back. Now it looks a little like spring the trees are begining to bud and a few garden seeds are coming up. Our Spring is considered very late. I think our fruit is mostly killed.

We have not sowed our garden yet, for the ground is still too wet. How are you and the boys getting along with your crop? I guess you have had better weather than the rest of us. How is Ma getting along gardening? I know she will have vegetables before we will.

I sent Ma the mustard seed by mail, but have not had an opportunity of sending your corn to Bryan yet, that is the nearest point at which I could have it expressed. I have concluded to risk it by mail for it may be sometime before I have a chance to send it to Bryan. I guess you will get it. You must write to tell us all about how Caroline come out in the Horace affair. We had a bad negro affair to take place about 4 miles below where we live last Sunday night. Some white men murdered a negro woman. We have not learned the particulars yet, the men have run away that did it, we understand she was most brutally killed. How are you getting along with your freedmen? Do they work pretty well? I hope they may do their part well and prove to be great help to you.

How is brother Childs getting along? and has he obtained board for his wife & daughter yet?

Tell Ma I have done a great deal of sewing since I got home and got over my fatigue. I am not troubled with headache now at all, and have had but one spell of headache since my return home. I expect to do my cooking with the help of a little negro girl & what the Capt can do untill I get sick, and then a widow lady by the name of Bird is to stay with me as long as I want her, she is a good nice old lady, about 58 years old, & loves me and the Capt as much as if we were her own children. Tell Ma she must not be uneasy about my having attention, for Love is a good nurse and a devoted husband & this old lady is a true friend and will do a mothers part. When did you hear from sisters Missouri & Lizzie? and how were they when you heard? The Capt received the letters Brother Jimmie sent him. He also received one from Marcilous. We were indeed rejoiced to get them, and learn you were all well. Love will write to the boys when he returns from court.

I will write to the boys when we get moved and tell them how I am getting along then gardening & raising chickens & pigs. Well Pa I will have to close for want of something to write. Tell Ma she must write to us. I have written to her twice & also to all the girls, but as yet have received no answers to any. Now Pa you must try and pen a letter once in a while if not often, and rest assured every word will be highly appreciated by us. Tell Indiana & the boys to write also. When you see Melia kiss her for me and tell her Aunt Mary is going to write her a little letter before long. Give our love to all the family & accept the same yourself. Please write to us as soon as convenient for we will be happy to hear from you all.

Remember us in your prayers.
I remain as ever your affectionate Daughter,
M. F. Hardison

P.S. Well Pa it is just a week this Evening since I wrote this letter, and here it is yet. I failed to get it off last mail but will be sure to send it this week, and your corn too. And hope you may receive them in due time. We are all quite well. I had a light cold the past week but not bad enough to lay me up at all. We will go to housekeeping the 7th of April. Love attended Court at Springfield, he made a handsome little sum too. Well you must be sure to write when you get this. Tell Ma I will write to her just as soon as I get home & get strait, for it will take me several days to get fixed up right. You all must write often.

As ever your Daughter
Mary F. H.
April 4th 1869

[A daughter, Amelia Randolph, was born to Mary and John on April 12, 1869.]

Mary Fletcher (Northington) Hardison and John Randolph Hardison to Mary's Fathers

Personville Texas Nov 17th 1869

Mr. Jas. F. Northington:
My Dear Father,

I have been thinking for several weeks that I would write to you, but something has transpired every day to prevent it either too much work or too much company, but now I will undertake it. I have not heard from home in a great while, what is the matter? why don't some one of the family write? I cant tell how anxious I am to hear, the last news I had Sister Lizzie's babe was sick. Well Pa cold weather has come again,—yes it is winter, it finds us all in good health, my health is better now than it has been in 18 months, I run from morning till night. We have two boarders, our same little merchant—Mr. Jones & his clerk. I have no negro, for it is impossible to get one here. I have a good Stove and get along very well, my stove is in my dining room, the room is 16 feet square. I never do my washing or scouring, there is a poor woman near who does it for me. I have a good deal of sewing to do. Some comforts to quilt. My old friend who was with me when I was confined will help me to do my sewing & knitting, She is a kind good lady, we all call her Grand-ma, her name is Bird. She has [been] with us now 5 weeks. Well Pa we get the finest lot of ducks now I ever saw, they are as fat as squabs and very sweet. I have enough feathers brought in this fall to make a large pair of pillows. Well Pa I must tell you a little about our sweet little "Millie Randolph." She is one of the best little children you ever saw, never cries unless hurt. She is as fat as a pig weighes 22 lbs, has dark hair, very fair white skin & deep blue eyes. Oh how I do want you & Ma to see your little Texas Grand-childe. Pa you must try and write to us when you get this, we are so anxious to get some news from home. Tell all to try and write at least once a month. I am very uneasy about you all, for it has been so long since we heard, we fear something bad has taken place, do write and tell us. Love got a letter from Bro Tom. Mims sometime ago, he wrote Sister Missouri was down home, and had been for three weeks, and that she would not write him a word, he said she was the strangest woman in the world. Pa how do they get along now? Tell me, for I want to know. Tell Ma I will try and write to her soon. How is Lizzie's family? Well Pa it is late so I will close for this time. Do write soon. Tell Indiana & the boys to write. Give my warmest love to all and accept the same yourself.

I remain your affectionate daughter
M. F. Hardison

Well Father, Do you think there was ever any thing new under the Sun? You will no doubt think so when you see this page, for it is certainly new for me to be caught writing letters outside of business ones, but really it has been so fearfully long since we heard from any of you that we have become almost alarmed. Is any thing the matter with any of the family? If so do write & let us know even if it should be bad. I have nothing new to tell you & if I had I am too tired to write much to night as I have picked cotton hard all day. My crop is short as are all other crops in this part of Texas. I will make 4 Bales—not ½ crop. Prices range from 15 to 17½c in gold with us but we expect a heavy rise before April. You know about as much about Politics in Texas as I do. We all are in fine health and our little Amelia is the prettiest thing I ever saw & the best child in the world. I recon Every body thinks so, and all our neighbors & children come to see us & make much of the baby.

I am anxious to know how your old red land field turned out this year in cotton & wheat, and all about your crop every way—Have you any Ducks and Turkeys to hunt this fall? Well I guess we have had plenty of fun thus far at our Home—Myself & a friend who boards with us have killed nine (9) Turkeys and 72 ducks already this fall. I wonder how the Boys will take the news. They would almost go wild if they were here. Fletcher gets plenty of Feathers & we all have fine eating all the time. I keep our table well supplied every day & only hunt a few hours at a time say twice a week. We have plenty of Deer within one mile of my House plenty of fat Hogs and the finest Beef I ever saw—I shall kill 2 large Beeves next month for winter use. I know this is the easiest country to live in I shall ever find, still I shall go back to Georgia for my wife's sake. We longed to be with you all at the State Fair this week in Macon. Do write soon—& give wagon loads of love to Ma, to Lizzie & family, to Sissie & all the family.

Your unworthy son, J R Hardison

Mary Fletcher (Northington) Hardison to Harriet Missouri (Northington) Mims and Thomas Mims s

Personville Texas Feb 20th 1870

Mrs. H. M. Mims:
My Dear Sister,

   It has been a long time since we heard from any of you. Love wrote Bro Tom a long letter sometime ago, but as yet has no answer to it. Why dont you all write, we would be so glad to hear from you often. I think you might write at least once a month. This leaves us in pretty good health. Love is gone to Louisannia, has been gone 17 days, will be home about the last of this month or the first of march. I am very anxious to see him return, I am so lonely when he is absent. Grand ma (that is Mrs. Bird) is staying with me. We have four boarders, one of them is gone most of his time. Our little merchant has run away, but I will get pay for his board, from a friend of his. It was a courting scrape that run him off we think, his name was Jones. I have planted some of my Garden, and the seeds are coming up finely, I will plant more tomorrow. I think we will have a good garden from the present prospect. I have been very busy for some time quilting and sewing. I have a fine quilt to quilt as soon as the weather gets warm enough, the others were comforts.

   Well how is little Annie coming on? I guess she can walk by this time. Amelia Randolph can get up by a chair, she will be walking by the time she is a year old or before may be. She is a fine healthy baby & very pretty indeed.

You must write and tell me all about little Annie. How is Mrs Lockett's health? does she still live near you? How is Mrs Wm Mims family? And when you write tell me all about your visit down home. What time did you go home? What is Bro Tom going to do this year? will you live at the same place? Love got a long letter from brother Haynes sometime ago, he informed us he intended to come to Texas in the summer to look for him a home. We were happy to hear it for this is indeed a far better country than Georgia. And Love will not consent to move back willingly. He gets a good practice here, and then provisions are so much cheaper here, that it is a great consideration with one who buys much. I have a fine lot of young hens and get lots of eggs. We have plenty meat, and a splendid lot of fat dried beef, we gave $2\frac{1}{2}$ cts a lb for it. We live well. There is but one objection here, that is society, that is a little bit rough. but we have some nice neighbors, some just come from Georgia & Alabama, very nice people.

When Haynes comes I want Pa & Tom to come and buy them a home too, if Pa cant come I want Jimmie to come. so they may be satisfied before coming to live.

You must write as soon as you get this and tell me what you all intend doing. I was much pleased with little Annie's dresses they were very pretty indeed. but you are misstaken about my making little Millie so many. I have never bought her a dress since she was bornd. Her Pa has bought her some little saques & stockings. You must send me scraps of all Annie's dresses for I love to look at them.

I have a cook this year, she has one child, she had two, but her oldest died last friday. The one living is four years old.

Well dear sister it is a bright beautiful sabbath evening, and how I do wish we could be seated together, O! how we could talk & enjoy ourselves. I wish often for your company, it would make me so happy to have some of my dear family to come to Texas. I hope it wont be long before we will all be living as neighbors. Kind Heaven grant, I pray. I must quit I guess for little Millie is on her palet by me & teasing me to take her. Love went to eastern Texas & from there to Louisana, he is on law-business collecting & selling land.

What are you doing these times with your little self. Do write me a long letter, and tell us a heap of news. I want you to have yours Bro Tom's & Annie's photograph taken and send them to me, especially Annie's. Now do have them. and as soon as I can get it I will send you Millies. I tried last week but she would not sit still. I will try again.

Give my love to brother Tom, tell him to write to us. Kiss little Annie for us, tell her of her little Texas cousin. I will try and write oftener in future, and you must do the same. Your letters are always so interesting I love to get them, I always know when I get one from you that I will hear a heap of news. Now please write soon.

I hope this may find your dear little family all well and happy. I remain your devoted sister

M. F. Hardison

A few lines to Brother Tom.

Well Brother Tom, I want you and sister Missouri to sell out and move to Texas and live neighbor to us. You must come with Bro Haynes when he comes, and then you can buy you a Home to suit yourself. I want Pa or Jimmie one to besure to come. I had rather Pa would so he could suit himself. I know it would be better for him to come here, then the boys could have good land to tend, and then they could settle around him, and we could all be neighbors. Oh! it would be so pleasant to have all my people near me.

You must try and come, now write and let us know all about it soon. I want you to try and come in july, then you can see and judge correctly. This is a good country no misstake of that. But you know that for you have seen it. You must write us a long letter and tell us all the news. Have you settled the law suit yet, hope you have, and got your Homestead. Tell us about it.

Please write soon and tell us all the news.

Accept our love & best wishes

I remain your true sister   Mary F. Hardison

P.S. The reason we want you to come in July, is that you may see the growing crops, so you may know exactly what can be done here. No more

Mary.

Mary Fletcher (Northington) Hardison and John Randolph Hardison to Mary's Parents s

Personville Texas March 13th 1870

Mrs M. R. Northington:
My Dear Mother,

I will now write you another letter, I commenced one to you two weeks ago today, but many things have occured to prevent my completing it. My sweet little Babe has been quite sick with a rising on the large Gland just behind her right ear, we have been endeavoring to scatter it for nearly two weeks, but we dont know how it will terminate, for it is still much swelled & very hard, Ma I have seen a great deal of trouble about my sweet little Millie, I have wished often for you to help me nurse her, I was alone in my troubles awhile for Love did not get home untill the 2nd of this month and Ma I cant tell you how glad I was to see him, and he never shall go off to be gone so long again, it throws so much responsibility on me, and then my anxiety about him is so great that I cant have it, he was gone for four weeks. I will be so glad when we all get to be neighbors, then when Love has to be absent some of you can stay with me. Ma little Millie was eleven months old yesterday, she has two teeth only, can crawl, stand alone and get up by a chair & then walk after it. But I fear this rising will put her back.

Well Ma how are you all getting along now? Well Dear Mother I will conclude my letter tonight March 15th. My sweet little Babe is still suffering from her rising neck. It has rise, we can have it lanced in the morning, we can now almost see the matter, it is a bad looking place. But I pray it may soon be well.

Ma I must tell you of my good success. Love has bought me a nice sewing machine, and the way I can sew is a fact. It is a splendid one. I have a good deal of work to do when my Babe gets well. I have four regular boarders that pays me well. I have a pretty good cook, one that is close & very saving, washes & irons well, she does all my work. Grand Ma has gone home, but I will send for her soon, she is a nice good lady. The children are at school and Grand Ma is good company to me.

Well Ma I must quit & take Millie. Write soon I do love to get your dear letters. Tell Pa to please write to us. Tell all to write. Give my love to all the family & accept the same yourself.

I am as ever your loving daughter, Mary F. Hardison

March 16 1870

Dear Pa & Ma,

Fletcher wants me to finish her letter, but I have nothing to write this morning only to say that we now have the coldest weather of the past season—night before last it turned cold, with a considerable fall of hail yesterday morning, every thing was frozen—the ponds frozen over—ice $1\frac{1}{4}$

in thick in the vessels about the house & though it was a clear day it continued freezing in the shade, all day. It has moderated a little, but this morning there is a heavy frost with plenty of ice. Our Gardens orchards and early corn are badly damaged & I think totally ruined. I had a splended garden, every thing growing finely—but my mustard Turnips Cabbage Peas Beets and early Corn are all killed. This will throw us back a week or so, though there is plenty of time yet to plant again. The fruit I guess is entirely destroyed.

Fletcher has told you about our little Melia. She has suffered a great deal. The absess is ready to be lanced this morning, and she has been remarkably cheerful and smart, all the time she has been sick, after it runs we think she will be better right off.

I have been off on a long trip, was in 18 counties in Texas and 4 Parishes in Louisiana, but I have not time to tell you much of what I saw. We hope you are all well. Do you think of coming out to Texas with Haynes next summer? We would be delighted to have you do so and would do all in our power to render your visit pleasant and agreeable. I will write more next time.

Your unworthy son
J R Hardison

John Randolph Hardison to Edwin T. Davis c

Person Ville, Texas 17th Octr AD 1870

Dear Edwin,

Your long-looked for and highly esteemed favor, the date of which does not at the present moment occur to me, came to hand some ten days since, and I accept the first opportunity afforded me of writing you in reply. To say that I was pleased—delighted—gratified—to hear from you again, would only express a very vague and imperfect idea of the pleasure and real gratification your well-timed letter afforded me, coming as it did freighted with so much of importance and interest, not only to myself, but to my entire family as well.

I am certainly greatly obliged to yourself and to Sister Liz & Sallie for your earnest expressions of affection for my dear Children and for the deep interest & concern you manifest for their welfare and prosperity. And I can well assure you all that I have long since determined to remove with them to Georgia for the purpose of paying timely attention to their Education, as well as to return my wife once more to the bosom of her family, from whom she has been long estranged. I am forcibly impressed with the necessity of having Lily and Winnie at a good school all of next year and sometimes I almost come to the conclusion to send my entire family over this winter so that the Children could enter school there at the beginning of another year, but it being impossible for me to wind up my business here now so as to be absent even for a single twelve months, I don't see how I could separate myself from all that is dear to me for so long a time together. You must therefore be forbearing towards me if I say that in all probability our return to the Home of our childhood will of necessity have to be deferred one more year. I have no hope of a school here for the next year worthy of my patronage & shall have to place my Children in a Boarding School. There are three very good schools within 30 miles of us, one of which I shall patronize so that I can bring the Children home at intervals without loss of time, & where I can hear from them speedily in case of sickness.

As your letter is where mine was when you wrote to me—absent from me—I may not be able to answer all your inquiries. As to the practice of the Legal Profession being at this time a paying business in this State is entirely owing to the circumstances surrounding each individual case. While the practice pays some Lawyers handsomely in all parts of the state, others of apparent equal ability and talent in the same localities do but little and many frequently have to look to other means for sustenance.

For my own part I cannot complain at the success which has attended my efforts since I have been in this county and Judicial District. I have made between $1500.00 & $2000.00 Gold since the 1st day of January last besides 160 acres of land in addition to an ample support at home, and a very short cotton crop which for this year turns out only four Bales. But when I remember this is the fruit of my individual labor almost entirely I try to be content. I live in very humble circumstances and try to economise in every thing but you know Economy is one virtue which is a hard matter for me to practice.

The corn crop in every part of our State so far as heard from is very good, but owing to the anticipated heavy Emmigration the coming winter Farmers in this section are holding at $1.00. The cotton crop, which up to July 4th promised to excell that of any previous year, was cut very short by the continued drought, which hereabouts and in many other localities lasted from July 4th until yesterday morning when it set in to rain down in good old fashioned torrents & has continued ever since without intermission to the present hour 10 P.M. Monday night—& now our county and small streams are flooded, greatly damaging the cotton still remaining in the fields. However the turnout of cotton thus far has been much better than was at one time anticipated and has proven to have been a very good and full-length staple.

Edwin you must really excuse me for deferring a chapter on the Political Status of Texas to some future letter for indeed I do not feel competent to do that vexed and complicated subject justice to night. For the present suffice it to say that we are ruled by a Tyrant in the shape of Governor whom we most frequently call "King Edmond J. Davis" instead of "Gov. Davis"—A man who has been imbued with unlimited power by our late Radical Legislature and who is mean enough to do the meanest and most diabolical acts for the sake of personal interest & benefit sits in the Gubernatorial Chair of Texas with his willing tools and emmisaries secretly stationed in every Town and Hamlet throughout the state, who like their Crown Head have the meaness to conceive and audacity to execute designs of the darkest die.

Were it not for the political troubles that are upon us and which hang about us like a choking stifling Incubus, and which, for the present we are wholly unable to shake off, our state would ere long unquestionable stand foremost in the south-west in all that "makes a State." With so many natural facilities, with a tide of Immigration to our Teritory absolutely without a precedent, with a populace of untiring energy and industry, with a mint of Capital seeking a channel of Increase in our midst—with an inexhaustable soil covering millions of acres of domain extending across not less than 8 degrees of latitude, most happily adapted to every species of vegetable Production—with a climate healthy and salubrious—with Rail Roads pushing their Heads towards almost every point of the compass—Texas, nothwithstanding her deplorable political thralldom, must ere long "Rise like Venus from the Ashes"—She will have soon "Builded her House," "Hewn out her seven pillars," "Put on her beautiful garments," and taken her wonted station in the great sisterhood of "Independent Sovereignties."

Our Texas Central Rail Road from Galveston has already reached this county. The cars now run daily within 23 miles of Personville and by next fall will cross the Navasota River and pass within 10 miles west of us & east a few miles of Springfield, our present county site. The first Depot east of

XIII. FAMILY LIFE IN TEXAS DURING RECONSTRUCTION 341

the Navasota River in this county will be in the beautiful country within 15 miles of this point and as our Court House will no doubt be moved hither and a large Town go up as soon as the Depot is permanently located, I am making ready to purchase 2 or 3 lots as soon as they are offered for sale by the R Road Co. This will undoubtedly be a business place and permanent, and is the first point on the line I have gotten my consent to move to.

I was pleased with your account of your trip to Macon, Atlanta, & to the old "Boro" [Davisboro in Washington County, Georgia] that place so "dear to memory" with me, and I traveled in imagination with you in all your rounds. Wish you had went up to 14 [Oconee] & called on our folks there. I was indeed gratified to hear all our friends and relatives were doing so well. Don't Till look nice with a fine Boy. But you forgot to say who Lawson D. married. I am more than anxious to learn? I was delighted to learn that Mr. H.[Hardwick] had done so well in business since his return to Ga. No doubt the move was fortunate for him. Glad Bobbie [Robert Hardwick] graduated with honor & know he will be of great help to his Father in business.

Well now, last but not least, I know your sweet little "Mattie Jr." is all that you say of her as to beauty if she resembles in any shape "Mattie Sr." for no beauty ever excelled hers when last it was my good fortune to behold her. And as to intellect—Smartness—she can't resemble you—unless she possesses all of that you allot to her, but with all this so happily combined she may equal, but not excell ours in either. I shall be so proud to see the day when I can see them together.

In conclusion will you forgive me for writing so much and for reminding you that you failed to answer many interrogations contained in my last, and will you be kind enough to remember me and mine most affectionately to your "Matties," to Sallie, J.W. & family & to Mr. H [Hardwick], sister Liz & family when you write them?

Lily & Winnie say they want to see you all very much but won't consent to go over there to school unless we go with them. Lily says she will try to write you something after she learns a little more about the art. I had nearly forgotton to say that Win has entirely regained her health and is now growing fast and is fleshier than I ever saw her—and as full of mischief as can be. Lily is inclined to be delicate.

Good night,
Your Tired Bro & friend,
J. R. Hardison

XIV

Family Life in Texas during Reconstruction Letters of John and Mary Hardison Part Two, 1871-1875

John Randolph Hardison to Mary's Parents s

Springfield Texas
Saturday June 17th 1871

Dear Father & Mother

I know you all are anxious to hear from us now, and I will at once relieve your suspense by telling you that my darling Fletcher was delivered of another fine Daughter on Thursday last the 15th inst. Fletcher had a pretty hard time for about four hours but she was strong and healthy and her labor was natural and this morning when I left home both Mother and Child were doing as well as we could desire. Our babe is large and healthy and we think very pretty. We have not named her yet but as that has been left with me we may call her "Nannie Misouri" for my sister and Sister Hattie. You must know we have a time of rejoicing at our house now, and you all will rejoice with us. I think Fletcher looks more beautiful and interesting now than she ever did before. It is a great time for our little Amelia she has a great deal to say about her little Sissie as she calls her, but she dont like the idea of sleeping away from her mother. Our Physicians and friends and neighbors

Personville Texas
March 31st 1873

Dear Mother—

Now that the Box of good things you all were so Kind as to send us has arrived in safety, I will write you a few lines to relieve your anxiety— We are certainly under lasting obligations to you all for such marked evidences of your Kind remembrance and tender affection but we fear from what you said in your last Kind letter you had too much on your hands already— in your advanced years —to justify you in favoring us so greatly— But we trust we appreciate the Kind motives which prompted you all and accept your tender offerings as tokens of your undying love and fond remembrance —

Letter of John Randolph Hardison to His Mother-in-Law,
Amelia Fisher Northington, March 31, 1873

Slaughter Collection

have been and are very kind to us and have given Fletcher & our Babe every attention. I am in Springfield to day in attendance on our District Court which is in session now for 3 weeks in this County, a good deal of business to be transacted. We are having a very dry hot time now and unless it rains soon crops must suffer. There will be a good crop made if we have seasons in time. There is no news of a general Character worth your attention. Our folks are well generally. We hope this may find you all well and prospering in life. Please write to us soon.

Your unworthy Son
J R Hardison

Mary Fletcher (Northington) Hardison to Her Mothers

Personville Texas
June 2nd 1872

Mrs. M. R. Northington
My Dear Mother,

It is a beutiful Sabbath evening and of course my thoughts are with you all, for a Sabbath never comes without my wishing to be with my Dear Ones at my sweet old Home. Ma I do want to see you all so much. I get heart sick sometimes when I get to thinking about you all & about the great distance which separates us. I shed many a tear of sorrow that none knows of, but he that knoweth all things. I was indeed rejoiced to get your kind and affectionate letter which was received in due time and greatly pleased to learn you were all well and getting on so pleasantly. You asked me about your letter before the last you wrote. I received it about three days after I wrote you the one you spoke of being so glad to get. I love to get your precious letters, they are full of such pure good encouraging advice, I always feel blest when I get one. Do write as often as you can. I do wish Pa would write to us. We would appreciate it so much.

Well Ma now about myself & family, first we are all well, getting on very well, we have the best & finest garden we have ever had, it is indeed beautiful. Various kinds of vegatables in abundance. We are going to try to send some to market, we have so many we cant near use them all. Ma we have the best prospect for a crop that I ever saw in my life, we have just had rain enough to answer every purpose so far. I never saw such corn as I now see, at this time a year before, it is certainly a show to most any one. The Capt has a pretty crop of corn & cotton & Potatoes. We all work very hard.

I do most all my cooking. I get dinner and supper & Elen gets breakfast and does the washing & her & Lillie does the milking. Ellen works out all the time except wash-day, she is a good negro to work and does it very well. I do trust we will have a good seasonable year & make a plenty.

I have a hundred little chickens some large enough to fry. I have had fine success raising chickens they grew off so fast. We make plenty of butter have more milk than four families like mine could use. My little children are quite well, & fat as pigs, & pretty as rose-buds. Amelia talks about you all every day, she will ask me to tell her about her Grand Pa & Ma & her uncles Jimmie & Marcellous & Capers, & aunt Annie. She loves to look at your Pi[c]tures and knowes you all. She wants me to take her to see you all very much. Ma I want to live near you so much, so my little ones could have your good training. I know you could teach them many things I am not able to. I do pray that we may all be permited to live together before a great while. Ma I dont know what to do, whether to try and go to Georgia this coming winter or not. I want to so much but still I am afraid I would be uneasy about the Capt, so much so that it might cause me trouble & anxiety to a great extent. I will study it all over and let you know in the course of two months. We will know in that time what we will make in the way of a crop.

The Capt is willing for me to go and stay a year if I think I can stand it, he says he knows he can bear it by working hard night and day, but knows he could never rest a moment idle. We wont be able to move this coming winter without something great takes place in our favor. You may rest assured we are more than anxious to go back, on account of living with you all. Who is your Presiding Elder this year? We attended a two days meeting last saturday & sunday week, 7 miles above us where our membership lies. I guess we will soon have a church near us, we had a good meeting. Religion among us is at a low ebb. The methodist are like "A[n]gels visits" "few & far between" most all Baptist & very poor ones too. What I mean is cold ones. Ma we have a good Preacher, a man full of Pure Religion, it does me good to hear him preach, he is just such a man as uncle Windfield Robison, gets shouting happy when he preaches. His name is George Turner, he is a Local minister. Our circuit riders name is Kid he is a very fine good preacher, but not as feeling a man as Brother Turner. We have no Sabbath school organized yet. Have you any? I am glad Caroline stays with you. Tell her she must stay untill I come & I will bring her a nice dress ready made. Ma what has become of Liza & her little children? and aunt Clarisa? [probably former slaves] Tell Pa we are going to write to Uncle Marshall this week, and when we hear from him, we will let him hear from us. We have never written to him yet. Ma I must close for this time, hoping to hear from you again soon. You can never realize how much we appreciate your dear good letters.

I received a letter from sister Lizzie a few days ago, it was truly interesting to us. Also a short one from sister Missouri after so long a time. I thought she never intended to write any more. She said they were all well & getting along well. Ma I know you will think this a strange composed letter, but I wrote just as I thought of things, so you must excuse me, Ma I did not think the least hard of you about the dried fruit, and you must never think that way about me, you know me too well for that kind of conclusion.

I kiss my little Darlings often for you & Grand Pa. Poor little things have no relatives to love them here.

Ma you must write as often as you can, and we will do the same. Give our warmest love to Pa & all the children & accept the same your dear self
I am as ever your loving & devoted daughter
Mary F. Hardison

P.S. Ma I told you why I did not write for so long a time, it was on account of sis Nan's confinement & her babes illness & death. I was there so much & so wearied I did not feel able to write, but I will not wait so long again, for I would never cause you a pain if I could avoid it, you may be assured of that dear Mother. Yours truly
Mary.

Mary Fletcher (Northington) Hardison to Her Mother s
Personville Texas Dec 3rd 1872

Mrs. A.R. Northington:
My Dear Mother,

I will try to pen you a few lines tonight in answer to your dear letter which we were the happy recipients of last week. I was so glad to hear from you all once more & hear you were all in good health. I think Pa must be getting young again, out hunting at night. Oh! it makes me happy to know he feels able to go and enjoy himself. I wish he would come & hunt some with the Capt. This is a fine country for hunting. We are all quite well and trying to do the best we can. We have lost another one of our fatning hogs since I wrote to Brother last week, we cant tell what is the matter with them, it seems to be their lungs or lights. The Capt examined one that died on yesterday, and he said its lights were entirely decayed, just in a mess. One of our finest sows seemed to be sick tonight, she is heavy with pig and just as fat as she can walk. If they continue to go, it will be severe on us, but we will submit to our fate without murmuring. While we are blest with good health I can bear most any trial and hardship.

My sweet little children are so rosy & bright as little stars. I feel so thankful, thankful for the precious "Gifts" for they are sweet "Angels of comfort & happiness" to me, they are my company from morn till night. Oh! how I do wish you could see them. I am as devoted a mother as you ever knew, people here think me the most careful and particular mother they ever saw, but Ma my husband & my dear little children are my all here, they are the only ones I have to live for, cut off as we are from our loved relatives. The dear little darlings talk about Grand Mama in Georgia and what good and pretty tricks she is going to send them. Ma I shall receive your precious gifts as true tokens of tender love & motherly affection. I will feel truly greatful for them, make the trunk or box you send secure from entrence on the route, if it were covered with bagging it would stand the jolts better, if you send in a box you can just nail hoop fast around it after nailing it fast and send it without any difficulty as common freight and it will come safe by itself, and if Mr. Ivey dont come, send it any how for the sake of the little ones. They are so eager about Grandma's Pretty things as Amelia calls them. You and Indiana beat me quilting. I will go about mine next week if nothing prevents. Ma if that was Dr G A Parsons that died, I want
[Remainder of letter missing.]
PS—If you send any thing without any one coming, direct it to Capt J R Hardison Groesbeck Texas—in care of J I Lewis

Mary Fletcher (Northington) Hardison to Her Mother s

Personville Texas Jan 21st 1873

Mrs. A.R. Northington:
My Dear Mother,

We have just received your kind and interesting letter. We were indeed truly glad to hear from you all once more, and hear you were still getting along well. I was sorry to hear you & Capers had been sick. I have been quite sick, am just able to walk about a little now, I am very poor & weak. I was sick four weeks. Sissie has been quite [page torn] but is a little better today, [page torn] are uneasy about her, she has fever and inflamation of stomach. I do trust the little darling will continue to improve. I am so weak & have nursed so steady, that I cant half write but may be you can read it.

All the rest of the family are well. Amelia is just as fat as a pig, and smart and pretty too. She parched coffee for dinner today, she says she is Ma's little woman.

Ma I do want you to see my sweet little children so much. But I cant tell when that time will come, for we have a rite smart family, and have made so little for the two past years we are very much behind in our affairs. We will have to work hard and live hard this year. But we will try and do the best we can. I received a letter from [page torn] today, the first we have [page torn] months, we were truly glad to hear from her and little family, she said she was going home to spend some time. Oh! how I wish I could be with you all then. You must remember me and my little ones in your happy meetings. The other girls have the advantage of me, they can visit home when ever they feel like it, but I am so far off I cant go alone.

Well Ma in refference to sending those things to me, I want you to send them if you can, for it will be quite a treat to me & my dear babes, you send them to Galveston & please pay the freight to that place, & we will direct the Firm to send it direct to our depot. I never did want any thing more than some of your good dried fruit, since I have been so sick and feeble. And tell Sister Indiana I will accept the dress she spoke of sending, with great pleasure for dresses with me are scarce & with my little children. I will send you scraps of the only dresses bought for myself last year. I dress plain and seldom go any where acept to our church. Tell Sister Indiana as soon as I get a little stronger & sissie gets well I will write her a long letter. Sister Lizzie has not written to us in a long time, what is the matter? Tell her to write. Sister Missouri [page torn] guess will be with you by the time this reaches you, if so, tell her I will answer her letter the first of February at Oconee. Well Ma you must write often, for your good letters cheer me so much I cry over them, but still they comfort me so much. I wish Pa would write to us too. Tell the Boys to remember me. Give your warmest love to all the family and accept the same your dear self. Ma you must excuse this sorry letter, for I am to weak and feeble to write much, or well. I will write in a few days & let you know how sissie is getting along. Tell Sister Annie not to wait for me to write, but write as often as she can. Kiss little Annie Mary & Jimmie for me. Tell them Aunty wants to see them so [page torn].

The Capt will tell you how [page torn] your box to us, he is going [page torn] some. Amelia brags to [page torn] folks here, that Granma in Georgia is going to send her pretty things, She is so proud of them. I do wish you could hear her talk, you would be astonished, she is so sensible & talk so plain too. Well Ma I will close for this time. Write dear mother as often as you can & tell all the rest to try and do so too.

I remain your devoted Daughter as ever
M. F. Hardison

John Randolph Hardison to Mary's Mother s

Person Ville Texas
March 31st 1873

Dear Mother—

Now that the Box of good things you all were so kind as to send us has arrived in safety, I will write you a few lines to relieve your anxiety. We are certainly under lasting obligation to you all for such marked evidences of your kind remembrance and tender affection but we fear from what you said in your last kind letter you had too much on your hands already in your advanced years to justify you in favoring us so greatly. But we trust we appreciate the kind motives which prompted you all and accept your tender offerings as tokens of your undying love and fond remembrance. Well I hardly know how nor where to begin to describe the scene that ensued in our little family circle when the Box arrived. It was brought to our Door by a kind neighbor while we were at Breakfast & when we realized it was sure enough from home & the veritable Box of which we had heard, our "Faith was at once lost in sight"—the little ones had been told over and over again what stores of good and nice things were coming from Grand Ma & Grand Pa and Aunties & Uncles in Georgia—all was excitement—expectation—everyone of us expecting something—we knew not—could only guest what. The Breakfast Table was deserted instanter of course and all hands made a general rush pel mel for Grand Ma's Box. The next thing was to open with great care & that was no small job I can well assure you—nailed together and bound as it was. But perseverence overcame all obstacles & soon the lid was gently raised & Oh! My—the little ones pitched at the pretty Dresses skirts cakes Doll etc. etc. with a deal of [?]. Nothing we could manufacture at home, however fine and tasty, could in their eyes compare with all these "pirties" as they call them—all the way from "Grand ma in Georgia" Little Nannie (Sissie we call her) took entire possession of Amelia's Doll at first sight & will allow her no voice or ownership in the matter whatever—The Dresses for Fletcher & Dito & Dress goods for the children are excellent. The aprons for Lillie & Winnie are superb. The cake Fruit & Preserves are Par excellance & the seed Corn & Cotton seed exceed them all in my eye of course. Lillie was absent at school and did not share our joy & happiness—but I have written to her telling the news & will send her apron by mail—She is boarding with my only Bro. Dr W. L. Hardison & is going to school at Birdston in Navaro [Navarro] Co, which place is 32 miles north of us. She will not be home before July & not then unless vacation is given in the school.

Well on Tuesday & Tuesday night last we had a heavy freeze which played havoc with our young crops which were generally very forward & the finest I ever saw to have been so early. Many have plowed up & planted over their corn & those who had cotton up did the same. My corn was ready to plow out was ½ leg high—but I am still risking the old stand which is now growing off again generally. My cotton then planted—was not up & was not hurt. It is now coming up pretty fast. The weather is now warm & pleasant. I planted my Ga. corn today with great care & about Saturday next will plant the cotton seed & will report to the Boys fully my success. I have and am putting in a heavy crop 22 acres in cotton 13 in corn besides potatoes garden and other patches. I have but little help besides myself—but am fully up with my work with health all the time as good as heart could desire—and this is one reason why I am trying to turn my entire attention to farming. My health is always much better, & my mind composed & at rest & besides I have more time to spend at Home with my little family. The people through out this entire country are doing more towards farming than was ever known before. Every farmer has enlarged his fields by taking in new lands. The farm work is well done & in ample time. Provisions are abundant & cheap. Corn only 40c to 50c yet with no demand whatever. Bacon of the finest quality at 12½ cts & dull sale at that. Health good generally.

Well we are anxious to hear from you all again. Write soon & tell us all the news, whether Sister Hattie is at Home & about her & her children's health now & how Bro Tom is & where he is farming this year etc etc—& how all the family & friends are doing etc. Is Father & Sis Annie & the Boys & Lizzie & her little ones & Haynes all well now? & is your own precious health still better?—Please send this letter to Lizzie & Haynes when you are done reading it, as I do not know when I may have time to write another as long. It is now growing late at night, Fletcher & the children long since fast asleep, not a soul up on the place save me & my eyes are growing heavy as this is the 7th letter I have written since dark and 3 others still waiting to be written but from my feelings now they must of necessity stand over until another night. I sincerely hope and believe the good Lord will sustain and uphold you in the trials you are brought to encounter in your declining [years], for He is a Buckler and a Shield, a very present help in time of trouble. Remember us tenderly and affectionately to all without distinction, Fletcher will probably write some thing to send with this.

Your unworthy
J. R. Hardison

John Randolph Hardison to Lilly Hardison c

Person Ville
Monday Mar 31st [18]73

Dear Lily

I guess you are anxious to hear from home by this time & I will write you to day for the up mail on Wednesday. Well I reached home in safety about dark on the day I left you & found all well but a little lonesome because of our absence. Monday night a heavy Norther blew up as you doubtless remember & on Tuesday we did little else than make fires and sit by them. The freeze was severe here & killed every thing to the ground, some have planted over their Corn. Others are waiting to see if it will grow out again. I think mine will do best to stand, therefore I shall only replant & risk the old planting. The young fruit is killed generally I believe, I saved our watermellons & some of the young plants in the garden. We are now planting Cotton again this week. Well I must tell you now that your Ma received her case of goods from Georgia the other day, & what a time we had opening it and looking over every thing it contained, nice little Dresses Dress goods underskirts Chemises etc for the Children, 2 nice Dresses for your Ma—A beautiful Doll in full Dress for Amelia from her cousin Amelia, A whole lot of Peach & Pear Preserves Dried Applies & Peaches Some fine Corn and Cotton Seed for me, & among other things a beautiful Apron for you and Winnie. You Ma says she will send you yours by mail so you may look out for it each mail Day. It will be addressed like your letters to the care of your Uncle Doc's. I know you will regret not being here, but I have told you about all the Box contained & when you come home you can see everything. Well nothing new or comical has turned up here since you left. Your Uncle Doctor Reeves preached a big Hard Shell Sermon at Lost Prairie Church on yesterday & a multitude of people were out to hear him. Mrs. Rambo & her Mississippi Daughter came to see us on Saturday evening. Grandma has returned from Ben's & we look for her this week. Now my Daughter you must strive to improve your mind in every way you possibly can. Pursue your studies closely and dilligently and accept every opportunity to improve your Knitting Sewing Crocheting etc. Endeavor to be as useful and agreeable to your Uncle Doc & Aunt Josie, as you well can. You must preserve all our letters & bring them home with you when School is over. They may form in future years a pleasant reminescence of the past, & as this is my first ever written to you, you will take great care of it of course. You must write to us occasionally. We can read your writing, & your Aunt Joe can direct your letters for you —Good bye for this time. Be a good girl.

Your affection father
J R Hardison

Amelia (Fisher) Northington to Marcellus Northington s

Sandersville May the 6, 1873

Dear Marcillus

I received your kind letter to night and was glad to heare from you all but was very sory to heare that Anne was so sick. I truste she may be restored to health if it is our Heavenly Fathers will. I wanted to visit her before I came up here but I did not feele able to make the walke. I havent felt well in several weeks my breste still hurts me. I take good care of my self and I want you all to do the same. well in refference to Lizzie she has not been confined yet. She is in a very strange condition, she has been in a graite deal of pain for the laste weeke and suffers dredful with her feete. She has had feever for sevrel days. The Dr. thinkes she is taking the measles she is not able to be up. Bobbie is up. Amelia is down with the measles Allis hasn't take them yet They are all over this plaise. I cant tell when I can come home it is unreasonable to think of leaving Lizzie in her condition unless some of you gets sick at home. I wish all was well that I could come home be it ever so humble theres no plaise like home.

I never felt my dependance more upon my Heavenly Father then I do now. I pray that the good Lorde may guide us all over the see of life and finely in to the Haven of repose. there are meny things that appeares harde for us to bear but the good Lorde never sends more upon us then he will give graise to bare. if we will only look to him and believe his worde. Lizzie sais if you all could only k[n]ow what she suffers you all would not blaime her for wanting me to stay with her she sais toung [tongue] cant dis cribe what she suffers. write soon for I am anxious to heare from all. fare well my loved ones to night my love to al write soon.

Your devoted Mother
M. Northington

John Randolph Hardison to Lilly Hardison c

Person Ville Texas
Monday Night May 12th [18]73

Dear Lillie,

As I promised I will write you a line to Night. We are all well & hard at work. Grand ma came on Friday evening and is still with us. Sarah Bird came up Saturday evening & remained with us until yesterday afternoon. Ginnie Rambo came home on Friday & went back Sunday evening. She is looking quite pretty. Dr Glass escorted her to Church yesterday. The Girls and Boys are driving along just about as they were when you left. Grand ma says you must learn a heap before you come home. Melia & Sissie are as pretty as ever. Your Aunt Nan is much better—No one married—Crops are growing finely now, Grass & weeds ditto. I am tired & can't write much to night. Let us hear from you occasionally. Our kind love & regards to Josie & the children.

In haste your Devoted Father
R Hardison

John Randolph Hardison to Lilly Hardison c

Person Ville Texas.
May 25th 1873

Dear Lily

I will write you a few lines to night as I may not have another opportunity before Wednesday which you know is our up mail day. We are all on foot but not very well. Sissie has been quite sick with a bad cough and high fevers for over a week past. She is now nearly well, coughs only a little & is a little fretful when her Ma ma is out of sight. She can talk very well and is more interesting than ever. She knows your picture as well as ever & will no doubt recognize you when you return home. Amelia is as sprightly and prety as ever and talks a great deal about you. Winnie is about as usual—I have her to help me in the farm some but she is not much fond of farm work. Jimmie is well and full of mischief. His Sister Mary keeps him quite busy helping her. Your Ma is not very well, she is fatigued a good deal at her house work and nursing the Chidren.

Tuesday Night, June the 3rd 1873 Well Lily we are disappointed in the Mail last week. I did not finish my letter, but will conclude it tonight in time for the up mail to morrow. Your kind letter of the 23rd of May came to hand to day, & I can assure you we were glad to see it for it was the first word we had had from you since I left you. We were gratified to know that you are all well, & that your Aunt Josie's crop was looking so finely.

We are all very well here except your Ma. She is grieving bitterly on account of the sudden and unexpected death of her Dear Sister Lizzie—Mrs Renfroe who lived in Sandersville Ga. She died on the 14th of May & we got news last week in the paper and then received the particulars in a letter from your Ma's Mother. Poor Lizzie was one of the best women I ever saw. She was loved by every body. A long piece in the paper concerning her death. She died perfectly happy & rejoicing in the good Lord. She gave directions about her children and all her effects. Talked to every body present, & sent kind messages to her absent friends—she leaves 4 children, one only a few days old. We will tell you all the particulars when you come home. I got a kind letter from your Aunt Lizzie Hardwick—your Mother's sister, last week. She made many inquiries about us all, and you and Winnie in particular, and begs me to let one of you spend a year with her if no longer. She is a good woman and I am anxious for you both to see her. You can read her letter when you come home & then you must write to her. I have wrote her a long letter and told her all about you and Winnie. Your Ma says she will try to compose herself enough to write to you in time for our next week mail. I will try to go after you on the day you name—but if I shall fail on that day I will be there without fail on Saturday after & we can come home on Sunday. We all want to see you very much, and then you could be of so much comfort and consolation to your Ma in this day of trouble. I told Amelia to day I had a letter from Lily & that you were coming home in 3 or 4 weeks & she jumped up and clapped her hands & said "My Lily's coming back" Pa you must go and bring my Lily home tomorrow" etc. Dear little

Children they do love you so much. Well it has rained too much & I am bad in the grass over the Creek, but keep pulling away. Crop looks well, & I will make a plenty. All the folks here abouts are well I believe. Mrs. Gilbert spent the day with us on yesterday. I must close for I have another Letter to write to night. Our best Love to Josie & the children. Write again before I come. Good Night.

Your Affectionate Father
J R Hardison

John Randolph Hardison to Mary Elizabeth (Davis) Hardwick c

Person Ville, Texas   Sunday June 1st 1873

Mrs. M. E. Hardwick.
My Very Dear Sister.

You may imagine but I can not describe my feelings—my real pleasure and gratification, when, on returning home the other evening I found your very kind and affectionate letter of the 4th prev. I perused its pages time and again & I sat for hours musing over the fond and tender memories its every sentence yea every line & word brought so vividly to mind. I was certainly most surprised for I had long abandoned almost the last hope of ever again being the happy recipient of a friendly and affectionate line from under your pen. And now that it has come—now that I am in the timely possession of other & further evidence of your fond remembrance and lasting affection, I am greatly buoyed up and encouraged to write you as in "Days of Long ago."

You say My Sister you have written to me often during the past 3 or 4 years, well then what evil has befallen all your letters—What horrid fate has driven all of them far far astray of their destination? for I assure you Dear Sister not one word have I had from any of you since the receipt of Edwin's letter written in answer to some mention I made to you of his long silence. His letter reached me soon after my return from Ga. (& I replied to it at full length immediately) and is the only tidings I have had from any of you since until yours acknowledged above found its way to me. True it was I did not expect you considering your situation every way to write often and I here acknowledge my cruelty in not writing to you at least once a month regularly, but I did think Edwin might have written as often as I did & he having failed to answer my last which I intended to have been as interesting as possible—the correspondence between us ceased.

Well Dear Sister, you seem so anxious to hear all about the children Lily & Winnie I will tell you about them first, even to the exclusion of other things until I write again. Lily was 14 years old the 13th Jany 1873 & is tolerably well grown to her age & certainly is one of the most industriously disposed children I ever saw. This trait is remarked by all who know her. She loves books—History, Literature, science, Art & Romance, but does not at all like to be confined closely to the study of any scholastic branch—neither is she fond of close confinement to tedious and dificult manual Labor such as needle work Embroidery knitting crotshinging [crocheting?] etc. etc. I fear she never will be proficient and quick in these useful branches of a Lady's acquirements. She has a fair complexion—a little inclined to freckle—with very light hair—she has a great deal of discretion and has more the appearance of a woman of mature years than a Girl of only fourteen. She is now off at Birdston in Navarro Co at school. Has not been home since March & will not return until the first of July.

Winnie is quite diferent. She was Eleven years old in March last, Is well grown—Inclined to be slender—Has a clear white skin—No inclination to freckle or tan, Is the very image of her mother and Edwin—If you ever see her you will be forcibly struck with the favor, She will no doubt make a prettier woman than Lily—and will be equally apt to improve her mind but not now so industriously inclined to manual labor. She has a gentle disposition when not irritated and likes to be petted & noticed a good deal. No I have not forgot my promise to take them back to Ga & am striving hard now to be able to accomplish that end if they can remain only one short year. I am anxious that they should see and learn to love and revere their Mother's people, and nothing but the great distance and my many sad reverses of fortune have caused me not to have already taken them to you. We have two other nice sweet intelligent children—both Girls, one 4 & the other nearly 2 years old. Our first born before we went to Ga was a nice little Boy but it died at a few days old.

Well my Dear Sister, I am beginning to feel myself almost a lone in the world. Not one of my Father's family left now save myself and my Sister Mrs. Reeves. You know that Bro Thos & Clark & Mother died before the war & Sister Mary just after—well in October 1871 our old Father went to his long home, leaving to Sis Nan. & myself a little half Sister & Bro. as our only legacy. We have them yet—She the Girl & I the Boy & they are smart industrious children & we intend to do the best we can for them. Five weeks ago to day, Bro William sent for Dr Reeves & myself & Sister to go to see him as he was very sick. He lived about 35 [miles] north of us in the upper edge of Freestone Co, We reached his Residence next morning, but Oh! My God—only to find him cold cold in Death. He was taken on Wednesday before with something like Pneumonia which awakened afresh his old Asthmetic affections & his disolution was rapid & poor poor fellow he died—died died before he had the least warning or expectation of Death's near approach—without a relative near him save his poor wife & 2 little children and my little Daughter Lily, who was boarding at his House. Dr. Reeves & I reached his House 2 hours after he expired and Oh the heart rending cry of his weeping wife & my little Daughter when they met us exclaiming "Too late!—too late! If you could have come sooner you might have saved him." It appeared he had but little done for him although two Physicians were in constant attendance. The scene and my feelings were altogether beyond my powers of description. He was burried On Tuesday Evening with Masonic honors and thus another great and good man has fallen, leaving a widow and 2 children with many relatives & friends to mourn his loss. On my return home on the following day I found news of the untimely death of a little child of my wife's sister Mrs. Renfroe of Sandersville Ga. and the other day when the *Sandersville Herald* of the 16th May reached us—what should first meet our eyes on opening it but the death of that most excellent Christian and [blot] lady (Mrs Renfroe) herself—an account of whose [blot] you no doubt have seen before this time. This was my wife's favorite sister and when we read the sad sad news it did seem like it was more than we could bear & it appears like my poor wife can never become reconciled to her death. She was one of the best women that ever lived—and I have always loved worshipped and Idolized her—Just like I always have you—Great God—what evil god is holding sway over old Washington County? Nothing but Death after Death & scores of Deaths in every week's news we get from there. Truly they are fast passing away. We have had no letters since Mrs Renfroe's death—but are looking for the sad tidings with all the particulars on Tuesday next.

And Bobbie is married, is a Father and yourself a Grandmother? How odd this seems to me—for but yesterday as it were Bobbie was but a boy and only just the other day my Sister Lizzie was but a young mother with only two little Babes—Bobbie and Trudie. "Time is winning us away—To our Eternal home"—And John West and Sallie are at Americus and still working by the Rule of Multiplication! Ed & Mattie are still at Thomas Ville I guess though you omitted to tell me as much. Well Dear Sister you can scarcely imagine how grateful I am to hear from you all once more and I naturally infer you all are doing very well in this world. You promised me a long letter next time & you must tell me every thing—what all of you are doing—all about Uncle Joel, Aunt Win, Sister Tempa, Uncle Billie's folks and all their children are doing. Is Temp & Bell Davis and Billie married—How old does Aunt Win look now—Does Mr Hardwick begin to look old—how is it with your precious self? Oh! How delighted I would be to place my foot on Old Washington County soil once again and be with you all once more. Remember me tenderly and affectionately to all without distinction and never my Dear Sister for a moment doubt the earnestness and never ending constancy of my true affection and tender feeling for you—No—nothing cold in my breast—I am now as ever I have been—& I beg you to believe me when I tell you so.

Where does Till Davis live & how many children has she? Has sister Tempa [wife of Thomas Davis] ever married again—where is Lawson, Charles & Billie Davis & what are they driving at.

I will conclude my checkered letter on this page by telling you I have almost entirely quit the practice of Law & am devoting my attention to farming simply. This seems to suit my feelings more and agrees with my Temperament better. Crops are elegant here notwithstanding the late cold & Dry March & April, May has been too wet—a rare occurrence here—Corn is tassling out with some silks, cotton full of forms & knee high—gardens splendid and vegetables of all kinds in abundance—Beets squashs Cabbage—Beans Peas Irish potatoes etc. & Poultry Butter & Eggs by the bushel—I have 4 cows in my Pen—from which we get 8 gallons milk pr day—Buff[?] is fine & fat—Our small game & fish are plentiful—Health perfect—No sickness—No Deaths here since winter—Fruit all killed by the heavy freeze last of March & again the 9th April—Corn planted since then is now taller than a man, & Tassling out, June 2nd Rain yesterday & to day too wet for farm-work, & grass growing distressingly. Heavy provision crop doubtless secure already, so imigrants need fear nothing, but may come along. Our best love to you all. Write—Do write Dear Sister immediately. Tell Bobbie to write—Tell me all.

Your unworthy Bro-
J R Hardison

Mary Fletcher (Northington) Hardison to Her Mother s

Personville Texas
July 8th 1873

Mrs. M. R. Northington,
My Dear Mother.

I received your long kind sad letter telling us all of the particulars of our sweet precious Lizzie's sickness & death some weeks ago, but as I had just written to you a few days before, I did not think it worth while to respond immediately. Your dear letter was a good one indeed & I was glad to receive it! But Oh! it hurt me so much to know our dear Lizzie suffered so much. I am afraid she neglected herself on account of her little ones, perhaps if she had taken remmedies in time she would have cured her throat & mouth. But it will do no good to speak of that now. She is gone, & it grieves me so much, it appears like I cant get over it, I never knew what trouble was before. Dear Dear Lizzie was always good, yes good from a child. I have often looked at her and wished I was as mild & good as she was. The Capt. has often said she was a model of a woman, he said he loved her just as dearly as his own sister. I wish I lived near enough to help you with the sweet little ones. I would love to work for them, just as I would for my own. Bless their sweet little lives. May Heavens richest Blessings ever rest on them. Ma I am still up, but clumsy & sometimes very feable. I will be confined sometime about the 12 or 15th of August. you know I dread it, I wish you could be with me, but I know that is impossible. Grand-Ma Bird will stay with me. She is like a mother to me. I dont know who would attend to my babies if she was gone. She is as mild and pleasant as a summer's day. Ma tell me if you received my letter I wrote to you some weeks ago, asking you about our dear Lizzie's death. Lillie has returned from school and is larger than I am, she is a great help to me, takes all the milking and nearly all the cooking off my hands. I just cook when I feel like it. Lillie is a good girl treats me well. She is a great comfort to me, & is devoted to my two little ones, loves them like herself. Amelia is one of the smartest children to her age I ever saw, she is a heap of help to me, and just as affectionate as she can be. Sissie has grown to be very pretty, and is very bright, loves her Papa better than every body else. The Capt thinks they are the prettiest little things under the sun. And they are all we could desire in children. Ma I want you to write as often as you can, we do love to get your good letters. Tell Pa & the Boys & Sister Annie to write. Ma pray for me, that I may get through with my confinement safely. We received a letter from Bro Haynes today, the first since Sister Lizzies death, it was truly a sad one too. Poor Haynes, I feel so sorry for him in his lonely condition. Ma I want you to save the things for me that Sister Lizzie made for my children, she wrote to me about them before her death, said she was going to save them & send them. She spoke of all she had made, in particular Amelia's apron, she said it was the prettiest she ever made. I want them because she was so anxious for me to have them. I want them for keepsakes for my little ones to look at, and know that Aunt Lizzie's precious fingers made them, they shall just keep them to look at. Ma please write soon. Give my love to Pa & all the children and accept the same your dear self.

Your affectionate daughter
Mary F Hardison

John Randolph Hardison to Mary's Parents s

Person Ville Texas
August 5th 1873

Dear Father & Mother

I am again priviliged to write to you and to tell you the glad news that My Dear Fletcher has another sweet little Babe—the prettiest little Doll you ever looked at, & just as good as it can be, with black hair deep blue eyes & skin as purely white as alabaster, our other dear chidren are pretty enough but this one we think just a little excells them all in beauty & how very small it is! —and looks like it was 2 or 3 months old, it is so cheerful & has such good use of its sweet little self, but la-me here I am half way down the page & have not told you what it is yet—How cruel you will judge me to be to have written this much and still kept back that important Item?—Well now for it. It is—is—well it is another Boy? just like all the others—and how proud we are of it. All the children from Lillie down are delighted—and little Sissie seems more delighted and loves it better than them all. Some 25 or 30 of the Neighbor Ladies have been in to see us already and every body treats us with the utmost kindness and attention. We lack for nothing—Our sweet Babe was born on Monday morning the 28th of July at half past 2. 0. clock—Fletcher suffered less than ever before only an hour or two & that quite light—she did not have time to get frightened before all was over, & she is now setting up & walking about the room—nearly well and by far the sweetest & handsomest woman in Texas. Good old Grand Ma Byrd is with us again & just as good to us as an Angel from Heaven could be. Fletcher has named her Babe for Grand ma Byrd & for Dr Glass, her Physician with all her children—here is the name "Annie Glass"—how do you like it? Annie is also for Sister Annie in Ga.

Well Dear Parents, we are all well and doing well—abundant provision crops are already secure & the cotton never looked better at this season. There has been too much rain at times but the crops have stood the excess of wet very well & an abundance of every thing will be made in this entire section of our State. I have the best crop I ever had in Texas—am sooing [sowing] fodder now. It has been very healthy all this year up to a short time back when, owing to too much rain we think, sickness began to make its appearance in some families & now I hear of a good many cases of Billious fever in the country & our Doctors have some practice.

We had a letter today from Bro Haynes stating all were well which good news we were glad to hear. I deeply sympathize with Haynes in his sore affliction. You must not expect a long letter from me to night for it is now quite late & I have just gotton in from the fodder field an hour since dark, tooke a bite of supper & sit down to scribble this poor thing of a letter to you knowing you were anxious to hear from us about now, would have written last week but our mail failed to come through. To night I am quite tired & my hands are very sore from pulling fodder 3 or 4 days. Haynes told us that you & the Boys had a good crop this year & we are glad indeed to hear this for we know you all have worked hard and we are thankful that Providence has smiled upon your efforts.

Well Dear Parents, If I am not I ought to be the happiest man in the world, for I have the best wife, the healthiest children, a host of good friends all around me, a good country & excellent health myself & a plenty to live on. We hope you both will favor us again before long with another one of your good prayerful letters for we are at all times grateful to you for such unmistakable testimonials of your lasting affection & tender regard for us. We beg to be remembered affectionately to all the family without distinction. Good night.

Your Unworthy Son
J R Hardison

XIV. FAMILY LIFE IN TEXAS DURING RECONSTRUCTION

Mary Fletcher (Northington) Hardison to Her Parents s

Personville Texas Nov 24th 1873

Mr & Mrs Jas F Northington:
My Dear Parents.

   I will try and write you some kind of a letter. I am weak, and dont feel much like writing. I have been very sick indeed since I wrote to any of you last. I will tell you something of my sickness first. I was taken first with a very sore throat; in a day or two afterwards I was taken with a bad cough and severe soreness all through my body, I was then confined to my bed several days, and the soreness after severe treatment gave way a little; but the cough grew worse and worse untill I was completely prostrated, and in that feeble state I was taken with Pleurisy, then I thought death would certainly be the result. I can never tell you dear parents what I suffered, either in body or mind. I did pray that I might not leave my poor little girls here among strangers with no dear Grandmother or kind Aunt to look after the dear little infant's wants. It was indeed a bad time with me. Well I recovered from the Pleurisey, but still the awful cough continued for several weeks, and I discharged as much from my lungs as any one with consumption, and I do believe I [page stained and torn] if I had not heard of the Celebrated "California Vinegar Bitters", I am convinced it saved my life, for the Capt got every thing that could be had and nothing done any good so we could see, untill we got the Bitters. In a week my cough began to give way, I then began to mend and in two weeks was able to go in the dining room. Now my cough is about well, and I can do a little work. But I suffered more since the first of Sept. than I ever did in all my sickness put together, since I left you in 1866. My dear little ones liked to have went naked, for Grandma Bird was taken down pretty soon after I was with a kind of rheumatism in her back, so I had no help atall. But thank the dear Lord I am again up and able to work a little. But wont begin to ever get up with my work. I need quilting done, but that will have to go undone. I wont be able to quilt any this winter. Ma I thought of you and Dr Palmer many times during my long illness, and wished you by my bedside, but fate it seems has ordered it otherwise, and we must try and submit to our fate without murmuring, but Oh! it seems so hard to be so far from you all when I am so sick and low. I tried to get the Capt to write, but he said he could not give you so much pain, he said it would be more than you could bear to tell you my situation when I was so low. I thought I had the consumption and others thought so too. I pray I may never have another cough like it. My Babe was sick for three weeks before I was taken down, she had a bad cough also, but not as severe as mine. I took cold siting up with her. She is now well and as plump as a little chick. All the family are well & looking well, except myself, and I trust soon to be able to do my work & look once more like myself. Lillie was my constant nurse during my illness, for the Capt was oblige to attend to some work, and after laboring hard all day he had to rest some at night, so Lillie was constantly with me day and night, when she had to sleep she would fall down on my bed and sleep. So about the time I began to mend, she was taken with a cough like mine, but she was so healthy and stout she did not give way under it, like I did, but it made her feeble and reduced her in flesh too. Lillie was just as kind to me as she could be and done all she knew how to do, and I appreciated it too, and the Capt's kind nursing and kindness & trouble for me was all appreciated, but Ma no one can take your dear place and fill it. And then I had a young babe, and it needed tender treatment, and Lillie and the Capt was the chance [?] to attend to her little wants.

I could write pages and then not tell all, but it would do no good, and so I had better quit. Sis Nan has never offered to sew a stich for me or my little ones, or either of her girls (they are both grown and married) and they have one of these fine splendid sewing machines like sister Lizzie's was. I do think hard of them. I cant help it. But I pray that the good Lord may bless me with perfect health once more and I will try by his help to live right, and I hope to show them that I can live without their assistance. Carrie the oldest daughter lived in sight of us, and never did she put her foot inside of my house to see me while I was sick. But when I got up and went to work, she came to get me to make her a fine Pin cushion on a paper box (like Missouri had one) and wanted me to cut some patterns also. I told her I could cut the Patterns, but I had too much work to do for my little ones to make a fine cushion. I did not think it was my duty to do it, and neglect my poor little children. Lillie is a poor hand with a needle, for she had a bonefellon on her right thumb that took out the bone, and of course that made a bad thumb for sewing. She seldom ever sews any.

Well I dont want to weary you reading my sad stories so I will talk of something else. How is my dear Lizzies sweet little ones getting along? Oh! Ma you dont know how lonely I feel away off here when I get to thinking and grieving over the loss of our darling Lizzie, sometimes it does appear like

I cannot feel right any more, that is feel like I could ever enjoy the world again, as I once did. I did love her so dearly, and I did appreciate sister Lizzie's virtues so highly, and the Capt loved her like his own sister, he says she was one [of] the noblest women he ever knew. I try to live like her, and pray that I may die like her. Ma & Pa you have all with you this year, but me I woul[d] like to share some of your company too. But it seems there is but little hopes of that. Some of you might come to see me if you would. We spent all we made clear in three years, to go to see you all, and I dont regret it. I only regret one thing that is, I did not go last winter again, then I could have seen my precious Lizzie once more & her sweet little Foster, and I could have shown her two of my dear children. Now Marcellous I want you & Haynes to fix up and come out any how. I know Ma wont let Capers come yet, but may-be she will let you come with Haynes. Jimmie is so much attached to home I have but little hopes of his ever coming, he never as much as speakes of such a thing in one of his letters. Now Marcellous we want you to come, as it is a long route to come, and some what dangerous, we would be glad you could have company, we are more than anxious for you to come. I am nearly crazy to see you all. Tell Haynes when you see him the Capt says if he will come, he can make an independant fortune at Mexia, a little city just building up, 16 miles above us, it is where we
[Remainder of letter missing.]

Amelia (Fisher) Northington to Mary Fletcher (Northington) Hardison and Her Familys

Oconee Jan the 20, 1874

Dear Children once more I will try to write you a letter, it has been some time since I attempted to write one, for I have so meny things to get along that I can hardly ever feel like writing, it is not because I donte think enough of you, for I can assure you that you are never forgotton by me. I was very sorry indeed to heare of your sickness, I would gladly be with you in all your sickness and do all I could for you if it was so that I could, our separation gives me as much trouble as it does you, but I comforte my self in this way, our seperation wonte be long at beste, life with us all will soon pass by, the moste important thing with us should be to live so that we may meete in the good worlde to parte no more, that should be our greate object in life, and I can tell you dear Children that is my greateste concerne, to try to live write. I am determin by the grace of the good Lorde, and I am happy to say I often look foward to the time when I shall be releaste from the toils and sorrows of earth. Dear Children live for God, there is nothing like living for God and heaven, let the world and its affairs go as they may, live write dear Children, take an intruste in your prayers that as I go down the steepe of time that my hopes may be charde [shared?] and my prospects britened for the good Worlde and I can assure you all you have all the aide my feeble prayers can afforde you day by day. It dose my sole good to know I can pray for my loved ones, my minde often follars them through life in to the good worlde whare parting will be no more.

I will quit this subject though I had rather talk on this subject and write on it then any thing else. The little trancient news that is passing I leave for the Children to write. We are all in comon health at this time. Hope this will finde you all quite well. Many kinde thankes to dear Lillie for her kindness to you and your little ones. I pray that the good Lorde may bless her through life and give her heaven in the ende. Haynes was with us last sunday he and his children are well. Bobbie will boarde with us this yieare and go to Schooll. There is a Camelite Preacher teaching School at Antioch Church by the name of Waddel, a very fine teacher. Haynes is boarding this yieare with his brother in law Weden. When Haynes comes down it allwais makes me feele as bad as I can to see him with his little Motherless Children and then see him go off alone. I cant tell you how bad I feele. I will never get over my dear Lizzies death. I pray that I may not out live eny more of my dear Children. My dear Children you donte know what a greate comforte [it] woulde be to us if you could live neare us but I suppose the Capt thinks you would be more liable to die here then in Texes. I donte thinke soe. We are liable to die any whare, that is a good way to put you off but I will be by you as I am by the Children here abou[t] going there. I all wais tell them to do what they think beste for the Worlde is before them and I am nearly done with it. There fore you must do what you think will be for your good. We have commenced worke for another yeare, the Boys are all at home. We have no negroes this yiear except the old man and his wife that was here when you ware here. I will bring my letter to a close as Indiana wants to write some, please write as often as you can for it is a greate comforte to heare from you all, kiss all the Children for me and press your s[w]eete little babes to your bosom for me. I love your darling Children with all my hearte.

My love to you all your devoted
Mother M. Northington

John Randolph Hardison to Haynes Renfroe s

Groesbeck   Limestone Co Texas
26th Feby 1874

My Dear Haynes

After an unaccountable and inexcusable delay I once more find myself seated for the purpose of writing you, I scarcely know what, until I get further along with my letter.

To attempt to explain the many reasons for my long silence would be utterly futile, hence I will not presume to do so, but content myself with assuring you that since the astounding truth of your sad bereavement and irreparable loss was announced to me & I forced to believe it, I have been in too much distress—my heart has been too full of sorrow for you and your orphaned babes to permit me to attempt even to write you. And now, having gathered myself up sufficiently to attempt to commune with you and while I would be the last one to open afresh in your bosom a wound which time and the consoling influences of a Holy Religion had perhaps partially healed or made bearable at least, yet I would beg even now to assure you of my deep-lasting-heart felt sympathy, for scarcely a day has passed since the news of Dear Lizzie's untimely and lamented death brought grief and sorrow, Oh how deep! to our far distant household that I have not wept grieved and prayed for you and your dear children.

Turning now to a brighter view of the sad picture I rejoice that you can rejoice in the reflection that you have a companion in Heaven waiting your arrival, that you are blessed with the best of grandmothers to care for your babes and to train them up in the way they should go. I rejoice with you that you have the happy influences of the Religion of our Lord & Savior to sustain you in your sorrowful & lonely pilgramage from Earth to Heaven. Many many things come up before me about which I would like to write but I am away from home & have been now for 3 days so I will not write much more now. I have sold out at Person Ville for $700.00, made 9 bales Cotton last year & have just got moved to a new place I have leased, a rich farm or as much of it as I want for as many years as I may want it & I never expect to move again until I move home again. I sold out because my place was too small. My folks were all well when I left them. I would be glad to hear from you all once more. How & what is Tom Mims doing now & what is he doing & where is he this year. Fletcher was badly upset because no one of the boys would come to see us. Haynes treat me better than I have you and write me all the news. Our best love to your dear children, to Pa & Ma and all the family.

Your Unworthy Bro J R Hardison
Cotton Gin   Freestone Co
Care Maj. Bean

John Randolph Hardison to Mary's Parents s

At Home   Freestone Co Texas
June 22nd 1874

Dear Father & Mother

    After an unpardonable delay I will join Fletcher in writing you some thing in the shape of a letter. I will attempt to offer no apology for my long silence for that would only be adding insult to injury. A multiplicity of business affairs and trouble & disappointment in our expectations with regard to our domestic matters often cause us to neglect our dearest friends but I can assure you that you are by no means forgotton by us, for we think and talk about you all every day of our lives. Ma's last letter of the first of May together with one from Hattie in the same Envelope did not reach us until last week. It had no doubt lain in the office at Cotton Gin several days, this Letter of Ma's fired up Fletcher to a high degree, and by then she was done reading it amid tears & sighs she had resolved to go home in November, let come what would. The news of Ma's feeble health, her conclusion that she would never live to see Fletcher & her children was too much for Fletcher, and armed her at once for the undertaking the journey alone in case she finds no one going that way when she is ready to start. The trip can now be performed all the way by Rail Road via Memphis Atlanta etc and in about three days and nights. I am perfectly willing for her to go and stay 12 months or longer if she wishes to and I will take great pains in fitting her out so that she can perform the journey with no great deal of ill-convenience. I would be more than delighted to [go] with her and stay a long time with you all, but the expenses would be too great and time too long for me to lose from my business at this particular time as fortune as to money affairs has been a little hard on me of late. My Bro-in law old Dr Reeves speaks of going over to Ga. & says if he concludes to go he will take great pleasure in seeing Fletcher & the children safely to your Door. He is the best friend I ever had & I think more of him to day than I do of any man in Texas.

XIV. FAMILY LIFE IN TEXAS DURING RECONSTRUCTION

Well there is no general news here worth your attention, save that the health and crops are good generally, and this is assuredly a great blessing to any people. We have no sickness this year save tooth ache with Fletcher & occasional chills with the children & they now are as fat and rosy as they well can be. I was very much disheartened about my crop up to last Thursday. In the first place I had to build and move over here and did not get to work in the farm untill after the 1st of March. It then began to rain in great floods which continued until the last of April. I got my Corn planted the 2nd time the last of April, after the last great rain had fallen, which left our lands in a miserably beaten & sobbed condition, & only for the great fertility of the soil the Corn could not have grown but little and as it was it grew but slowly & was only about waist & shoulder high up to last Thursday when we were visited by a gentle wetting rain which was repeated the next day, & now Monday it is as high as I can reach in many places & about as promising as I could ask for. I shall make an abundance with another rain about the time it is silked out. I got my Cotton planted on the 7th of May, a part came up & a part failed, until the last of May when a light shower brought it all came up. My oldest is now knee high & higher & my youngest—only 22 days old is now half leg high—the oldest well formed—full of branches young blooms & squares and all of it as good as it can be for young cotton. I shall make as much as I can possibly gather if no disaster befalls it in future. I have a fine crop of Potatoes also & they are growing rapidly—you know I always go in for "taters."

You can't imagine how much better I feel since the good rains have fallen, I am now laying by my Corn at the rate of 5 acres per day and will have finished—planting my Corn Crops—plowing 3 times & laying by all within 2 months or 60 days from the moment the first seed was dropped in the ground. I have been over my entire crop once every 2 weeks since planting. I have in 27 acres. Enough of this. We truly hope this will find all of you in good health and doing well. We are under lasting obligations to you for your many tender expressions and fervent prayers in our behalf—& we trust they are not altogether in vain. Remember us to all affectionately and without distinction. I am due the boys letters and will write to them as I can. I wrote to Haynes the first of March and afterwards sent him a Texas paper for 12 months. I will write more next time.

As ever yours etc
J R H

Mary Fletcher (Northington) Hardison to Indiana Northington⁵

[Salutation, date, and first page or pages are missing, but the contents indicate the letter was written to Indiana in 1874 after the family's move to Freestone County.]

I wish you could come and spend a year with me. Come out next year and stay a year if we all live. I hope we will be better situated by that time, & be able to treat you well. Now come, say cant you?

The Capt says he intends to make 12 bales of cotton this year if he keeps his health, and corn enough to do him. The Capt has to work very hard, for we have a large family and all girles, except little Jimmie, and he is too small to do much. The Capt has fine health. I use all the economy I can, so as to get along.

When you answer this letter. Direct yours to Cotton-Gin Frestone County Texas, in the Care of Maj Wm Bean, the old maj sends for his mail regular and is well known there, and we will by that means get ours regular also. Now I will close for this time, hoping to hear from you soon, and try and prevail upon the rest to write also. Tell Marcellous I hope he will make his promise good by fulfilling it some day. The little children talked a great deal about Uncle Marcellous coming to Texas, but poor little things were sadly disappointed. Tell Pa & Ma to write when convenient. Give our love to all and accept the same your dear self. Is Missouri with you all yet? If so tell her to write too. I love to get her long letters, they are always interesting. Give our love to Her & Bro Tom & the children & Kiss them for me. Kiss Sister Lizzies sweet children too. Tell them aunt Mary loves them dearly. Be kind to them, dear sister and raise them right. Give our love to Bro Haynes, I will write to him soon. Please write soon dear Indiana.

I remain your devoted sister,
Mary F. Hardison.

John Randolph Hardison to the Northington Family⁵

At Home Texas
Wednesday Night Nov 11th [18]74

Dear Father & Mother
Brother & Sisters

Your surprise at securing another letter from me, should this ever reach you, cannot surprise my own astonishment at finding myself attempting to write you again after such a protracted [silence], but true it is the pleasure I always realize in letter writing to friends has at last over balanced the antipathy I have always had to settle myself down to the starting point. In other words "Once I get at it I love it so well I never know when to quit" as you may be able to testify ere you have done reading what may be scribbled out on these rumpled pages ere my pen is stayed. As my thoughts may flow so shall I write, & leave you to do the correcting as you read for above all things I like an easy flowing letter, when addressed to friends.

You see from my heading that this is night and finds me a little lonesome for the good reason that My Dear Fletcher, Lily & the 3 little children have all gone off on a visit since monday leaving me & Winnie & Jimmie my little Bro, to make the best we could of things at home. They 2 have gone to bed & I am left all alone scribbling away to you. I shall go after my runaways in the morning for I know they are becoming as anxious to get back home as I am to have them here. Fletcher had a good deal of sewing to do, & had broken her Machine & besides wanted to see some of her old neighbors over at Person Ville, hence her visit. We all are in good health now & have been for a long time with the exception of sore eyes, whooping cough & one little spell of continued fever which attacked little Nannie Misouri, after she had had the cough for a long time, & which was very bad for 9 days. She is now as fat & plump as ever, while all have gotton along with the cough surprisingly well, in fact it has hurt them but little & is now abating. Fletcher & I both had Nurses cough which troubled us a good deal while it lasted, we have all had sore eyes from which we suffer a great deal. I had 2 attacks, & now my eyes are very dim & sight weak, this is the first letter I have attempted to write in months.

Well this has been a remarkable year in many respects, remarkably healthy in the first place, remarkable wet & dry & now remarkably warm for the season. In the Spring we were drowned out which was followed by a hot dry Summer which lasted uninteruptedly until Sep. 1st, we then had a good season for the time being & no more rain up to the present time, & now it is as warm as summer & as dry as it has been at any time this year. On the morning of the first day of this month we had a dry frost with a little ice, which is all the cool weather we have had this fall. It has been cloudy for 8 or 9 days past but no rain since september. We look for a cold snap when the change does come. From the above statement of things you can guess we have made poor crops, yes very poor in deed. I planted for 12 bales of cotton & only gathered four (4) with barely enough corn to make out with by sowing small grain. Though I saved about 4000 lbs of good fodder which will help out a great deal—& strange to say I made 100 bushels of Potatoes which no one else has done any where in my knowledge. We have an abundance of Flour at only $7.00 per bbl which is lower than it has been here for years. Farmers generally are sowing largely of Wheat and other small grain this fall. Pork will be scarce here. The mast which was plentiful has been almost entirely destroyed by what we call the mast bug & there is no corn to fatten Hogs on. A great deal of beef will be killed & baconed up for winter & spring use. I have 10 large hogs which are now pretty fair pork on the mast & I thought I would pin them up & feed them a little corn so as to make them do me with some beef which I shall put up as soon as the weather turns cool.

(This to the boys) The game season has set in with us & I have had my share of the sport and the spoils thus far. I have killed one Deer 5 Turkeys & 30 Ducks up to today. Can any of you beat this, Boys? I didn't mention all the features which has tended to make this a remarkable year with us. In a religious point of view it has like wise been remarkable—wonderful revivals have occurred on every hand, Methodists Baptists & even Hard Shells have all enjoyed refreshing seasons—56 were immerced at one time by the Missionaries, 27 at another & Dozens at various other times & from 30 to 125 were added to The Methodist Church at different times & places. The good old Hard Shell Church (we have but one among us) got ten or twelve new members during the year or rather the meeting season, so you see we must have had rousing times to have gotton the whole mass of people so thoroughly stirred up on the subject of Religion. But the Hard Shells say "a bad crop year always for a great religious revival"—any how I hope every body was in earnest & that lasting good was done.

You have doubtless ere this received Fletcher's last letter stating that it was a doubtful case about her getting off on her intended visit to Ga this fall & no one regrets her inability to go more than I do for although her long absence from home would prove a sore trial to me yet I was anxious for her to go on account of her Dear Old Parents.

[Remainder of letter missing.]

*Mary Fletcher (Northington) Hardison to Her Father*s

Fre[e]stone Co Texas Jan 2nd 1875

My Dear Father,

I am ruined—ruined forever, Oh! my dear husband is no more, he died 30th of Dec was sick but three days & 4 nights, I never saw any one suffer like he did. I was taken sick & very sick first a week before he was, and was not able to sit up or do any thing for him, Pa I have lost one of the best men that ever was, he was all kindness & love. O I am hea[r]t-broken, it looks like grief will wear me out. Pa I am too weak to write but a few lines, I am suffering now with a dreadful cough. Pa I want to come home, cant you send some one to help me there. I want to go just as soon as I am able to travel. If the boys dont want to undertake the trip, try & get Haynes to come, now dear Pa send someone for I dont feel like I can ever make it alone & send them just as soon as possible, for it looks like it will almost take my life to stay here. O! I never never knew what trouble was till now Pa send some one if you can. If you cant I wont think hard of you for I know you will do the best you can.

Pray for me & my little ones. I must quit let me here from you soon.

Your poor daughter
Mary F Hardison

*Mary Fletcher (Northington) Hardison to Her Mother*s

Personville Texas Jan 20th 1875

Dear Mother,

I have just recieved your good kind letter, and was glad in deed to hear from you all, was sorry to hear of Missouri's ill health, but hope ere this she is much better. Tell her, she is not alone with her trouble, for mine is allmost more than I can bear [page stained] out live my trouble. The Capt was truly a good kind & affectionate husband, always done all in his power to make me happy. Oh! Ma it is so hard to give him up, it does seam like it will almost take my life. Ma I cant manage to get along here, and can I come home? write & let me know as soon as you can. If I can, I will try & wind up my little affairs as soon as possible & go home. My health is improving slowly, my dear little children are all well. I guess you have received the letter I wrote you telling you of the Capt's death & my severe sickness, before now. I wrote the day after he was buried. Ma pray for me that I may have grace & strength to bear my troubles. I dont know when I will be able to get off. I wrote to Pa to send for me, but if my health becomes good, perhaps I can make it alone. I hope to be with you all as soon as possible.

Lillie has written to Mrs Hardwick to know if she wants her & Winnie to come & live with her, she is their mother's sister. If she wants them, they will go with me, if not they will stay here. I hope she will take them, for I hate to leave them here to be imposed on by their kinfolks here.

Well Ma I will close for I dont feel like writing.

Write soon,
Your devoted daughter
Mary F. H.

Edwin T. Davis to Lilly and Winnifred Hardison c

Thomasville, Geo.   Feb-y 3d, 1875.

My Dear Little Nieces,

A few days ago your Aunt Lizzie wrote me the very sad news of your dear Father's death. Since then she has sent me Lilly's letter, which has added to my sorrow. Yes, dear Children, God has grievously afflicted you, your little Sisters, your Ma, and us! I know it seems to you that your troubles are greater than you can bear. Your Father was a true gentleman, a kind-hearted, generous, noble man, and I mourn his death almost as [if] he were my own Brother. You nor we must not complain at the providences and dispensations of a great and just God. He is too wise to ere and too good to do wrong. Though we can not understand His ways. He has smitten us for some wise purpose. Let us love and trust Him, and some day in the coming years He will take us to Himself far beyond the Stars, where we fondly hope your sweet, sweet Mother and dear Father are for ever rejoicing in His presence!

Your Mother! Ah! You can never know how true, pure and amiable she was! She loved your Uncle Ed so tenderly, and was always so prompt and ready to provide for him, and assist and encourage him in his struggles in early life. I returned an ardent and devoted affection, and rejoice to honor her memory, and recall her goodness and love. Your Father too was ever prompt to assist and encourage me in every way he could. Especially do I gratefully recall his numerous deeds of kindness and generosity when we served near together as soldiers in the Confederate Army, during the memorable campaigns in the West.

Your troubles and sorrows are very great, but you must bear them with as much patience and fortitude as you can. It will not always be a night of gloom and sadness: Light and sunshine will fall across your pathways and hope and happiness will spring in your young and tender hearts. God has promised His special care for the Widow and Orphan. Love Him and give him your hearts while you are young, and you will never be alone in the World. Be cheerful and hopeful. You are not forgotten, though you are so far away from your Mother's relatives and friends. Your Aunt Liz & Uncle Bill, Aunt Sallie & Uncle John, Uncle Ed & Aunt Mattie sympathize with you very deeply, and are taking necessary steps to have you brought back to them, where they can give you comfortable, happy Homes, and assist in raising you up to be useful, smart and good women. Show this to your Ma, and give her assurance of my kindest feelings and sympathy. It is not necessary for you to ask her not to leave you in Texas. I know she will not do it. That is no place for you. We want you here, and must and will have you. You and your Ma must keep us informed as to your condition and wants, and when you are ready to start to Georgia, so that we may send money to bear your expenses. I sent Lilly's letter to your Aunt Sallie. She has written to you, and your Aunt Lizzie has already done likewise. Your Aunt Mattie, and little cousin Mattie join Uncle Ed in much love and many kisses to you both. May Heaven preserve and bless you!

Your loving & affectionate Uncle,
E. T. Davis

෴ ෴

John's death was indeed a calamity, for it meant the break-up of the household which included the two daughters from his first marriage, his half-brother Jimmie, and his and Mary's three daughters. The cause of his sudden death is not given in Mary's letters nor known by his descendants. According to recollections of John's eldest daughter, Lilly, who was sixteen years old at the time the family left Texas, both John and his father, Seth, were buried in the cemetery of Lost Prairie Church, a few miles from Personville in Limestone County. As noted previously, there are in that cemetery two unmarked adult size mounds between the markers for members of the family of Seth's youngest son, James Harvey Hardison, and members of the William J. Reeves family. They are probably the burial sites of John and Seth.

With John's death, five of the six adult children who had accompanied Seth Hardison from Florida to Texas were deceased. Only daughter Nancy (Hardison) Reeves was left, along with the young daughter and son, Lula and James, who had been born to Seth's Texas marriages of the 1860s. The surviving males who carried on the Hardison name for Seth's branch of the family were James and the two sons of William L. and Josephine (Elkins) Hardison, William and Alva. With his large family of twelve children, James left a number of Hardisons to carry on the family name in Limestone and surrounding counties and elsewhere in Texas.

Mary had wished throughout her years in Texas to return to Georgia, but she had envisioned a move with her husband. Instead she left as a grief-stricken and almost destitute widow with three small children. Fortunately the Davis family was eager to have Lilly and Winnifred return to Georgia and they provided homes for them. Mary expressed regret in having to leave John's half-brother James [Jimmie] in Texas and his descendants have stated that he had a harsh childhood, as he was abandoned by Seth's last wife and passed around to various relatives. Mary's letters of the years after her return to Georgia indicate that she realized little or nothing from the small amount of property the family owned in Texas. She supported herself and her daughters by teaching and was aided by the Northingtons.

The brief nine years of John and Mary's marriage, while marred by disappointments in their material expectations and deaths among their kinsmen, were characterized by mutual affection and joy in their family life. Mary's feelings about those years are summed up by her remark in her letter of April 6, 1882 to her step-daughter Winnie, "I often think of Texas and sigh over the precious hours, that form some of the most pleasant 'Reminiscences' of my life."

THE ODYSSEY

⁕ Part 4 ⁕

Georgia
1875-1889

XV

Home to Georgia
Washington County, 1875-1889

When Mary Northington Hardison left her home in Washington County, Georgia as a bride in January, 1866, the county was struggling to recover from the destruction visited upon it by Sherman's army at the end of the Civil War. By the time she returned as a widow almost ten years later, much of the damage had been remedied by repairs and rebuilding. The courthouse in Sandersville, which Sherman had ordered burned in 1864, had been rebuilt and the wrecked and burned depots and rails of the Central of Georgia Railroad had been restored. Farms and plantations had returned to operation and schools had reopened. However, the emotional scars from defeat and destruction and the loss of many young men remained, while the political, social, and economic changes wrought by the war and reconstruction permanently altered the way of life of both the black and white members of the population.

Mary's father and the other planters and farmers of Washington County, who had depended in large part on slave labor to help produce the cotton which was the basis for the county's economy, were unable to cultivate their former acreages. The struggles which both her father and her husband experienced in the decade following the

Bay Spring Ga Apl 7th 1882

Miss Winnie C. Hardison,

    Dear Sister,

I have decided to pen you a few lines to let you know how we all are. We are all well at present. I wrote to sister Lillie about a month ago, and directed it, to Turnville thinking that she was there but have not heard a word from her. I suppose she had gone to Davisboro. Mama has a very good school now. I remained home all last week to make me a dress, it is very pretty. What are you going to give me for a birthday present? Mrs. McBride & Dr. McB say they are going to give me a present. We are going to have a picnic sometime the first of May for the benefit of the children. Why dont you write to me, I have been looking for a letter for a long time, but never get one. We are all going a fishing at the mill pond next Saturday. Kiss little Lucy for me. You must come to see us. Well I must close for this time, write soon I am anxious to hear from you, when you write tell me how many April fools you got. Lillie and Annie sends their loves to you. Well I must close. Write soon.

        Amelia J. R. Hardison

Letter of Amelia Randolph Hardison to Her Half-Sister,
Winnifred Cornelia Hardison, April 7, 1882

Ryan Collection

war have been alluded to in the letters included in the preceding chapters. Deeds pertaining to the division of James F. Northington's land among his children after his death in 1893 seem to indicate that he retained ownership during his lifetime, but many holdings were broken up and sold in smaller parcels after the war.[1] During the antebellum period Washington County had had a higher ratio of small farmers relative to planters than the surrounding counties of central Georgia. In the decade of the 1860s the preponderance of small farms was heightened as the plantations of the county began to break up due to the emancipation of the slaves and other losses suffered by the planters. During that decade the number of farms in the county increased from 697 to 1,652 as both farmers and planters found themselves unable to cultivate their former holdings.[2] The smallest farms produced so little of the money crop that their owners were often in need and in debt. The decades following the war were hard years for both black and white citizens, as a new labor system was developed and many of each race became share-croppers and tenant farmers. Their plight was made worse by a major drought and the effects of two nation-wide financial crises, the Panic of 1873 and the Panic of 1893.

In the midst of these difficult times Mary returned to her mother and father with her three small daughters, Amelia, Nancy (Nannie or Sissie), and Annie. Her two step-daughters, Lilly and Winnifred, now ages sixteen and thirteen, were cared for by their mother's sisters and brother, Mary Elizabeth (Davis) Hardwick—Aunt Lizzie, Sarah (Davis) Sheffield—Aunt Sallie, and Edwin T. Davis. The Hardwicks were prosperous landowners in Washington County; Aunt Sallie's husband, John West Sheffield, was a successful merchant in Americus; and Uncle Edwin was a lawyer in Thomasvillle. At first Mary and her children lived with her parents on their farm in the Bay Spring community, a few miles from the village of Oconee, and then in a home built for her on her father's land.[3] As noted previously, Oconee had come into existence when its site in the southwestern portion of the county was chosen as Station Number Fourteen on the route of the Central of Georgia Railroad from Savannah to Macon in the 1840s. The railroad had literally put Oconee on the map and figuratively Washington County, as it tied the county to the markets the major towns of Georgia and the nation beyond.

Mary was fortunate in having a profession to which she could turn to augment the help given by her parents and brothers, Jimmie, Marcellus, and Capers. She had been a teacher before her marriage and she returned to the classroom in Bay Spring Academy, the school where she had taught before her marriage. Public education was minimal throughout Georgia's nineteenth century history, beginning with what were known as the "old field schools" in the ante-bellum era, one-room schools scattered throughout the county where poorly trained teachers taught the 3 R's a few months of the year. A number of private schools, usually called academies, were chartered in this era and they were attended by children whose families could afford the tuition. A number of the privately supported schools were associated with the churches of the county. One of the best of the academies was located in the town of Davisboro and probably John Hardison's first wife, Winnifred Davis, and other members of her family attended it. Since John had so many happy memories of Washington County, it is possible that he had been sent to school there while his family was living in Early County in the early 1840s.

In 1871 Georgia attempted to provide for a system of state-wide elementary schools, supported by specially designated tax revenue which was apportioned to the counties, but the schools were of poor quality and short terms geared to the agricultural seasons. The academies continued to flourish and provided the only high school level education until 1912, when state funds for high schools became available. The letters which Mary wrote after her return to Georgia indicate that she taught for several years in the Bay Spring Academy and also in the Bethesda Academy, probably associated with Bethesda Christian Church in the southwestern portion of the county. The school to which she sent her daughters, Antioch Academy, was established in 1868 in association with the Antioch Christian Church in Oconee. The property of John's uncle, William L. Hardison, was located near this church and gifts of land to the church were made by members of his family.[4] William, who died on March 15, 1870 at the age of seventy-one, and his family are buried near the church in a small private cemetery currently known as the Posey Family Cemetery.[5]

The school building for the Antioch Academy, which was under construction in 1867, was described by Dr. James M. Palmer, a prominent citizen of the area who was physician and friend to the Northingtons, in a letter to his daughter: "Framed house 30 by 20 feet with 10 glass windows. Will get it done in 10 days. Will have a stove to warm it. It stands about 40 or 50 steps from the church."[6] This was one of the numerous one-room school houses typical of the county and the nation in this period, when poor roads and little public transportation made it necessary to carry on daily life within the confines of the small rural communities in which most people lived.

The lives of Mary and her daughters and step-daughters are depicted in a small group of letters written from 1877 through 1882. They are a part of the two previously cited collections, the Cain Family Genealogical Collection and the Nancy Louise Brown Slaughter Collection, augmented by a few in the possession of Elizabeth Shreve Ryan. As with the previous letters, their source will be indicated by a small letter at the end of each heading—"c" for Cain, "s" for Slaughter, and "r" for Ryan. Half of the twelve letters were written by Mary to her step-daughter Winnie, with whom she seems to have maintained a close relationship. There are also a few other letters to Winnie, from her Uncle Edwin, her sister Lilly, her half-sister Amelia, and her fiance, George Washington Wood. The collection includes a letter to Mary from a friend in Texas, J. C. Morton, who was attempting to collect money owed to John Hardison at the time of his death, and another from a cousin, the Reverend William Fisher Robison, concerning the education of William's brother John. The Cain Collection includes a transcript by Winnie of the war-time entry in Mary's autograph book which her father John had made in January, 1864, and indicates that she copied it when she visited Mary in October, 1880.[7] Probably they had sat together and reminisced about John and their years with him in Texas. The letters indicate that Lilly and Winnie moved about among the homes of their Davis relatives and friends and family members in Washington County during the years covered by the correspondence, with Winnie marrying in 1882 at the age of twenty. The letters of 1879 speak of the death of their uncle Edwin Davis in that year.

Edwin T. Davis to Winnifred Cornelia Hardison c

Thomasville, Geo.
April 18th, 1877

My Dear Winnie:

I thank you for your kind and affectionate letter, received several days ago. I should have sent you an earlier answer, but for absence from Home and pressing professional engagements. And even yet I am hard pressed for time, and write you this letter in the Court House, while Court is in session and mouthy, saucy lawyers are jawing each other and the witnesses they are examining. I would postpone my letter to a time when I could write you a better and more interesting one but fear you might think that I do not appreciate your letters as fully as I should. You must not allow such an idea [to] disturb you for a moment. I have so many cases at this time, and so many things to engage and occupy my time, that I am often compelled to delay for a time answers to the letters of my dearest and best friends. I love you and Lilly very much indeed and am always deeply concerned in all that relates to your welfare and happiness.

I am very glad you were thoughtful enough to send me your Monthly Report—and you must continue to do this so that I may have the pleasure of noting the steady improvement and progress in your studies which I feel confident you will make. Your Report, with three exceptions, is an average good one. In Arithmetic it is unusually good, and shows you have a fine turn for Mathematics. Ninety (90) is a very fair average—but you must not be satisfied with less than 100, which is the mark of highest excellence.

Be thorough and perfect in all that you do or undertake.

Adopt this rule while you are young and follow it up closely through life. I would not like to appear as a critic of your teacher, but fear you have rather too many studies on hand. They are all important studies and probably you should take them up at some time or other, but I think it is bad policy for a student to be grappling with too many at the same time.

German, French, Latin & Chemistry are difficult and better suited for students who have been several years at school. Why are you not studying Grammar and English composition?—As you asked my advice in regard to your studies, let me urge you to pay good attention to spelling. Whenever you write a letter or composition, or anything else, you should be absolutely certain that every word in it is spelt correctly.

Keep a good Dictionary upon your writing Desk, and if you have any doubt at all about the correct spelling of any word consult your Dictionary. Then it is a most excellent practice for you to write your Letters or Compositions as carefully as you can, then correct the spelling, punctuation, and grammatical constructions and then write it all over once or twice. You will soon notice very material improvement, and it will learn you to be careful as to what you say, and the style in which you say it.

There are, my dear child, a good many things about your studies, and other matters equally or more important that I would like to advise you about, but can't well do so in this letter. I think I will see you in a few days, which will give me a much better opportunity than writing.

[Remainder of letter missing.]

Mary Fletcher (Northington) Hardison to Winnifred Cornelia Hardison c

Bay Spring Academy
April 30th 1877

Miss W. C. Hardison,
Dear Daughter,

I have been thinking for a long time of writing to you, but I have but little time to devote to my correspondents. I am teaching at the above named place again this year. I resumed the exercises of my school on the 12 of Feb last. I am quite busy at school through the week, and Saturdays I have very many little cares to look after and Sabbaths I have to attend church and Sabbath school, we have a good Sabbath school. So you will perceive at once my situation. I hope you are well and doing well. I received a letter from Texas a few days ago, from Mattie Rambo, she wrote a long interesting letter. Said Mrs Rogers (Mrs Gilbert that was) was dead, also Ellen Reeves old-man, (John Burtton) also Mrs James Morton. Mrs Morton died the 15 of Feb last. I also received a letter from Mrs Rambo; she told me Grandma Byrd's health was very bad; her son High is married again, he married "Symantha Mullins" I know you will be astonished at that marriage, for I was, High's friends were greatly astonished also. Your uncle Dr Reeves has moved to Freestone Co., but left little Jimmie with Mrs. Lucius. Don't you think that is a shame! for that poor woman could not feed her own children without her neighbor's help. I know poor little Jimmie often thinks of me.

He said he meant to go to sister Mary just as soon as he was large enough. They (Dr Reeves & wife) took Lula with them to Freestone. I have not heard a word from Mr. Morton in refference to my affairs there since last fall, he said he had not succeeded in collecting my notes up to that time, he said that some had refused to pay, after promising faithfully to pay by the first of Oct last. He said that he would do the best he could for us. He said it was no use to sue for he could not obtain anything in that way. I shall not grieve about it, I shall do the best I can, and humbly trust in God. He has promised to be a husband to the widow and a father to the fatherless and I believe every promise in his precious word. I have been taken care of so far (and will too) by my dear Parents & precious brothers, and my brothers says we (I and my little children) shall never want as long as they live and they are noble pious young men. They make a great pet of Annie. She is a very bright child. Amelia and Sissie both go to school and learn fast. Well Winnie I will desist for the present. You must be a good girl, read your Bible daily, and pray too. I remember you daily at a Throne of grace. May God bless you, comfort you, and lead you through a happy christian life, and save you at last in Heaven is the sincere prayer of your devoted mother. Write soon.

Mary F. Hardison

Do you ever write to any of your Friends in Texas?

[Mary wrote frequently to Winnie about former neighbors in Texas and the family of her husband's sister and brother-in-law, Nancy (Hardison) and Dr. James Harvey Reeves. Carrie (Caroline) Persons and Sallie (Sarah) Ivey were the Reeves' married daughters and Jimmie and Lula were John Randolph Hardison's half brother and sister, who were children at the time Mary left Texas in 1875.]

William Fisher Robison to Mary Fletcher (Northington) Hardison s

Lumpkin Ga
July 9th 1877

My dear dear Cousin

Yr sweet letter dated May 14th has not been forgotten. I've been engaged nearly all the time since it came in a long protracted meeting resulting in great good I hope. Rest assured my dear Cousin that I fully appreciated you[r] kind letter. It breathed a spirit of true christian love. You have no idea how often my poor soul goes back to other days & associations when you & I were children walking over the old hills & roads around old Bay Spring & how my young heart was filled with the love of God & then how often I would go to my regular places of secret prayer & how God would meet with me & bless me. But my dear Cousin little did we dream of the many sad changes that have overtaken us. What a trial has life been since our childhood days & how poorly prepared have we been for it! God has been good to me every day of my life. I gave my young heart to him when a boy & I have never withdrawn it. My devotion to God has been constant, yet I have had my ordeals & embarrassments like all others, my seasons of doubt & gloom, yet I would hold on & pray till God would reveal himself to me in great Grace and Mercy. You [asked?] when & how I started the Ministry. Since connection with the Conference I have had but one work to do & that I have endeavored to do well. I should say I have been blessed with good appointments—better probably than I deserved yet I have done the best I could & I have had the help of the good Spirit.

As touching John's case I will say that I have just written Winfield about him. I had made arrangement for him but as I've lost sight of him at present probably he had better wait till the opening of another year. In the mean time he can make more money to clothe himself. John should not think hard of me as the express understanding between us was that he—John should get up what money he could collect & come on to me whenever I wrote for him. So the failure was his not mine. I am willing to give John two years schooling board & all if I can have any security that he has any interest in the estate & that I can be paid when he becomes of age. As you know our land is in litigation & may continue so for years to come. I am not in secular business at all & must look to the Church for my support. Each of my brothers in this particular has had a better chance than I have. If I were able it would afford great pleasure to educate John without any consideration at all, but I am not & then I have a wife & three children to care for & my children will soon be at a very expensive age. I will need all & more than I have. I have sought to be useful & serve my day & generation by the will of God, those next to me have the first claim upon me. Our trust in which I claim an interest has not as yet been of any benefit to me, though it may be after a while. As you know my people have not done just as I have desired. No man loves his kin people more than I do I dare say & yet I don't have much influence over them. I know I am true to my kin & my friends & I love them all. I don't hear from the old homestead & why I cannot tell.

I saw the paper notice of Mr. Mims' death—poor Missouri like yourself is a widow. May God take care of her. Now my dear cousin I've written you enough for this time do as [?]. Give love to all the family, I love them all & if we nevermore meet again in the flesh we will meet on a better & brighter Shore than this. Pray for me daily, God hears prayer, yet I want that perfect love of which you speak in your letter. We are all well. The weather is hot & dry. May God bless you & your dear little ones.

Affectionately
Yr Cousin
William

PS Savannah joins me in great love to you all

[William's mother was Elizabeth Fisher Robison, aunt of Mary Northington Hardison and daughter of Metcalf Fisher, who left a portion of his property to her to be held in trust for her children. The Robison property adjoined the Northingtons' land in the Bay Spring Community. Missouri was Harriet Missouri, sister of Mary Northington Hardison, and her husband was Thomas Mims. William's brother John became a physician.] [8]

Mary Fletcher (Northington) Hardison to Winnifred Cornelia Hardison c

Bay Spring Ga
Dec 12th 1877

Miss W.C. Hardison,
My Dear Daughter

I have thought for several weeks, that I would write to you every day, but this has been indeed and in truth a very busy year with me. I have been teaching school again this year. And since my school closed, I have been quite busy making up winter clothing and quilting. I have a nice pretty quilt for you too! I hope you will not think unkind of me for not writing more. You must not think you are forgotten, no I remember you daily at a Throne of Grace. I would be glad to see you. You must write to me soon and tell me how you are, and how you like Thomasville.

I hear from Mrs. Rambo and Mattie Rambo often. I have not heard from Mr. Morton since last May, he wrote me that his wife was dead. She died with consumption and since her death, little Annie her daughter has died.

The old lady Baldwin is dead also and your cousin Sallie Ivey lost her youngest child. He died in Sept. sometime. Henry Reeves lost his wife and baby both, Mattie did not say when they died. There has been a great many deaths in our old neighborhood in Texas since we left.

Mr. Jeff Rogers has married again, he married quite a young lady this time, Mrs. Ellen Burton, your uncle Jay Reeves daughter. Mr. Burton her former husband died last winter I think. I was very much astonished to hear that she had married so old a man as Mr. Rogers.

Dr. Harrison Gregory is married (he was Mattie Rambo's old beau) he married Allie Bean. I guess you remember her. Mattie wrote me she had joined the church at Lost Prairie and was trying to live a pious life. I want to know if you have joined any church yet. Winnie youth is the time to give the heart to God, it is purest then. And the holy command is "Seek now thy Creator in the days of thy youth." Read the Bible and don't forget to pray. There is nothing that can afford us the true happiness in this life that the Religion of Jesus can, especially when it becomes the ruling principle of the soul. And then it prepares us for a purer home beyond the skies.

The children are quite well. My health is very good indeed. My Father's family are quite well. Winnie, I have a good home, kind parents and the best brothers in the world, they are so kind to me and my little ones. They are indeed noble young men. Winnie I will send you a beautiful bookmark in my next letter, would send it now, but it is not completed. You must write soon.

Mr. Morton has not been able to collect the notes yet, or sell the land. I don't much expect he will ever collect the notes.

I remain your devoted mother.
M. F. Hardison

Mary Fletcher (Northington) Hardison to Winnifred Cornelia Hardison r

Bethesda
May 13 1879.

Miss W.C. Hardison,
My Dear Daughter,

I was the recipient of your kind interesting letter some weeks ago, was truly glad to hear from you and to learn you were well. I intended responding sooner, but various things have transpired to prevent me from complying with my desire. I am teaching a school at the above named place, a very pleasant place too, situated about five miles southeast of Pa's. My little girls are with Ma. I will send Amelia and Sissie to school next term to Mr. Snelling, he teaches very near to Pa's, and is a good teacher. They are very anxious to go. Their Uncle Capers told them, he would dress them & send them to School. Their relatives are very kind to them. Annie will go to school to me. I will take her to my boarding house, and keep her with me, she is so small I dont like to be away from her. I go to Pa's once in two & three weeks. Amelia & Sissie often talk about you & Lillie and wish to see you both. I was truly sorry to see the death of your Uncle Edwin Davis. He was indeed a fine looking man, and bid fare to live a long while when I saw him four years ago. But how uncertain is all that pertaining to this life. This life is but a dressing room for Eternity. And dear Winnie let us so live that we may be properly attired when we are call[ed] hence, then we shall meet where parting sickness & death will never come. What was the matter with your Uncle? I would like to know the particulars.

I have not heard from Texas in sometime, and the truth is I have not answered my correspondents. I wrote to Mattie some days ago, in answer to a letter I received from her last fall, I know she thinks unkind of me. But I am always busy, especially when teaching. I have a good school & a good boarding house also. I love to teach, I feel perfectly at home in the School-room. My health is very good, I don't think I ever had better health in my life, I am much fleshyer than when I resided in Texas. My little girls are quite well & pretty as rose-buds. I must close for the present. You must write to me often, I am always glad to hear from you, and I will try in future to write more frequent. Winnie I think of you, and remember you daily at a throne of Grace. You must strive to be a good christian, for if we miss Heaven, we miss all. May God bless you is the fervent prayer of your devoted mother.

Mary F. Hardison

J.C. Morton to Mary Fletcher (Northington) Hardison s

Personville Tex.   June 14th [18]79

Mrs M F Hardison
My Dear Friend.

You have perhaps expected a letter from me ere this, but I have made no collections for you & thought it unnecessary to write.

I had suit brought against Little on the notes this Spring and got judgment, dont know whether I will ever get the money or not, think he never intended to pay. The notes would have run out of date this Spring. Will do my best to make it if he ever has any thing subject to execution. I will get pay ($4.00) for the bed stead this fall. The other little articles left are here & I have been unable to dispose of them.

This leaves myself & family up. Lula has been in poor health all the Spring, has a chill & some fever occasionally. I have been in feebler health for 2 years than formerly though I keep up. The health of the community is good.

Money matters have been extremely tight ever since you left here, though provisions have been abundant. We had 10 weeks of drouth in Feb, Mar & Apr. two weeks of heavy rains the latter part of Apr & now 6 weeks of dry weather is finishing it. Old corn has gone up from 25 & 30 to 75 cts per bu. The present crop is estimated will make about 10 bu. per acre though a good season now would make the yield greater. Oat crops were generally good in this part of the Co. but very poor in most of the State. Wheat was good. Gardens are poor, fruit is fair. Cotton is promising though most of the crop was planted too late. I have 10 acres which I manured well & prepared & cultivated with extra care. It is about 18 inches high & is as handsome a sight as I ever saw. It is the Cheatham variety & is fruiting well. I have had but one hand hired this year who is a Chinaman. I find him the best worker I ever had, has done nearly all the work about the place and cultivated 28 acres with some occasional help, is polite, cleanly & behaves well. Would like to have a dozen if all were like this one etc.

I have rented most of my land out, have about 60 acres left out this year. The tenantry system is very unsatisfactory and to hire help is worse. Farming with either has paid very poorly for several years. Most of the tenants have to be supplied and fail to make as good crops as they might. Our system of labor is worse than when you were here and I see no prospect for improvement. Reeves, Ivey & Persons are here yet & all doing reasonably well. Rambo, Glass, Byrd, the Rogers & others are getting along well. Most of the transient population have changed about & moved off. As I have no news of interest I close. Would be pleased to hear from you at [your] convenience. Where is Lillie & Winnie? Tender my regards to them.

Yours Respectfully
J. C. Morton

Mary Fletcher (Northington) Hardison to Winnifred Cornelia Hardison r

Bethesda Georgia
July 19th, 1879

Miss W. C. Hardison,
My Dear Daughter,

I received your kind interesting letter the 4th inst, was glad to hear from you, and to hear that your health was so good. We are all quite well. My health is splendid. I am going to send you a photograph of your dear Father & myself, you can keep it, if you wish to. I have another. It is a good one, very much like him. It was taken in Sandersville Ga, 10 years ago, by a splendid artist. I had two letters from Texas recently. One from Mr Morton & one from Matt Looke, (Matt Rambo that was) Matt wrote that old Brother Sikes was dead, also Old Mr Duncan & Fairer his son & Sallie his youngest daughter. All died within two weeks of each other. Mr Morton said he had not been able to collect anything from Mr Little. Said he had sued him and got judgement against him, but did not know as he would ever get any thing. I think Little ought to be ashamed of himself. Mr Morton inquired after you and Lillie, and said present you with his regards. He said his health was feeble and had been for two years, said also Lula's health was bad. Mrs Rambo's health is also bad. And they said Grand-Ma Byrd was failing very fast.

Well Winnie I was sad indeed when I read the account of your uncle Edd's death. It was truly heart-rending. Amelia and Sissie are going to School and are learning fast. They go to Antioch. Mr Snelling is their teacher. Annie came out and staid with me five weeks, whilst here, she attended school and learned well, she is nearly through the first Reader. The children all have bright minds and learn well. They are anxious to see you, talk much about you & Lillie.

I never hear a word from Lillie. I wrote her a long letter sometime ago, but she has never responded to it. You must write to me often, you write good letters, I love to get them. I will close for the present time. Write soon. Be good & holy. May God bless you is my prayer. As ever your devoted mother. Direct your letters as heretofore.

M. F. Hardison

Lilly Mary Hardison to Winnifred Cornelia Hardison c

Sunday Evening
Feb. 1st, 1880

My Dear Sister

I received your letter last Tuesday and thought I would write every day last week but first one thing and another prevented. I have been right busy every since I came home, have been sewing and visiting, have been out a good deal with Aunt Liz. The young mens library fair has been going on for two weeks. We went out one evening to the fair and went two nights. They had several very handsome articles to be raffled off, had a fine brussels carpet, a [?] dollar piano, a 5.00 dollar state bond, a fine sewing machine, a gentlemans and a ladies writing desk, a handsome set of china and a great many other things. I took a chance at the set of china but of course I never got it. I had a letter from cousin Henry last week, they are all well except Cousin H., he had rheumatism. I am expecting a letter from Lou Harris this week and one from cousin Bel and Mollie.

Winnie write me soon and let me know if you know what month you will go to Davisboro in or what month you think you will go in. Aunt Liz is not going to keep house this year but will board, her health is so poor and she stays at home so closely that the physicians have advised her to quit house keeping for a while any way and she has decided to do something that I never thought she would do. She told me that [I] could board with her or rather at the place she staes [stays] or visit my friends and relatives. All of my friends and relatives in Washington Co. are just begging me to come and spend the year with them and I guess I will go, know I will have a delightful time. Mrs. Matthews wants me to spend two or three months with her. Mamie Harris in Sandersville is begging me to spend some time with her. Miss Bessie Newsome wants me to stay some with her. Sallie Frances, Mrs. Hensman, the Harris girls, Aunt Tempie Davis in Riddleville all are after me to come and stay with them. Cousin Henry and all his family just begged me if Aunt Liz did board to come and stay all the year with them. I will stay some with Ma and cousin Add and cousin Sallie Joiner and with Uncle Joel Davis. All my friends are very anxious to have me go and spend the year in Washington and if nothing happens to prevent I will leave here the first of March. Don't know where I will stop first but think I will stop at 14 [Oconee] to see Ma as I will pass by there but don't know yet, will let you know, don't say anything about my stopping at 14 for I don't think Aunt L.

wants me to go there much but I am going, intended going while I was down there but did not have time. You must be sure to go to Washington for I am very anxious to see you, have many things to tell you. You must go to Davisboro by the time the big meeting commences any way. We will have such a nice time. Come as soon as you can.

I will be very busy from now until the time we move, have lots of sewing to do, a good deal for Bel and some for my self. I made two pairs of drawers, two chemise for Bel last week & a skirt for Aunt Liz. I will get my Spring and Summer dresses before I leave as the Spring goods will be in by 1st March. Cousin Henry's family all said they enjoyed your stay with them last Spring so much and are very anxious to have you come again and you must not fail to go. We can go over and see Albert Cook teaching the "young idids [?] how to shoot" I know he looks funny, don't you. We had a postal from Cousin Bob yesterday written the 29th, said Cousin [?] would be home in about a week from the time he wrote and he would be here by the 7th or 8th so we will expect them both the last of this week. Have not heard from Cousin Zem since she left Americus. Guess she is well though, tell Aunt Sallie to be sure to come home with Cousin Zem, we are all very anxious to have her come. I don't wonder at your loving her so, don't know who could help loving her, she is so good and kind. I tell you she won me over completely. I am truly glad to hear that you like to cook and hope you will continue so and please them all and do the very best you can. Winnie, you have such a good home and I hope you will do your part and I know that Uncle John and Aunt Sallie will do theirs. Give much love to all from me and let me hear from you soon. Uncle Bill has written to Aunt Sallie. Guess he has written all the news and Aunt L. is improving right fast I think. I have been at home all day, did not go to church, feel right lonely.

With much love and best wishes
I am your loving sister,
Lillie

[The place of residence of Lilly and her aunt, Mrs. Hardwick, at the time the letter was written is not indicated. "Cousin Bob" was the son of the Hardwicks and "Cousin Zem" was his wife, Zemula Matthews. "Ma" refers to Lilly's step-mother, Mary Northington Hardison.]

XV. HOME TO GEORGIA, 1875-1889

Mary Fletcher (Northington) Hardison to
Winnifred Cornelia Hardison c

Bay Spring Academy   June 1st 1881

Miss W. C. Hardison
My Dear Daughter,

After waiting for long weeks, for a letter from you, I received one that had been written a great while from Washington City. But old as it was, it met a warm reception. Yes Winnie I was truly glad to hear from you once more.

I have been thinking for some time that I would write to you but the truth is, I have so much to do and look after that I seldom ever write a letter. I have lost one of my dear Texas correspondents, one whose letters were all good and highly entertaining to me and truly appreciated. Mr. J. C. Morton, is the one I have refference to. He died last July with consumption. Lula Morton his daughter died in January before he did, with consumption also. Did you ever know a family to die up so fast! First Mrs. Morton then Annie the same year. Then Mr. Morton & Lula so soon afterwards. I never think of them without having the blues badly. O! this Life is so full of trouble.

I received a letter from Mrs. Rambo some time ago, also one from Matt. Mrs. Rambo said that Mr. Sam Morton (Mr. J. C. Morton's Brother) had brought the children that were left back to Georgia to live, Winnie, Ned & Frank. Mrs. Rambo said Old Dr. Reeves was dead also, said your aunt Nancy was still keeping house.

Sallie Ivey has 3 children living, one dead. I think she said Carrie Persons has 3 living, 2 dead. Carrie lost one the same day she wrote to me, a babe about 3 months old. Mrs. Rambo wrote the last of April. Matt has a boy, little over a year old. She said he is fine looking. Matt said her Pa's health was very poor. She did not say anything about Jimmie or Lula Hardison. I wrote to her, to tell me all about them in her next letter. I wish them well, for they were both good children. When did you hear from Lillie? Annie is going to work you and Lillie a Bookmark. She has worked Dr. Glass one, and it is beautiful. She is one of the most apt children to learn I ever saw. You would be astonished to see her work. I have a class of young ladies & large girls taking lessons in all kinds of needlework, and nothing would do Annie

[Remainder of letter missing.]

Mary Fletcher (Northington) Hardison and her Eldest Daughter, Amelia Randolph Hardison, to Winnifred Cornelia Hardison r

Bay Spring Ga   Apr 7th 1882

Miss Winnie C. Hardison,
Dear sister,

    I have decided to pen you a few lines to let you know how we all are. We are all well at present. I wrote to sister Lillie about a month ago, and directed it to Tennille thinking that she was there but have not heard a word from her. I suppose she had gone to Davisboro. Mama has a very good school now. I remained home all last week to make me a dress, it is very prety. What are you going to give me for a birthday present. Mrs McBride & Dr McB say they are going to give me a present. We are going to have [a] picnic sometime the first of May for the benefit of the children. Why dont you write to me, I have been looking for a long time for a letter but never get one. We are all going a fishing at the mill pond next saturday. Kiss little Lucy for me. You must come to see us. Well I must close for this time, write soon I am anxious to hear from you, when you write tell me how many april fools you got. Sissie and Annie sends their love to you. Well I must close write soon.

Amelia J R Hardison

[Apparently Amelia appropriated her father's initials to include with her name.]

School Room.   Apr 6th [1882]

Dear Winnie, I know you think hard of me for not writing to you, but Winnie if you could only see me, and see how crowded I am with business, you would excuse me. I am teaching, and have to do all my sewing at night, many a night I sew untill 12 and one O clock. It makes me look & feel very badly next day but I am oblige to do it to get along. I intended to send you some nice birthday presents, I failed to get to Sandersville, and there was nothing at #14 [Oconee] suitable to send you. But it will do you just as well to have a Christmas present wont it? I regreted your disappointment very much indeed.

    Winnie you can have those buttons made for me, and send them to me, and you can have the other one. I am living with Dr McBride, he is a nice kind gentleman. And his wife a nice lady. They are very kind to us. I have a pleasant beautiful home. But dear Winnie I often think of Texas and sigh over the precious hours, that form some of the most pleasant

"Reminiscences" of my life. I have not heard a word from Texas in nearly a year. When did you hear last? Amelia has written you a short letter, she will be 13 years old the 12th of this month, and is much larger than I am. Amelia is a smart girl and a great deal of help to me, and greatly beloved by all who know her. Winnie I would be so glad to see you, and talk with you, it would do me so much good, some times I do feel so lonely and desolate. I often retrospect the past and it never fails to give me the blues. Sissie and Annie both grow fast and learn well. I have a tolerable good school. What are you doing? How do you and your aunt Liz get a long now? does she treat you with more respect than she did formerly? How does poor little Lucy get along? Well I will have to desist for this time. Please write soon and do please write a long letter too.

I remain as ever your true
Mother M F Hardison.

George Washington Wood to Winnifred Cornelia Hardison c

Gordon Ga. June 16, [18]82

My Own Darling Winnie,

I sent you a box yesterday containing a album & badge. The badge was the present of the Alpha Tau Omega fraternity of which I have the honor of being a member. This society can claim among its members some of the most prominent men in the country. Almost any graduate of a modern coledge can tell you of the fraternity. My badge has some historic worth attached to it. It was once the property of Otis A. [Glanyebrook?] who married a cousin of Gen. Lee and by her inherited from the celebrated Custis family. I have nothing that I prize more highly than this. It was, I trust, you will pardon me for saying, given to me as a compliment for excellency in oratory. Whether I deserve the compliment or not remains for others to say.

I wore the beautiful little bouquet that you was kind enough to send me. I appreciate these little acts of kindness very muchly, and it makes me proud to think that my little sweetheart is so interested in me. I never felt more fearful for the success of a side that I represented than I did last night. Not because I felt that I was not on the safe side but because all the good speakers were on the other side. We have some splendid speakers all on the other side. We had a tremendous house, every available seat was full in the house. Many was standing. All the girls and women in the whole county was present. You bet I was fearful. All knew that I was the principle speaker on my side and the whole crowd of women seemed to look for a vindication of themselves to me and then to fail, what a disgrace! But still I was never more impatient to get to my feet and claim the floor. The whole crowd thought my side was gone but I turned the tide of affairs when I got the chance. I had the perfect attention of the house and I knew that that was the time to make a telling speech. Suffice to say that the president decided in my favor in ¼ of a moment after I finished. But you must not show this letter to any one, they would surely think me vain but I owe every thing to the subject. You ought to see what nice bouquets I got. They are real pretty.

I think I will come so soon as I can. You surely cannot be more impatient to see me than I am to see you. I have a great many things to tell you & want to see you any way. I mean I just want to look at you. Besides I would make you tired talking to you.

Remember me as your own devoted
Geo W Wood

Mary Fletcher (Northington) Hardison to Winnifred Cornelia Hardison r

Bay Spring   Oct 5th 1882

Miss W. C. Hardison,
My Dear Daughter,

Your letter containing the information of your marriage, was warmly received on yesterday Evening. I was truly glad to hear from you. You said in your letter, that I would be surprised at your choice. But you were mistaken. I had decided in my own mind before I received your letter that it was "George." I am much pleased with your selection, I think G.W.W. will make you a kind good companion. I formed a very favorable opinion of him the first time I met him. I wish you both much happiness, Together may you sweetly live. Dear Winnie you are now going to make a most important step in life, and permit me to give you a word of advice. Strive to be a good Christian wife, always kind and truly respectful to your husband. Always greet him with cheerful loving wellcome. Love honor and obey him, do nothing without consulting him. Dont never allow yourself to become angry with your husband, but strive to please him in every respect. Love and confide in him always. If you will do this, you may be confident that you will be truly the happy recipient of his purest love. You told me of your

XV. HOME TO GEORGIA, 1875-1889

marriage, but did not tell me when it would take place. I would like to see you married, but I would not think of attending without an invitation from your Uncle. If I attend, that will be all, the children cannot, for it will not be convenient. Will your aunt Lizzie be there? Where is Lillie now? Winnie you are truly blest in having such a kind and benevolent uncle. He does certainly possess a most noble heart. I hope kind heaven will reward him abundantly for his kind and loving favors bestowed upon you. I will have you a beautiful quilt ready by your marriage, and will make you others afterwards.

Amelia is well pleased at your marriage, but Sissie and Annie are not satisfied about it, they think and feel like you are lost to them. Annie walked in just now and said "Tell Sister Winnie she did not want her to marry" You can imagine how they feel about it. The children all love you devotedly. Annie has just recovered from a severe illness. She had Remittant Malarial fever and some symtoms of conjestion of the stomache. Dr McBride was her Physician, and he staid with her day and night most of the time. Annie is now able to walk about in the house. I was very uneasy about her for some time. Well I will desist for the present. You must write soon, and don't forget to tell me when you intend to marry.

Where does your Aunt Lizzie live now? Will you live in Gordon?

Please write soon and a long letter, I am ever pleased to hear from you. What will it cost to go to Americus? I would be glad to see you and assist you in your preparation for your marriage.

Truly your devoted Mother,
M F Hardison

෴ ෴

Winnie and George Washington Wood were married on November 2, 1882 and settled in the village of Sunny Side in Spalding County, a short distance from Atlanta. George, the son of the Reverend James R. Wood and Martha Chester Wood of Washington County, had a general merchandise business and was a Baptist minister, who served in a number of rural churches in middle Georgia. On his gravestone are written the words "He preached Jesus." Winnie maintained a close relationship with her sister Lilly and her half-sisters, Amelia, Nancy, and Annie, and the Wood home became a favorite place for them and their children to visit. Winnie and George had four sons, Dean Osgood, George Washington, Jr., Boyd Emory, and

Roy Smith, and a daughter, May Lydia, between 1885 and 1896, before Winnie's untimely death in 1905 at the age of forty-three. After Winnie's death, Lilly joined the household to care for the children and she and George were married on December 21, 1909. He died in 1920 and she continued to live in the Wood home until her death in 1937, greatly loved by two generations of nieces and nephews. The inscriptions on the gravestones of Winnie, "She was a friend to the needful," and Lilly, "She lived for others," are memorials to their dedication to family and community.

Winnie's and George's eldest child, Dean, died as an infant and Boyd died as a teenager. The careers of their daughter May and sons George, Jr. and Roy and their descendants show the influence of the value placed on education by Winnie's father, John Hardison, and uncle, Edwin T. Davis, and by George's education at Mercer College. May became a teacher and married a lawyer, James Robert Cain of Savannah. Their children pursued careers as editor, civil engineer, accountant, and naval officer and their grandchildren in varied callings, including editor and computer data administrator. George, Jr. and Roy became lawyers and settled in Miami, Florida. Their children and grandchildren have followed a great variety of professions, including law, journalism, and nursing. George Jr.'s granddaughter, Janet Reno, daughter of Jane Wood, was appointed Attorney General of the United States in 1993 in the Clinton Administration. Janet's aunt, Winifred Wood, a member of the Women's Airforce Service Pilots in World War II, remarked in speaking of the varied careers of her nieces and nephews, from rain forest expert to county commissioner to Attorney General, "They have done many interesting things . . . I'm never surprised at what they do."[9]

The letters of 1882 are the last for that decade in the previously cited family collections. Information about the lives of Mary Northington Hardison and her family in the remainder of the 1880s is drawn from Washington County records and a small group of newspaper clippings, which are reproduced below. Washington County deeds indicate that Mary's father gave her land for a home and that a residence was built for her in 1883.[10] At the end of the decade two deaths and a marriage marked the end of life for the matriarchs of two generations and the passage into adulthood of Mary's eldest daughter. In February of 1887 Mary's mother, Amelia (Milly) Fisher Northington, died and Amelia Randolph Hardison, the elder Amelia's namesake, was married to John Evers Granade. A little more than two years later, on May 23, 1889, Mary died a few months before her fiftieth birthday.[11]

> NORTHINGTON. Mrs. Millie Northington, *nee* Fisher, was born April 28, 1814. Professed religion and joined the Methodist Episcopal Church in 1825, when eleven years old; died in great peace and triumph, February 10, 1887. She was happily married to James F. Northington, of Sandersville, May 14, 1834, by the late James B. Payne, of the old Georgia Conference. Her wedded life was blessed with a goodly number of children, six of whom survive her. For more than six months previous to her death she was a great suffer[er] from heart disease and dropsical affection, yet in the weary months of pain and helplessness she maintained an uncomplaining Christian spirit, and recognized in it all the finger of God. This good woman was a sincere and devout Christian wife and mother, a blessing to her home, the Church and the community in which she lived. Among the purest pleasures of her life was the entertainment of the itinerant preacher. Though limited in this world's goods, she had ever in her heart that godliness, with contentment, which is great gain. The aged husband, deprived when most he seems to need the loving companionship of such a wife, feels bereft indeed. May the prayers of God's people ascend on his behalf, and God's Grace sustain him until he will be called to join her on the other shore.
>
> W. F. Robison
>
> [Mary's father, James Foster Northington, who was born in North Carolina on Nov. 11, 1809, died on Jan. 31, 1893. A memorial to him by the Methodists of Washington County honored him as "a worthy and valued citizen" and "a faithful and honored member" of the Methodist Church, which he had joined in 1829 and served in many capacities throughout his life.] [12]

The clipping about Amelia Hardison's marriage does not include the date of the wedding, but her marriage license, which was dated February 2, 1887, records that it took place on February 3. The account seems to indicate an elopement on the part of Amelia, not quite eighteen years old, and John Evers Granade, who was eleven years older.

Came to Macon to Wed.

There arrived in the city on the Central railroad train from Oconee yesterday the following party: Mr. J. E. Grenade [Granade], Mr. James Fiser [Fisher], Miss Amelia Hardison and Miss Nannie Hardison. They seemed somewhat disappointed at not meeting some particular person at the depot, and then went over to Brown's Hotel where they remained but a short while. They then boarded the street cars and returned to the hotel shortly after 7 o'clock. Their movements were somewhat explained by the names that were then written on the register. "J.E. Grenade and wife, Oconee," meant that Mr. Grenade and Miss Amelia Hardison had been married. They expected to meet Rev. John A. Harrison, pastor of Jones Chapel, at the depot, but he was not there, and if the mountain would not come to Mahomet, Mahomet would go to the mountain, and they went to the minister's residence.

The party will remain in Macon to-day and return to their home tonight, when it is hoped all will be forgiven and that the young and happy couple will receive the parents' blessing.

John Evers Granade, from a family of Wilkinson County, was a bridge superintendent for the Central of Georgia Railroad.[13] After their marriage, he and Amelia lived in Oconee on property which adjoined that of W. J. Hardison, the son of Amelia's great-uncle, William L. Hardison. Amelia, like her father John Hardison, loved the land and farming and on the few acres which surrounded her home she grew peaches and other crops which she marketed.[14] The Granades had four daughters, Mary Elizabeth, Effie Evers, Lillie Marie, and Helen Lanier, born between 1888 and 1901. About 1908 the Granades moved to Milledgeville in adjoining Baldwin County, in order to have their four daughters educated at the recently founded women's college, Georgia Normal and Industrial College. In a letter of January 31, 1912 to her sister Annie, Amelia wrote, "It certainly is a long and tedious undertaking to educate children—you won't know anything about expenses till you start yours off, but I rather mine were educated than to have the money that it has taken. I know they can keep an education and be independent if they half try. I feel so glad we have been able to do as much as we have."[15] All four of the Granade daughters graduated from the college and became teachers. They lived at various times in Georgia, Alabama, Florida, and South Carolina. Their children and grandchildren have pursued a variety of callings, including teacher, musician, economist, lawyer, business man and woman, writer, and computer analyst.

On May 23, 1889, a little over two years after her mother's death and Amelia's marriage, Mary Northington Hardison's life came to an end. Like her mother, she was remembered for her piety and dedication to her family.

OBITUARY
MRS. MARY FLETCHER HARDISON

was born in Sandersville, Washington county, Georgia, December 13, 1839. Her maiden name was Northington. She was the daughter of James F. and Amelia R. Northington of Bay Springs. Her mother, one of the best of women, died a few years ago, but her father still lives at the advanced age of 80 years.

Being brought up in the lap of piety, it was quite natural for her to unite with the church at an early age. Accordingly on the 2nd of November 1852, at the age of thirteen, we find her casting in her lot among God's people, giving her heart to God, her hand and name to the preacher, and her influence and life to the church. She united with the church at Bay Springs, under the ministry of Rev. Milton C. Smith, then a member of the Georgia Conference, and that year in charge of the Sandersville Circuit; and the consecration then made was adhered to with marked fidelity throughout her life. She never regretted, and never for a moment thought of retracing the step then taken. It was made with deliberation, and "with purpose of heart." But she was not converted at that time. Into this blessed experience she intered [entered] three years later, in September, 1855, when just budding into the freshness and bloom of young womanhood. From that date till her death there were but few times when she could not say truthfully and consciously, "I know that my Redeemer liveth," "I know whom I have believed." Hers was not a doubting and doubtful religion, cold, cheerless, comfortless, but warm, loving, and active. She enjoyed religion; it was her main business, and she carried it into all the concerns of life. Thus, she was ever ready to "give a reason of the hope that was in her." She loved God's people and His house, and His service, and was always willing to assist in the latter in any manner in which she might be able.

On the 23rd day of January, 1865 [1866], she was happily married to Captain John R. Hardison of Personville, Liberty [Limestone] county, Texas, a lawyer by profession, with whom she lived most congenially and joyously until his death, which occurred on the 31st [30th] of December, 1874. Thus, early widowed, she was left with three small children—all girls—to raise and educate. Indulging no vain regrets and useless repinings, she addressed herself heartily to the task of maintaining herself and children, and educating the latter. And through the blessing of God she was enabled to accomplish this purpose, and was spared to see her girls all grown, and the eldest favorably and happily married.

Her end was that of the "perfect and upright" "peace." Her last sickness was short and death made rapid advances. She was taken sick on the 16th of May, and surrendered to the grim monster on the morning of the 23rd, not quite one week. While her sickness was painful, her death was calm and serene. Looking upward toward Heaven just before the breath left her body, she smiled lingeringly, and then passed away, leaving her face still wreathed with a Heavenly smile which seemed to affirm that she and not death had triumphed.

Sister Hardison was one of the best christians I ever knew. Uniform, regular, and consistant, yet always rather quiet, her life was not like the noisy brook, but like the deep river that moves quietly and smoothly on to its destination. "Her children rise up to call her blessed." And may God ever bless them, [page torn] each of them to meet [page torn] happy world beyond.

R. B. B [page torn]

In the early years of the decade following Mary's death, her two younger daughters followed Amelia in marriage. The middle daughter, Nancy ("Nannie") Missouri, was married to John Ackbar Darsey, a lawyer and later a judge in Spalding County, on January 1, 1890 at the home of her half-sister Winnie, Mrs. George Washington Wood, in Sunny Side.[16] The Darseys lived throughout their lives in Sunny Side, a few miles from Griffin, the county seat of Spalding County. Their children were Ralph Hardison, Annie Mary, John Ackbar, Jr., and Lillie Winifred, born between 1890 and 1908. Ralph, a teacher, farmer, and building contractor, married and reared his family in Sunny Side, and Winifred, a music teacher, married and lived with her family in Griffin where her husband Carl N. Richardson was an executive in the cotton manufacturing industry. Annie Mary died unmarried in early adulthood. John, Jr. became a lawyer and from 1941 to 1947 was special assistant to the United States Attorney General, serving as associate prosecutor in the Japanese war crimes trials. He later practiced law and was county attorney in Jackson County, Georgia.

Annie, the youngest daughter, was also married in Sunny Side, indicating the on-going warm relationship between the two sets of sisters. Her husband was Jarrett Irwin Brown of Washington County, who had been employed in the mercantile business of his uncle in that county. After their marriage in January, 1895, they settled in Dodge County in south-central Georgia, where Jarrett acquired a large holding of 1,500 acres. He died in 1916, but the family continued to live on their land in a spacious home, which they built soon after 1900, until the 1930s and then in adjoining Telfair County. The children were Willis Neal, Jarrett Irwin, Mary Elizabeth, Nancy Louise, and Lillie Hardison, all of whom remained in Georgia except Nancy Louise. She entered nurses training in 1933 and pursued her career for over thirty years. She married a doctor, Earl Charles Slaughter, who was one of six sons of a Nebraska family who were physicians, and they settled in Norfolk, Nebraska.[17]

In returning to Washington County, Georgia, Mary Northington Hardison reversed the direction of the journey which had taken her husband and his grandfather, John, and father, Seth, across the South. Three generations of Hardison men had sought riches through the acquisition of land and the cultivation of cotton. They would probably have agreed with the advice of Gerald O'Hara to his daughter Scarlett: "Land is the only thing in the world that amounts to anything, for 'tis the only thing in this world that lasts, and don't you be forgetting it! 'Tis the only thing worth working for, worth fighting for— worth dying for."[18] John Randolph Hardison and thousands of other young men fought and many died in order to preserve the way of life they had established on the lands of the South. After the Civil War, many grew poor trying to farm the land they had fought for. If John had had sons, perhaps they would have shared their father's enthusiasm for farming. Instead the daughters of John and his wives Winnifred and Mary were inspired by another enthusiasm—the love of learning, which had been shared by their parents. As they married and had families, they and their husbands labored to make possible the education which their children needed to succeed in a variety of careers. As Mary and John's eldest daughter Amelia said in 1912, "I know they can keep an education and be independent if they half try." If Amelia were living at the end of the twentieth century, she would agree with Winifred Wood's statement, "'They have done many interesting things . . . I'm never surprised at what they do."

NOTES

Background information on the history of Washington County has been drawn from the previously cited *Cotton to Kaolin, a History of Washington County, Georgia, 1784-1989*, edited by Mary Alice Jordan. Chapters 4 and 5 pertain to the years 1860-1910.

1. A number of Washington County deeds of 1882-1912 record transactions within the Northington family concerning the land of Mary's father, James Foster Northington. James gave small acreages to daughter Mary and sons James, Jr. and Capers (W. C.) before his death in 1893—Deed Book F, p.503 (to James, Jr.) and p.645 (pertains to lien on Mary's house for construction materials), Deed Book K, p.709 (to W.C.), and Deed Book M, p.469 (to James, Jr.). After James, Sr.'s death, James, Jr. and Capers (W. C.) came into possession of the remainder of their father's land through various transactions within the family, which included their brother Marcellus A. Northington, sisters Hattie Missouri (Mrs. Thomas Mims) and Indiana (Mrs. Joseph Etheridge), and niece Amelia Hardison Granade (acting through her husband John Evers Granade), representing her mother's claim—Deed Book O, pp.465-66, Deed Book Q, pp.558-60 and 598, and Deed Book V, p.383.
2. Jordan, *Cotton to Kaolin*, p.37, quoting information from C. Mildred Thompson, *Reconstruction in Georgia* (Atlanta: Cherokee Publishing Company, 1971), "Farms over 1000 acres decreased in number from 20 to 2; farms from 500 to 1000 acres decreased from 52 to 9. The number of small farms in the county increased during these years. Farms from 50 to 100 acres increased from 151 to 464 and farms from 20 to 50 acres increased from 81 to 886.".
3. Washington County Deed Book F, p.645 (lien on Mary's house for cost of construction materials); Deed Book Q, p.598 (refers to property deeded to Mary F. Hardison and subsequently deeded by Mrs. A.[Amelia] R. Granade to W. C. Northington in 1896).
4. Jordan, *op. cit.*, p.247, a statement in the history of Antioch Church that Mrs. Fannie Hardison gave the land on which the church was built in 1857; Washington County Deed Book T, pp.680-81, records a gift of land in 1910 by Delia F. Hardison, widow of W. J. Hardison, for a parsonage for the church.

XV. HOME TO GEORGIA, 1875-1889   407

5. Hardison markers in the Posey Family Cemetery include William L. (died Mar. 15, 1870, age 71), his wife Sarah, (d. Feb.20, 1866, age 69), William J. (Mar.22, 1829-Sept. 1, 1904), his wife Delia Frances (1845-1914), Charles A. (May 29, 1827-Jan. 1, 1885), Susan A. (July 28, 1825-Dec. 16, 1895), Seth L. (Feb. 10, 1837-Jan. 15, 1847), and Nancy, (d. Aug. 20, 1849). According to data in the Cain Family Genealogical Collection, the cemetery is located on land which had formerly belonged to William L. Hardison. It is located a short distance into the woods on the east side of State Highway 272, south of Antioch Church in Oconee. In a deed of Oct. 29, 1903, W. J. and Delia Hardison deeded additional land to "the Hardison Cemetery," Deed Book Q, p.444. Amelia Granade was a witness to the deed.
6. Jordan, *op. cit.*, p.36.
7. The autograph book entry of John Randolph Hardison is quoted in full in Chapter 10.
8. Ruby Robison Penton and Joel R. Penton, *Samuel Robison of Washington County, Georgia*, p.490, in a section on the family of Elizabeth (Fisher) and William Robison, the authors state that Dr. Winfield Robert Robison, their son and the brother of the author of the letter, purchased all the estate property of Elizabeth and William. Metcalf Fisher's will of 1859 is found in Washington County Will Book B, pp.135-37.
9. Letter from Winifred Wood, January 23, 1994, Idyllwild, California, to Elizabeth Shreve Ryan; data on the Wood family is based on a survey of the family graves (Lilly, Winnie, George Washington Wood, and all of George and Winnie's children except George, Jr.) in the cemetery of Sunny Side, Georgia, and the Cain Family Genealogical Collection.*
10. Washington County deeds relative to Mary's house and land, cited in footnote #3.
11. Newspaper clippings in Elizabeth Shreve Ryan Collection (obituaries of Amelia Fisher Northington and Mary Northington Hardison were a gift from Nancy Louise Brown Slaughter). The latter obituary does not include the year of Mary's death, but the year 1889 appears in legal notices printed on the reverse of the page. There is no indication on the clippings of their sources. The obituary of Amelia Northington may have appeared in a Methodist publication or in the *Sandersville Herald*, the marriage write-up in a Macon newspaper or the *Sandersville Herald*, and the obituary of Mary Hardison in the *Sandersville Herald*. Amelia's marriage, which took place on Feb. 3, 1887, is recorded in Washington County Marriage Book F, p.144.
12. *Sandersville Herald*, Sandersville, Georgia, April 6, 1893.
13. Eighth Federal Census, 1860, Georgia, Wilkinson County, p.883, John E. Granade, age 5, is listed in the family of Dr. James Granade and Elizabeth Granade, with brother Adam and sister Fanny. John's age in the census records does not agree with the year of his birth as given on his gravestone in Memory Hill Cemetery, Milledgeville, where his dates of birth and death are June 29, 1858 and Dec. 15, 1933. Like the Hardisons, Northingtons, and Davises, the Granades had North Carolina roots. John Granade appeared in the Revolutionary War army accounts of the New Bern District of North Carolina (D.A.R. #492916) and later Granades appear in the records of New Bern and Craven County.
14. The Granade home, which is still standing (1996), is located on Brown Street in Oconee, now also State Highway 272; the Militia District Map of Washington County of 1897 (original in Georgia State Archives and Records, Atlanta) shows its location in District 88 between the property of T. F. Brown to the north and W. J. Hardison to the south, with Antioch Church located just south of the Hardison

property.*
15. Nancy Louise Brown Slaughter Collection.
16. Fred R. and Emilie K. Hartz, *Marriage and Death Notices from the Griffin (Georgia) Weekly News and the Griffin Weekly News and Sun, 1882-1896* (Vidalia: Gwendolyn Press, 1987), p.166, quoting from the Jan. 10, 1890 issue of the *Griffin Weekly News and Sun*.*
17. Data on the Brown family from Nancy Louise Brown Slaughter.*
18. Margaret Mitchell, *Gone with the Wind* (New York: Macmillan Company, 1936), p.36.

* Names and genealogical data on the families of Lilly, Winnifred, Amelia, Nancy, and Annie Hardison are found in the Appendices.

⁂ *Epilogue* ⁂

From the founding of Jamestown in 1607 to the settlement of Texas in the middle decades of the nineteenth century, the American South was peopled by successive waves of land-hungry settlers. At first they came directly from England to the tidewater area of Virginia, but soon from all of Great Britain and from the other colonies, pushing south from Virginia through the Carolinas to Georgia. After the Revolution the restless and ambitious from the original thirteen colonies were soon on the move into the lands they had won from Great Britain and later acquired from Spain, France, and Mexico. Those who chose the South as their destination populated the back country of the older states and then the areas which became Tennessee, Kentucky, Florida, Alabama, Mississippi, Louisiana, Arkansas, and finally Texas. The possession of land was seen as the means to security and prosperity in all of the colonies throughout the colonial era. For the South it continued to be so in the nineteenth century, as agriculture dominated its economy. Its vast, fertile lands were the treasure sought by the families who were willing to risk their lives to the enmity of the desperate Indians and the harsh conditions of successive frontiers.

Jasper Hardison came to North Carolina in the early 1700s as a mature man with a large family. Their British and previous American origins have not yet been documented, but their acquisitions of land from North Carolina to Texas are recorded in the county courthouses of the South. From Jasper's appearance on the banks of the Roanoke River and Albemarle Sound in North Carolina in 1723 to the settlement of a group of his descendants on the banks of the Trinity River in Texas in the 1850s, the records they left have been searched and their story told. Other chroniclers have written and continue to write of the journeys of their branches of the family in the migrations from North Carolina after the American Revolution.

Jasper and his sons came to North Carolina to exploit its great forests and their descendants remained in the South to clear and farm its land. Their migration through those lands and their successes and failures have been presented as an unfolding odyssey—"a long wandering marked by many changes of fortune." They and their companions on the migration trails were shaped by and they helped to shape the South's distinctive way of life. While there were many variations in that way of life from area to area, the similarities were great enough to weld them into a political entity, willing to do battle with the rest of the American states when their institutions and their understanding of the federal union were attacked.

In the aftermath of their defeat and the wreckage of the South's agricultural economy following the Civil War, the generations of Hardisons who came of age at the end of the nineteenth century turned increasingly from farming and the obsessive pursuit of land. Just as leaders of the New South preached economic diversity, so did many Hardison descendants teach their sons and daughters to look to varied choices for their careers. Law, teaching, and medicine had been popular choices among family members in the mid-nineteenth century and continued to be in post-Civil War years. To them have been added an increasing variety of callings, which have taken succeeding generations far from the land and from their Southern roots. However, few, if any, have lost their affection for the South, for its fields and woodlands, and for its bitter-sweet memories of lost battles and a lost way of life. This study was written for Hardison descendants who wish to know more of their past, the odyssey which brought their ancestors to and through the South. It is also for readers whose interest in the South and its role in the history of our nation will be enriched by sharing the story of an American family in transition.

Photographs

Winnifred Cornelia Davis (1834-1862)
Married John Randolph Hardison in 1857

Cain Collection

Mary Fletcher Northington (1839-1889)
Married John Randolph Hardison in 1866

Slaughter Collection

Mary Northington Hardison and John Randolph Hardison (1834-1874)
Ryan Collection

Lilly Mary Hardison (1859-1937)
Daughter of John Randolph Hardison and Winnifred Davis Hardison
Married George Washington Wood in 1909

Cain Collection

Winnifred Cornelia Hardison (1862-1905)
Daughter of John Randolph Hardison and Winnifred Davis Hardison
Married George Washington Wood in 1882

Cain Collection

Amelia Randolph Hardison (1869-1958)
Daughter of John Randolph Hardison and Mary Northington Hardison
Married John Evers Granade in 1887

Ryan Collection

Nancy Missouri Hardison (1871-1951)
Daughter of John Randolph Hardison and Mary Northingon Hardison
Married John Ackbar Darsey in 1890

Ryan Collection

Annie Mary Hardison (1873-1956)
Daughter of John Randolph Hardison and Mary Northington Hardison
Married Jarrett Irwin Brown in 1895

Slaughter Collection

May Lydia Wood (1886-1972), on left, daughter of George Washington Wood and Winnifred Hardison Wood, and Mary Elizabeth Granade (1888-1974), on right, daughter of John Evers Granade and Amelia Hardison Granade. May married James Robert Cain in 1908 and Mary married Reuben Thomas Shreve in 1913.

Ryan Collection

Family and friends at the home of George Washington Wood and Winnifred Hardison Wood, about 1904, Sunny Side, Georgia. Family members are front row seated, first from left, Roy Smith Wood, second from left, Mary Elizabeth Granade, and far right, George Washington Wood, Jr.; second row standing, second from left, Lilly Mary Hardison, and third from left, Winnifred Hardison Wood; second row seated, second from left, Annie Mary Darsey, and fourth from left, May Lydia Wood; third row, second from right (standing) Nancy Hardison Darsey; and fourth row, first from left Boyd Emory Wood (standing).

Ryan Collection

The Wood and Cain families, Sunny Side, Georgia, 1913. Standing on far left, James Robert Cain; front row seated, left to right, May Wood Cain, James Robert Cain, Jr., George Wood Cain, and Roy Smith Wood; second row seated, Lilly Hardison Wood, George Washington Wood, holding granddaughter Jane Wallace Wood, and sister of George Washington Wood; third row standing, George Washington Wood, Jr. and Daisy Hunter Wood (parents of Jane).

Cain Collection

Daughters of John Evers Granade and Amelia Hardison Granade with their husbands, Milledgeville, Georgia, about 1938. Standing left to right, Mary Elizabeth Granade Shreve, Helen Lanier Granade Long, Effie Evers Granade Nelson, and Lillie Marie Granade Bloodworth; seated left to right, Reuben Thomas Shreve, Robert Edgar Long, Patrick Alfred Nelson, and William Gastin Singleton Bloodworth.

Ryan Collection

Grandchildren of John Evers Granade and Amelia Hardison Granade, gathered for the wedding of Elizabeth Randolph Shreve to John Morris Ryan, July 30, 1949, Milledgeville, Georgia. Left to right, John Allen Bloodworth, Helen Evers Long, Helen Anne Bloodworth, Elizabeth Randolph Shreve, Lillie Marie Bloodworth (Mrs. Robert Bruce White), Mary Miles Bloodworth, and William Granade Bloodworth.

Ryan Collection

Elizabeth Shreve Ryan, daughter of Reuben Thomas Shreve and Mary Granade Shreve, and her daughters, Susan Randolph Ryan, on left, and Nancy Elizabeth Ryan, on right, 1968.

Ryan Collection

Appendices

Appendix I

Hardison Heads of Household in Federal Census Records of Georgia, 1820-1860

As always when writing about Federal Census population enumeration records for Georgia, it is necessary to state the regrettable fact that the three earliest, 1790, 1800, and 1810, have been lost. The list below is based on entries in the commercially produced indexes to the Federal Census records. Only in the case of the 1820 records of Washington County has a name by name search of all the heads of household in the microfilms of the original census record been made. Because of the varied spellings of the name Hardison, it is inevitable that some names have been missed, although listings for such obvious ones as Harderson and Hardisson were investigated. It is probable that some of the people listed as Hardiman were actually Hardisons.

Using the microfilms of the original records for 1820-1860, the entries for each head of household who was judged to be a Hardison were read in order to learn about the make-up of the family. Until 1850 only the name of the head of household was given, with the rest of the family enumerated in groups by sex and age. In the 1850 enumeration, and thereafter, the names of all family members, their ages, and place of birth were included. Information on the make-up of the families who are the subjects of *The Hardisons, a Southern Odyssey* has been included in the text.

As noted previously there are many problems in using Federal Census records. All for the 1820-1860 period are handwritten and the script is often difficult to read; names are often misspelled; and ages vary, depending on the accuracy of the member of the family who happened to be at home when the census taker made his call. Despite all these shortcomings, the Federal Census records are an invaluable resource for a great variety of research and have shed much light on the Hardisons' migrations and family make-up. The indexes also present problems, for there have been omissions and numerous misreadings of names, but they are a useful guide and a great time saver. The lists below do not attempt to include all the information on the Hardisons in each of the census enumerations from 1820 to 1860, but to help determine the identity and location of the families who settled in Georgia in the first half of the nineteenth century. Names marked with an asterisk indicate those which have been included in the text.

1820, Fourth Federal Census

> WASHINGTON COUNTY
> *Elizabeth, p.144
> *Frederick, p.128
> *John, p.146
> *William, p.133
> JONES COUNTY
> *Cullin, p.115 (Hardison spelled Hadason)
>
> (Also possibly Felix Harderson in Irwin County, p.126)

1830, Fifth Federal Census

> CRAWFORD COUNTY
> *Frederick, p.403
> TALBOT COUNTY
> William, p.336
> WASHINGTON COUNTY
> *William L., p.248
> WILKINSON COUNTY
> H., p.342
> (Possibly Widow Harderson in Irwin County)

1840, Sixth Federal Census

> EARLY COUNTY
> *Seth, p.127

1840, Sixth Federal Census (cont.)

    HOUSTON COUNTY
        James W., p.391
    MARION COUNTY
        William, p.73
    TALBOT COUNTY
        Harry, p.194
    WASHINGTON COUNTY
        *William L., p.228

1850, Seventh Federal Census

    CRAWFORD COUNTY
        F., p.428
    HOUSTON COUNTY
        Henry, p.314
        James W., p.315
        Thomas, p.314
        Thomas, Jr., p.316
    MARION COUNTY
        William B., p.286
    WASHINGTON COUNTY
        *William L., p.228
        C. Acman (son of William L.), p.212

1860, Eighth Federal Census

    BALDWIN COUNTY
        Charles S., p.150
    COWETA COUNTY
        Luther W., p.723
    CRAWFORD COUNTY
        Allen G., p.879
        George, p.879
    HOUSTON COUNTY
        Frances E., p.1060
        Hardy, p.1074

1860, Eighth Federal Census (cont.)
> HOUSTON COUNTY (cont.)
>> James W., p.950
>> Martha, p.1074
>> Theofilus, p.1075
>> Thomas, p.1075
> STEWART COUNTY
>> William B., p.362
> WASHINGTON COUNTY
>> *William L., pp.246-47

Appendix II

Genealogy (Selective) of the Hardison Families of Georgia, Florida, and Texas

The eleven generations who are listed below represent a selection based on the branches of the Hardison family which are the focus of *The Hardisons, a Southern Odyssey*. The initial chart is an outline of the four generations beginning with Jasper Hardison, the founder of the family in the South, who lived in North Carolina in the eighteenth century. They are the ancestors of Generation 5, the siblings William L., Seth, Temperance, Nancy, John M., Winnifred, and Elizabeth Hardison, who lived first in Washington County, Georgia in the first decade of the nineteenth century and then participated in the migrations which pushed the boundaries of the American South to Texas in the years preceding the Civil War. The names of the children of these siblings are listed as Generation 6, while the subsequent lists reflect the focus of the text of this study—the children of Seth Hardison, of his son John Randolph Hardison, and of selected branches of John's family. A number of blank pages have been provided at the end of the book to allow family members to add new members and to enter names of branches of the family not included in the lists.

The sources of the data for the lists are those on which the text of the study is based, primarily Federal Census records, marriage records, and information furnished by descendants. Many dates of births and deaths and of marriages are approximate, since such records were poorly kept in the South in the first half of the nineteenth century. As noted previously, ages and spelling of names of family members vary from decade to decade in the Federal Census records and in the absence of more dependable records, such as a family Bible or a gravestone, must be guessed or approximated.

The following abbreviations have been used:
   b.—born   d.—died
   ca.—approximate

Generations 1-5
See chart on opposite page

Generation 6
John Hardison Line

Children of WILLIAM L. HARDISON (1799-1870) and SARAH (1797-1866), formerly Mrs. Sarah Lewis, married ca.1820
1. SARAH
2. SUSAN ADDERAM, b.1825, d.1898
3. CHARLES ACMAN, b.1827, d.1885
4. WILLIAM J., b.1829, d.1904
5. NANCY, b.ca.1833
6. JOHN W., b.ca.1834
7. SETH L., b.1837, d.1847
8. MARY LOU, b.1839, d.1907

Sources—Federal Census records for Washington County, Georgia, 1830, 1840, 1850, and 1860, indicating William L. was born in North Carolina and Sarah and all their children were born in Georgia; Posey Family Cemetery (located on land formerly belonging to the Hardison family, Oconee, Georgia) where William L., wife Sarah, and children Susan Adderam, Charles Acman, William J. and wife Delia Frances (1845-1914), Nancy (who married a Willingham), Seth L., and Mary Lou (wife of John A. Joyner) are buried; and Cain Family Genealogical Collection. A male named Adrian, age 29, was listed in the 1860 Federal Census enumeration for the family, but his name does not appear in the other sources. Members of the family of Aaron Lewis, son of Sarah Hardison by her first marriage, are buried in the cemetery with the Hardisons

Children of SETH HARDISON (ca.1803-1871)

First married MARY BARFIELD ca.1824 (probably in Washington County, Georgia, no marriage record, name from Cain Family Genealogical Collection)
   1. MARY ANN, b.ca.1825 in Georgia, d.ca.1866 in Texas

Descent from Jasper Hardison of North Carolina to the John Hardison Family of Georgia and Florida

Generation 1   Jasper* — died in North Carolina, 1733

Generation 2   John — died in North Carolina, ca. 1780

Generation 3   Benjamin — died in North Carolina, ca. 1785

Generation 4   John — born between 1760 and 1770 in North Carolina, died in Florida, 1832

Generation 5

William Lanier
b. 1799 in North Carolina
d. 1870 in Georgia

Seth
b. ca. 1803 in Georgia
d. 1871 in Texas

Temperance
b. ca. 1805 in Georgia
d. ca. 1846 in Georgia

Nancy
b. 1806 in Georgia
d. 1890 in Texas

John M.
b. ca. 1810 in Georgia
d. 1836 in Georgia

Winnifred
b. 1812 in Georgia
d. 1877 in Georgia

Elizabeth
b. ca. 1815 in Georgia
d. ca. 1849 in Florida

*See Chapter 2 for chart of Jasper's sons and their children.

Chart created by Margaret H. Cannon

Second married MARY BLANDFORD (d.ca.1861) May 31, 1829 in Leon County, Florida

    2. NANCY, b.ca.1830 in Florida, d. after 1880 (listed in 1880 Federal Census for Texas)
    3. THOMAS G., b.ca.1832 in Florida, d.1859 in Texas
    4. JOHN RANDOLPH, b.1834 in Georgia, d.1874 in Texas
    5. CLARK B., b.ca.1836 in Georgia, d.ca.1861 in Texas
    6. WILLIAM L., b.ca.1836 in Georgia, d.1873 in Texas

Third married SARAH TIPTON (d.ca.1864) November 30, 1862 in Polk County, Texas

    7. LULA (given name probably SARAH LOUISE), b.1864 in Texas, d.1916 in Texas

Fourth married MARTHA JOHNSON (d.ca.1866) January 31, 1865 in Polk County, Texas

    8. JAMES HARVEY, b. 1866 in Texas, d.1943 in Texas

Fifth married MRS. MARY ANN DOWDEN June 16, 1867 in Polk County, Texas. No children.

Sources—Federal Census records for Jefferson County, Florida, 1830, Early County, Georgia, 1840, Gadsden County, Florida, 1850, Polk County, Texas, 1860, and Limestone County, Texas, 1870; marriage records of Leon County, Florida and Polk County, Texas; Cain Family Genealogical Collection; and Lost Prairie Church Cemetery, Limestone County, Texas, gravestones for Lula (married J. W. Sandifer) and James Harvey Hardison, but none for Seth or son John Randolph who Cain Collection records state are buried there.

Seth migrated from Washington County, Georgia to Jefferson County, Florida with John Hardison, presumed to be his father, and John's wife Winnifred Hardison in the late 1820s, to Early County, Georgia in the mid-1830s, to Gadsden County, Florida in the mid-1840s, to Polk County, Texas in 1857, and to Limestone County, Texas in the late 1860s. He died in Limestone County in October, 1871.

Children of TEMPERANCE HARDISON (b.ca.1805, d.ca.1846) and ENOS A. DAVIS (d.ca.1848), married in Washington County, Georgia ca.1822

    1. JAMES H., b.ca.1823, d.ca.1847
    2. THOMAS L., b.ca.1826, d.1864

3. BENJAMIN, b.ca.1828, d. in youth
4. MARY ELIZABETH, b.ca.1830, d.1900
5. JOHN N., b.ca.1832, d. in youth
6. WINNIFRED CORNELIA, b.1834, d.1862
7. SARAH ANN, b.ca.1836
8. JOEL A., b.ca.1839, d.ca.1850
9. EDWIN T., b.ca.1842, d.1879

Sources—Federal Census records for Washington County, Georgia, 1830 and 1840; *A Davis Family Record,* by Sara Jane Overstreet and Barbara Davis-Stovall (1983), pp.4-11, and *Elm Hill and Its People,* by James Porter Davis, p.40 (unpublished manuscripts, copies in collection of Washington County Historical Society, Sandersville, Georgia); entries on the Davis families and the Hardwick family (Mary Elizabeth Davis married Thomas William Hardwick and was the grandmother of Thomas William Hardwick, Governor of Georgia, 1921-1923) in *Cotton to Kaolin, a History of Washington County, Georgia, 1784-1989* (Sandersville: Washington County Historical Society, 1989), edited by Mary Alice Jordan; and Cain Family Genealogical Collection. Both Temperance Hardison Davis and Enos A. Davis died in Washington County, Georgia.

Children of NANCY HARDISON (1806-1890) and EMERALD BRIGHAM (1793-1863), married in Jefferson County, Florida, March 18, 1830

1. SETH (possibly a son of Emerald Brigham by his first wife)
2. ELIZABETH, b.1832, d.1905
3. WINEFORD (WINNIFRED), b.1834, d.1868
4. W. L., b.ca.1836
5. M. A. (female), b.ca.1839
6. BENJAMIN, b.1843, d.1935
7. JOHN, b.1843
8. NANCY TEMPERANCE, b.ca.1846

Sources—Federal Census records of Jefferson County, Florida, 1830, Early County, Georgia, 1840, Randolph County, Georgia, 1850, De Witt County, Texas, 1860, and Blanco County, Texas, 1870 and 1880; marriage records of Jefferson County, Florida and Randolph County, Georgia; federal pension application of Nancy Hardison Brigham as widow of a veteran of the War of 1812, #43568, August 12, 1884; pension application to Texas by Benjamin Brigham for service in the Confederate States Army, 1916; Blanco County News, *Heritage of Blanco County, Texas*

(Dallas: Curtis Media Corp., 1987), pp.372-73; and John Stribling Moursund, *Blanco County Families for One Hundred Years* (Burnet, Texas: Nortex Press, 1981), pp.25-26. Seth married Mary Jones, Elizabeth married Matthew Stubbs, and Winnifred married Lemuel Stubbs while the family was living in Randolph County in the 1840s. The Stubbs families migrated to Blanco County, Texas with the Brighams and Nancy Temperance married Lemuel after Winnifred died. Both Nancy Hardison Brigham and Emerald Brigham died in Texas.

Child of JOHN M. HARDISON (ca.1810-1836) and MARY FAIN, married in Early County, Georgia in 1834

    1. ANNABELLA, b.ca.1835

Sources—marriage and estate records of Early County, Georgia, the latter recording the disposal of the possessions of John M. after he died of wounds received in the Battle of Chickasawhatchy Swamp in Baker County, Georgia in July, 1836; reference to his death in the *Columbus Sentinel*, Columbus, Georgia, July 22, 1836; and listing of Annabella Hardison, age 15, as a member of the household of Charles Applewhite (relationship unknown) in the Federal Census of 1850, Stewart County, Georgia.

Children of WINNIFRED HARDISON (1812-1877) and JOEL A. DAVIS, married in Washington County, Georgia ca.1830

    1. GEORGE B., b.1832
    2. ENOS A., b.1834, d.1862
    3. LOUISA W. (later called Matilda), b.1836
    4. ELIZABETH E., b.1838
    5. JOHN LAWSON, b.1839
    6. TEMPERANCE, b.1841
    7. CHARLES E., b.1843
    8. WILLIAM P., b.1845
    9. ISABEL F., b.1846
    10. JAMES PORTER, b.1850
    11. JEFFERSON BUTLER, b.ca.1852, d.1942
    12. THOMAS JOEL, b.ca.1854, d.1927

Sources—Federal Census records for Washington County, Georgia, 1830, 1840, 1850, and 1860; *A Davis Family Record*, by Sara Jane Overstreet and Barbara Davis-Stovall, pp.12-26; *Elm Hill and Its People*, by James Porter Davis, pp.36-40, which describes the lives of the descendants of Winnifred and Joel Davis at their farm in Washington County, Georgia in the second half of the nineteenth century; and entries on the Davis families in *Cotton to Kaolin, a History of Washington County, Georgia, 1784-1989*, edited by Mary Alice Jordan (a portion of *Elm Hill and Its People* is reproduced on pp.320-26). Both Winnifred Hardison Davis and Joel A. Davis died in Washington County, Georgia.

Children of ELIZABETH HARDISON (ca.1815-ca.1849) and ABNER JACKSON (1813-1864), married ca.1835, probably in Florida

1. THEOPHILUS HARDEE, b.1836, d.1917
2. WINNEFRED, b.1838, d.1876
3. SARAH, b.1840, d.1913
4. ELIZABETH A. SAPHRONIA, b.1845, d.?
5. MARY ANN, b.1846, d.ca.1864

Sources—Federal Census records of Early County, Georgia, 1840 and Gadsden County, Florida, 1850; Alma Walker Jackson Genealogical Collection; and application by Dr. Theophilus Hardee Jackson to Florida for a pension for service in the Confederate States Army, 1909. After the death of Elizabeth Hardison Jackson in Florida in the late 1840s, Abner married Sarah Jane Holland and moved with his daughters to Catahoula Parish, Lousisana, where he died in 1864. His son remained in Florida.

Generation 7
Seth Hardison Line

Children of MARY ANN HARDISON (ca.1825-ca.1866) and JOHN GRAY, married in Early County, Georgia in 1842

1. DAVID, b.ca.1844
2. MARY A., b.ca.1848
3. J. (John?) H., b.ca.1850
4. SARAH, b.ca.1854

Sources—Federal Census records of Gadsden County, Florida, 1850 and Polk County, Texas, 1860; Early County, Georgia marriage records; tax records of Liberty County, Texas, 1860s; and Cain Family Genealogical Collection, including letters referring to Mary Ann. Mary Ann was the child of Seth Hardison's first marriage and was probably born in Washington County, Georgia. After her marriage to John Gray in Early County, Georgia in 1842, they migrated to Gadsden

County, Florida with the Hardison family in the late 1840s and to Polk County, Texas in the late 1850s. They moved to Liberty County, Texas in the 1860s and Mary Ann died shortly after the Civil War. The history of her family after her death has not been researched. The names and ages of her children are based on the Federal Census for Polk County, Texas, 1860.

Children of NANCY HARDISON (b.ca.1830, d.after 1880) and JAMES HARVEY REEVES (d.ca.1881), married ca.1849, probably in Gadsden County, Florida
  1. CAROLINE, b.ca.1851
  2. SARAH CLARK, b.ca.1857
  3. JAMES, b.ca.1863
  4. JOHN W., b.ca.1865

Sources—Federal Census records of Gadsden County, Florida, 1850, Polk County, Texas, 1860, and Limestone County, Texas, 1870 and 1880; tax records of Gadsden County, Florida, 1850s and Liberty and Limestone counties, Texas, 1860s; data in the records of Bethel Baptist Church of Polk County, Texas, Oak Shade Baptist Church, Liberty County, Texas, and Lost Prairie Baptist Church, Limestone County, Texas; and the Cain Family Genealogical Collection, particularly the letters of the 1860s and 1870s written when the Reeves and the family of John Randolph Hardison were living near each other in Limestone County. The Reeves family moved from Gadsden County, Florida to Texas, first to Limestone County in the late 1850s and to Polk County in the early 1860s, next to Liberty County and Limestone County during the 1860s, and to Leon County in the 1870s. The list of their children and their ages is based on data in the 1860 Federal Census for Polk County and 1870 Federal Census for Limestone County. Dr. Reeves was a physician and a lay minister in the Baptist Church. Caroline married Lewis R. Person and Sarah married Elijah Ivey and they lived in Limestone County. The lives of James and John have not been researched.

Child of THOMAS G. HARDISON (ca.1832-1859) and ANN (maiden name not known, formerly married to a Walker and a Jackson while living in Alabama and Florida), married in 1857, probably in Florida
  1. THOMAS, b.1859, d.before 1870

Sources—Federal Census records of Polk County, Texas, 1860 and Liberty County, Texas, 1870; deed records of Polk County, 1857-59; data on Ann Hardison and her Walker and Jackson children in *History of Polk County*, by Emma Haynes (Livingston: Keen Printing Co., 1968), vol.1, pp.104-05; and Cain Family Genealogical Collection. Soon after Thomas, a physician, and Ann were married, they migrated to Polk County, Texas in 1857 and he died in 1859. A son, Thomas, was listed as nine months old in the 1860 Federal Census for Polk County, but is not listed in the household of Ann Hardison in the 1870 Federal Census for Liberty County, where she had moved in the 1860s with her Walker and Jackson children. Presumably he died in early childhood. Ann and her other children lived in Polk and Liberty counties in the 1860s and 1870s.

Children of JOHN RANDOLPH HARDISON (1834-1874) and first wife, WINNIFRED CORNELIA DAVIS (1834-1862), married in Washington County, Georgia, November 26, 1857, and second wife, MARY FLETCHER NORTHINGTON (1839-1889), married in Washington County, Georgia, January 23, 1866

Children of first marriage
1. LILLY MARY, b.January 13,1859, d.January 28, 1937
2. WINNIFRED CORNELIA, b.March 10,1862, d.May 26, 1905

Children of second marriage
3. JOHN RANDOLPH, b.July 10, 1867, d.1867
4. AMELIA RANDOLPH, b.April 12, 1869, d.May 5, 1958
5. NANCY MISSOURI, b.June 15, 1871, d.March 21, 1951
6. ANNIE GLASS (later changed to ANNIE MARY), b.July 28,1873, d.1956

Sources—marriage records of Washington County, Georgia; Federal Census records of Polk County, Texas, 1860 and Limestone County, Texas, 1870; tax records of Polk County, Liberty County, and Limestone County, Texas, 1860s and 1870s; family data and letters of 1857-1882 of John and his wives in the Cain Family Genealogical Collection, Nancy Louise Brown Slaughter Collection, and Elizabeth Shreve Ryan Collection; and Compiled Service Record of John's service in the Confederate States Army, National Archives. John, a lawyer, and his first wife migrated with the Hardison family from Gadsden County, Florida to Polk County, Texas soon after their marriage in 1857 and lived in Polk County and adjoining Liberty County from 1858 to 1862. Winnifred died on March 12, 1862 and John volunteered for service in the Confederate Army, leaving his daughters Lilly and Winnie with his sister Mary Ann Hardison Gray in Liberty County. He married Mary Fletcher Northington in 1866 and they lived briefly in Liberty County before moving to Limestone County in 1867. In 1874 they moved to adjoining Freestone County and John died there on December 30, 1874. Mary and the five daughters moved to Georgia in 1875 and all remained there throughout the remainder of their lives. Mary died in Washington County, Georgia on May 23, 1889.

[CLARK B. (probably BLANDFORD) HARDISON (ca.1836-ca.1861), twin brother of William L. Hardison, no children]

Sources—Federal Census records of Polk County, Texas, 1860 list Clark as a bookkeeper; letter of June 1, 1873 by John Randolph Hardison states that Clark died before the Civil War, Cain Family Genealogical Collection.

Children of WILLIAM L. HARDISON (ca.1836-1873) and JOSEPHINE ELKINS, married in Savannah, Georgia, December 12, 1860

1. WILLIAM CLARK, b.ca.1873, d.1944
2. ALVA

Sources—Federal Census records of Polk County, Texas, 1860 (unable to find a listing for William in Federal Census records of Texas of 1870, probably living in Liberty County at that time); marriage records of Chatham County, Georgia; tax records of Liberty County, Texas, 1860s; deed records of Freestone County, Texas, 1873; data in Cain Family Genealogical Collection, including mention of William in the letters written by John Randolph Hardison in 1873, the year of William's death; and Compiled Service Record of William's service in the Confederate States Army, National Archives. William, a physician who received his medical training in Savannah, Georgia, migrated to Polk County, Texas with the Hardison family in the late 1850s. He enlisted in the Confederate Army in 1862 but was able to serve only intermittently due to ill health. He lived in Liberty County after the Civil War until the early 1870s when he moved to Freestone County, where he died in April, 1873. His widow married a Mr. Jones and she and her sons remained in Texas. Son William Clark was active in the petroleum industry in Limestone County and other areas of Texas. His obituary in the *Houston Chronicle*, June 26, 1944, mentions wife Pixie, daughters Camille, Fannie Beth, and Lucylee Wallace, and son Clark Hardison.

Children of LULA HARDISON (1864-1916) and J. W. SANDIFER (1863-1919), married in Limestone County, Texas, in 1885

1. LILLIE, b.1887
2. JOSEPH, b.1889
3. AMELIA, b.1891
4. HOLLAN, b.1894

5. WINNIE, b.1896
6. CECIL, b.1898
7. WILLIE, b.1902
8. FERRAL, b.1903
9. BOBBIE, b.1908

Sources—data from Violet Harris of Fairfield, Texas; marriage records of Limestone County, Texas; gravestones of Lula and her husband in Lost Prairie Church Cemetery, Limestone County; and Cain Family Genealogical Collection. Lula was born to Seth Hardison's third marriage, to Sarah Tipton in 1862 in Polk County, Texas. After Seth's death in 1871, she lived with her half-sister Nancy Hardison Reeves and her husband Dr. James Harvey Reeves.

Children of JAMES HARVEY HARDISON (1866-1943) and CLARA BELLE SIMS (1870-1929), married in Limestone County, Texas in 1886

1. LEONARD CLARK, b.1887, d.1979
2. MAGGIE, b. 1890, d.1910
3. WILLARD K., b.1891, d.1974
4. LELA, b.1893, d.1904
5. JAMES ALLEN, b.1896, d.1957
6. CLAUD, b.1898, d.1915
7. CLYDE, b.1899, d.1978
8. LARUE, b.1901, d.1988
9. LYDIA, b.1905, d.1986
10. ARVIN A., b.1908, d.1978
11. ALGIE O., b.1910, d.1974
12. ALVIS R., b.1913, d.1971

Sources—data from James Garvis Hardison and Ruby Hardison Hitt of Limestone County and Linda Hardison Smith of Dayton, Texas; marriage records of Limestone County; and from gravestones of James Harvey Hardison and his family in the Lost Prairie Church Cemetery, Limestone County. James Harvey Hardison was born to Seth Hardison's fourth marriage, to Martha Johnson in 1865 in Polk County. After Seth's death in 1871, he lived during his childhood with his half-brother John Randolph Hardison until John's death in 1874 and then with his half-sister Nancy and her husband Dr. James Harvey Reeves. In his adulthood, he farmed and reared his family in Limestone County.

Generation 8
John Randolph Hardison Line

[LILLY MARY HARDISON (1859-1937), married GEORGE WASHINGTON WOOD (1856-1920) on December 21, 1909 in Spalding County, Georgia. No children.]

Children of WINNIFRED CORNELIA HARDISON (1862-1905) and GEORGE WASHINGTON WOOD (1856-1920), married on November 2, 1882 in Americus, Georgia
1. DEAN OSGOOD, b.January 14, 1885, d.January 21, 1885
2. MAY LYDIA, b.July 15, 1886, d.February 11, 1972
3. GEORGE WASHINGTON, JR., b.October 3, 1889, d.June 5, 1962
4. BOYD EMORY, b.November 28, 1891, d.December 6, 1905
5. ROY SMITH, b.July 19, 1896, d.October 26, 1982

Children of AMELIA RANDOLPH HARDISON (1869-1958) and JOHN EVERS GRANADE (1858-1933), married in Macon, Georgia on February 3, 1887
1. MARY ELIZABETH, b.March 22, 1888, d.March 20, 1974
2. EFFIE EVERS, b.August 21, 1892, d.December 28, 1993
3. LILLIE MARIE, b.April 1, 1895, d.May 21, 1991
4. HELEN LANIER, b.June 14, 1901

Children of NANCY MISSOURI HARDISON (1871-1951) and JOHN ACKBAR DARSEY (1869-1953), married in Sunny Side, Spalding County, Georgia on January 1, 1890
1. RALPH HARDISON, b.December 1, 1890, d.October 17, 1983
2. ANNIE MARY, b.July 19, 1892, d.March 14, 1915
3. JOHN ACKBAR, JR., b.August 15, 1904, d.November 15, 1973
4. LILLIE WINIFRED, b.October 31, 1908, d.May 30, 1957

Children of ANNIE MARY HARDISON (1873-1956) and JARRETT IRWIN BROWN (1873-1916), married in Sunny Side, Spalding County, Georgia in 1895.

1. WILLIS NEAL
2. JARRETT IRWIN
3. MARY ELIZABETH
4. NANCY LOUISE
5. LILLIE HARDISON

Sources—data for the Wood family based on the Cain Family Genealogical Collection and information from the Wood and Cain families; data for the Granade, Darsey, and Brown families from descendants. The Wood family and the Darsey family lived in Sunny Side, Spalding County, Georgia and a number of their members are buried in the cemetery of the Sunny Side Methodist Church. The Granade family lived in Oconee, Washington County, Georgia until about 1908 and then in Milledgeville, Georgia, where Amelia Hardison Granade and John Evers Granade, their daughter Mary Elizabeth and her husband Reuben Thomas Shreve, and son-in-law Robert Edgar Long are buried. The Brown family lived in Dodge and Telfair counties, Georgia and Annie Hardison Brown, her husband Jarrett Irwin Brown, and daughter Lillie Hardison Brown are buried in the Erick Christian Church Cemetery, near Alamo, Georgia.

Generation 9
John Randolph Hardison Line—Grandchildren of His Daughters

Grandchildren of WINNIFRED HARDISON WOOD and GEORGE WASHINGTON WOOD

Children of MAY LYDIA WOOD (1886-1972) and JAMES ROBERT CAIN (1866-1948), married on March 25, 1908
1. JAMES ROBERT, JR., b.January 28, 1909, d.April 5, 1979
2. GEORGE WOOD, b.September 22, 1910, d.July 20, 1990
3. JOHN HARDISON, b.July 10, 1914, d.November 9, 1957
4. LILLY MARY, b.August 13, 1916

Children of GEORGE WASHINGTON WOOD, JR., (1889-1962) and DAISY SLOAN HUNTER (1884-1975)
1. JANE WALLACE, b.May 8, 1913, d.December 21, 1992
2. DOROTHY PARKS, b.July 23, 1915, d.September 23, 1973
3. DAISY HUNTER, b.April 28, 1917, d.February 1991
4. MARGARET WINIFRED, b.July 6, 1919
5. GEORGE WASHINGTON III, b.December 5, 1921

Children of ROY SMITH WOOD (1896-1982) and HELEN BALCH (1915-1965)
1. ROY SMITH, JR., b.January 28, 1937
2. FRANK BALCH, b.October, 12, 1942
3. ADAM, b.December 6, 1955

(Second marriage of Roy Smith Wood to Eleanor Murrah Wilson—no children.)

Grandchildren of AMELIA HARDISON GRANADE and JOHN EVERS GRANADE

Child of MARY ELIZABETH GRANADE (1888-1974) and REUBEN THOMAS SHREVE (1878-1958), married in Milledgeville, Georgia on June 25, 1913
1. ELIZABETH RANDOLPH, b.July 22, 1926

[EFFIE EVERS GRANADE (1892-1993) and PATRICK ALFRED NELSON were married in Milledgeville, Georgia on September 25, 1923, no children.]

Children of LILLIE MARIE GRANADE (1895-1991) and WILLIAM GASTIN SINGLETON BLOODWORTH (1891-1969), married in Milledgeville, Georgia on February 3, 1917
1. WILLIAM GRANADE, b.February 26, 1918, d.November 8, 1979
2. JOHN ALLEN, b.January 10, 1921, d.September 16, 1956
3. LILLIE MARIE, b.November 18, 1923
4. HELEN ANNE, b.August 27, 1926
5. MARY MILES, b.March 22, 1931

Child of HELEN LANIER GRANADE (b.1901) and ROBERT EDGAR LONG (1892-1951), married in Milldegeville, Georgia on August 24, 1921
1. HELEN EVERS, b.January 22, 1934

Grandchildren of NANCY HARDISON DARSEY and JOHN ACKBAR DARSEY

Children of RALPH HARDISON DARSEY (1890-1983) and MAGGIE FREEMAN (1893-1970)
1. RALPH HARDISON, JR., b.September 13, 1917, d.July 11, 1990
2. SARAH MARGARET, b.June 28, 1919
3. FRED FREEMAN, b.July 12, 1922, d.February 7, 1980
4. JOHN ACKBAR, b.December 4, 1924
5. WILLIAM NOVIN, b.December 18, 1928

[ANNIE MARY DARSEY (1892-1915)—no children]

[JOHN ACKBAR DARSEY, JR. (1904-1973) married first MARY BELLE WOODRUFF, second EMMA KEYES, no children]

Child of LILLIE WINIFRED DARSEY (1908-1957) and CARL NEWTON RICHARDSON (1908-1996)
1. CARL NEWTON, JR., b.May 21, 1938

Grandchildren of ANNIE MARY HARDISON and JARRETT IRWIN BROWN

Children of WILLIS NEAL BROWN and NELLIE MCCLENDON
1. WILLIS NEAL
2. ANNIE OLA
3. LILOUISE

[JARRETT IRWIN BROWN—no data]

MARY ELIZABETH BROWN—two marriages, second to Haslett, one daughter

[NANCY LOUISE BROWN married EARL CHARLES SLAUGHTER in 1944—no children]

[LILLIE HARDISON BROWN—no children]

Generations 10 and 11
John Randolph Hardison Line
(Hardison-Wood-Cain and Hardison-Granade)

HARDISON-WOOD-CAIN LINE (descent through May Wood Cain, daughter of Winnifred Hardison Wood and George Washington Wood, and her husband James Robert Cain)

Child and grandchildren of JAMES ROBERT CAIN, JR. (1909-1979) and KATHERINE HAWTHORN (1916-1984)
1. JAMES ROBERT CAIN, III, b.July 4, 1943, m.CASSANDRA MARIE SWEATT
   1. KAREN MARIE, b.December 21, 1976
   2. CHRISTOPHER HAWTHORN, b.August 28, 1981
   3. LISA ANN, b.August 23, 1983

[GEORGE WOOD CAIN (1910-1990) married MARY LOU ELLIOTT CAIN (1924-1986) on February 14, 1962—NO CHILDREN]

Children and grandchildren of JOHN HARDISON CAIN (1914-1957) and MARY LOU ELLIOTT (1924-1986), married on October 5, 1946
1. JOHN RANDOLPH HARDISON CAIN, b.July 9, 1948, married LYLLIAM LOYRETT CORBELLO on September 10, 1985
   1. MARIA ISABELLE, b.October 4, 1991
   2. LYLLIAM AMERICA, b.March 16, 1994
2. CORNELIA WINNIFRED CAIN, b.August 17, 1951, married THOMAS LEIGH BIEN, JR. on January 2, 1983
   1. THOMAS LEIGH, III, b.April 16, 1984
   2. JULIA ELLIOTT, b.October 23, 1987
3. MAY LYDIA WOOD CAIN, b.August 1, 1953, married JOHN DAVID CAVANAUGH on June 23, 1990
   1. GEORGIA WOOD, b.January 2, 1992
   2. JOHN DAVID, JR., b.May 5, 1993

[LILLY MARY CAIN, b.August 13, 1916—no children]

HARDISON-GRANADE-SHREVE LINE (descent through Mary Elizabeth Granade Shreve, daughter of Amelia Hardison Granade and John Evers Granade, and her husband Reuben Thomas Shreve)

Children of ELIZABETH RANDOLPH SHREVE, b.July 22, 1926, and JOHN MORRIS RYAN, married on July 30, 1949
1. NANCY ELIZABETH, b.July 9, 1960
2. SUSAN RANDOLPH, b.January 15, 1962, married THOMAS ALFRED SULLY, III on April 25, 1992

HARDISON-GRANADE-BLOODWORTH LINE (descent through Lillie Marie Granade Bloodworth, daughter of Amelia Hardison Granade and John Evers Granade, and William Gastin Singleton Bloodworth)

Child and grandchild of WILLIAM GRANADE BLOODWORTH (1918-1979) and HELEN RENFROE, married on March 24, 1945
    1. WILLIAM HARRIS, b.February 10, 1958, married BARBARA LEE EPPELSHEIMER on April 23, 1994
        1. MARGARET MAY MARIE, b.September 26, 1995

Children and grandchildren of JOHN ALLEN BLOODWORTH (1921-1956) and SHIRLEY ANN MOORE, married on December 4, 1943
    1. JOHN ALLEN, JR., b.June 7, 1945, married SANDRA KAY TRUITT on April 13, 1967
        1. JOHN ALLEN, III, b.November 22, 1974
    2. DAVID BELVIN, b.September 15, 1948, married SUSAN COLLEEN CAMPBELL in 1979
        1. HEATHER KATHRINE, b.July 2, 1980

Children and grandchildren of LILLIE MARIE BLOODWORTH, b.November 18, 1923, and ROBERT BRUCE WHITE, married on May 18, 1946
    1. ROBERT BRUCE, JR., b.December 4, 1952, married SANDRA MARIE MOTYL on October 17, 1987
    2. WILLIAM CHANDLER, b.September 18, 1954, married CANDICE LYNETTE OLSEN on May 12, 1990
        1. ALEX CHANDLER, b.February 19, 1992
        2. NATALIE CANDICE, b.May 24, 1995

[HELEN ANNE BLOODWORTH, b.August 27, 1926—no children]

Child and grandchild of MARY MILES BLOODWORTH, b.March 22, 1931, and MORTIMER MEYER WEINBERG, JR., married on March 10, 1957
    1. MORTIMER MEYER WEINBERG, III, b.June 30, 1960, married NANCY LANE SINGLETON, on June 13, 1987
        1. MEREDITH AMANDA, b.February 12, 1990

HARDISON-GRANADE-LONG LINE (descent through Helen Lanier Granade Long, daughter of Amelia Hardison Granade and John Evers Granade, and Robert Edgar Long)

Children and grandchild of HELEN EVERS LONG, b.January 22, 1934, and WESLEY EDWARD BASS, JR., married July 2, 1955
    1. ELIZABETH LANIER, b.December 23, 1964, married JAMES TIMOTHY SHANDS on August 31, 1991
    2. CATHERINE RANDOLPH, b.June 19, 1967, married RONALD LAWRENCE PERONA on May 8, 1993
        1. COREY ELIZABETH, b.June 24, 1995

Index

The repeated use of given names in succeeding generations of Jasper Hardison's descendants, particularly in eighteenth century North Carolina, necessitates the use of a system of identification. The identifications listed below have been used in the index for Jasper, the founder of the North Carolina family, his sons Charles, Jasper, John, Joseph, Joshua, Richard, and Thomas, and their male progeny who share their names. Also included are two of Jasper's grandsons, Benjamin and William, whose names were shared by several other North Carolina Hardisons, and Benjamin's son and grandson, Seth. Middle names or initials are known for several of the nineteenth century men who were given the favorite names and these have been used to identify these men. Mary, Elizabeth, Nancy, and Winnifred Hardisons abound and they have been identified by the name of husband or father and by cross refernces to their married names. To help establish the identity of all Hardisons listed in the index, the reader should consult the descent chart of Jasper, founder of the North Carolina family, on page 32 and the genealogical data in Appendix II, a selective listing of Jasper's descendants through the twentieth century.

    HARDISON, JASPER I, founder of North Carolina family, d.1733

    HARDISON, CHARLES I, son of Jasper I

    HARDISON, JASPER II, son of Jasper I, also known as Jasper, Sr.

    HARDISON, JASPER III, son of Jasper II, also known as Jasper, Jr.

    HARDISON, JOHN I, son of Jasper I

    HARDISON, JOHN II, son of John I, also known as John, Sr.

    HARDISON, JOHN III, son of John II, also known as John, Jr.

    HARDISON, JOHN IV, grandson of John I, son of Benjamin I, moved to Georgia ca.1800, d.1832 in Florida

    HARDISON, JOSEPH I, son of Jasper I

HARDISON, JOSHUA I, son of Jasper I

HARDISON, JOSHUA II, son of Joshua I, also known as Joshua, Jr.

HARDISON, RICHARD I, son of Jasper I

HARDISON, RICHARD II, son of Richard I, also known as Richard, Jr.

HARDISON, THOMAS I, son of Jasper I

HARDISON, THOMAS II, great-nephew of Thomas I, grandson of John I, son of Benjamin I, moved to Georgia ca.1800

HARDISON, BENJAMIN I, son of John I

HARDISON, BENJAMIN II, son of William I

(There are also several Benjamins who could not be identified.)

HARDISON, SETH I, son of Benjamin I

HARDISON, SETH II, son of John IV, grandson of Benjamin I

HARDISON, WILLIAM I, son of John I

HARDISON, WILLIAM II, son of Benjamin I

HARDISON, WILLIAM III, son of Joseph I

Names of the counties and communities of the Hardisons' residence have been listed under the states in which they lived—North Carolina, Georgia, Florida, and Texas.

INDEX

Adams, Elizabeth, 136
Alabama-Coushatti Indians, 208
Alford, Bias, 139
Anderson, F., 216, 217
Ann (slave), 191
Annee (slave), 49
Anthony (slave), 191
Anthony, J. D. (Rev.), 281, 320
Apalachee Indians, 147-48
Applewhite, Charles, 170
Applewhite, Julia, 170

Barefield. *See* Barfield
Barfield, Mary, 152
Barfield, Mary, family of, 434, 436
Barfield/Barefield family, of Ga. and Fla., 152, 172
Barfield/Barefield, Catherine, 185
Barfield/Barefield, James, 172, 176, 185, 194
Barfield/Barefield, Jesse, 172
Barfield/Barefield, John, 185
Barfield/Barefield, Mary Riley, 172
Barfield/Barefield, Nancy, 185
Barfield/Barefield, Rachel, 185
Barfield/Barefield, Sarah, 185
Barfield/Barefield, Sarah Conyers, 172, 185, 194
Barfield/Barefield, Thomas, 185
Barfield/Barefield, William, 152
Barksdale, William, 324
Bean, Allie, 389
Bean, William (Maj.), 368, 370
Beasley, Mary Hardison, 75, 78
Bell (slave), 49
Benjamin (slave), 191
Bently, James, 52
Bird family, of Limestone Co., Tex. *See* Byrd
Blackshear, David, 123
Blackshear, Elijah, 123
Blandford family, of Ga. and Fla., 152
Blandford, Champ (Champion?), 152, 170, 173, 184, 185, 186, 187, 191, 218
Blandford, Clark, 152, 170, 184
Blandford, Clark, Jr., 152
Blandford, Mary, 152, 153, 170, 172, 173, 176, 183, 184, 187, 191, 215, 216, 219, 220, 298, 357

Blandford, Mary, family of, 436
Blanford. *See* Blandford
Blocker, Stephen, 176
Bloodworth family, of Ga. and S.C., 446, 449-50
Bloodworth, Lillie Marie Granade, 402
Blount family, of N.C., 41
Blount, John, 23
Blount, Sarah Hardison, 102, 104
Bob (slave), 77, 103
Bozman, Leven, 48, 49
Brice, William, 50
Brigham family, of Fla., Ga., and Tex., 153, 171
Brigham, Benjamin, 171, 231
Brigham, Elizabeth, 171
Brigham, Emerald, 153, 155, 171, 173, 177, 194, 207, 231
Brigham, Emerald, family of, 437-38
Brigham, John, 171
Brigham, M. A., 171
Brigham, Martha Mott, 153
Brigham, N. T., 171
Brigham, Nancy Hardison, 128, 132, 153, 156, 158, 163, 170, 171, 176, 193, 194, 207, 231, 299
Brigham, Nancy Hardison, family of, 437-38
Brigham, Seth, 171
Brigham, W. L., 171
Brigham, Wineford, 171
Brooking, ____ (Major), 320. *See also* Brookins, Haywood
Brookins, Haywood, 320
Brooks, James, 156
Brown, Annie Glass/Mary Hardison, 309, 313, 362, 364, 381, 386, 390, 392, 395, 396, 397, 399, 402, 405
Brown, Annie Glass/Mary Hardison, family of, 445, 447
Brown, Jarrett Irwin, 405
Brown, Jarrett Irwin, family of, 445, 447
Brown, Lillie Hardison, 405
Brown, Mary Elizabeth, 405
Brown, Morgan, 135, 139
Brown, Nancy Louise, 309, 383, 405
Brown, Willis Neal, 405

INDEX

Browney family, N.C., 48
Browney, John, 49. *See also* Browning
Browning family, N.C., 42, 48
Browning, John, 22
Burgess, John, 205, 212, 218, 219, 302
Burton, Ellen Reeves, 385, 389
Burton, John, 389
Buttrey, Silvanus, 55
Byrd family, of Limestone Co., Tex., 326, 337, 354, 385, 391
Byrd, Annie (Grandma), 312, 333, 334, 337, 354, 360, 361, 362, 363, 385, 392

Cain Family Genealogical Collection, 309, 312, 383
Cain family, of Ga., 445, 448
Cain, James Robert, 400
Cain, May Lydia Wood, 400
Caksky (slave), 77
Call, Wilk, 329
Capers, F. W. (Major), 281
Capers, Henry D. (Col.), 320
Capers, William (Bishop), 290, 320
Carkeet family, of Maine, 4-8
Carkeet family, of N.C., 24, 41, 96
Carkeet family, of N.C., land records, 42-46
Carkeet, Benjamin, 6, 23, 26, 42, 43, 44, 46, 48, 49, 52, 58, 91, 96
Carkeet, Lydia, 42, 44, 45
Carkeet, Lydia Glanfield, 5, 6
Carkeet, Mary Hardison, 6, 23, 26, 32, 46, 88, 91
Carkeet, Mary Hardison, land records, 42-46
Carkeet, Mary Smithwick, 44
Carkeet, Robert, 6, 42
Carkeet, Sarah, 44
Carkeet, William, 42, 43, 44, 45, 46, 49, 50, 55, 58, 59, 78, 91, 93, 96
Carkeet, William, of Maine, 5, 6
Carkeete, 96. *See also* Carkeet
Carkete, 5. *See also* Carkeet
Caroline (former slave), 328, 331, 346
Carter, Isom, 123
Census Records. Hardison Family in: N. C. State Census, 1784-1787, pp. 89-91; Federal Census of 1790, N. C., 91-93; Federal Census of 1800, N. C., 93-97; Federal Census of 1810, N. C., 109-10; Federal Censuses of 1820-1860, Ga., 429-32; Federal Census of 1820, Ga., Washington Co., 130-32; Federal Census of 1830, Ga., Washington Co., 137-38; Federal Census of 1830, Fla., Jefferson Co., 151-52; Federal Census of 1840, Ga., Early Co., 170-71; Federal Census of 1850, Fla., Gadsden Co., 184-85;Federal Slave Census of 1850, Fla., Gadsden Co., 185-86; Federal Census of 1860, Tex., Polk Co., 215-17; Federal Slave Census of 1860, Tex., Polk Co., 217-18; Federal Census of 1870, Tex., Limestone Co., 306-07
Cerkeet, 43. *See also* Carkeet
Charity (slave), 101, 126
Chason, James, 27
Cherry family, of N.C., 41
Chesson, 27. *See also* Chason
Choate, Moses L., 208
Civil War: Atlanta campaign, John Randolph Hardison participation in, 255-72; Brigham, Benjamin, C.S.A. service, 231; Davis family of Washington Co., Ga., C.S.A. service, 231, 235, 246, 263, 267; Granbury's Texas Brigade, 239-45, John Randolph Hardison's service in, 255-86; Hardison, John Randolph, C.S.A. service, 231-86; Hardison, John Randolph, courtship during War, 245-52, 264-71, 285; Hardison, William L., C.S.A. service, 235; Jackson, Theophilus Hardee, C.S.A. service, 231; Texas Brigade, *see* Granbury's Texas Brigade
Clarisa (former slave), 346
Collins, Elizabeth Duggan Hardison, 99, 101, 102, 106, 126. *See also* Duggan, Elizabeth and Hardison, Elizabeth Duggan
Collins, John, 99, 102, 126
Collins, Mary Ann, 56
Comanche Indians, 299
Conyers, Sarah, 172, 185, 194
Cook, Albert, 394
Cooper, Edward, 103
Corey, Benjamin, 53

INDEX

Cowart, William, 139
Cravy, Henry, 175
Creek Indians, 113, 119-23, 148-50, 152, 165, 167-68, 208
Crowell, John, 130, 135
Crum (slave), 292
Curkeete, Lydia Glanfield, 5, 6
Curkeete, William, of Maine, 5, 6
Curkeete, 5. *See also* Carkeet
Curkeitt, Ellis, 5
Curkeitt, 5. *See also* Carkeet

Daley, John, 44, 56
Daly, John, 44, 54. *See also* Daley, John
Daly, Mary Carkeet, 44. *See also* Carkeet, Mary Hardison, and Hardison, Mary
Darsey, Annie Mary, 404, 405
Darsey, John Ackbar, 404
Darsey, John Ackbar, Jr., 404, 405
Darsey, John Ackbar, family of, 444-45, 447
Darsey, Lillie Winifred, 405
Darsey, Nancy/Nannie (Sissie) Missouri Hardison, 313, 343, 345, 348, 350, 354, 360, 361, 371, 381, 386, 390, 392, 396, 397, 399, 402, 404
Darsey, Nancy/Nannie (Sissie) Missouri Hardison, family of, 444-45, 447
Darsey, Ralph Hardison, 404, 405
Davis family, of Washington Co., Ga., 136-38, 359, 393
Davis, Benjamin, 190
Davis, Charles I., 188
Davis, Diocletian, 136, 137
Davis, Edwin T., 190, 193, 194, 209, 222, 223, 225, 226, 231, 234, 235, 246, 263, 267, 313, 328, 329, 330, 338, 340, 356, 357, 359, 374, 375, 381, 383, 384, 385, 390, 392, 400
Davis, Elizabeth (daughter of Joel Davis), 194
Davis, Elizabeth Adams, 136
Davis, Enos, 125, 136, 137, 140, 190, 193, 218, 231, 245, 267
Davis, Enos, family of, 436-37
Davis, Enos (son of Joel), 188, 194, 209, 226, 231, 246
Davis, James, 190
Davis, James P., 188
Davis, James Porter, 136, 137
Davis, Joel, 125, 128, 136, 137, 138, 188, 190, 193, 194, 209, 225, 231, 245, 246, 313, 359, 393
Davis, Joel, family of, 438-39
Davis, Joel A., 190
Davis, John, 173, 175, 190
Davis, John (father of Joel and Enos Davis), 136
Davis, Lawson, 231, 246
Davis, Mary Elizabeth (Liz), 190, 193, 209, 225, 313, 329, 338, 341, 355, 356, 374, 375, 381, 393, 394, 397, 399
Davis, Mattie Jones, 330, 341, 359, 375
Davis, Sarah (Sallie) Ann, 190, 209, 225, 313, 330, 338, 341, 358, 375, 381, 394
Davis, Selah, 190
Davis, Temperance (daughter of Joel Davis), 194
Davis, Temperance Hardison, 125, 128, 129, 132, 136, 137, 140, 158, 163, 190, 193, 231, 245, 246, 267
Davis, Temperance Hardison, family of, 436-37
Davis, Thomas L., 190, 193, 194, 209, 226, 231, 246, 267
Davis, William P., 231, 246
Davis, Winnifred Cornelia (wife of John Randolph Hardison), 140, 163, 172, 180, 190, 191, 192, 193, 194, 209, 214, 215, 216, 218, 222, 223, 225, 226, 235, 245, 246, 287, 309, 357, 382, 406
Davis, Winnifred Cornelia (wife of John Randolph Hardison), family of, 441-42, 444, 445-46, 448
Davis, Winnifred Hardison, 125, 128, 129, 132, 136, 137, 138, 158, 163, 188, 193, 231, 245, 246, 313, 359
Davis, Winnifred Hardison, family of, 438-39
Devore, C., 209
Dewberry, Sallie, 328
Dowden, Mary Anne, 219
Duggan, Elizabeth, 99, 101, 102, 106, 126
Duggan, Ivy W., 250
Duggan, Mary Smithwick, 99
Duggan, William, 99

INDEX

Duncan family, of Limestone Co., Tex., 392
Dunnam, Maggie, 213

Easter (slave), 101, 126
Elkins, Josephine, 219, 221, 299, 353, 354, 355, 356, 376
Elkins, Josephine, family of, 442
Elm Hill, Washington Co., Ga., 137
Etheridge, Elijah, 105, 106
Etheridge, Elizabeth Hardison, 105, 106
Etheridge, Indiana Northington, 290, 310, 312, 319, 322, 324, 325, 326, 327, 328, 331, 333, 348, 349, 366, 370
Everard, Richard, 24, 25, 34, 51, 54
Everard, Richard (Gov.), 24, 54
Everett, Thomas, 48
Everitt, Elizabeth Hardison, 102, 104
Evins, Alse, 49

Fain family, of Fla. and Ga., 170
Fain, Mary, 166, 168, 170
Fain, Mary, family of, 438
Fain, Matthew, 168, 170
Federal Census Records, Hardison family in. *See* Census Records, Hardison family in
Fisher family, of Washington Co., Ga., 287-93
Fisher, Amelia, 327
Fisher, Amelia (Milly), 246, 287, 290, 292, 390, 403
Fisher, Amelia (Milly), correspondence with daughter Mary Hardison, 1866-70, pp. 309-41
Fisher, Amelia (Milly), correspondence with daughter Mary Hardison, 1871-75, pp. 343-76
Fisher, Amelia (Milly), death of, 401
Fisher, Elizabeth, 287, 290, 291, 292, 388
Fisher, Elizabeth Schaffner, 289
Fisher, Harris, 325, 328
Fisher, James, 402
Fisher, John, 287, 290, 291, 292
Fisher, John, of Mass., 289
Fisher, Lavinia, 290, 291
Fisher, Mary, 318, 325
Fisher, Mehitable Metcalf, 289
Fisher, Metcalf, 247, 287, 289, 290, 291, 292, 388

Fisher, Sallie, 318
Fisher, Sarah Ann, 290
Fisher, William, 290
Florida, China Hill, 182, 194
Florida, colonial history, 147-51
Florida, Gadsden Co.: Barfield/Barefield family in, 185; establishment and early history, 179-83; Gray family in, 184, 188, 191-92; Hardison family in, 179-98; Jackson family in, 185, 188-90, 193; Reeves family in, 184-85, 188
Florida, Hardison family, in census records: Federal Census of 1830, Jefferson Co., 151-52; Federal Census of 1850, Gadsden Co., 184-85; Federal Slave Census of 1850, pp. 185-86
Florida, Hardison family, slaves, 152 (Jefferson Co.); 185-88, 191, 194-95 (Gadsden Co.). *See also* Slaves (listing by name)
Florida, Jefferson Co.: Brigham family in, 153; establishment and early history, 150-51; Hardie/Hardy family in, 153-55; Hardison family in, 145-61
Florida, Monticello, 155, 156
Florida, northern counties in ante-bellum era, 145-51
Florida, Quincy, 181-83
Florida, Tallahassee, 183-84
Fonville, Isaac, 50
Foster, Samuel T. (Captain), Confederate Army diarist, 237, 242, 257, 260, 261, 268, 272, 275, 276, 277, 237
Francis, Cordell, 139
Francis, Sallie, 393

Gainer, Benjamin, 40, 41, 45
Gardner, Hannah Hardison, 102, 104
Gardner, Isaac, 102
Garrat, William, 26
Garrett family, of N.C., 27, 41
Garrett, Daniel, 48, 49
Garrett, James, 48
Garrett, Mary, 27
Garrett, William, 26, 27, 48, 53, 54, 56
Garrott, William, 26
Garvey, Florida Walker, 221
Garvey, Gustavus, 221

George (slave), 292
Georgia, Bay Spring, 245, 250, 290, 381-82
Georgia, Blakely, 165-66
Georgia, colonial history, 113-19
Georgia, cotton culture, 133-34, 139
Georgia, Davisboro, 136-38
Georgia, Early Co.: Brigham family in, 171; establishment and early history, 165-68; Hardison family in, 163-78; Jackson family in, 171-73, 176
Georgia, Elm Hill, 137
Georgia, Fort Gaines, 165, 167
Georgia, Hardison family, in census records: Federal Census of 1820, Washington Co., 130-32; Federal Census of 1830, Washington Co., 137-38; Federal Census of 1840, Early Co., 170-71
Georgia, Hardison family, slaves, 126, 127, 131, 135, 138 (Washington Co.); 172-73 (Early Co.). *See also* Slaves (listing by name)
Georgia, Hardison heads of household in, Federal Census Records of 1820-1860, pp. 429-432
Georgia, Oconee, 245, 381
Georgia, Randolph Co., Brigham family in, 171
Georgia, Washington Co.: Davis family in, 125, 136-38, 140, 190, 231, 245-46; establishment and early history, 119-125; Fisher-Robison-Northington families in, 287-93; Hardison family in, 113-43, 379-408; in Civil War, 245-52, 272-73, 280-82; in Reconstruction, 379-80; map, 109; Northington family in, 290, 312, letters to and about Northingtons, 309-76
Gilmer, J.N., 320
Glanfield, Lydia, 5, 6
Glanfield, Lydia Ward, 5
Glanfield, Robert, 5, 6
Glass, ____ (Dr.), 312, 354, 362, 395
Glass family, of Limestone Co., Tex., 391
Granade, Amelia (Melia/Millie) Randolph Hardison, 313, 332, 333, 334, 335, 336, 337, 338, 343, 346, 348, 349, 350, 351, 352, 354, 355, 360, 361, 380, 381, 383, 386, 390, 392, 396, 397, 399, 401, 402, 403, 404, 406

Granade, Amelia (Melia/Millie) Randolph Hardison, family of, 444, 446-47, 449-50
Granade, Effie Evers, 402
Granade, Helen Lanier, 402
Granade, John Evers, 401, 402
Granade, John Evers, family of, 444, 446-47, 449-50
Granade, Lillie Marie, 402
Granade, Mary Elizabeth, 402
Granbury, Hiram B., 240. *See also* Granbury's Texas Brigade
Granbury's Texas Brigade, C.S.A., formation of, 239-45
Granbury's Texas Brigade, C.S.A., John Randolph Hardison's service in, 239-45, 255-86
Gray family, of Ga. and Fla., 171
Gray, D. L., 216
Gray, David, 184
Gray, J. H., 216
Gray, John, 171, 184, 186, 188, 191, 192, 209, 212, 216, 218, 220, 298, 302
Gray, John, family of, 439-40
Gray, Mary, 184
Gray, Mary A., 216
Gray, Mary Ann Hardison, 152, 170, 171, 183, 184, 186, 188, 191, 192, 215, 216, 220, 224, 226, 293, 298, 313, 357
Gray, Mary Ann Hardison, family of, 439-40
Gray, Sarah, 216
Gregory, Allie Bean, 389
Gregory, Harrison (Dr.), 389
Gregory, Isaac, 47
Griffin family, of N.C., 41

Halston, David, 216, 217
Hannah (slave), 77
Hardee family, of Ga. and Fla., 153
Hardee family, of Maine, 7
Hardeson, Charles, of Onslow Co., N.C., 50
Hardeson, John, of Onslow Co., N.C., 50
Hardeson, 6. *See also* Hardison
Hardie family, of Ga. and Fla., 153
Hardie family, of Maine, 7
Hardie, Allen, 155

INDEX

Hardie, Mary, 156
Hardie, Theophilus (Rev.), of Ga. and Fla., 152, 153, 154, 155, 156. *See also* Hardy, Theophilus
Hardie, Thomas, 155
Hardie, William, 154, 156
Hardie. *See* Hardy and Hardee
Hardin, William B., 209, 214, 215
Hardison Creek, N.C., 15
Hardison Mill Swamp, N.C., 53, 55
Hardison Mill, N.C., 15
Hardison Slough, Tex., 212
Hardison families, of Lamar Co. and Harrison Co., Tex., 207
Hardison family, of Maine, 4-8
Hardison family, of N.C., participation in American Revolution, 70-74
Hardison family, of N.C., acquisition of land, 21-25, 34-57
Hardison family, of N.C., descendants of Jasper I, 32
Hardison family, of N.C., way of life, 31, 33-36
Hardison family in Federal Census Records. *See* Census Records, Hardison family in
Hardison heads of household, Federal Census Records. *See* Census Records, Hardison family in
Hardison, Alcy, 32
Hardison, Allen Crosby, 7
Hardison, Alse Evins, 49
Hardison, Alva, 376
Hardison, Amelia (Melia/Millie) Randolph, 313, 332, 333, 334, 335, 336, 337, 338, 343, 346, 348, 349, 350, 351, 352, 354, 355, 360, 361, 380, 381, 383, 386, 390, 392, 396, 397, 399, 401, 402, 403, 404, 406
Hardison, Amelia (Melia/Millie) Randolph, family of, 444, 446-47, 449-50
Hardison, Ann, 32
Hardison, Ann (daughter of John I), 75, 78
Hardison, Ann Walker Jackson, 189, 191, 209, 214, 216, 217, 218, 221, 222, 299
Hardison, Ann Walker Jackson, family of, 440-41
Hardison, Ann, wife of John Hardison of Onslow Co., N.C., 51

Hardison, Anna, 95
Hardison, Annabella, 166, 168, 170
Hardison, Annie Glass/Mary, 309, 313, 362, 364, 381, 386, 390, 392, 395, 396, 397, 399, 402, 405
Hardison, Annie Glass/Mary, family of, 445, 447
Hardison, Asa, 32, 95, 96
Hardison, Benjamin, 32, 60, 72, 73, 92, 94, 95
Hardison, Benjamin I, 32, 39, 41, 42, 59, 60, 72, 73, 74, 75, 76, 77, 78, 79, 85, 88, 89, 91, 98, 99, 100, 104, 105, 106, 108, 121, 125, 126, 130
Hardison, Benjamin I, will, 101-02
Hardison, Benjamin II, 32, 59, 93, 94, 95, 96, 97, 102, 103, 104, 105
Hardison, Benjamin, of Ga., 130, 131, 134
Hardison, Benjamin, of Maine, 7, 73
Hardison, Catherine, 32
Hardison, Catherine, daughter of Charles Hardison of Craven Co., N.C., 51
Hardison, Charles, 32, 96
Hardison, Charles (son of Joseph I), 88
Hardison, Charles I, 23, 26, 32, 43, 44, 53, 55, 58, 88, 89, 90, 92, 94
Hardison, Charles I, descendants, 32
Hardison, Charles I, land records, 49-51
Hardison, Charles, Jr., 32
Hardison, Charles, of Craven Co., N.C., 51
Hardison, Charles, of Hyde Co., N.C., 92
Hardison, Charles, of Onslow Co., N.C., 95
Hardison, Charlotte, 32
Hardison, Churchill, 32
Hardison, Clara Belle Sims, family of, 443-44
Hardison, Clark B., 152, 170, 183, 184, 216, 219, 220, 226, 298, 313, 357
Hardison, Cloah, 32
Hardison, Cullen, 22, 32, 89, 94, 95, 97, 102, 103, 104, 105, 106, 113, 121, 127, 130, 131, 134
Hardison, Cullin, 97, 102, 103, 104, 127. *See also* Hardison, Cullen
Hardison, Daniel, 32
Hardison, David, 32, 53, 59, 90, 91, 92, 94, 95
Hardison, David (son of Jasper II), 49

Hardison, Delilah, 32
Hardison, Edward, 32, 53
Hardison, Elijah, 32
Hardison, Elijah, son of Charles Hardison of Craven Co., N.C., 51
Hardison, Eliza, 32
Hardison, Elizabeth, 32
Hardison, Elizabeth (daughter of Benjamin I), 32, 105, 106
Hardison, Elizabeth (daughter of John I), 32, 75, 78
Hardison, Elizabeth (daughter of William I), 32, 102, 104
Hardison, Elizabeth (wife of Abner Jackson), 8, 128, 132, 151, 154, 156, 158, 163, 167, 170, 171, 172, 176, 185, 188, 193, 231
Hardison, Elizabeth (wife of Abner Jackson), family of, 439
Hardison, Elizabeth Duggan, 99, 101, 102, 106, 126
Hardison, Elizabeth, daughter of John Hardison of Onslow Co., N.C., 51
Hardison, Elizabeth, of Washington Co., Ga., 97, 131, 132, 135
Hardison, Elzey, 32
Hardison, Emily J., 32
Hardison, Ezekiel, 32, 95, 96, 102, 105, 106, 125
Hardison, Ezra, 32
Hardison, Frances (daughter of John I), 32, 75, 76, 78, 79
Hardison, Frederick, 32, 95, 96, 107, 127, 131
Hardison, Frederick (son of Jasper II), 49
Hardison, Frederick (son of Richard I), 55
Hardison, Frederick, of N.C. and Ga., 89, 97, 106, 107, 113, 121, 132, 134, 135
Hardison, Gabriel, 32, 90
Hardison, Gabriel, son of Charles Hardison of Craven Co., N.C., 51
Hardison, George W., 32
Hardison, Hannah, 32
Hardison, Hannah (daughter of John I), 32, 75, 78, 79
Hardison, Hannah (daughter of William I), 32, 102, 104
Hardison, Hansel, 32

Hardison, Hardy, 8, 32, 72, 73, 74, 154
Hardison, Hardy (son of Benjamin I), 32, 102, 105, 106
Hardison, Hardy, son of John Hardison of Onslow Co., N.C., 51
Hardison, Harmon, 32
Hardison, Humphrey, 32
Hardison, Ira, 32
Hardison, Isaac, 32, 92, 95, 96
Hardison, James, 32, 60, 72, 73, 74, 90, 91, 92, 94, 95, 96
Hardison, James (Jimmie) Harvey, 219, 301, 312, 355, 370, 371, 375, 376, 385, 386, 395
Hardison, James (Jimmie) Harvey, family of, 443-44
Hardison, James (son of Richard I), 55
Hardison, James W., 32
Hardison, James Y., 32
Hardison, James, of Craven Co., N.C., 92
Hardison, Jasper I, 4, 6, 8, 13, 15, 20, 26, 27, 43, 58, 65, 87, 88, 98, 108, 113, 125, 409, 410
Hardison, Jasper I, descendants, 32, 433-50
Hardison, Jasper I, settlement in N.C., 21-25
Hardison, Jasper I, will, 25-26
Hardison, Jasper II, 27, 58, 88, 90, 92, 93, 94, 94, 96, 107
Hardison, Jasper II, descendants, 32
Hardison, Jasper II, land records, 48-49
Hardison, Jasper III, 48, 49, 88, 90, 92, 93, 96, 107
Hardison, Jasper, of Craven Co., N.C., 95, 96
Hardison, Jasper, of Washington Co., N.C., 95
Hardison, Jemima, 32
Hardison, Jese, 74. See also Hardison, Jesse
Hardison, Jesse, 72, 74
Hardison, Jesse, Jr., 32
Hardison, Jesse, Sr., 32
Hardison, Jesse, son of John Hardison of Onslow Co., N.C., 51
Hardison, Jessey, 95, 96
Hardison, Jessie, 32
Hardison, Jessie, Jr., 32
Hardison, Joel, 32

460   INDEX

Hardison, John (grandson of John I), 76, 78
Hardison, John I, 15, 17, 22, 23, 26, 27, 43, 44, 45, 47, 52, 55, 56, 58, 59, 60, 73, 87, 88, 98, 99, 100, 108, 125
Hardison, John I, career in public service, 67-71
Hardison, John I, death and will, 74-79
Hardison, John I, descendants, 32
Hardison, John I, land records, 39-42
Hardison, John II, 41, 52, 58, 59, 60, 75, 77, 78, 79, 88, 90, 92, 94, 95, 98, 99, 100, 102, 104, 127
Hardison, John III, 59, 90, 91, 92, 94, 95, 97, 100, 104, 127
Hardison, John IV, 42, 78, 89, 94, 97, 99, 101, 102, 105, 106, 108, 113, 121, 126, 127, 128, 129, 130, 131, 132, 135, 136, 139, 140, 145, 150, 151, 152, 154, 155, 156, 158, 163, 193
Hardison, John IV, family of, 434-39
Hardison, John M., 32, 128, 132, 151, 155, 156, 158, 163, 164, 166, 167, 168, 169, 170, 173, 193
Hardison, John M., family of, 438
Hardison, John Randolph, 140, 152, 163, 170, 170, 171, 180, 183, 184, 186, 187, 190, 191, 192, 193, 205, 208, 209, 211, 212, 214, 215, 216, 217, 218, 220, 221, 222, 225, 226, 256, 298, 382, 383, 386, 387, 400, 402, 404, 405, 406
Hardison, John Randolph, C.S.A., 1862-63, pp. 231-54
Hardison, John Randolph, C.S.A., 1864-65, pp. 255-86
Hardison, John Randolph, burial site, 375
Hardison, John Randolph, courtship of Mary Fletcher Northington, 1863-66, pp. 231, 232, 245-52, 256, 264-68, 270-71, 285
Hardison, John Randolph, death, 373
Hardison, John Randolph, family of, 441-42, 444-50
Hardison, John Randolph, law license, 288
Hardison, John Randolph, letters by and about John and family, 1866-70, pp. 309-41
Hardison, John Randolph, letters by and about John and family, 1871-75, pp. 343-76
Hardison, John Randolph, poem, 257-59
Hardison, John Randolph, second marriage and move to Limestone Co., Tex., 287-307
Hardison, John Randolph, service in Granbury's Texas Brigade C.S.A., 239-45, 255-86
Hardison, John Randolph, Jr., 321, 323, 325
Hardison, John, of Craven Co., N.C., 50
Hardison, John, of Ky. and Tex., 203, 207
Hardison, John, of Maine, 7
Hardison, John, of New Hanover Co., N.C., 50
Hardison, John, of Onslow Co., N.C., 51
Hardison, Joseph, 32, 72, 74, 95
Hardison, Joseph (son of Jasper II), 49
Hardison, Joseph H., 32
Hardison, Joseph I, 26, 27, 39, 41, 43, 44, 52, 53, 58, 59, 90, 91, 94, 97, 100, 105
Hardison, Joseph I, descendants, 32
Hardison, Joseph I, land records, 55-57
Hardison, Joseph I, will, 88
Hardison, Joseph, of Hyde Co., N.C., 95
Hardison, Joseph, of Pitt Co., N.C., 92
Hardison, Josephine Elkins, 219, 221, 299, 353, 354, 355, 356, 376
Hardison, Josephine Elkins, family of, 442
Hardison, Joshua, 32, 95, 97
Hardison, Joshua (son of Jasper II), 49
Hardison, Joshua I, 26, 39, 41, 43, 55, 58, 59, 73, 88, 90, 91, 92, 94, 100
Hardison, Joshua I, descendants, 32
Hardison, Joshua, Jr. (II), 53
Hardison, Joshua I, land records, 52-53
Hardison, Joshua, of Pitt Co., N.C., 92
Hardison, Judah, 32
Hardison, Judah/Judith, 26, 32, 47, 88, 91, 93, 96
Hardison, Judah/Judith, land records, 46-47
Hardison, Judith, 32
Hardison, Judith (daughter of Joseph I), 56, 88
Hardison, Judy, 32
Hardison, Judy (daughter of Jasper II), 49
Hardison, Lamb, 32
Hardison, Lavinia, 32
Hardison, Lemuel, 32, 95
Hardison, Lemuel (son of Jasper II), 49

Hardison, Lewis W., 32
Hardison, Lilly Mary, 214, 215, 216, 224, 226, 293, 309, 313, 330, 339, 341, 346, 351, 352, 354, 355, 357, 358, 360, 361, 364, 366, 371, 374, 375, 376, 381, 383, 384, 390, 391, 392, 393, 394, 395, 396, 399, 400
Hardison, Louisa, 32
Hardison, Lucretia, 92, 95, 96
Hardison, Luke, 32, 94, 95
Hardison, Lula, 219, 376, 386, 391, 395
Hardison, Lula, family of, 443
Hardison, Luther, 32
Hardison, Margaret, 32
Hardison, Mark, 32, 53, 94, 95
Hardison, Martha, 32, 102
Hardison, Martha Johnson, 219
Hardison, Martha Johnson, family of, 436
Hardison, Mary, 32
Hardison, Mary (daughter of John I), 32, 75, 78
Hardison, Mary (daughter of William I), 32, 102, 103, 104
Hardison, Mary (wife of Benjamin Carkeet), 6, 23, 26, 32, 46, 88, 91
Hardison, Mary (wife of Benjamin Carkeet), land records, 42-46
Hardison, Mary (wife of Jasper I), 13, 26
Hardison, Mary (wife of Joseph I), 88, 92, 93
Hardison, Mary Ann (wife of John Gray), 152, 170, 171, 183, 184, 186, 188, 191, 192, 215, 216, 220, 224, 226, 293, 298, 313, 357
Hardison, Mary Ann (wife of John Gray), family of, 439-40
Hardison, Mary Ann Collins, 56
Hardison, Mary Anne Dowden, 219
Hardison, Mary Barfield, 152
Hardison, Mary Barfield, family of, 434, 436
Hardison, Mary Blandford, 152, 153, 170, 172, 173, 176, 183, 184, 187, 191, 215, 216, 219, 220, 298, 357
Hardison, Mary Blandford, family of, 436
Hardison, Mary Fain, 166, 168, 170
Hardison, Mary Fain, family of, 438
Hardison, Mary Fletcher Northington, 163, 232, 246, 247, 248, 249, 250, 251, 252, 256, 264, 265, 269-71, 279, 285, 368, 400, 403, 404, 405, 406
Hardison, Mary Fletcher Northington, death of, 403
Hardison, Mary Fletcher Northington, family of, 441-42, 444-45, 446-47, 449-50
Hardison, Mary Fletcher Northington, in Washington Co., Ga., 1875-82, pp. 379-403
Hardison, Mary Fletcher Northington, letters by and about Mary and family, 1866-70, pp. 309-41
Hardison, Mary Fletcher Northington, letters by and about Mary and family, 1871-75, pp. 343-76
Hardison, Mary Fletcher Northington, letters of, 1877-82, pp. 379, 384-99
Hardison, Mary Fletcher Northington, marriage and move to Limestone Co., Tex., 287-307
Hardison, Mary Mizell, 99, 102, 103
Hardison, Mary Taylor, 7
Hardison, Mary, of Washington Co., N.C., 95, 96, 97
Hardison, Millicent (daughter of Joseph I), 32, 56, 88, 105
Hardison, Mittie, 32
Hardison, Nancy, 32
Hardison, Nancy (daughter of Joseph I), 56, 88
Hardison, Nancy (wife of Emerald Brigham), 128, 132, 153, 156, 158, 163, 170, 171, 176, 193, 194, 207, 231, 299
Hardison, Nancy (wife of Emerald Brigham), family of, 437-38
Hardison, Nancy (wife of James Harvey Reeves), 152, 184, 185, 213, 214, 215, 216, 298, 301, 312, 321, 325, 343, 347, 354, 357, 358, 364, 376, 386, 395
Hardison, Nancy (wife of James Harvey Reeves), family of, 440
Hardison, Nancy, daughter of John Hardison of Onslow Co., N.C., 51
Hardison, Nancy/Nannie (Sissie) Missouri, 313, 343, 345, 348, 350, 354, 360, 361, 371, 381, 386, 390, 392, 396, 397, 399, 402, 404

Hardison, Nancy/Nannie (Sissie) Missouri, family of, 444-45, 447
Hardison, Noah, 32
Hardison, Olive, 39, 75, 76, 77, 79, 100
Hardison, Penelope, 32
Hardison, Peter, of Maine, 7
Hardison, Rebecca (Rebekah), 55, 88, 90, 91
Hardison, Richard B., 32
Hardison, Richard I, 25, 26, 27, 44, 50, 51, 52, 53, 56, 58, 59, 73, 88, 107
Hardison, Richard I, descendants, 32
Hardison, Richard I, land records, 54-55
Hardison, Richard II, 32, 59, 90, 91, 92, 94, 95
Hardison, Robert, 32
Hardison, Robert (son of John I), 76
Hardison, Rosanna, 41
Hardison, Samuel, 32, 92, 102, 105, 106
Hardison, Sarah, 32
Hardison, Sarah (daughter of John I), 32, 75, 78
Hardison, Sarah (daughter of William I), 32, 102, 104
Hardison, Sarah Lewis, 132, 138, 407
Hardison, Sarah Lewis, family of, 434
Hardison, Sarah Tipton, 219
Hardison, Sarah Tipton, family of, 436
Hardison, Seth I, 32, 102, 105, 106, 125, 126, 127
Hardison, Seth II, 125, 128, 129, 132, 134, 135, 136, 139, 140, 151, 152, 153, 154, 155, 156, 158, 163, 166, 167, 168, 169, 170, 171, 172, 173, 174, 175, 176, 182, 183, 184, 185, 186, 187, 188, 190, 191, 192, 193, 194, 205, 207, 208, 209, 212, 213, 214, 215, 216, 217, 218, 219, 220, 221, 298, 299, 301, 302, 357, 405
Hardison, Seth II, burial site, 375
Hardison, Seth II, family of, 434, 436, 439-44
Hardison, Simon, 32
Hardison, Stephen, 7, 8, 154
Hardison, Temperance, 194
Hardison, Temperance (wife of Enos Davis), 32, 125, 128, 129, 132, 136, 137, 140, 158, 163, 190, 193, 231, 245, 246, 267

Hardison, Temperance (wife of Enos Davis), family of, 436-37
Hardison, Thomas, 32, 94, 95
Hardison, Thomas (son of Thomas G.), 216, 217, 221
Hardison, Thomas G. (Dr.), 152, 170, 183, 184, 187, 188, 191, 192, 194, 208, 209, 214, 215, 218, 220, 221, 226, 298, 299, 313, 357
Hardison, Thomas G. (Dr.), family of, 440-41
Hardison, Thomas I, 26, 27, 32, 52, 58, 59, 88, 90, 92, 93, 94, 95, 127
Hardison, Thomas I, land records, 53-54
Hardison, Thomas II, 89, 94, 97, 102, 105, 106, 113, 121, 125, 126, 127, 128, 129, 130, 132, 135
Hardison, Thomas, of Houston Co., Ga., 132
Hardison, Thomas, of Maine, 7
Hardison, W. J., 402
Hardison, Wallace Libby, 7
Hardison, Wiggins, 32, 56, 88, 94, 95, 105
Hardison, Wiggins, Jr., 32
Hardison, William, 32
Hardison, William (son of Joseph I or Benjamin I), 95, 96
Hardison, William (son of Joseph I), 56
Hardison, William Clark, 376
Hardison, William F., 216. *See also* William L.
Hardison, William I, 32, 41, 52, 59, 60, 75, 76, 77, 78, 79, 88, 89, 90, 91, 92, 94, 98, 99, 100, 130
Hardison, William I, will, 102-04
Hardison, William II, 99, 101, 102, 105, 106, 126, 127
Hardison, William III, 56, 57, 88, 105
Hardison, William J., 32
Hardison, William Jonathan, 32
Hardison, William L., 32
Hardison, William L. (Dr.), 152, 170, 183, 184, 188, 208, 219, 221, 222, 225, 231, 235, 298, 309, 312, 315, 316, 353, 358, 376
Hardison, William L. (Dr.). family of, 442
Hardison, William Lanier, 125, 128, 129, 130, 132, 134, 135, 136, 137, 138, 139, 158, 163, 193, 245, 281, 359, 402

INDEX

Hardison, William Lanier, death and burial site, 382
Hardison, William Lanier, family of, 434
Hardison, William, Jr., 32
Hardison, William, of Jefferson Co., Fla., 156
Hardison, William, of Washington Co., Ga., 131, 132. *See also* Hardison, William Lanier
Hardison, William, son of Charles Hardison of Craven Co., N.C., 51
Hardison, Winaford/Winnifred (wife of John IV), 128, 135, 140, 151, 156, 163, 170
Hardison, Winnifred (wife of Joel Davis), 32, 125, 128, 129, 132, 136, 137, 138, 158, 163, 188, 193, 231, 245, 246, 313, 359
Hardison, Winnifred, family of, 438-39
Hardison, Winnifred (Winnie) Cornelia (wife of George Washington Wood), 224, 226, 293, 313, 330, 339, 341, 351, 352, 355, 357, 371, 374, 376, 380, 381, 383, 384, 385, 386, 388, 389, 390, 391, 392, 393, 394, 395, 396, 397, 398, 399, 400, 404
Hardison, Winnifred (Winnie) Cornelia, family of, 444, 445-46, 448
Hardison, Winnifred Cornelia Davis (wife of John Randolph Hardison), 140, 163, 172, 180, 190, 191, 192, 193, 194, 209, 214, 215, 216, 218, 222-26, 235, 245, 246, 287, 309, 357, 382, 406
Hardison, Winnifred Cornelia Davis, family of, 441-42, 444, 445-46, 448
Hardisson, 6. *See also* Hardison
Hardiston, 6. *See also* Hardison
Hardwick family, of Washington Co., Ga., 194, 329, 356-59, 381
Hardwick, Mary Elizabeth (Liz) Davis, 190, 193, 209, 225, 313, 329, 338, 341, 355, 356-59, 374, 375, 381, 393, 394, 397, 399
Hardwick, Robert (Bobbie), 329, 341, 394
Hardwick, Thomas William (Bill), 190, 193, 375, 394
Hardwick, William P., 138
Hardwick, Zemula Matthews (Zem), 394
Hardy family, 153
Hardy family, of Maine, 7, 8
Hardy, Mary Sullivan, 8

Hardy, Theophilus, of Ga. and Fla., 8, 135
Hardy, Theophilus, of Maine and N.H., 7, 154
Hardy family, of N.C., 8
Hardy, 155. *See also* Hardee, Hardie
Hareson, 6. *See also* Hardison
Harison, 6. *See also* Hardison
Harris, Lou, 393
Harris, Mamie, 393
Harrison, John A. (Rev.), 402
Harrison, 6. *See also* Hardison
Harry (slave), 190, 194, 218
Hatch, Verena, 51
Hawkins, Mary, 301
Henry (slave), 191, 218
Henry, Francis, 100
Henry, Sarah, 100
Hill, Whitmel, 60, 69, 70, 72, 73, 97
Hodges, Foreman, 135
Holland, Sarah, 172
Holliday family, of N.C., 41
Horace (former slave), 331
Hudson family, of N.C., 41
Hunter, Thomas, 60, 68, 69, 70, 78

Indians. *See* Alabama-Coushatti, Apalachee, Comanche, Creek, Seminole, and Tuscarora
Ivey family, of Limestone Co., Tex., 391
Ivey, Sarah (Sallie) Reeves, 386, 389, 395

Jackson family, of Ga. and Fla., 167, 172, 185
Jackson, Abner, 8, 154, 167, 170, 171, 172, 173, 176, 185, 188, 193, 231
Jackson, Abner, family of, 439
Jackson, Ann, 189, 191, 209, 214, 216, 217, 218, 221-22, 299
Jackson, Ann, family of, 216-17, 221-22, 440-41
Jackson, Clark, 172, 173, 176
Jackson, Elizabeth Hardison, 8, 128, 132, 151, 154, 156, 158, 163, 167, 170, 171, 172, 176, 185, 188, 193, 231
Jackson, Elizabeth Hardison, family of, 439
Jackson, Elizabeth Saphronia, 172, 185
Jackson, Emily, 216, 217

INDEX

Jackson, Ira, 173
Jackson, Isaac, 217, 222
Jackson, J., 216, 217
Jackson, Jane, 216, 217
Jackson, Mary Ann, 172, 185
Jackson, Sarah, 172, 185
Jackson, Sarah Holland, 172
Jackson, Theophilus Hardee (Dr.), 8, 154, 172, 183, 185, 188, 189, 193, 231
Jackson, Winnifred, 172, 185
Jamesville, N.C., 15, 57, 100-01
Joe (slave), 191
Johnson, James, 40, 41, 45
Johnson, Lydia Carkeet, 45
Johnson, Martha, 219
Johnson, Martha, family of, 436
Johnston, James, 45. *See also* Johnson, James
Joiner, Moses, 319
Joiner, Sallie, 393
Jones, Harding, 50
Josey, John W., 290
Josey, Mary, 290

Karkeet, 43, 46, 93. *See also* Carkeet
Kate (slave), 191
Kerkeet, 43. *See also* Carkeet
Kerkeitt, 5. *See also* Carkeet
Kerkite, Lydia Glanfield, 6. *See also* Carkeet
Kirkeet, 5. *See also* Carkeet

Landingham, Frances, 320
Lanier family, of N.C., 128
Lawson, Hugh, 320
Lee family, of N.C., 41, 48
Lee, Stevens, 48
Lee, Thomas, 22, 48
Leroy (slave), 190
Lewelling, John, 45
Lewis, F., 130
Lewis, J. I., 348
Lewis, Sarah, 132, 138, 407
Lewis, Sarah, family of, 434
Lim (slave), 194
Litchfield, Ysobel DuPree, 57
Liza (former slave), 325, 346
Long family, of Ga., 447, 450
Long, Helen Lanier Granade, 402
Looke, Mattie Rambo, 392, 395

Louisa (slave), 209, 218
Lucius, ____ (Mrs.), 385
Lucy (former slave), 246

Mackay, William, 100
Maine: Carkeet family in, 4-8; colonial history, 4-8; Glanfield family in, 5-6; Hardie/Hardy family in, 7-8; Hardison family in, 4-8; York Co., 4-8
Manger (slave), 77
Manning, Benjamin, 155
Marshall (former slave?), 347
Martin, Josiah (Gov.), 69
Mary (slave), 191
Matthews, Zemula, 394
McBride family, of Washington Co., Ga., 396, 399
McCarty, C. L., 209
McDaniel, David, 139
McKenzie, Kenneth, 60, 68, 70
McLeod, Angus, 211, 212, 221
Meazle, Sarah Hardison, 75, 78
Meazle, 75. *See also* Mizell
Metcalf, Mehitable, 289
Milley (slave), 191
Mims, Annie, 334, 335, 336
Mims, Harriet (Hattie) Missouri Northington, 290, 312, 314, 319, 323, 325, 331, 333, 334, 336, 343, 347, 349, 351, 364, 368, 370, 373, 388
Mims, Thomas, 312, 323, 333, 334, 335, 336, 351, 367, 370, 388
Mims, Wm. (Mrs), 335
Mizell, Ann Hardison, 75, 78
Mizell, Luke, 100
Mizell, Mary, 99, 102, 103
Mizell, 78. *See also* Meazle
Mizelle, Edward, 52
Moore, Elizabeth Hardison, 75, 78
Morris, William, 22
Morton family, of Limestone Co., Tex., 312, 385, 386, 388, 395
Morton, Annie, 388
Morton, J. C., 383, 389, 390, 391, 392, 395
Mott, Martha, 153
Mullins, Symantha, 385

INDEX

Nelson, Effie Evers Granade, 402
Newsome, Bessie, 393
Nicholson, Malcolm (Dr.), 189
Norris (former slave), 319
North Carolina, Albemarle Co., 16, 17-18, 21, 22, 25, 34
North Carolina, American Revolution, Hardison family in, 65-74
North Carolina, Beaufort Co., 57, 94-96
North Carolina, Bertie Co., 21, 22, 34
North Carolina, Chowan Co., 22, 34
North Carolina, colonial era, Hardison family in, 13-64
North Carolina, Craven Co., 50-51. 92, 94-96
North Carolina, early statehood, Hardison family in, 83-110
North Carolina, Hardison Creek, 15
North Carolina, Hardison Mill Swamp, 53, 56
North Carolina, Hardison Mill, 15
North Carolina, Hardison family, in census records: Federal Census of 1790, 91-93; Federal Census of 1800, 93-97; Federal Census of 1810, 109-10; State Census of 1784-87, 89-91
North Carolina, Hardison family, land records, 21-25, 34-57
North Carolina, Hardison family, slaves, 47, 49, 77-78, 93, 96-97, 99, 101, 103-04, 126. *See also* Slaves (listing by name)
North Carolina, Hardison family, way of life, 31, 33-36
North Carolina, Hardison family, wills: Benjamin I, 101-02; Jasper I, 25-26; John I, 74-79; Joseph I, 88; William I, 102-04. *See also* Garrett will, 26-27
North Carolina, Hardison, village of, 15
North Carolina, Hyde Co., 90, 92, 93, 95, 96
North Carolina, Jamesville, 15, 57, 100-01
North Carolina, Martin Co., 22, 34, 36-37, 39-60, 68-70
North Carolina, Onslow Co., 50-51, 90, 92. 94-96
North Carolina, Plymouth, 104-07
North Carolina, Roses Plantation, 13, 22, 23, 26, 54, 55, 56

North Carolina, Tyrrell Co., 22-25, 34. 36-37, 39-57
North Carolina, Washington Co., 22, 27, 34, 49, 95-96, 104-07
Northington family of Washington Co., Ga., 281, 287-93
Northington family, of Washington Co., Ga., letters by and about, 1866-70, pp. 309-41
Northington family, of Washington Co., Ga., letters by and about, 1871-75, pp. 343-76
Northington, Amelia (Milly) Fisher, 246, 287, 290, 292, 390, 403
Northington, Amelia (Milly) Fisher, correspondence with daughter Mary Hardison, 1866-70, pp. 309-41
Northington, Amelia (Milly) Fisher, correspondence with daughter Mary Hardison, 1871-75, pp. 343-76
Northington, Amelia (Milly) Fisher, death of, 401
Northington, Annie, 312, 346, 349, 351, 360, 362
Northington, Capers. *See* Northington, William Capers
Northington, Harriet (Hattie) Missouri, 290, 312, 314, 319, 323, 325, 331, 333, 334, 336, 343, 347, 349, 351, 364, 368, 370, 373, 388
Northington, Indiana, 290, 310, 312, 319, 322, 324, 325, 326, 327, 328, 331, 333, 348, 349, 366, 370
Northington, James (Jimmie) Fisher, 290, 312, 319, 324, 325, 326, 331, 335, 336, 346, 365, 382
Northington, James Foster, 246, 287, 290, 292, 323, 381, 390, 403
Northington, James Foster, correspondence with daughter Mary Hardison, 1866-70, pp. 309-41
Northington, James Foster, correspondence with daughter Mary Hardison, 1871-75, pp. 343-76
Northington, James Foster, death of, 401
Northington, Jesse, 290
Northington, Jesse A., 290
Northington, John, 290

Northington, Marcellus Addison, 290, 312, 319, 320, 324, 331, 346, 353, 365, 370, 382
Northington, Martha Elizabeth (Lizzie), 290, 312, 313, 314, 319, 322, 325, 331, 332, 333, 334, 347, 349, 351, 353, 354, 355, 358, 360, 361, 364, 365, 366, 367, 370
Northington, Mary Fletcher (wife of John Randolph Hardison), 163, 232, 246, 247, 248, 249, 250, 251, 252, 256, 264, 265, 269-71, 279, 285, 368, 400, 403, 404, 405, 406
Northington, Mary Fletcher, death of, 403
Northington, Mary Fletcher, family of, 441-42, 444-45, 446-47, 449-50
Northington, Mary Fletcher, in Washington Co., Ga., 1875-82, , pp. 379-403
Northington, Mary Fletcher, letters by and about Mary and family, 1866-70, pp. 309-41
Northington, Mary Fletcher, letters by and about Mary and family, 1871-75, pp. 343-76
Northington, Mary Fletcher, letters of, 1877-82, pp. 379, 384-99
Northington, Mary Fletcher, marriage and move to Limestone Co., Tex., 287-307
Northington, William Capers, 290, 312, 319, 320, 326, 346, 348, 365, 382, 390

Palacios, M. R., 302
Palmer family, of Washington Co., Ga., 325, 328
Palmer, James M. (Dr.), 317, 363, 383
Parker, Cynthia Ann, 299
Parker, Quanah (Chief), 299
Parsons, G. A. (Dr), 348
Payne, James B., 401
Penney (slave), 191
Perry, A.M., 326
Person family, of Limestone Co., Tex., 391
Person, B. D., 300
Person, Caroline (Carrie) Reeves, 216, 364, 386, 395
Person, Laura, 325
Phibb (slave), 101, 126, 127
Phibea (slave), 103, 127
Phillips, William, 173, 174, 175

Phoebe (slave), 135
Poldo (slave), 191
Pollock family, of N.C., 40, 41
Pollock, Cullen, 22, 23, 24, 26, 40, 43, 48
Pollock, George, 22, 40
Pollock, Thomas, 21, 22, 23, 40
Pope, Owen C., 190
Pope, Selah Davis, 190
Pritchet, Aaron, 156

Rambo family, of Limestone Co., Tex., 312, 326, 353, 388, 391
Rambo, Ginnie, 354
Rambo, Mattie, 385, 388, 389, 390, 392, 395
Randolph, John, of Virginia, 171
Reeves family, of Fla. and Tex., 185, 214, 391
Reeves, Caroline (Carrie), 216, 364, 386, 395
Reeves, Ellen, 385, 389
Reeves, Henry, 389
Reeves, James Harvey (Dr.), 184, 185, 188, 213, 214, 216, 219, 220, 222, 227, 298, 301, 312, 321, 325, 353, 358, 368, 385, 386
Reeves, James Harvey (Dr.), death of, 395
Reeves, James Harvey (Dr.), family of, 440
Reeves, Jay, 389
Reeves, John W., 185
Reeves, Mary, 185
Reeves, Mary Hawkins, 301
Reeves, Nancy Hardison, 152, 184, 185, 213, 214, 215, 216, 298, 301, 312, 321, 325, 343, 347, 354, 357, 358, 364, 376, 386, 395
Reeves, Nancy Hardison, family of, 440
Reeves, Sarah (Sallie) Clark, 216, 386, 389, 395
Reeves, William J., 375
Reeves, William Jay, 301
Reeves, Willie, 214, 216
Renfroe, Allis (Alice?), 353
Renfroe, Amelia, 327, 353
Renfroe, Foster, 365
Renfroe, Haynes, 312, 313, 314, 319, 325, 335, 336, 338, 351, 361, 362, 365, 366, 367, 369, 370, 373

INDEX

Renfroe, Martha Elizabeth (Lizzie) Northington, 290, 312, 313, 314, 319, 322, 325, 331, 332, 333, 334, 347, 349, 351, 353, 354, 355, 358, 360, 361, 364, 365, 366, 367, 370
Renfroe, Robert (Bobbie), 319, 327, 353, 366
Reno, Jane Wallace Wood, 400
Reno, Janet, 400
Rhodes, Arthur, 56, 105
Rhodes, Millicent Hardison, 56, 88, 105
Rhodes, William, 24
Richardson, Carl N., 405
Richardson, Lillie Winifred Darsey, 405
Riley, Mary, 172
Rives, 185. *See also* Reeves
Roach, Reuben, 216, 217
Roberson, John, 99
Robinson, Boling H., 192
Robinson, Henry, 49
Robison family of Washington Co., Ga., 287-92
Robison, Elizabeth Fisher, 287, 290, 291, 292, 388
Robison, John, 383, 387, 388
Robison, John G., 155
Robison, Mary, 292
Robison, William Fisher (Rev.), 292, 383, 386-88, 401
Robison, William H., 287, 290, 291, 292
Robison, Windfield, 317, 346
Robison, Winfield, 387
Rogers family, of Limestone Co., Tex., 391
Rogers, Ellen Reeves Burton, 389
Rogers, Jeff, 389
Rose (slave), 103, 104
Rose, Richard, 23
Roses Plantation, N.C., 13, 22, 23, 26, 54, 55, 56
Ross, Richard, 23
Ryan family, of N.C., 41
Ryan, Elizabeth Randolph Shreve, Collection, 383

Sandefer, 219. *See also* Sandifer
Sandifer, J. W., family of, 443
Sandifer, Lula Hardison, 219, 376, 386, 391, 395

Sandifer, Lula Hardison, family of, 443
Schaffner, Elizabeth, 289
Seminole Indians, 143-50, 157-58
Sheffield, John West, 313, 341, 358, 375, 381, 394
Sheffield, Sarah (Sallie) Ann Davis, 190, 209, 225, 313, 330, 338, 341, 358, 375, 381, 394
Shoffner, 289. *See also* Schaffner
Shreve family, of Ga., 446, 449
Shreve, Elizabeth Randolph, 383
Shreve, Mary Elizabeth Granade, 402
Shreves, Robert, 50
Simon (slave), 101, 126
Sims, Clara Belle, family of, 443-44
Slade, William, 60
Slaughter, Earl Charles, 405
Slaughter, Nancy Louise Brown, 405
Slaughter, Nancy Louise Brown, Collection, 309, 312, 383
Slaves (by name): Ann, 191; Annee, 49; Anthony, 191; Bell, 49; Benjamin, 191; Bob, 77, 103; Caksky, 77; Caroline, 328, 331, 346; Charity, 101, 126; Clarisa, 346; Crum, 292; Easter, 101, 126; George, 292; Hannah, 77; Harry, 190, 194, 218; Henry, 191, 218; Horace, 331; Joe, 191; Kate, 191; Leroy, 190; Lim, 194; Liza, 325, 346; Louisa, 209, 218; Lucy, 246; Manger, 77; Marshall, 347; Mary, 191; Milley, 191; Norris, 319; Penney, 191; Phibb, 101, 126, 127; Phibea, 103, 127; Phoebe, 135; Poldo, 191; Rose, 103, 104; Winny, 49
Slaves, Davis family, 190, 194
Slaves, Federal Slave Census, 1850, Florida, Gadsden Co., 185-86; Federal Slave Census, 1860, Texas, Polk Co., 217-18
Slaves, Fisher family, 292
Slaves, Hardison family. *See* listings under Fla., Ga., N.C. and Tex.
Smith, Milton C. (Rev.), 403
Smithwick family, N.C., 44
Smithwick, Edmondson Samuel, 45
Smithwick, Edmund, 44, 45, 101, 102
Smithwick, Edward, 44, 60, 70
Smithwick, John, 44, 99, 100
Smithwick, Mary, 44, 99

INDEX

Smithwick, Samuel, 60, 69
Sreaves, Robert, 50
Stewart family, N.C., 44
Stewart, John, 102
Stewart, Thomas, 44, 68
Stubbs, Anne, 49
Stubbs, John, 49
Sullivan, Mary, 8
Sutton family, of N.C., land records, 46-47
Sutton, Deborah, 46
Sutton, Elizabeth, 46, 47
Sutton, George, 47
Sutton, Jasper, 47
Sutton, John, 47, 91
Sutton, Joshua, 47
Sutton, Judah/Judith Hardison, 26, 32, 47, 88, 91, 93, 96
Sutton, Judah/Judith Hardison, land records, 46-47
Sutton, Judith, 47
Sutton, Lemuel, 96
Sutton, Mary Elizabeth, 47
Sutton, Parthenia, 47
Sutton, Sarah, 47
Sutton, Thomas, 46, 47, 91, 93, 96
Sutton, Warren, 173, 174, 175
Sutton, William, 47, 93, 96

Tarkington, Burton B., 222
Tarkington, Sarah Berry, 222
Taylor, Mary, 7
Tennessee, Hardison family, 53
Texas, Blanco Co., Brigham family in, 207, 231, 299
Texas, Civil War, 231-39
Texas, colonial history, 201, 205
Texas, Cotton Gin, 368-73
Texas, DeWitt Co., Brigham family in, 207
Texas, Freestone Co., Hardison family in, 298-99, 368-73
Texas, Grayson Co., John Hardison of Ky. in, 203
Texas, Hardison Slough, 212
Texas, Hardison family, in census records: Federal Census of 1860, Polk Co., 215-17; Federal Census of 1870, Limestone Co., 306-07; Federal Slave Census of 1860, Polk Co., 217-18

Texas, Hardison family, slaves, 209, 216-18, 220-21. *See also* Slaves (listing by name)
Texas, Harrison Co., Hardison families in, 207
Texas, Lamar Co., Hardison families in, 207
Texas, Liberty Co.: Gray family in, 220, 226; Hardison family in, 219-27; Reeves family in, 220
Texas, Limestone Co.: Gray family in, 298, 307; Hardison family in, 298-374; Reeves family in, 298, 306; frequent mention of, in Hardison letters, 309-74
Texas, Lost Prairie (community and church), 300-01, 375
Texas, Matagorda Co., Brigham family in, 207
Texas, Personville, 300, letters written from, 309-74
Texas, Polk Co.: Gray family in, 209, 215-17, 218; Hardison family in, 207-19, 298, 302-03; Reeves family in, 213-14, 216
Texas, Reconstruction, 294-305
Texas, settlement in ante-bellum era, 201-07
Texas, Tarkington Prairie, 222, 223
Texas Brigade, C.S.A., 240. *See also* Granbury's Texas Brigade
Tipton, Sarah, 219
Tipton, Sarah, family of, 436
Turner, George, 346
Tuscarora Indians, 16, 19

Walker, Ann, 189, 191, 209, 214, 216, 217, 218, 221, 222, 299
Walker, Ann, family of, 216-17, 221-22, 440-41
Walker, F., 217
Walker, Florida, 217, 221
Walker, T., 216, 217
Ward, Francis, 52, 53
Ward, Lydia, 5
Ward, Philip, 48
Wilcox, Everitt, 192
Wilkinson, Reuben, 123
Williams family, of N.C., 68
Williams, Samuel, 60, 97
Williams, William, 69, 70
Winifred (name), use by Hardisons, 136
Winnifred (name), use by Hardisons, 136

Winny (slave), 49
Wood, Boyd Emory, 399, 400
Wood, Dean Osgood, 399, 400
Wood, George Washington (Rev.), 397, 398, 399, 400
Wood, George Washington (Rev.), family of, 444, 445-46, 448
Wood, George Washington, Jr., 399, 400
Wood, James N., 290, 317
Wood, James R. (Rev.), 399
Wood, Jane Wallace, 400
Wood, Lilly Mary Hardison, 214, 215, 216, 224, 226, 293, 309, 313, 330, 339, 341, 346, 351, 352, 354, 355, 357, 358, 360, 361, 364, 366, 371, 374, 375, 376, 381, 383, 384, 390, 391, 392, 393, 394, 395, 396, 399, 400
Wood, Martha Chester, 399
Wood, May Lydia, 400
Wood, Roy Smith, 400
Wood, Sarah Ann Fisher, 290
Wood, Winifred (daughter of George Washington Wood, Jr.), 400, 406
Wood, Winnifred (Winnie) Cornelia Hardison, 224, 226, 293, 313, 330, 339, 341, 351, 352, 355, 357, 371, 374, 376, 380, 381, 383, 384, 385, 386, 388, 389, 390, 391, 392, 393, 394, 395, 396, 397, 398, 399, 400, 404
Wood, Winnifred (Winnie) Cornelia Hardison, family of, 444, 445-46, 448

Yonge family, of Fla., 182